Between Two Worlds

Discovering New Realms of Goalie Development

Justin Goldman

Published by: Justin Goldman
Foreword by: Chris Koentges
Cover Art by: Carl Herring

 All content included in this manuscript is original literature produced by the author, Justin Goldman. Interviews were held during the Summer and Fall of 2014, between the months of May and December.

First Printing: 2015
ISBN-13: 9781507779804
ISBN-10: 1507779801

Justin would like to extend a special thanks to his friends for sharing their insights, which helped make this book possible: Josh Tucker, Jukka Ropponen, Hannu Nykvist, Ale Jääskeläinen, Jack Hartigan, Ted Monnich, Rasmus Tirronen, Mikko Ramo, Rasmus Reijola, Erno Suomalainen, Bobby Goepfert, Clare Austin, Larry Sadler, Eli Wilson, Corey Hirsch, Dave Rogalski, Corey Wogtech, Mitch Korn, Mike Valley, Thomas Magnusson, Garret Sparks, Dave Alexander, Kevin Reiter, Joe Exter, Mike Ayers, Nick Petraglia, Matt Millar, and Brennan Poderzay.

TABLE OF CONTENTS

ACKNOWLEDGEMENTS AND PHOTOGRAPHS

My list of acknowledgements begins with a quick story.

In January of 2014, I received an e-mail from a writer named Chris Koentges. At the time, Chris was crafting a lengthy article on Finnish goaltending and was looking for a specific quote in an ode I wrote a few years earlier to one of my idols, Miikka Kiprusoff.

A few months later, his article was published on The Atlantic's website, and it forever changed my life. *The Oracle of Ice Hockey* wove an intricate and sanguine tale about the legendary goalie coach Urpo Ylönen and the Finnish goaltending empire he helped build nearly 40 years ago.

I absolutely love it when a true literary master dives deep into the game of hockey and discovers the beauty of the goaltending position. This doesn't happen often, but when it does, their words always seem to create a new way for people to see the position, shedding a very different type of light on something we see all the time through their unique words and metaphors.

Talented sportswriters are able to take a vivid Polaroid of goalies and hockey games. But writers like Koentges are able to paint Picasso's and Dali's and Van Gogh's.

Part Five of Chris' article was titled "The System" and discussed Finland's sturdy goalie development program, which was put into action nearly three decades ago. Part Six was titled "The Soul" and brilliantly reflected the innate and ornate human nature of the Finnish goaltender.

I've read a thousand goalie articles, watched numerous Finnish goalies, and talked shop with hundreds of goalie coaches over the past five years. But it was Chris' article that acted as the genesis of this book project. Inspired by his words, Chris injected me with the motivation needed to finally invest in a trip to study Finland's goalie development and goalie coaching culture.

This is something I had wanted to do since I first committed to studying the position on a professional level after the 2004 NHL lockout. For all the reasons Chris illustrated in his article, Finns had always been my favorite goalies to watch and dissect. Few articles had catalyzed my motives like this, but after reading his article in the days that followed for a fifth and sixth time, I realized I had exhausted all of my silly superstitious excuses to stay home. It was time to put up or shut up.

A few weeks later, I applied for, and was fortunately accepted into, the prestigious GoaliePro Coaching Mentorship Camp, which was founded by the esteemed Finnish goalie coach, Jukka Ropponen.

Overwhelmed with excitement and gratitude for being accepted into Ropponen's exclusive program, I worked diligently to make sure everything would come together smoothly. Needing money to afford the trip to Helsinki and back, I sold my sleek and sexy black 1998 Acura Integra RS to a friend and used the cash to book my flights. Next, I set up a Kickstarter campaign and raised the rest of the money I needed to attend nearly 10 more high-level goalie camps between the months of May and August.

So I'd be remiss to not acknowledge Koentges for his inspiring storytelling. Few words have I read in the past decade that have moved me to write so extensively. He was the catalyst of my creative side, a side I embrace more than any other. This book is like the progeny of Chris' flawless portraiture of Finnish goaltending lore, so having him write the Foreword really brings everything full-circle. I'm honored to have some of his words appear within these pages, and I hope to one day be even half as skilled at storytelling as he is.

I must also extend a special thanks to Ropponen for accepting me into his mentoring program. Not being the traditional or typical high-level goalie coach, I'm so thankful he allowed me to actually participate. He was not only open to sharing his thoughts and ideas on goalie development, but he set aside extra time to enhance my learning experience. Until the last day in Finland, he was so hospitable. He even allowed me to spend an entire summer afternoon in his home, rummaging through his cluttered basement full of goalie memorabilia. I was like a loyal squire blissfully peeking through the closets and chambers of his knight's hidden armory.

I'll never forget the GoaliePro Coaches Appreciation Party, which was held on a silent shore of the Baltic Sea. Sharing a wooden sauna with Jukka in silent admiration of his influence on Finnish goaltending was a special moment. I would have sat there – naked as the day I was born – until the skin melted right off my bones if it meant spending a little more time in that sauna with him and the rest of the GoaliePro coaching staff.

I also want to thank my good friend Mike Valley, who is my biggest mentor and most reliable friend in the goalie world, for his support and guidance. Although I wrote this book on my own, it was his continued confidence in my abilities after we co-authored our first book that pushed me along. When I was invited to attend his NHL goalie camp in Madison, it was further proof that he genuinely cared about my development and what I was trying to accomplish with this book. After helping him breathe new life into NetWork Goaltending, we became partners for an organization that could truly revolutionize the way goalie coaches share new ideas. I can think of no higher honor than that.

To Mitch Korn, who continually amazes me with his tedious organizational skills, his ability to explain things in an easy-to-understand manner, and his ability to exhibit superhuman levels of energy. I can't thank him enough for the opportunities he has given me to shadow and learn from him. Being in his hotel room in Duluth while he made key phone calls to different members of the Washington Capitals coaching staff was an awesome glimpse into his world, and spending time breaking down videos of NHL goalies like Justin Peters and Chad Johnson was an unforgettable learning experience. Time and time again, he has shown me that I'm capable of seeing technical things on deep levels, and like Valley, he unselfishly supports my endeavors.

To Jack Hartigan, who I met for the first time in Finland. Because of his willingness to share information, we created a friendship that I know will last a lifetime. His egoless personality, especially at his age, was so refreshing to see. His insights on goalie development models also played a massive role in my newfound passion for improving what is currently taking place within the United States. Jack's one of the most ambitious goalie coaches I know, and I thank him for guiding and inspiring me to move in a certain direction with this book.

To Clint Elberts, one of the most animated and rib-tickling goalie coaches I've ever known. I'm so thankful for the friendship we created during the GoaliePro camp. I'll never forget what he told me in the Helsinki nightclub regarding my first book. I want him to know that I will forever hold him in high esteem for his honesty that night. And the photo I have of his old driver's license, to this very day, still makes me cry from laughing so damn hard. Finding the Olympic Gold Medal in that random little trinket shop in the heart of Tallinn was also a great memory of our time together.

I also have to thank the four goalie coaches that comprise NetWork Goaltending. Thomas Magnusson, Hannu Nykvist, David Alexander, and the aforementioned Valley were so kind and generous during our time together in Madison, and I'm so happy to be a small part of the new organization. I'll never forget the afternoon we all spent at Adam Burish's house; when I dropped onto the grass in his backyard in the lingering twilight, I stared up through the trees and realized I was, at least for that one night, in Goalie Heaven.

To the 33 backers that supported my Kickstarter fundraising project, I can't thank them enough for providing some of the financial support I needed to write this book. It was a very costly and exhausting endeavor, especially since I almost traveled non-stop from May to the end of August. Countless Uber trips to and from airports, all of those last-minute hotel arrangements, transferring money to and from different bank accounts, and endless stops at coffee shops and delis would have left me broke and jobless had it not been for their support.

I also want to extend a special thanks to my friend Scott Svare, who kindly created the intro video for my Kickstarter project page. His skills are top-notch and he has a very successful video and movie production career ahead of him.

To Bobby Goepfert and Clare Austin, I thank them for providing readers with some great supplemental content for the book. They both deserve to be recognized for their work, and I'm proud to promote them anytime, anywhere. Hopefully we get to meet someday down the road.

To everyone else I interviewed in this book, including Dave Rogalski, Corey Wogtech, Eli Wilson, Ted Monnich, Josh Tucker, Larry Sadler, Corey Hirsch, Scott Barry Kaufman, and the lengthy list of goalie minds that weren't mentioned within, I thank them all for sharing their honest opinions and ideas on goalie development. I hope that this book becomes known as a quality reflection of their brilliant perspectives, and less about my own (and sometimes avant-garde) ideas and ambitions. What these guys taught me over the years played a major role in shaping my own thoughts and motivations.

Finally, I have to thank my parents, Al and Michel. For everything they have done in my lifetime to allow me to follow my wildest goalie dreams, I thank them from the bottom of my heart. My father is an amazing man and even at age 77, still works harder than anyone I've ever known. My mother is full of grace and spirituality, and I have them to thank for being shaped into the man I am today. I am eternally grateful that they taught me about Faith and why it is the single most important tool a man can have.

About the Cover

I also wanted to carve out a little section here to express my gratitude for my good friend Carl Herring. The time and energy he invested into creating the book cover's original artwork was a testament to the dedication he has to his craft as a 3-D designer. It took quite a while for him to strategically place every single pixel on the canvas, and after tons of late-night live streaming sessions and Skype chats, I couldn't have been happier with the final result.

Carl is one of the most selfless people I know. For the past four years, he has driven all the way from southern Texas to Denver in order to volunteer his time at the annual charity adult hockey tournament I founded back in 2007. As if that wasn't enough, he has also put in countless hours to help me create artwork for not only both of my book covers, but for numerous other goalie-related projects as well. On top of all that, he always has a ton of enthusiasm and energy.

It was not easy to come up with a design concept to reflect the book's title, but after some time, I finally settled on the idea of the two worlds, Finland and North America, being represented by medieval goalie knights. Carl added sashes on each goalie to represent each country's colors, and since the United States and Canada represented North America as a whole, we chose red and white. The doorway behind them contains the "new realms" of various aspects of goalie development I discovered during my summer adventure.

There's also some hidden symbolism laced within the cover. For example, you have to personally determine whether the two goalies are blocking you from entering the new dimension, or if they're holding back the new realms from breaking out. If you look closely, you'll see more subtle subtext in there as well.

Overall, Carl brought my vision for the cover to life with true precision. So I hope you all take a moment to appreciate his original artwork. Also be sure to visit his design website at *www.carlherring.com* and check out all of his sick 3-D environment and logo artwork.

The Photographs

I took hundreds of photos throughout my summer adventure, but many of them were done on my phone, so they obviously weren't the highest of quality. It also would have been much more expensive to include them all in the book, so after thinking it over, I decided to post them on The Goalie Guild website.

Just head on over to **www.thegoalieguild.com/betweentwoworlds** and check them all out. These will help you visualize a lot of the moments, environments, concepts, people, and ideas I discovered during my wild summer goalie expedition!

FOREWORD: FINNISH GOALIES ARE MADE IN SPLENDID ISOLATION

By: Chris Koentges

"No man is an island, entire of itself; every man is a piece of the continent, a part of the main." —John Donne

Among the curiosities that found their way to Calgary during the 1988 Olympics – overshadowed by Eddie the Eagle and the Jamaican Bobsled Team – was "an exhibition of professional hockey masks." The masks came mostly from the late 1960's and 70's. Terry Sawchuk's primitive cat mask was displayed alongside Wayne Stephenson's Captain America and the demonic fiberglass veil of Yves Belanger. They possessed a straightforward spookiness that the elaborate scenes painted on today's masks don't always convey. (Made all the eerier by the fact that, in 1988, most of the teams no longer seemed to exist.) My grandfather bought me a poster featuring an hypnotic 6-by-5 grid of the exhibition's gnarliest masks. It went on the wall above my bed, and I couldn't take my eyes off it.

I would fall asleep backwards, inventing tales about the masked creatures that did battle for phantom teams in the night. The poster became my comic book and horror movie. Sometimes the Scotch tape that held the masks to the grainy wall would give, and I'd be startled awake in the middle of the night, face to face with Gilles Meloche's twisted black and red Cleveland Barons glower. Mom came to mistrust my preoccupation with the masks. When the poster suddenly disappeared, it was probably for the best. I didn't think too hard about goalies after that. My hometown Flames had become so boring, in fact, that I barely thought about hockey at all.

My mom died the same week the Flames traded a second-round draft pick for a goaltender from the southwest coast of Finland. Not quite knowing what to do with ourselves in the days that followed, I took my dad to a game at the Saddledome. It had been some years since either of us had been. Our heart wasn't in it that night. At least, not at first. Nobody knew how to pronounce the new goalie's name. He'd beaten Montreal, 2-1, in his debut. I realized a few days later when I found myself watching the Flames' next game that the forces, which had hooked me so long ago, had returned.

In the months that followed, the aloof Finn would carry Calgary to the seventh game of the Stanley Cup Finals, and I almost bankrupted myself going to games. Sometimes I would go with my pal Gavin, who would jump to his feet whenever Detroit – or any of those stacked teams that had dominated the Flames for so many years – would race in on an odd-man rush or build a cycle in Calgary's zone. It meant we were about to see Miikka Kiprusoff work. The snipers that had picked apart our listless defenses and overmatched goalies for more than a decade, suddenly seemed flustered. As they'd rack up shots, Gavin, in fits of ecstasy, would scream *feed it.* The creature became more powerful the more rubber it was fed. *FEED IT!* We would scare the other fans in our section, imploring Datsyuk and Marleau and the rest of them to *feed it,* until our vocal chords became raw. Kiprusoff was not a hockey goalie so much as a state of mind. The creatures that lurked in my childhood poster had come to life at the moment in my life I needed such a creature.

It wasn't the accumulation of desperation saves, nor the glove hand, which in stark contrast to Mike Vernon, barely seemed to move – nor the realization there were no longer rebounds to the slot – that made Kiprusoff a revelation. To really appreciate "Kipper," as he would come to be known in the dressing room, was to paradoxically wait for the moment after he let in the big goal. The bigger the better.

Where other goalies I'd seen would use their helmets as a shield from the intense isolation of that moment, this perpetually unshaven creature from the southwest coast of Finland would push the mask up over his head and casually grab for the water bottle on the net behind him, the way a broken Al Swearengen would fiddle with toothpicks, surveying the menace of Deadwood from his balcony at the Gem Hotel, as he knew his enemies were watching for evidence of weakness. I wanted to understand the sheer force of this indifference. I wanted to understand the movements that were barely human. I wanted to understand where this thing called Kiprusoff went after it left the ice. Sometimes I imagined him alone in a rundown motel, legs spread at jarring angles, stabbing his blocker hand at shadows creeping across the wall. Or maybe he went to the forest and waited until they called him back to the crease.

My curiosity about Kiprusoff turned into a full blown wonder about Finnish goaltenders. Who was making them? What had happened to the great Quebec goaltending factory? I assumed that people who knew hockey had thoughtful answers to these questions. It turned out, however, that this question was not so easily answered.

Eventually, I would find Kevin Woodley's stuff. And Ken Dryden. And Randall Maggs' dark narrative poem about the darkest of them all Terry Sawchuk, and his line that seemed to parse the soul of these noble creatures: "Like saints, they pray for nothing, which brings grace." If you look hard enough, you can piece together a small, scattered canon of goaltending literature. But the first things I read about goalies were riddled with clichés and contradictions. The writers, analysts—whatever they liked to call themselves—hinted that there was *something about Finland.* However, no attempt had been made by hockey's media machine to really understand it.

My first real clue came from a scouting report on Kiprusoff. It was impressively detailed for what appeared, in my Googled-out daze, to just be some dude's blog. I printed out the entry on Kiprusoff and underlined the parts of it that I wanted to reference later. When I realized that I had marked up the whole page, I began circling in a different color. Then I wrote down the line that summed up not just Kiprusoff, but the rest of this vast website, filled with equally detailed scouting reports, in which the author had tried to make sense of concepts like Kiprusoff's scorpion save.

> *"The nickname for this save reflects the animalistic nature of a sudden piercing movement based on pure survival. Like a stab to the heart, there is a purpose to his movements, despite the fact he has no time to think about it." –Goldman*

I was so consumed with finding the fountainhead of Finnish goaltending that I didn't stop until months later to ask, *who the hell wrote that thing*? It was evidence of a mind that took nothing for granted. That would consume itself so thoroughly with something called a scorpion save. The website's reports on Finnish goaltenders – which expressed equal measures of wonder – had been like breadcrumbs to a city called Turku on Finland's southwest coast, where the ultimate subject of my story lived. An old man named Upi Ylönen. The man who made Kiprusoff. Ylönen's fingerprints were all over modern Finnish goaltending, and consequently on the coaching systems that had tried to emulate Finland.

While, on the surface, the mystery had been solved, the undercurrents only deepened. Nobody tells you how to write about goalies. Writing about goaltenders is one of those tap dancing about architecture things. And because the loudest discussions about goaltenders still pay homage to entirely outdated ideas, I began my reporting with the hypothesis that whoever invented the butterfly, and whoever invented whatever it was that Finnish goaltenders did, represented two opposing philosophies, which I would have to pit against each other in the story I was writing. It was supposed to be a story about good versus evil. The stubborn orthodoxy versus the new Baltic way. And when I finally tracked down the guy who invented Kiprusoff and the guy who invented Patrick Roy – one spoke with a thick Québécois accent and one only spoke Finnish, they'd never met and were barely aware of each other's existence – but it was crystal clear that they believed in the *exact same thing*.

When I went back to figure out who that blogger was, confronting these exact questions, it finally occurred to me that this blog called The Goalie Guild wasn't at the edges of that scattered canon of goaltending ideas, but that, years from now, it would represent the center. It made perfect sense that its author Justin Goldman, who had dedicated his life to understanding these creatures, grew up on a horse ranch in rural Texas. Only an extreme outsider could be drawn to the thinking of other outsiders.

Goldman's attempt to synthesize a global perspective on goaltending – a profession still rife at the highest levels with xenophobia – is about more than technical expertise, or the latest philosophies about developing a goaltender. Goldman is on a madcap sociological pilgrimage. He's moving quickly, but not so quickly that he won't stop to point out some menacing little image that a hopeful teenage goaltender in the Baltic has sketched on a beaten up mask.

Chris Koentges
Vancouver, BC

Chris Koentges has written about goaltenders and other creatures for *The Atlantic, ESPN The Magazine, Deadspin,* and *CBC.*

PREFACE: STEPPING THROUGH THE GATES OF CHANGE

"With blood I soak my idols, with pride I set my sails. I scan the furthest horizon for the shores I am aimed to find." –Thyrfing

I was living on a horse ranch in a rural northern Texas town called Parker when I was first introduced to the game of hockey. I was 11 at the time, and everything I learned about being a goaltender came exclusively from watching them on TV.

But only a few of them, namely Mike Richter, Mike Dunham, John Vanbiesbrouck, and Ryan Miller, were American. The rest of the goalies I watched with unbridled fascination were Canadian or European, including my biggest idols: Chris Osgood, Felix Potvin, Miikka Kiprusoff, and the venerable Dominik Hasek.

By not only enjoying the process of watching and then mimicking their different playing styles, but also by being exposed to such a wide variety of styles at this impressionable age, I naturally created my own unique way of playing the game. And even though my Texas roots were as American as apple pie, you couldn't even call what I did a true "American" goaltending style.

During those key years of athletic development and physical maturity, because I was forced into being a self-taught goalie due to my location and birthright, I had no other choice than to develop an open-minded approach to learning the position. Without judgment or preconceived biases, I soaked up everything I could find about goaltending, and since ice and coaching was impossible to find, I took to the streets on rollerblades to develop my raw puck-stopping skills.

Since then, I've spent the past two decades blissfully entangled in an intricate web of discovery. Things like functional movement, biomechanics, progressive butterfly techniques, effective game-management tactics, efficient positional strategies, mental and emotional conditioning, and the winding journey of self-discovery have taught me valuable lessons that filter down into every aspect of my life. It was this bravura and artistry of the goaltending position that captivated me at a young age, and I've come to terms with the fact that this is my lifelong calling.

When I first started to plan my summer expedition and conceptualize this book, I simply wanted to answer a few questions that constantly sang and danced around my mind like natives around a bonfire.

> *How do cultural differences between North American and European goaltenders influence playing styles, coaching methods, and development models? What elements actually create those differences, and what significance do these differences have when I look at the current state of goaltending as a whole?*

Asking those core questions quickly led to even more questions, and the natives continued to sing, dance, and stoke the flames of the bonfire in my mind. Knowing I had already written a book about the key emotional factors of an elite goalie's mental game in *The Power Within*, now more than ever, I was curious about the cultural and social factors that influenced goaltending development.

I already knew things like environment, birthright, genetics, playing and training opportunities, coaching, family values, wealth, economics, education, and family influences played a key role in a goalie's development. But by how much? Were any of these things actually quantifiable? Furthermore, which factors mattered more than others? How much weight did each one pull? How much did pure, uninhibited raw skill weigh on the balance scale compared to mental conditioning? How much did coaching matter? How much did success rely on having the right attitudinal beliefs? How much stemmed from knowing the right people, meeting them at the right time, being scouted at the right time, and being on the right youth and junior teams?

I also realized that I had a growing passion for improving the way US-born goalies developed. I had seen both sides of the coin in this regard; I grew up in a very non-traditional hockey market, left to my own defenses without a goalie coach until I was 16. After college, I quickly became a volunteer goalie coach, then a private goalie coach, and then a head goalie coach for an entire youth hockey association. After I had enough coaching experience, I transitioned into goalie scouting, then became an analyst for NHL.com, a mentor for young goalies and parents, and then into a conglomerate of all these things with USA Hockey and the National Team Development Program (NTDP).

Since I knew all of those key learning experiences would allow me to write this book as an authority on the subject of goalie development, I really wanted to use this book to initiate and cultivate change within the United States. But the more I discovered about the current state of things, the more I became overwhelmed with the breadth and complexity of this daunting task.

> *Where do I start, what steps do I take, and what is the best way to separate fact from fiction in the realm of developing goaltenders in different regions and countries? What could I could glean from comparing not only the different playing and coaching styles found in Finland, Sweden, and North America, but what could I learn about their development programs as a whole? Knowing that Finland and Sweden were leaders in this field, how much could I learn from them, and more importantly, what could I bring back and inject into my world? What could unique regional coaching methods reveal about the path a young American goalie could or should take to become elite? Could I pinpoint hard evidence and universal truths that actually simplify, streamline, and purify the process of turning average goalies into elite ones?*

So many questions to consider, yet so many remained unanswered.

When I finally approached the Gates of Change and started gathering information for this book, I had no choice but to transform my way of thinking. Through copious amounts of research into the "new realms" I had discovered, I learned about the different development models found between the two worlds and then saw my entire life and mindset change even more drastically.

Fortunately, I've always loved change. A kid from Texas doesn't go from being a wannabe cowboy to a goalie scout for USA Hockey without embracing change. Totally against the grain and unheralded in the traditional path of a typical pro hockey scout, I knew first-hand that being adaptable was the key. My upbringing led me to embrace the fact that I didn't choose goaltending, goaltending chose me. And through the many learning experiences I've had over the years, my passion for researching different training methods and development patterns, and then trying them out on my own, turned me into a goalie alchemist of sorts.

I actually read a Taschen art book a few years ago that retold the history of the world's first alchemists through images and photographs. In one of the chapters, it briefly explained the story behind the *Opus Magnum*. This was often called "The Great Work" and was defined as the divine process of creation. It was considered a process of combination, extraction, purification, and unification, all of which was needed to turn iron and other "base" metals into pure gold. In order to accomplish this feat, the alchemist had to acquire the Philosopher's Stone. This object was the elusive ingredient that revealed and organized the specific combination of elements and necessary steps one needed to take in order to go from a state of high entropy (no organization or structure) to a state of low entropy (structured, refined elements).

After reading parts of that book, I gained even more confidence in the idea that alchemy was a legit archetype for goalie development. Because of this, I desperately wanted to go on my own mysterious adventure, just like those passionate intellects did when they learned new ways to understand the different elements that constructed their world.

For at least one summer, the Between Two Worlds excursion allowed me to be a real-life goalie alchemist, searching the world for the Philosopher's Stone of goaltending. I knew that so many questions would remain unanswered, but I also knew that I'd still learn more about the way elite goalies were made and refined. Knowing that every goalie's development process was different, I took solace in knowing that the end result was a rare but repeatable occurrence.

A child is born, falls in love with stopping pucks at a young age, trains hard, develops slowly, and eventually becomes an NHL star.

Metaphorically speaking, these select superhuman athletes start off as base metals and slowly transform into solid pieces of goaltending gold. Such is the circle of life, right? I mean, the only constant in life is change, and only by studying these changes with more depth can we truly comprehend the infinite complexities that exist alongside a goaltender's path of development. The changes will never disappear, the world will keep turning, and where we go from here will forever be shrouded in mystery. We just need to know what makes the process more or less effective.

So when this prelude ends and you start reading the first chapter, you'll approach the same Gates of Change that I did, and hopefully you'll take the time to step through to the other side and walk with me on what was the educational and inspirational journey of a lifetime.

The "journey" was an exhausting four-month international globetrot that stretched from May 7 to August 30, 2014. I traveled to Helsinki, Estonia, Buffalo, Toronto, Detroit, Duluth, Denver, Madison, Las Vegas, and many other cities in between in order to shadow some of the world's best goalie coaches. I met a number of amazing people along the way, spoke candidly with countless goalie coaches in Finland and North America, and was even a small yet integral part of the coaching staff at USA Hockey's most prestigious annual goalie camp.

Through it all, while I still choose to not call myself an expert (despite public flak in the past from other hockey journalists and experts, this remains my personal decision), I can now say with more authority that *there is no secret recipe to success*. There is no Philosopher's Stone to be found when it comes to 'proper' goalie development, no one way or right way of doing things. The same goes for coaching methods and anything else that influences the way a goalie evolves and improves.

Instead, I think it's a lifelong search, both within our hearts and through the relationships we build with all of our coaches and friends and mentors, in order to find what methods and ideas work best for us as individuals. The Philosopher's Stone, as cliché as it may be, is really found within you, and even though many of you may never end up finding it, that doesn't mean we should give up the search. Keep digging, keep learning, keep discovering, and keep mixing elements together.

So not only does this book document my summer adventures as I bounce from camp to camp, but it also maps out how I mixed my own ideas together in order to create and implement a basic Level 1 goalie coaching certification program here in the USA. I tried to answer as many questions as possible, all while being equal parts analytical, conceptual, and philosophical. I think it all tied together nicely, and with the voices of all the coaches I interviewed, I try to present you with a kaleidoscope of colorful prisms on goalie development.

I also wrote this book in order to create a platform and launching pad for you to come up with some of your own ideas. Once you see how this summer excursion steered my career in a positive direction, it should motivate you to share your ideas with everyone in the goalie universe. You surely have answers to some of my questions, so maybe we can discuss them together over a beer sometime. I'd actually really like that, no matter who you are or where you're from.

Beyond the inclusion of my own creative ideas, which comes at a point in time when North America is finally recognizing the need for structured goalie development at the grassroots levels, I also chose to put a lot of personal reflection in here. And I did it for a very specific reason.

I did it because I learned that development, whether you're a goalie or a coach, is greatly influenced by the environment you're in and the people you're surrounded by. It's not just about what you know or how skilled you are, but who you know and how you treat everyone around you. It's all about relationships.

Now that I've told you what this book is about, I also want to tell you what this book isn't.

This book isn't a historical account or a timeline of goalie development models in Finland and North America. It isn't a full dissection of techniques and styles found in Finnish and North American goalies, either. It's also not a comprehensive scientific dissertation on epigenetics and the current state of goalie stats and analytics. It's merely my way of recapping a personal and enlightening path of discovery combined with some in-depth interviews in order to create an in-depth comparative analysis of goalie development culture and ideas between the two worlds.

The evolution of goalie development methods stretch across a timeline of many decades, but depending on your view of things, you may come to realize that goalie development, as a whole, is still very much in its infancy. That being said, by sharing my experiences, I hope this book is a gift that keeps on giving; I hope it opens up new doors for the way you see the position. I hope it helps you realize that there are so many things to learn about the way we train, teach, and develop goalies.

In the end, I witnessed a black and gold Phoenix rise from the ashes of what I used to know. As you will see, there are some amazing people out there willing to help us create solutions to issues that have plagued our goaltending culture for decades. But unless key players in youth and national hockey programs in North America are willing to make the trek overseas and witness first-hand the major gap between the two worlds, we'll continue to stagnate.

Unless we learn how to build and implement some form of a goalie development model using ones that are already in place elsewhere, then the vast majority of the goalie community in North America will continue to miss the point. This prevalent and unsettling issue of uncertified volunteer goalie coaches erroneously teaching advanced techniques at the wrong time will continue to widen the gap between the two worlds.

Fortunately, just in the past few months, Hockey Canada has made swift and decisive changes to their culture. After sending a delegation over to Europe in late-2014, they met many of the same people I did during my summer trek and quickly saw their perspectives on goalie development change. It opened the doors for major change to take place, change that will have a positive impact on Canadian goalies forevermore.

An article on *TheProvince.com* by Jim Jamieson regarding these new changes included a great quote from Pasco Valana, who is a goaltending advisor for Hockey Canada and a good friend of mine. His words reinforced much of what I discovered first-hand regarding the massive cultural differences:

> *"We were humbled. Everyone in Canada had this big ego. Everyone used to hide their stuff, it was a big secret. Now everyone shares. We have group discussions on how to help each other. Everyone realized to a man that our system is flawed. When you find that, as any good coach, you work to change it. In Europe, everyone works together."*
> *–http://www.theprovince.com/sports/goalie+solution+Hockey+Canada+getting+ready+institute+European+teaching+model/10363867/story.html*

I wrote this book with the hope that USA Hockey does something similar to Hockey Canada, and if that trip ever transpires, I hope my commitment to goalie development warrants a spot on the delegation. It would be an honor, because I really care about creating a legitimate solution to some of the key problems we've been facing with goalie development in the States.

Regardless of what happens, I believe I have created a piece of enjoyable and educational literature that will help you realize what I did; the only way to create a more refined and intelligent goaltender is to bridge the gap between the two worlds. But the only way we strengthen the bonds between North America and Scandinavia is if we choose to accept and reinforce Europe's culture of sharing. And sharing only happens if we proclaim a willingness to reach out and exhibit a desire to learn from those we usually perceive to be the enemies.

I believe the only enemy in the world of goalie development is ignorance, and I believe that ignorance stems from being too proud, too ashamed, or too afraid to learn from others.

When I finally finished writing the book, all of the questions and answers I found came together like the closing ceremony of that tribe of natives dancing around my mind. Their final song echoed my ultimate purpose for taking on this project – to give you an inside look at the amazing complexity of goalie development, and to help you realize that your path, and more importantly your own ideas and methods, are beautifully perfect in their own special way.

I'm not sure why, but I'll always remember the idea of those natives dancing around a blazing fire in my mind.

Until the day that I die, their voices will continue to chant songs and tell stories about the relationships I created, like chemical bonds that burned immeasurable wisdom into the halls of my soul and painted new ideas with earthen hues on the walls of my mind.

Between Two Worlds Travel Itinerary: Summer, 2014

May 7-11: *Warren Strelow Goalie Camp | Ann Arbor, MI | 36 goalies | 512 miles x 2 = 1,024 miles*

May 12-19: *Colorado Summer Getaway | Denver, CO | 700 miles x 2 = 1,400 miles*

May 23-24: *ProHybrid USHL Prospects Tour | Eagan, MN | 24 goalies | 10 miles*

May 28-June 8: *GoaliePro Mentor Program | Finland | 24 goalies | 5,105 miles x 2 = 10,210 miles*

June 9-12: *GGSU Legends Camp | Chicago, IL | 20 goalies | 355 miles x 2 = 710 miles*

June 13-16: *Korn Goalie Camp | Duluth, MN | 40 goalies | 155 miles x 2 = 310 miles*

June 17-18: *Vaughn Factory Tour | Oxford, MI | 528 miles x 2 = 1,056 miles*

July 3-10: *Home Trip to Colorado | Denver, CO | 700 miles x 2 = 1,400 miles*

July 13-20: *Select 15's Festival | Amherst, NY | 24 goalies | 733 miles x 2 = 1,466 miles*

July 24-25: *Dave Peterson Goalie Camp | Blaine, MN | 50 goalies | 40 miles x 4 = 160 miles*

July 26-31: *Eli Wilson Elite Prospects Camp | Toronto, ONT | 24 goalies | 677 miles x 2 = 1,354 miles*

August 1-6: *ASD Trade Show | Las Vegas, NV | 1,298 miles + 628 miles = 1,926 miles*

August 9: *Flight from Colorado back to Minneapolis | 700 miles*

August 16: *The sudden move back to Colorado | 925 miles*

August 25-29: *Elite Goalies NHL Camp | Madison, WI | 8 NHL goalies | 825 miles x 2 = 1,650 miles*

TOTALS: 24,291 miles traveled and 250 goalies scouted

1

THE COMPARATIVE ANALYSIS OF GOALIE DEVELOPMENT

"In the last ten years, goalies have gone from Gumby-like stick figures to net protecting objects as big as a house." –Ken Dryden

The technical and tactical realms of goaltending are more serious subject matters than ever before. They're not only essential to playing the position successfully, but they're essential to winning hockey games and championships. In fact, I've learned that a pro goalie's "positional strategy" is often the main focal point of their training. At this level, their collection of physical skills and instincts, in relation to all other amateur and junior goalies, are considered to be elite, so knowing how and when to use those skills appropriately and efficiently is of utmost importance.

"Positional Strategy" can be defined as a goalie's set of physical skills and techniques that are combined with the cognitive, tactical, and analytical tools needed to execute those skills in an effective manner that is successful for each and every type of situation a goalie faces. When done in an effortless and consistent manner, goalies with sound positional strategies are usually considered to have higher upside, or are perceived to have more potential skill, than others.

When goalies with certain technical and physical features (or positional strategies) begin to establish a resemblance in form and function (their style) too strong to have been accidental, and when these features are observable throughout different regions and cultural environments, then it is impossible to ignore the fact that some sort of connection exists between them.

The study of these strong resemblances and connections is my definition of *Comparative Goaltending.*

A goaltender in their primeval "raw" state is reflecting a very specific sequence of internal and external environments, so how they evolve from day to day is a matter of causation between their bodies, minds, and surroundings. With that visceral connection permeating every aspect of the way an athlete plays and 'thinks' the position, deliberately speaking, I believe *Comparative Goaltending* is a creative and effective way to take a deeper look at national and regional development and training methods in order to see what may or may not enhance potential.

When analyzing an individual goaltender, one that has a certain set of parameters limiting what he or she is capable of doing, *Comparative Goaltending* also acts as the study of the effects or changes that occur when adding or subtracting certain elements within those same parameters.

I've taken this idea one step further through the concepts of *Universal, Diffusionary*, and *Monogenetic* comparative goalie analyses.

Universal comparative analysis in goaltending is when you break everything down to specific accordances and differences by appealing to certain universals. In simpler terms, it's the deconstruction or dissection of the position into common denominators based around key athletic psychological and physiological traits, like reflexes, skating, angle play, catching, or techniques.

Diffusionary comparative analysis in goaltending studies how different training methods and playing styles travel across the globe. This is my favorite of the three; I love charting the spread of information and ideas across vast oceans of social media and online superhighways. This is also the main type of analysis you'll find in this book, as I become more passionate about goalie development models in Finland and Sweden, and how those models are traveling overseas and taking influential roots in Canada and (slowly but surely) in the United States.

The trouble with this type of comparative goalie analysis is that, six or seven years ago, personal ideologies were developed by many different goalie coaches in many different areas, but the information they created and provided didn't have the means to travel very quickly. When this rare information did cross borders, especially prior to the mid 1990's, it traveled very quietly.

Only now are North Americans really seeing and discovering very valuable information disseminate from inside dominant pockets of goalie development, namely in Finland and Sweden, and at the same time help diffuse it around the globe. This book is a perfect example of that Diffusionary type of analysis; so much of what I learned ends up in a device that others can learn from and quickly apply to their own goalie coaching methods and ideas.

The diffusion or dissemination of information in the goalie world is exploding like a previously dormant volcano. In the early 2000s, I didn't have the capability to call, text, or Skype a goalie coach in Finland. I had to discover information through much narrower channels, or through my own way of naturally discovering new ways to stop the puck.

Today, I can cruise the World Wide Web on a daily basis and discover fresh ideas, alternative coaching methods, new ways to refine techniques, and a plethora of unique and legit perspectives on how to approach evaluating and scouting the position. I'm learning new things and reinforcing old things at a faster rate than ever before, but this ability to discover and then share new information is not possible without the means to *spread* or "diffuse" the information.

All of these new pieces to the puzzle were invisible in certain parts of the globe for many years. But with the technological revolution thrusting goaltending into a new age of dominance, almost everyone has the four corners and edges in place – the ability to learn through a computer. Now, more than at any time in the history of hockey, goalies and goalie coaches are working together to fill in the middle. But resistance still exists out there, and it's slowing us down.

There's a third and final realm of comparative goalie analysis, one I call *Monogenesis.* This is a method that traces information back to a common "ancestor" or originator. This is fun to ponder, because it includes the ancient roots of our history. But this type of analysis is not the main focus of this book, although it would certainly make an excellent subject matter.

For example, the majority of the goaltending community knows that Patrick Roy was the "godfather" of the modern butterfly, and while we all agree that Roy implemented this technique and save selection into his game with the help of legendary goalie coach Francois Allaire, it is only fair to consider the possibility that the two of them may have gleamed an influence or some sort of information about this new save selection from someone or somewhere else.

If this didn't happen and Allaire and Roy truly were the genius catalysts that ignited a goaltending revolution, then there is even more merit to *Monogenesis* in goaltending. The birth of the butterfly is not only a very important moment in our history, but what we can learn from that process of enlightenment can aid the process of development for the future of goalies everywhere.

Another one of my favorite examples of Monogenetic analysis is the *Hasek Roll.* The goalie world agrees that this move was 'invented' by one of the greatest European goalies of all time. Now a member of the Hockey Hall of Fame, one would need to speak directly to Hasek in order to know whether or not he actually discovered and created this movement all on his own, or if he gleaned the movement from someone else.

Fortunately, my good friend Kevin Woodley from *InGoal Magazine* was able to procure the amazing quote below straight from the horse's mouth regarding the Hasek Roll's genesis.

> *Some of the saves may only be possible because of his Gumby-like flexibility and Jedi powers of concentration and anticipation, but Hasek worked hard to perfect his methods. They included never giving up on a save and always having one last limb (or even his head) left to throw out at a shooter. Even the famous barrel roll was planned. As he told InGoal, it was actually a well-planned save selection he used in very specific circumstances. The barrel roll was easy to brush off as a fluke if you only saw it executed once, but after watching Hasek use it over and over again – and use the same "technique" in the same save situations each time – you realize there is a science to the style.*
>
> *"I was doing it in 80s, I do it in 90s, I do it in this century, it's nothing new," Hasek said. "I know I was doing it in the Czech Republic in the 80's and I don't know if some older goalie taught me or if I seen it. It was too many years ago."– http://ingoalmag.com/news/retiring-hasek-wasnt-the-unorthodox-flopper-many-believed*

The moment when a new movement pattern turned into a tried, tested, and true technique; the long-term influence that process had on the position as a whole; the exponential growth of the movement around the globe and ensuing mutations; how it altered the way in which goalies all over the world developed. That, at least in a basic sense, is a combination of the three types of comparative analyses I discussed above.

With these laying the foundation for how I approached writing this book, I quickly realized I would be considering cultural influences just as much as technical influences. This was what really resonated with me in Koentges' article, and what pushed me to finally take my own trip to Finland. Cultural differences play such a vast role in development patterns, so it's not just what type of technique certain goalies adopt, or what type of training umbrella a goalie works under, but how his or her external environment shapes their ability to improve through adaptation.

The vast role that culture has on shaping a goalie's personality is so great today because, as a whole, I believe our teachings are more streamlined and consistent than ever before. For the most part, every goalie is essentially learning the same thing when it comes to efficient puck-stopping and what type of drills we use. Furthermore, as we continue to share ideas and network together, we build bridges and new alliances that cause goalies to become more refined, thus looking more and more similar.

To a degree, this is not a bad thing; we're finding better ways to reach goalies worldwide and provide them with the coaching they need to stop the puck at a more efficient rate. At the same time, the unique marks that created our regional differences decades ago are being buffed away by the polish of progress, and we're slowly losing some of those unique and creative traits.

As one who may be considered a reductionist, I've come to learn that goaltending ultimately operates on the fundamental science of movement; all technique is a result of the body acting or reacting in certain ways, depending on the situation being presented to a goalie at any given moment in time. As it was in the beginning, movement is and forever shall be the driving force behind the goaltending position.

This is why I believe so strongly that goaltending is a *sacred* and *timeless* art. In fact, I can confidently go so far as to say that it is my faith, theological in nature. It's a dogmatic way of life for an athlete, one that is unlike any other position in sports.

The *sacredness* comes from the fact that success as a goalie relies on *who you are*, both physically and psychologically, not so much about *the tools you use* or the methods you employ. The *timeless* aspect is rooted in the fact that change is eternal, and it is how we manage those changes in different external and internal environments that allows us to properly develop.

Time is immemorial. If a goalie doesn't take the time to understand why they must be willing to change certain habits and training methods, and if a goalie doesn't take time to discover who they truly are, their success will always be limited.

2

GOALIE DEVELOPMENT IN THE AGE OF SOCIAL NETWORKING

"Information flow is what the Internet is about. Information sharing is power. If you don't share your ideas, smart people can't do anything about them, and you'll remain anonymous and powerless." –Vint Cert

As each day passes, the hockey community continues to realize that North America no longer dominates goaltending at the highest levels. The rise of Finnish, Swedish, Russian, and even Swiss talent over the past few seasons in the NHL was the straw that broke the camel's back, and now even the most casual hockey fan knows that good goalies come from everywhere.

For so many years, young American goalies like myself were only exposed to what we could see in person and on TV. It was 1993 when I was first able to watch a televised NHL game. So I, along with thousands of other competitive goalies, didn't see the hidden potency of Czech goaltenders before Hasek. We didn't see the silent but deadly style of the Slovaks before Rastislav Stana and Jan Lasak and Jaroslav Halak. We didn't see the flair and bravado of the Swiss goaltender before David Aebischer and Jonas Hiller. And we certainly didn't know about the scintillating hands of Finnish goalies before Miikka Kiprusoff.

Today, the world of is a very different place. Jump on your computer and you can watch KHL (Russia), SHL (Sweden), SM-liiga (Finland), and even NLA (Switzerland) games at any time. Hell, you could even watch hockey in Greece and Asia if you wanted. Turn on NHL Network and beyond the hundreds of NHL games they broadcast on TV and the internet, you can watch the World Juniors, the CHL Top Prospects Game, and even the World Championships. Even NBCSN now broadcasts a plethora of NCAA games, while ESPN2 still airs the NCAA Men's Ice Hockey Frozen Four Championship.

Thanks to the dawn of online streaming technologies and the age of social networking, there are more avenues available to not only watch different types of goalies from different countries, but readily and easily learn from them, interact with them, and research them.

If you told me six years ago that I would be having a friendly conversation with Eddie Lack or Jhonas Enroth online, I would have called you crazy. But thanks to Twitter and Facebook, it has happened more than once, and as time goes on, it will happen with more regularity.

This constant expansion of information and communication in today's world is, in my opinion, the most influential and powerful vehicle driving the evolution of goalie coaching culture. This force not only impacts what we see on a daily basis, but what we learn and who we learn it from.

When I started to consider this factor in relation to global goalie development, I reflected on my life experiences. America Online (AOL) and Netscape started to put its stamp on my view of the goaltending society in the mid 1990's, which was the same exact time hockey came into my life. It was not a coincidence, merely good timing. I moved from my farm in Parker, Texas to a suburb of Dallas the same year the Minnesota North Stars relocated to Dallas. That also happened to be the same year we were able to get a dial-up internet connection and satellite TV.

When both of those technologies were introduced to the Goldman household, one that was transitioning from a country lifestyle to living in the big city, my ability to absorb information on goaltending increased exponentially. Now I had all the time in the world to surf AOL chat rooms and talk about the Stars, the Red Wings, Ozzie, Potvin, goalie pads, and masks.

If I didn't move to the city, this most likely would never have happened. Instead, I would have continued to muck out stalls every morning, ride horses, and play basketball. If AOL didn't start to connect all of North America through the archaic process known as dial-up, I would not have been able to learn so much so quickly.

I can remember when I first subscribed to *The Hockey News*. It was in 1994 and I was in seventh grade. Every time I got a new issue, I devoured it cover-to-cover. But I also spent a lot of time examining the photos and letting my imagination run wild. Back then, we didn't have a computer pummeling our faces with random articles, Tweets, Vines, and animated .gif images. We only saw legitimate goaltending actions as they unfolded in a game or a single moment in time. The highlights weren't the over-glorified, enriched special-effect packages like they are today either, so to see a simple action photo of your favorite goalie in the top hockey magazine that existed at the time was a rare treat. It led to plenty of days clipping out articles of goalies, gluing them into a photo book, and letting those images burn into the far reaches of my subconscious. They seeped into my dreams and turned into desires for a pro career.

Examples of goalies learning on their own before having a legitimate goalie coach can be found everywhere. Mike McKenna, an AHL goalie currently in the Arizona Coyotes organization, grew up in the St. Louis area and told me (via Twitter, of course) that he didn't have a legit goalie coach until he was 24 years old. That's amazing for a guy that is more than skilled enough to be a full-time NHL backup.

During the 2015 World Junior Championships, NHL Network broadcaster Dave Starman was discussing USA Hockey's Thatcher Demko. In between whistles, he mentioned how Demko learned a lot about how to play the position by downloading videos off the internet. His goalie coach for Team USA (as well as for Boston College) is Mike Ayers, who was on the Warren Strelow Goalie Camp staff (you'll read about him later on). Starman relayed how Ayers told him that he didn't have to "un-teach" a lot of things that Demko had already brought to the table.

These are just two of a myriad recent examples of late-20 and early 30-year-old goalies having similar experiences. In fact, I can safely say that it's more common than uncommon, and it further proves the power that comes from combining technology with the ability to learn things by emulating and mimicking what you see (the science of shadowing) on TV and the internet.

But as interesting as it may be to ponder and reflect on where we would be without online and social networking, I think the more important question to ask is where we should be *with* it.

Whether you're a goalie coach, a budding goalie, or a goalie parent, now is not the time to be stubborn or set in your ways. Those who choose to seek out new information by listening to others will be rich with new ways to teach, understand, and play the position.

Now more than ever before, there lies a growing amount of knowledge on the position. It's dwelling in all corners of the internet – all you have to do is reach out and grab it. You can see its immense depth at any time, and you can take what you learn one step further by *sharing it* and discussing it with others. No matter what role you play in the goalie community, no matter how small your reach may be, I believe now is the time where you must accept a so-called 'duty' to share and interact with others.

What can you do to raise more awareness about certain aspects of goaltending? What can you do to share a few drills you learned at that summer camp you went to or worked with in Canada? What can you do to share one or two on-ice props when you got that rare chance to work with Mitch Korn? These are important questions for you to ask right now.

At the root of this expansion, and with the dominance of social networking permeating all areas of our culture, I find two key components that make the engine of progress work – people and information. Intimately tied together, information can't be shared in today's world without people willing to share and learn that information, and these people can't grow without the information existing out there, waiting to be found. This is how a subculture grows; people with similar passions and goals share and learn and repeat the process.

This was rarely possible 15 years ago. But today, sharing and interacting within the online goaltending world is happening every moment of every day. I can talk to a bunch of Finnish goalie coaches at the same time I'm watching an NHL game. I can access a plethora of resources that were once faint whispers in the wind. As a result, a good portion of my time as an independent pro goalie consultant is spent sharing links and providing online resources to different goalies, goalie coaches, parents, and fans. In fact, in just over five years, I was able to carve out an entirely new niche in the goalie development industry. Thanks to the internet, I simply collected, allocated, and dispersed new information and previously unknown resources.

As one of the only 'goalie-only' pro consultants out there, I can say with authority that the rise in social networking has also eliminated many regional barricades in the world of goalie scouting. Many North American scouts almost have an unhealthy obsession for finding the next great European goalie prospect now, all while we are starting to see more European clubs call upon veteran North American goalies to fill spots in a ton of different leagues (Josh Robinson, Jeff Deslauriers, Jeff Glass, and many others are recent examples).

At the same time, influential goalie coaches in North America have been able to create new working friendships with goalie coaches in countries like Switzerland, Sweden, Finland, the Czech Republic, Russia, and even Denmark. This has led to a plethora of new international summer goalie camps, overseas scouting trips for draft-eligible prospects, and a crucial component of new sharing. Russians are being taught by Swedes, Estonians are being taught by Finns, Latvians are being taught by Canadians, and Danes are being taught by the Swiss. I've even seen a Swiss goalie named Reto Schurch host summer camps in California, but he's teaching a lot of the same methods that his Canadian friend Francois Allaire teaches. Over the past few summers, Erik Granqvist, one of the best goalie coaches in Sweden, has also come to California to work with Team Canada goalie and Winnipeg Jets prospect Eric Comrie.

While these things are happening due in large part to the powerful influence of social networking in North America, imagine the impact it had on European countries in the mid-1990s. Usually restricted to watching goalies in their own regions, now a Finnish goalie coach can tap into an NHL game at any time. Remote coaching with Finnish goalies playing in North America strengthens the bond between native training and international play, all while giving European goalie coaches a taste of North American hockey culture and methods.

They are no longer isolated, they are now integrated. The world shrinks, thousands of high-level goalies and goalie coaches are able to interact on an easier basis, and the links that bind us together ultimately strengthen the position as a whole. This serves the greater good. This thrusts us forward and expands the spectrum of knowledge and progression.

We need this. I mean, where would we be without it? It's hard to imagine, but it's not impossible to consider that it can also pose threats.

The first threat is big business. Goalie coaches have an easier time monetizing their services through affordable technologies that allow for remote coaching and remote video analysis. They can charge users to access a databank of drills and videos. This is not always a bad thing; some information is more valuable than other stuff you'll find out there. But at the same time, monetizing stuff online in the goaltending industry ultimately acts as a restrictor, a barrier that becomes a wall in the wide open sprawl of a world where free information should coexist with new voices and new ideas.

Monetization also opens the door for another threat in the age of social networking – ego.

When one believes that their information is too valuable to share in an open and free forum, it can turn off a lot of other people, because it comes off as being egocentric. As I've said before, there are no real hidden secrets in today's world of goalie development. There are new technologies that come at a price, but in terms of teaching technique, or in terms of having different ways to explain positioning and angles, or even something more indescribable like mental conditioning or eye trajectory, we've reached a point in this highly-refined subculture where there are few hidden training methods. So many free resources already exist that you usually end up looking 'holier than thou' if you try to charge for these types of insights.

Coming off like you have a big or inflated ego due to charging large dollar amounts for camps and private lessons is more commonplace in North America, where you see coaches with strong resumes and pro coaching or playing experience at the center of their sales pitch. Or they're selling a gimmicky product. Again, in today's economic environment, this is to be expected, and it should not be exclusively frowned upon. But it can still stymie growth and opportunity.

As I'll continue to point out throughout the book, one of the biggest problems that faces North American goalie development lies in the size of our two countries. There are so many goalies in the Greater Toronto Area that high-level coaching is at a premium demand. That demand allows the goalie coaches to charge higher amounts, and that is another socio-economic plight that may never be broken. In more sparse areas, say in California for example, the supply of goalies is much smaller, so you won't find many high-end coaches. But the demand is quickly rising, because more and more kids are playing hockey and wanting to become full-time goalies.

This is the current state of affairs as we know it. Without coaching certification models in place in either country, pockets with smaller numbers will suffer and areas with larger numbers will also suffer. Goalies in non-traditional areas won't get the chance to work with certified goalie coaches because so few exist, and goalies in saturated markets won't get the chance to work with certified goalie coaches as often as they'd like, unless they're willing to pay a pretty penny.

I've witnessed countless goalies from smaller markets traveling to bigger markets where the opportunities to develop are more promising and plentiful. They pay more, but they get the chance to train and play in areas where scouts have found goalies in the past and hope to find a gem once again. It just goes to show you that it's not always how good you are, but where and when you're seen, and by whom.

But in the age of social networking, one can still gain a lot of knowledge by doing their own research and taking their development into their own hands. It's not the same as having a personal coach or a mentor, but with a little sacrifice and ambition (and a computer), you too can learn just as much as I have. Americans, now more than ever, have to be able to manage their own game a little bit.

The concept sharing was one of the most vital lessons I learned over the summer. It's something that seems so simple to achieve, but when you get to know individuals on a personal level, you find it rather curious that sharing isn't nearly as commonplace or as embraced as it is in Europe. It became one of the starkest differences between the two worlds, and something that I feel has to change in North America as soon as possible.

I repeatedly asked myself (and others) this summer, "Why is sharing so difficult for goalie coaches in North America?" Is it their paranoia? Is it their ego?

I think it's a combination of both. I also think it's a product of fear.

From what I've witnessed and experienced over the years, I think many goalie coaches are afraid to share ideas and information, because there's a real chance that someone else, maybe someone with more coaching knowledge than them, may consider or label their ideas and information as erroneous, logically flawed, archaic, non-institutionalized, shoddy, or amateurish.

Many coaches struggle with this, because they rely on proper teachings and information to make a living. So if a parent or potential student sees information that other goalie coaches consider to be flawed, it will damage that coach's reputation. And nobody who wants to make a living coaching goalies can afford to have that happen. So rather than take a chance and publish stuff on the internet that could be considered wrong, they silence themselves and keep it away from the eyes of others.

This is an unfortunate part of the current goaltending culture in North America. We live in a world where everyone loves to hate, where chiding, mocking and breaking people down is more enjoyable for some people than building others up and cheering them on. So this fear of sharing is, in my opinion, a very real and unfortunate thing.

It's also something I've experienced in my career. For someone who never played a game of NCAA or pro hockey, you can imagine the type of resistance and negative feedback I've received over the years. At first, I was oblivious to it, but then I became paranoid of it. I didn't want to believe it, but I knew many goalie purists thought that a kid from Texas would have very little knowledge about goaltending. Due to my upbringing and lack of pro experience, I figured it would act as a stigma or Scarlet Letter I'd have to deal with for the rest of my life.

But when I first started to publish information and scouting reports on goalies, I didn't know any better. I wasn't aware of the negativity that thrived in the shadows of the current social networking culture, and I didn't really care what people thought of my work, because I knew I was no expert to begin with.

Fortunately, my sheer passion for writing and studying goalies mixed together in such a way that The Goalie Guild garnered enough success for me to push through the resistance and keep on going. But believe me, there were many nights where I cowered in fear at the idea that somebody with a lot of authority in the hockey community would call me out for being a fake, or try to damage my reputation by refuting everything I said.

Despite these fears, I readily and openly shared hundreds and thousands of pages, posts, articles, and ideas on goaltending. Although I may have lost many financial opportunities to become a coach or start running goalie camps in Colorado, I did not care, because I simply way more passionate about scouting and writing and learning more from pro goalies and coaches.

The more I shared, the more I learned, because writing things down was a way for me to process what I saw and experienced. I made a few thousand dollars writing for NHL.com and through *The Power Within*, and I might make a few thousand dollars more from writing this book. But the real gratifying part of this whole thing has been the sharing of ideas and information.

In fact, to be perfectly honest, I owe almost all of my recent success to social networking. The online goalie community, mainly confined to the Goalie Store Bulletin Board (GSBB) and a few other similar online communities, was extremely small before The Goalie Guild launched in 2009. That's the same year that InGoal Magazine started, and between both of our sites, we've gathered together thousands of goalies and goalie coaches together into a very strong subculture. And that subculture continues to grow on a daily basis.

As a result, when it comes to sharing, I believe it's not just the decision one must make to actually disseminate information openly and without fear, but how you go about doing it. It's like the same thing you get when you tell a goalie to work smarter, not just harder.

Many goalie coaches I've come across have tremendous wisdom and plenty of ideas worth sharing, but they don't have the knowledge, time, or capacity to share it. Building websites are easier for kids from our generation, but much tougher for the previous generation. Staying relevant in the midst of all these new technologies and social media platforms limits their reach and their capacity to share, and that puts more experienced coaches at a disadvantage.

Many have been able to create Twitter profiles, but not many have the time to post enough content to remain relevant, especially those with families and full-time coaching jobs,

There is much pride to be had in building up a brand single-handedly, but in all reality, the success goes to the timing of it all. Had I not started that meager Wordpress blog in 2009 and that random Twitter profile a few months later, where would I be?

I see not only this type of pattern repeating in many other places with many other passionate goalies, but the amount will keep growing. The Greg Balloch's and Aaron Goldstein's and Clare Austin's of the world will keep popping up, and their ability to utilize new technologies will give them a voice regardless of their amount of experience. And since they're open to sharing ideas and spreading information, their voice will echo throughout the ages as the light we shed shines brighter and brighter.

This idea of continual growth and constant expansion is so important right now. It helps us spread value and passion to the areas that don't get exposed to these things. The goalies in Alaska, Iowa, Florida, Arizona, and everywhere else that seems fairly uncommon now have more ways than ever to become fans of goaltending, and to learn the same sort of things that goalies in Toronto, Minnesota, and New York are learning.

Because the world relies so heavily on these social norms, I've seen it influence every corner of goaltending, from coaching to recruiting.

Therefore, my advice is pretty simple. If you're a goalie, learn how to manage your online identity properly. You know the risks of saying the wrong thing at the wrong time, and you know the rewards that comes with free exposure. If you're a coach, please find ways to share your information, and don't be afraid to do so. Break through the fear and know that, regardless of your experiences, your views and opinions do matter. If you're just a passionate goalie lover, never let your thirst for new content and articles be quenched.

And to all of you, register a domain, create a Twitter feed, and get out there and share. Your ideas are unique, your voice is meant to be heard, and it is your duty as a lover of goalies and goaltending to speak up and speak loud. We need you now more than ever before.

I have listened and learned from some of the top goalie coaches in the world, as well as hundreds of younger and less-experienced goalie coaches. Through it all, I can tell you that those with the most wisdom are those that are willing to share openly and freely, and without fear of damaging their ego or reputation. Those that have a narrowed-minded point of view, think their way is the only way, think they must protect certain insights and secrets, or have this need to mock others, actually have less wisdom. Remember, there is no need to feel like you have to protect something. There is no reason not to share everything. There is no reason to try and 'dress up' or 'repackage' what can easily be found and learned elsewhere.

What matters is that you showcase a genuine work ethic, a solid coaching philosophy, and a fair value for the services you provide. And if you're willing to learn as much as you teach, you will never have a problem earning income in the age of social networking. The more you learn, the more you have to teach, and the more you have to teach, the more positive influence you have on the goaltending community.

We need this more than ever, because stagnation and fear are limitations to evolution. We constantly need to filter in new voices, new ideas, new goalie websites, and platforms for collaboration. Push forward with this idea, and we all win. Hold back from doing your part, and we all lose. It's that simple.

We must cherish the ability to share in order to break apart the prison cells of ignorance.

3

THE SCIENCE OF SHADOWING AND IDEOKINESIS

"Consciousness is only possible through change; change is only possible through movement." –Aldos Huxley

In December of 2010, I wrote an article on The Goalie Guild introducing a concept I called *Shadowing*. This article was fledgling in form; it was one of the first times I went beyond the reach of ordinary goalie analysis and discussed an idea that was my own creative genesis.

Shadowing was my way of explaining how goalies naturally emulate their idols, counterparts, and various other goalies they cross paths with throughout their lives. We see this at all levels of hockey and in many different situations, from mini-mites all the way to the pros.

When this happens, goalies gradually begin to experience changes in their postural and muscular patterns. This happens subtly and superfluously, but it can also happen substantially and swiftly, depending on the way a goalie's unique genetic and athletic blueprint interacts with their surroundings. It also depends on the type of interactions a goalie has with the characters found within his or her Web of Influence. Like I said in the prelude, relationships really matter when it comes to goalie development.

The Web of Influence was a way for me to visualize the impact that other goalies had on my own technique and stylistic tactics. Why did I have the same faceoff stance as Chris Osgood? Because he was my idol and I watched nearly every game of his entire NHL career. Why did I start wearing my jersey like Sergei Bobrovsky? Because I loved his style and quietly fierce attitude.

Why did you start doing certain things as a goalie, and where did you learn to do them? Consider the ways in which the world around you allowed you to create a meaningful connection and build a strong correlation between your conscious and subconscious interactions with these goalies. Through progressive coaching and training methods, we've developed the ability to alter our mannerisms and mechanics in swift and effective manners. Scientists have even proved that our DNA can be altered just by thinking, eating, and drinking the proper things. So it is no stretch of the imagination to understand that, by watching (and playing with) certain goalies, for better or for worse, *we are constantly changing*.

Like a diamond reflects different prisms of color in the sunlight, our movements, habits, routines, mannerisms, body language, and techniques can constantly change just through the sheer act of seeing and watching what other goalies are doing.

The roots of imagery and visualization, and the body's capacity to display dynamic alignment, is deeply embedded not only in athletes, but in performance artists as well. Dancers, singers, musicians, and even astronauts have used the power of the imagination to improve their posture, dexterity, mobility, and overall competitive prowess.

While this chapter focuses on the different ideas I've studied and formulated regarding the relationship between Shadowing, imagery, functional movement, and goaltending (I could write an entire book on this subject), please realize that this concept is nothing new. But it is the deep and drastic influence these sciences have on a goalie's body that I believe has yet to be discovered by the vast majority of the goalie community.

In the original article I wrote on Shadowing, I spoke with NHL goalie coaches Mitch Korn (Washington Capitals) and Mike Valley (Dallas Stars). Since many of you probably never read that original article, I wanted to re-publish a few quotes before I start trudging deeper into the dense forest of connecting this type of science to goalie development.

In one part of the article, I asked Valley about his own idol as a kid, Eddie Belfour.

> *"I put together over one hundred clips of Belfour on video and then watched it every single day," Valley reflected. "Because I saw it so many times, I naturally started mimicking what I saw and it was a big part of how I learned when I was younger."*

Surely we have all gained vital wisdom on playing the position by simply watching our favorite goalies play. Day after day, year after year, we allowed our bodies to naturally mirror that crease choreography, which unconsciously developed our own kinesthetic senses as young goalies. This, over time, enhanced our movements through the similar usage of our joints, bones, and muscles. Years later, some of us may have created very organized areas of similar postural patterns in the goalies we've idolized the longest.

At the highest level imaginable, however, Shadowing happens more on purpose and less on accident. In another section of my original article, I asked Korn about the on-ice learning dynamic between two former Nashville Predators goalies, Mike Dunham and Tomas Vokoun.

> *"Over time, Vokoun was no longer a pure butterfly goalie and was starting to stay up more, displaying more patience, and reacting to and saving pucks rather than just blocking," Korn explained. "And even though Dunham never became a true butterfly goalie, he was willing to leave his feet more and use the butterfly as a save selection."*

Another example of this was witnessed by Valley between Alex Auld and Marty Turco.

> *"Alex changed his stickhandling style to the over-hand grip last year due in large part to Turco's use of it on a daily basis," Valley said. "Because Alex saw Marty successfully handle the puck with the over-hand technique, as well as seeing the great decisions he made in every*

> *game, he knew there were certain options available to him."*

But it wasn't just a simple technical change that altered Auld's style. There were also postural changes:

> *"Auld started bending his knees more and got his butt lower to the ice so that he had better balance and more control," Valley added. "Marty gets lower to the ice and bends his knees as well, and also does an excellent job of getting his head up in order to read plays and improve his vision."*

I'm sure if you've watched NHL goaltenders over the past five years, you've also witnessed Shadowing at this level for yourself. Anders Lindback started looking like Pekka Rinne while he was in Nashville, and then, as I witnessed during the NHL Goalie Camp in Madison, Lindback started emulating a couple of Kari Lehtonen's traits in just a few short days. So even NHL goaltenders, as extremely gifted and as highly-refined as they are, will still get influenced and altered by who or what they see. They're adaptable, capable of changing on a daily basis.

Knowing an infinite number of Shadowing examples were out there, it simply came down to learning and understanding more of the science behind it, including how it impacted a goalie's development on a larger scale. From this, I was introduced to some beautiful concepts, a few of which I'm quite excited to briefly introduce you to in order to shed a little more light on just how intricate the goaltender is as an athlete, and just how difficult it is to solve the development riddle.

Embracing Biochemical Individuality

I'll start with the science of *Biochemical Individuality*, which essentially proves that there is no 'one-size-fits-all' training or development "path" for goaltenders.

Biochemical Individuality is an idea originally developed by Roger Williams. A world-renowned scientist, Williams contributed greatly to the notion that anatomical and physiological variations among people are a result of individual responses to their specific environments. More specifically, his work focused on nutritional needs and optimal health among people in different areas. He even contributed to the idea that identical twins, while still in utero, have different needs depending on their mother's living environment.

When the scientific community established the Human Genome project, Biochemical Individuality gained more attention, so it started reaching beyond nutrition into fields such as disease and medicine.

It didn't take long for me to realize that Biochemical Individuality clearly played a vital role in the way a goalie develops. Tying the two worlds together was easy, because we now know that every goalie has their own unique technical, mental, and emotional profile. Based on their genetics, their environment, and how their mind interacts with their body, goalies with similar potential will play very differently.

This comes as no surprise to the coaching community. We all know by now that we have to be open to teaching and treating goalies of the same age or physical stature differently. What works for one athlete may not work for another, even if that technique or strategy is mechanically sound and efficient. This idea has slowly seeped into the collective consciousness of goalie coaches since 2000, and finally, in 2015, it has become a staple, a fact, a no-brainer in almost everyone's coaching philosophies.

Unfortunately, very few goalie coaches in North America have a strong background in kinesiology, physical education, or exercise science, so there's a lot the average goalie coach doesn't know in terms of how the body develops, why age-specific training is important, and what type of methods out there exist to improve and enhance a goalie's functional and instinctual movements.

For those that are more informed about Biochemical Individuality, I know that this science is focused mainly on gene expression, nutritional needs, and metabolic processes. But even those aspects of a developing body have an impact on how a goalie performs. If they're not eating the right foods, they may be at higher risk for physical burnout in a game where they face a lot of shots. They may also struggle to breathe properly in a close game, or they may be more prone to dehydration in a lengthy bag skate.

These things matter, and these things may lead to a day where something like body mapping becomes a common practice for goalie and hockey scouts. The more we can evaluate, gauge, measure, and monitor a goalie's body, the better we can understand their unique physiological and biochemical traits, and the better we can strengthen their weaknesses.

It's only a matter of time before we begin to gain access to new and readily available technologies that measure things like a goalie's metabolic efficiency, their speed of physical recovery, their heart rate, and their muscle imbalances while in the crease. There is so much going on beneath the surface of what a goalie coach can see, so the next step in properly developing a goalie is gaining information on some of the realms of athleticism we can't see.

The Benefits of Pilates

Whenever a goalie asks me what they can do to improve their game, I give them all the same answer.

"Try Pilates," I say. "It will make you a better goalie in one month, without ever stepping a foot on the ice."

I was fortunate to discover Pilates over 12 years ago thanks to my sister Gina, who is regarded as one of the top Pilates instructors in Colorado. Throughout her years as a teacher, I was able to read some of her textbooks, glean from her deep knowledge of the body, and most importantly, take a handful of her mat, chair, and reformer classes.

I'll always remember my very first Pilates lesson with Gina. I was 20, a junior at CSU, and just starting to get interested in functional movement.

"You're only as old as your spine is flexible," she said to me.

Since then, that quote has stuck with me, forever changing my skill development as a goaltender. Her training placed the proper emphasis on balancing my muscles and improving my body awareness. Now at age 32, my body is still fit and highly functional, at least enough to play competitively on a daily basis without any back, hip, or knee issues. In fact, my body and spine is even more flexible and durable than it was at age 20.

As a result, I've taken the time to learn first-hand how Pilates can improve a goalie's coordination, balance, core strength, and overall body awareness.

To many people, Pilates is seen as a female-dominated practice. While that may be true, it's important to realize that the original creator, Joseph Pilates, was as manly as it gets. He was a broad-bodied German weight-lifter, gymnast, and boxer that previously suffered from numerous childhood sicknesses.

After reading many of my sister's books on Pilates, I learned that Mr. Pilates originally described his teachings through an idea called *Contrology*. This method was mainly focused on using the mind to better direct the body. Control was not about getting into one static position and holding it, but rather improving the way the central nervous system acts as a vehicle for improved and more refined movements. *Contrology* was for all of life's unexpected movements, so as to improve awareness within the body and mind, while also increasing the confidence and coordination needed to move in tricky and highly reactionary ways.

Pilates also wrote in numerous ways that the goal of his work was to enhance the coordination of the mind, body, and spirit. Three key ingredients needed to do this was awareness, alignment, and relaxed movements of all joints in the body. When those elements are harmonious, an athlete can truly achieved an efficient and elite level of functional movement.

As a goalie, no matter what style you play or what physical limitations your body may have, moving in a controlled manner from your core, with concentration and proper breathing, can create a more natural, relaxed, and efficient flow from one movement to the next. As such, I strongly believe Pilates is a powerful way to enhance a goalie's movements, because it single-handedly strengthens the steady connection of coordination, balance, muscle control, and focus.

Over the past few years, we have seen a rise in the number of goalie-related Yoga activities. Extremely beneficial for the mind-body connection and proper breathing, I've done my fair share of Yoga as well. Adding a dose of both practices to your training regime is quite complimentary, but if I had to choose one or the other, I would continue to practice Pilates.

One of the main reasons Pilates is my functional movement practice of choice is due to the engagement and strengthening of the Powerhouse. The Powerhouse is comprised of the abs muscles, the hips, lower back muscles, and the buttocks. It covers an area that begins at the base of the pelvis floor and extends to the bottom of the diaphragm, including the *transverses abdominus,* which is the deepest muscle in your abs. It surrounds the entire Powerhouse area and is one of the most important core muscles a goalie can use when attempting to move with a combination of strength and control.

Although I have no reason to discredit anything Yoga related, I often notice that many goalies who take Yoga classes end up over-stretching. A team practice or private goalie session is actually enough stretching and flexing of the hips and legs and knee joints for 36-to-48 hours. You're also stretching before and most likely after that practice as well. With so much emphasis placed on the butterfly save selection, if you're doing Yoga often on top of playing daily, you may in fact be over-doing it quite a bit.

Pilates, however, is very different. Every exercise, whether you're doing basic mat routines or working on the reformer, is aimed specifically at developing a symmetrically strong torso, and therefore an even stronger Powerhouse. This allows a goalie to move more from their core and less from their knees and ankles and hips. It reduces strain, decreases the likelihood of injury, and never exacerbates the potential copious amounts of stretching you may already be doing. Furthermore, Pilates brings many of the same awareness elements you get with Yoga. It develops self-awareness, places a strong importance on proper breathing, and improves the spine's functionality.

So if you're a goalie coach and want to improve all of your students, regardless of their style and skill level, now is the time to learn more about the benefits of Pilates.

Beyond the benefits of functional body movement practices like Pilates and Yoga, a number of other Somatic disciplines can really enhance a goalie's posture and mobility, including Functional Relaxing, Moshe Feldenkrais, Body-Mind Centering, the age-old discipline of simple Meditation, and my favorite of them all, Ideokinesis.

'New-age' disciplines like Pilates may be outside of the regular scope of a goalie's training habits, but they are actually not new-age at all. In fact, without a shadow of doubt, I guarantee that they can improve the movements and coordination of any type of goalie, regardless of their age or physical limitations.

In fact, I will never forget the time Gina and my mother saw Belfour taking a class in a small Pilates studio in Dallas way back in 1998. They told me how he was the only guy surrounded by a bunch of older women, but he was working very hard on a reformer, trying to eliminate the onset of back pain issues. Sure enough, it was his practice of Pilates that helped extend his NHL career during his time with Toronto and Florida.

Yes, as strange as it sounds, an NHL goalie was benefitting from Pilates more than 15 years ago. Yet only in the past few years has a mind-body practice like Yoga become more commonplace in enhancing a goalie's development. Even fewer goalies have discovered the amazing benefits of Pilates, so I hope this book and my future efforts can spread more awareness about this practice as time goes on.

An Introduction to Ideokinesis

Beyond Pilates, I'm really curious to know how many goalie coaches are familiar with Ideokinesis. If you've never heard this term before, have no fear; you've probably used this method with your students in the past, or have learned from a coach who liked to explain things in metaphors.

So let me break it down for you and include a brief history.

The etymology of the word *Ideokinesis* is simple. "Kinesis" means motion, or in this instance, a physical movement. "Ideo" means idea, or in this instance, a concept of a specific movement developed and visualized through an empirical thought process. Put the two words together and Ideokinesis is defined as a discipline where *an image or a thought acts as a facilitator for enhanced movement and posture*.

Ideokinesis gained prominence mainly in the dance industry, but it has also proven to be therapeutic, so it is often used with physical therapy patients, people with debilitating genetic disorders, and the elderly. But for goalies, I strongly believe that it can improve skills by making conscious, deliberate movements more unconscious. By creating imagery in our minds through simple visualization exercises, we can fuse technique together with the natural learning process in an educational and enlightening manner.

My idea of using Ideokinesis to improve a goalie's movements is rooted in its usage in the arts of dance and music. In the 1920s and 1930s, the famous pianist Luigi Bonpensiere originally coined and fathered the term as a way to describe some of his training methods, both as a player and a teacher.

From there, the life-long works of Mabel Todd (1880-1956) and Lulu Sweigard (1895-1974) further developed the idea that "thinking" rather than "doing" produced measurable changes in a person's postural and spinal alignment. Sweigard is probably most famous for creating her "Nine Lines of Movement", an idea that forever changed the way a dancer ploys and teaches his or her craft.

Visualizing lines of movement through the body (done while not moving) has been scientifically proven to change the habitual patterns of messages being sent from the brain through nerve pathways and to the muscles. As long as this new thinking pattern is able to be activated during movement, the proper muscle activity will automatically follow. This results in new muscle and movement patterns that can lead to improved balance, better alignment, and more relaxed "flow-state" mindset.

Other pioneers in Ideokinesis included Barbara Clark (1889-1982) and Sally Swift (1913-2009). Researching Swift's work was really intriguing to me, because she focused a lot of her time assisting horse riders. Growing up on a horse ranch in Texas, even though I didn't ride often, I watched my mom do it every day. So I was immediately drawn to creating connections between her methods and ways to better develop goaltenders. Sure enough, her work was so compatible with goaltenders that it didn't take long at all.

In 1985, Swift wrote a book called *Centered Riding* and introduced four basic Ideokinesis teaching points.

The first of the four points was called Soft Eyes. This involved her way of teaching riders how to relax the usual hardened focus of a rider that occurs when they try to concentrate. Swift found that relaxing the eyes in order to *openly receive* visual cues, as opposed to straining the eye muscles in order to *aggressively find* those cues, actually helped riders relax their entire bodies. As a result, they became better aware of the horse's movements through their other senses.

Just for fun, take a second to test this idea with me. Close your eyes and tune out the world around you.

Now imagine this: *warm water being poured on a dry sponge.* As the image is being processed in your mind, it should help facilitate a change in your body by naturally allowing yourself to relax your eyes. Easy. Effective. Exciting! The image you created in your mind through my simple visual cue is the facilitator of change in your eye's muscle movement and activity.

That, in a nutshell, is Ideokinesis.

Swift also taught the "anatomy of breathing" as the second of her four basic teaching points, which helped riders release upper body and core tension. The third teaching point was called Centering, which helped riders better center their gravity at the base of their pelvis.

The fourth basic teaching point was called Building Blocks, and it emphasized the importance of the rider visualizing alignment and body balance. By teaching them how to imagine a line running through the center of their head and down through their pelvis, Swift helped her students understand the specific and intimate balance and counterbalance needed when jumping, trotting, and cantering.

Like I said above, taking these four basic points and applying them into the realm of goalie development was no stretch at all. In fact, "Soft Focus" and "Hard Focus" is a term commonly used by Canadian goalie coach Eli Wilson during his training camps, and breathing exercises are finally starting to become more commonplace in the lexicon of goalie training. And of course we know the importance of being able to visualize having good balance on our edges.

But it is the integration of imagery and visualization, a lot of which can be done off the ice in a classroom or training room environment, that can take coaching skills and personal development to the next level. By visualizing efficient save movements using unique images found in nature, we can activate those tricky and complicated neurological pathways to help us better accomplish movements in the crease. Over time, Ideokinesis opens up the floodgates for the nervous system to better engage the main muscles goalies use, replacing old processes that were previously considered inefficient.

As I learned more about Ideokinesis, I also gained a deeper understanding of my own game. For example, a proper reverse-VH is not something I developed by seeing it in a book or having a goalie coach tell me how to position myself. Proper reverse-VH is a feeling within your body; it's a balance between sufficient *stimulation* of certain muscles and a sufficient *restraint* of muscle activity, which in turn makes the reverse-VH as relaxed, balanced, and as effortless as possible.

The science behind Ideokinesis and goalie development also has a lot to do with the brain. The wide and active areas of the brain involved in imagery, especially visualization, is very important. The body and mind responds as a single unit – no thought or emotion exists without a biochemical or electrochemical response or accompanying activity. This activity touches every cell, so even something like the act of dreaming about making big saves is a form of practice. The mind can influence the body on a cellular level, and thus have the power to modify, and eventually improve, your body's movements.

This is not mystical wisdom. It's real sports science.

This is why I'm of the strong opinion that more time must be spent *observing* a goalie at a young age, and less time spoon-feeding them answers to complex technical questions that don't really need answering until they're a little older and more ready to process advanced technique with greater success. Getting to know their unique genetic blueprint and biochemical individuality, then catering the teachings and guidance to what you've learned about the individual is much more effective than doing the opposite. For in many places, we teach first and observe later.

Because of this, you have to let the goalie learn on their own, especially at a very young age. Don't be afraid to observe and take notes and stress basic principles for a while, then buff out some of the technical flaws a little later. Young goalies are naturally flawed since it takes years to master body control, or things like having optimal balance on your inside edges. Some will excel in some areas and struggle in others, so the focus at a young age has to be on the evaluation of the athlete's genetic limitations, all while creating an environment that is fun and positive.

The more I learned about functional movement and dynamic alignment, the more I realized that a goalie's posture is constantly changing, and it often changes in a manner that reflects the current state of mind. Dynamic alignment is not static or a finality. You don't work towards the moment where you reach perfect alignment and then stay there forever. Rather, there is always room for improvement, always a better way to be more efficient or relaxed.

The following quote comes from Sweigard, who discussed somatic disciplines and the use of imagery in an article originally published back in 1961:

> *"The unattainable 'perfect posture' shows the skeletal framework in perfect alignment, in strict agreement with all principles of mechanical balance. Approaching the ideal promotes those attributes so important to the performing artist: a slenderized figure; optimum flexibility of all joints; and minimum expenditure of energy, both in the maintenance of the body in the upright position and in the performance of movement."*

A body is a function of its unique relation to their center. One goalie may need to move their hips a little higher to reach that optimal balance point. Another goalie standing in the same exact spot, may need to move lower. Ultimately, things like 'proper ready stance' is an imaginary point because it's slightly different for everyone.

To leave you with one last idea, I think it's important to understand how movements influence instincts and vice-versa. Postural patterns, with proper guidance and training, leads to postural precision. And postural precision leads to instinctual balance. Instinctual balance then leads to mental and physical readiness, both on and off the ice. Physical readiness allows a goaltender to focus more of his energy on tracking pucks and reading plays with a clearer mind – in a thoughtless, instinctual manner.

I've also learned that a goalie's muscle memory and instincts can be enhanced when they move at a slightly slower pace. So consider at what speed you or your goalies execute certain drills. Speed is a bodily limitation, and far too often I see goalies moving way too fast in drills, thus lacking proper body control. But when a coach has the capacity to recognize this bad habit, they can improve their goalie's neural feedback and cognitive ability to learn a skill by having them slow things down.

In the world of Martial Arts, Tai Chi routines are almost exclusively done very slowly. This methodical execution of movements allows the performer to become more aware of their breathing and muscle usage. But at the same time, some Korean Monks are known to complete their routines in less than a minute. They can be so fast that some people can't even see some of the movements taking place.

This is a good example of how you shouldn't get stuck in one mode of doing things. I often tell goalies to do at least one thing each day that they otherwise feel a certain resistance towards doing. It could be running, squats, biking, or in my life, it's lunges. I hate lunges. They hurt. But if you can overcome the comfort of routine and do new things, it will introduce new pathways in the mind-body relationship and generate new patterns in how you view and understand the way you move.

Especially at a younger age, you can't be overly concerned with speed. Remember, slow is smooth and smooth is fast. The mastery of a new or advanced skill follows a pretty simple process. Technique comes first, then accuracy, then power, and then speed. If you try going too fast before you've nailed down the technique of the skill, and if you're still inaccurate with your execution, speed means nothing and ultimately becomes a hindrance to execution. So it's important to recognize when you or your goalies are moving too fast. If you see it, don't be lazy and don't let it slide by. Tell them to slow down, give them proper feedback, and don't be in a rush. Structured, proper development equals quality reps first, and then you aim for quantity.

At the end of the day, everything relating to the way a goalie moves and improves depends mainly on the relationship between their body, their mind, and the ground. Through this idea, the science of Shadowing unlocks the doors to a massive new world just waiting to be discovered. This world is full of methods that have rarely been connected to goalie development, but at least now you have the keys needed to unlock doors and explore more.

What can you discover about the influence of biochemical individuality, the positive impact of Ideokinesis, or the teaching methods that exist in other athletic and artistic domains? More importantly, how can these things make you a better goalie or goalie coach?

The Epistemology of Head Trajectory

A few years ago, I stumbled across a goalie training company called *Optimum Reaction Sports.* The founder, a goalie coach named Lyle Mast, spent more than a decade studying and training clients from the novice to the NHL levels in order to determine if there was some special trait they all had in common.

He discovered that the special trait was proper visual attachment. From there, he trademarked a term called Head Trajectory™, which is defined on the OR Sports website.

> *"Head Trajectory™ impacts the ability to efficiently execute every aspect of your training,*

> *development, and game play, based on your set-up. It empowers the athlete to train on the values of efficiency versus just speed and seeing the puck versus just looking at it. It exposes the difference between being able versus unable to execute your save and post-save responses, eliminating delays. Simply put, OR Sports teaches you what your body requires in order to perform your best. They train the athlete how to properly track the puck using Head Trajectory™, eliminating delays in visual attachment, movement, rotation and access to the puck in all game play situations." –www.orsports.com/about*

Knowing what Head Trajectory™ claimed to do, I wanted to know how it worked. But I couldn't really get a good grasp of that through their website, so I repeatedly tried to get in touch with Mast. Unfortunately, I was unsuccessful, as he seemed very busy working on this trademarked technique with numerous major-junior and pro-level goalies. He was getting results, so I knew there had to be something substantial to it.

Since I couldn't speak directly with Mast, I had to try and figure it out on my own. So I read every single thing I could find on the subject, including their website's extensive testimonials page, a couple of short videos, and a few other random quotes and article quips. Still, there was nothing out there that directly explained the actual process or the technique behind the trademarked term.

Finally, as the months rolled along, I started to hear from a few more goalies and coaches that were more familiar with Mast's work. I eventually learned that, at its core, Head Trajectory™ improved the way you moved and positioned your head so that your eyeballs were more centered in their sockets and in total sync with the actual head movements. It was also the idea of 'closing in' on pucks, as opposed to 'lifting' the head away from them. Further research revealed that Head Trajectory™ taught goalies how to keep their head slightly tilted down like a boxer in order to better track pucks coming off a stick blade.

There was obviously more to it, but I felt like the principles of Head Trajectory™ had been around for decades. Beyond just actually watching the puck into the body, a goalie with good head trajectory moved less, stayed more patient, and had the ability to know how much space they filled in the net.

So what was the difference between teaching these commonplace skills and teaching Head Trajectory™? I still wasn't sure, and as time moved along, I kept struggling to uncover any legitimate specifics.

After speaking with a few former and current pro goalies that had worked with Mast, it turned out that the majority of them seemed to be telling me the same thing; it was simple to understand, but it was hard to tell when they were doing it right or doing it wrong. Some guys were able to feel it a bit more easily than others, but even then, the nomenclature used to explain the technique seemed quite complicated.

As much as I wish I could explain the science behind Mast's Head Trajectory™ technique, unfortunately, it still eludes me. Even after a few articles were recently published on NHL.com and InGoal Magazine regarding

Head Trajectory™, it remained a mystery for many. Due to these articles, thousands of goalies and coaches everywhere were wondering what it was, and how they could teach and implement it. There was a lot of confusion out there, and that became a very problematic situation with younger goalies.

In my opinion, head trajectory (not the trademarked term, but the idea that has been around for many years), is a mind-body awareness tool, not a rigid definition of what we generally call a new technique. It's a philosophy, a different way of thinking and teaching core skills. It's a way to further improve postural patterns and a way to help goalies understand how the head interacts with the eyes.

I am sure that Mast does an excellent job of improving the body awareness of his student through detailed explanations and video feedback, and I am sure he has a trained eye in order to see how the head is the manipulator of what a goalie's eyes are seeing. But I think many goalies understand that less movement improves overall body balance and mechanics.

So while I have no doubt that Head Trajectory™ has tremendous value for some goalies (many feel it's more beneficial for taller goalies), I think it's important to understand that it should not be categorized in the same realm with the likes of the reverse-VH or the back-side recovery technique. Simply put, you have to be careful with what you read and how you process the information. As time goes on, more and more of these new technical terms and analytical elements will pop up, so you have to be aware that some of them could possibly be re-packaging skills and components of goaltending that have been around for quite some time.

The epistemology (the study of knowledge) surrounding Head Trajectory™ is a fascinating thing, because how we acquire information on new ideas and then turn that into "knowledge" that we filter into our coaching and training methods plays a massive role in the development of our young goalies.

Therefore, I believe the most important thing you can do regarding Head Trajectory™ is to get educated. I've been doing this for a few years, ever since I added it to my Periodic Table of Goaltending Elements. Conversely, the worst thing you could do is go out there, over-think how you teach a goalie to center their eyeballs in their sockets, and force a goalie to push their head over their body way more than necessary.

Remember, every goalie has a very unique postural pattern. While some goalies may benefit from extending their neck further out or tilting it slightly downward, it may negatively impact others. At the end of the day, nothing can replace the importance of a goalie being able to understand when he or she feels comfortable. Coaches can certainly guide that learning process and help goalies discover the right feel, but ultimately, it's something only the goalie can accomplish on their own. This takes time, it takes awareness, and it takes discipline to be patient with the way in which you implement these techniques.

My fear is that many goalies will be prone to overthinking how their head is positioned atop their spine. When this happens, they may be more likely to tense up, or try controlling their neck and head by squeezing neck and shoulder muscles and wrongfully holding it in place. Doing that could cause more problems than it solves.

So, until you get a chance to learn what the trademarked form of Head Trajectory is all about (what it feels like when you do it right or wrong), please don't over-think it. Just keep doing what you're doing.

I've seen so many new techniques introduced to the goalie community before, and it's rarely pretty at first. Some coaches simply refuse to go beyond their realm of personal experience in order to understand potentially new solutions, so they automatically dismiss what they don't truly know. Others coaches are way too over-enthusiastic about those potential new solutions, so they automatically assume they understand it, only to erroneously integrate it with the goalies they teach. Both instances are bad.

I think there's plenty of merit to Mast's work, and I really hope I can finally get a hold of him someday and learn more about it. I just hope that the emergence of his trademarked technique doesn't cause a bunch of goalies to go out there and start straining their necks and negatively altering their spines and postures.

The Dangers of Text Neck

Speaking of strained necks and head placement, over the past few years, I have noticed that the growing amount of science behind the "Text Neck" epidemic may be revealing some negative effects on goalies. That being said, there's definitely a lot of truth to the fact that the media has vastly overblown this issue; everyone's heads protrude forward at times, and we're still able to be very highly functional humans. But from what I've seen with my own two eyes, I still feel that it's something the goalie community needs to consider and monitor.

"Text Neck" is loosely defined as the altered and detrimental posture we create when we excessively use our phones and computers.

Kenneth K. Hansraj, MD, a Chief of Spine Surgery in New York, published a brief but poignant study in 2014 regarding Text Neck. *Assessment of Stresses in the Cervical Spine Caused by Posture and Position of the Head* created a model that showed how much weight the spine had to support when flexing the head forward. As the head starts to tilt forward, the force on the neck surges all the way up to 60 pounds at a forward flex of 60 degrees.

In the most basic sense of the term, good posture equals little to no stress on the spine. But poor posture takes place when the head is tilted forward and the shoulders drop into a rounded position, which adds excessive stress on the spine.

I often look at the shoulders and necks of young goalies when I see them off the ice or hanging around with their buddies. To my dismay, I see more and more kids with really rounded shoulders, their heads slightly protruding forward more than what I consider to be normal, and in what appears to be an unnatural or uncomfortable position. But the problem is that these slight delineations happen so slowly over the years that it's impossible for many young kids to even realize they're hunched over or protruded. It is literally just a part of their natural anatomy.

That's why it's really hard to know whether it's actually a negative effect, or if it's just part of who they are. I don't have the expertise to know what is anatomically efficient or inefficient, but again, I do think it's important to ask these questions.

Furthermore, it's important to realize that it's not the phone or the tablet that causes this issue, but the habits of the individual who uses his or her phone way too often. I mean, even reading a book can cause this issue, and people have been reading books for centuries. So when humans with normal spinal alignment spend a few hours every day with their heads tilted forward, they can become numb or unaware to the fact it's happening. If it's not causing immediate or tangible pain, it begs the question of whether or not it's actually detrimental or a hindrance to goaltending.

Either way, this is capable of affecting the way a goalie moves on the ice. Even if the effect of Text Neck happens very slowly and is unable to truly be reversed, we still need to consider its impact on development. That is why I chose to discuss this topic directly following Head Trajectory. I mean, what kind of influence does that new 'technique' have on goalies that may be victimized by this idea of Text Neck? Should we really be teaching goalies to push their heads forward and tilt it down when they're already doing this on a daily basis through the excessive use of cellphones and tablets?

The head has a high center of gravity relative to the rest of the body, so any deviations from 'optimal' alignment will have a huge impact on everything else below it. That means the cooperation between the head and the neck plays a huge role in a goalie's alignment and proper movement control. This advocates the importance of a goalie understanding their head trajectory, but also reinforces the importance of educating people on what it is actually all about, how to properly execute it, and how certain daily habits can negatively impact on-ice habits.

What I've discovered through further research is that the small cervical vertebrae of the neck have a shape designed to increase their stability, so our neck muscles already do a very good job of naturally positioning the head on top of the spine. That doesn't mean we shouldn't try to improve that cooperation, it just means that even the slightest adjustment could make a huge difference.

I think the issue of Text Neck in goalies also brings up a number of concerns regarding how the head and neck interacts with the shoulders, chest, arms, and core.

First of all, consider the impact of Muscle Armoring, which takes place when a goalie tenses up their body when facing a heavy shot. This often happens on shots to the head and shoulders area, and it's something that is an instinctual part of who we are. You can't expect a goalie to completely relax their shoulders, but so often in practice, players are screaming down Main Street, wiring clappers up high and naturally forcing the goalie to continually tense up time and time again.

Another thing I notice that continually impacts the neck-head connection is when goalies back up into their crease. This is part of muscle armoring, as it becomes an instinct to backpedal, give up depth, and not set your feet. This alters all aspects of a goalie's postural pattern, which can make it even more difficult to implement proper head trajectory techniques on a younger goalie.

As you can see, there are a lot of different kinetic elements coming into play when you start to consider the impact the head and neck has on overall posture. I would love to make this section much more robust, but I think the most important thing is to simply consider it in relation to the topics above.

I have to admit, I'm actually quite concerned with the amount of young athletes that have bad head and neck alignment. It's no surprise to find that this is becoming more of an issue with goalies – like football players, we're wearing a pretty heavy full-caged mask that further alters every movement we make.

Coming to Conclusions

Learning about the different 'sciences of shadowing' over the past five years has been an eye-opening experience. Clearly I'm no scientist, but learning about these things has helped me formulate new ideas regarding goalie development. I love mixing science together with goaltending in ways that have rarely been explored before, because it proves that the more I learn, the less I actually know.

I firmly believe these are realms worth researching if the goalie community wants to further improve the way our athletes develop in different external and internal environments. I hope that someday these terms and practices become more commonplace in discussions and literature regarding goalie development.

On a global scale, it's interesting to see what kind of functional movement methods are being used in different parts of the world. Environment is a part of your culture and culture is a part of your environment, and while race and birthplace pose certain genetic barriers to athletic development, no matter where you're from or who your parents are, one-half of one percent of your genetic code is completely unique to you. That .5 percent is very important, because scientists now know that our DNA loves to gamble; it adapts and changes depending on your situations, surroundings, diets, and attitudes. That's why traveling, playing more than one sport, and trying new things can be so beneficial to development.

Have you read David Epstein's book, *The Sports Gene*? How about *Outliers* by Malcolm Gladwell? Two of the most influential books on the topics of athletic development and the potential for success, these masterpieces further enhanced my passion for finding answers to questions about the science of shadowing. These books also made me want to learn more about the age-old "Nature versus Nurture" debate, and how our individual differences shape our paths to the top of the goaltending food chain.

From reading these books, another set of questions plagued me this summer:

How do we distinguish or determine a goalie's ability to improve compared to their actual rate of improvement? Those are two very different things altogether, but how often do we actually consider it when we're caught up in the chaotic and complicated stages of goalie training?

Because I'm limited in my scientific knowledge on these topics, I make very few claims here. I mean, what differences between styles are actually real? That being said, my only agenda is to continue the learning process and share my findings with goalie coaches that can in turn reveal different perspectives. I'll gladly talk to kinesiologists and scientists and anyone with a background in exercise science.

For example, one question I often ask people is what they think about teaching a six-year-old goalie how to butterfly. Some of you may believe that the sooner they learn this skill, the quicker they will master it. In my opinion – and I'm not saying I'm right – I think that's crazy.

At that age, a goalie hardly has the capacity to even understand it's only one of many save selections, much less distinguish when and where to properly use it. Goalies at that age also seem to process it as a singularity; it's what they start doing every time a puck is shot at them. But if a goalie is not forced into learning the butterfly too soon, they will naturally learn how and when to use it through their own free will. Their decision-making will develop naturally instead of being pre-programmed in ways that may hinder instincts or cause more physical damage, like hip impingement in their mid-20s.

Eventually, a six-year-old will see enough NHL goalies butterflying to the point that it will filter into their mind and become a part of his or her natural playing style. From there, as the goalie ages, coaches then come in and clean up the technical issues while allowing his or her body to move naturally. In this regard, the goalie has already started to establish his or her own unique framework for how he or she moves and reacts to pucks, and the butterfly can continue to remain a save selection instead of an automation.

In my own experience, I started learning by watching NHL goalies at age 12. By age 15, even though I learned the basic skills at a later age, I was more aware of how and when to use them properly. So maybe I was less talented than other kids my age, but by the time I was 18, my ability to read plays and make sound decisions with my save selections was well above average. Even with zero coaching, my instincts developed quite fluidly. Reflecting back on my path as an American goalie, just like so many others, those instincts were nicely honed all on their own well into my teenage years.

Although this is clearly just my personal path and my own way of how I perceive development, if you are a goalie coach or parent, maybe you can take some time to consider the external influence you have on a goalie's instincts. Do you allow the goalie to learn for himself, or do you try hammering instruction into their minds before they have a chance to naturally progress?

For all goalies, I sometimes think this process of developing instincts is not only organically and naturally beautiful, but it's also a plight. Mastery of a skill is nearly impossible to achieve, because the world around you is constantly changing. Whether you're forced to wear new gear, suddenly playing on a different team, living in a different city, you suffer a serious injury, or your body continues to age and change, externally and internally, you're almost always forced to make conscious and subconscious adjustments to the way you process and play the position.

Again, this is one of those areas where certain basic questions opens up Pandora's Box. Which skills should be taught at a certain age and which skills should be left alone for a while? What constitutes over-coaching and what constitutes proper age-specific training methods? What is right and what is wrong?

This was one of the major differences in approach to goalie development in Finland and North America. As I learned first-hand, Finland has a major advantage, because they have a strong foundation of in-season goalie coaching, which allows kids to spend their summers playing other sports and doing other physical activities. There is also way more emphasis placed on the off-ice conditioning.

In North America, however, things are detrimentally different. After a long and tiring hockey season, many goalies spend their summers doing more position-specific training at camps and clinics, because they don't get enough personalized coaching during the season. So compared to Finland, many goalies in North America are forced into being over-coached, over-taught, and over-worked. If kids in North America can't get goalie training in-season, how can we expect them to play other sports and do other things during the off-season? That's the only time they really have the chance to attend quality goalie camps.

As you can see, the vast differences in the way goalies develop are cultural. Of course not all goalies are cleanly and neatly organized into this cultural paradigm, but clearly there is a significance to the systems currently in place. Goalies in Finland are more aware of how to use off-ice training models and programs to their advantage, because their playing and coaching environment allows them to do so.

How can goalies in North America instill good training habits into their pre-game routine if we don't have an environment that facilitates this type of learning? By the time goalies in the USA realize the importance of some of the things I've explained in this chapter, it's already too late. I'm a perfect example of that.

As we continue to learn new ways to develop goalies, we leave shells of our past culture behind and create a new skin in which we understand the position and the proper development methods with more clarity and a higher level of consciousness. So I can defend the current state of affairs in the USA since we're still early in the process compared to Finland, but sometimes it just feels like we never quite know what we're doing, because we still don't have a development program or model for our youngest goalies.

As a result, I'm afraid that my biggest fear becomes a reality far too often. I keep finding and scouting goalies that appear to have had their own beautifully poetic instincts silenced, or their biomechanics mangled by uneducated or inexperienced goalie coaches. This unknowingly destroy a young goalie's natural senses, only to replace them with robotic responses and rigid movements the goalies don't understand, yet still execute, but only because they're told to do it.

This is why functional movement practices like Pilates, Ideokinesis, and Yoga are so crucial to the development of North American goalies. We need it in order to help goalies better discover and understand themselves. Without a standardized educational program for goalie coaches, educating ourselves on some of these concepts of functional movement is a way to bypass the current roadblocks.

More importantly, we need to promote a culture of self-teaching. Goalies must learn some aspects of playing the position on their own. They must be able to develop dynamic thinking patterns and creative ways to problem solve before they are spoon-fed all of the answers. Implanting certain techniques and methods at the wrong time kills the tree of creativity, and combined with a discouraging lack of multi-dimensional, well-rounded athleticism, they fall further behind in the marathon (not race) of development.

But what exactly do I mean by "creativity" in a goalie?

4

GOALIE DEVELOPMENT AND THE DEATH OF CREATIVITY

"Creativity itself doesn't care at all about results – the only thing it craves is the process. Learn to love the process and let whatever happens next happen, without fussing too much about it." –Elizabeth Gilbert

Everyone is paranoid of the robotic goaltender. A form of *Automatonophobia,* the fear of an inanimate, non-sentient goalie haunts us all. Coaches don't want to develop one. Goalies don't want to become one. General Managers don't want to invest in one. Scouts don't want to be tricked into drafting one. Parents don't want to raise one.

The concept of the "robotic" goaltender has fascinated me for years. While I feel it has no legitimate or consistent definition – it's one of those 'eye of the beholder' things – the term 'robotic' has carried a negative connotation in the goalie community for the past decade.

But what does "robotic" goaltending mean?

My personal definition of a robotic goalie is one that relies so much on technique that they no longer think or play in the moment. They rigidly or blindly 'default' into certain positions at the wrong time, or they execute certain movements in the wrong situation. A robotic goalie always appears to move the same exact way, even when a similar situation or sequence unfolds a little differently.

Robotic goalies don't read plays coherently or accurately. They take the path of least resistance when filling space. They give the shooter the same 'look' every time, so they're easy to read. They are predictable, monotone, vanilla. They often lack the ability to process information as it unfolds in front of them and therefore erroneously utilize muscle memory.

On Twitter, I asked my followers to send me their definition of the robotic goalie. Alex Corley, an 18-year-old goalie playing for the Hartford Wolfpack in the EHL, had an excellent response.

> *"A goalie who allows his teaching and technique to override his natural reactions and instincts, often impairing performance." –Corley*

I felt a sense of accomplishment when I read this. Most goalies at Alex's age and skill level get it. They know what a robotic goalie looks like. NHL goalies always do an excellent job of bringing in real-life experience on this topic as well. Martin Biron once said to Ken Campbell in an article for The Hockey News (the October 27, 2014 issue), "The butterfly is a safe skill, not a reactive one. When I was in junior, one of my assistant coaches came to me one day and said, 'You know, you have to start reacting to the puck. Stop always going butterfly.'"

Robotic goaltenders are made on assembly lines. They always move the same. They over-use the butterfly save selection when a half-butterfly or keeping their feet would work just fine. They drop early on high shots. They execute a back-side push when the puck is nowhere close to the crease. They somehow opt to butterfly slide on cross-ice passes just inside the blue line. They drop into the VH or reverse-VH when a shooter streaking down the wing and along the half-boards is still well above the faceoff dot. They do things and make movements for no reason whatsoever.

Robotic goalies are technically efficient, but they have no dynamic off-the-cuff problem solving skills. If they are presented with a problem, they don't have the mental skills to execute the proper movements needed to get out of trouble. They have no answers, and part of this could be due to sheer fear. Over-coached goalies are often afraid to delineate from the technical blueprint laid out before them by their coach. They want to allocate the right movements in the back of their minds, but the instincts have been coached out of them – or transformed into negative feedback – to the point where all they do is default to what they've been previously told to do.

Knowing that more and more robotic goalies are populating the earth, the global goaltending community shrieks in terror at the thought of coaches, camps, and companies running factories that create these mechanized, soulless demons.

Unfortunately, you can't target or blame a single person or place for this issue; it's very much a cultural thing. In order to determine the root of the issue, and in order to fight back against development methods that lead to the creation of robotic goalies, we must therefore ask some very important questions.

How does this happen? Why does it continue to happen despite our efforts to create the opposite, despite our exponential evolution in training methods? Does a goalie become robotic at a young age or when he's older? If it happens when he's younger, at what age should we be altering our coaching methods in order to bypass or eliminate this trigger? When and where do these real boys turn into proverbial Pinocchio's? How do we educate goalies about roboticism? When does the dynamic switch flip to the 'off' position?

Those are some basic technical and developmental questions, but I'm curious about the sociological and cultural elements as well. For example, how come robotic goaltending developed such a negative connotation? How come a legend like J-S Giguere is considered the poster child of the robotic goalie if he played in a manner that actually allowed him to be successful in the NHL for so many years? Those questions are posed in a somewhat hypothetical manner; they're philosophical, difficult to answer.

Of course, there is a counterpoint, a validation so to speak, to the robotic goalie. At the NHL level, we all know that efficiency is king. The less you move, the better. The deeper you play, the less you have to move. Having set feet and being extremely stable, square, and still when shots are taken is the key to efficiency, as it allows you to remove any unnecessary lateral, forward, or backward flow in your movements. Because of this, many people fail to distinguish the difference between robotic *movements* and robotic *mindsets*.

To be honest, robotic movements (think Giguere or Corey Crawford, for example) are not exclusively bad. Furthermore, bigger goalies – the Ben Bishops of the world – are more susceptible to looking robotic because they are usually trained to rely more on their body and less on their hands and feet. They do less extending and more blocking, and that's not a bad thing, because it's safe, reliable, consistent, and most likely to be the best in terms of percentage-based net coverage.

Efficiency. Does it have a threshold? Is there such thing as being *too* efficient? A fair question to ask.

Movement-based roboticism aside, in regards to the robotic mindset, in my opinion – and please remember I'm no scientist – a goalie is improperly programmed at a fairly young age. My educated guess is that it happens when an eight or nine or 10-year-old goalie gets over-coached and spends too much time in a private lesson setting, receiving excessively detailed training from a goalie coach that doesn't recognize the importance of moderating the implementation of certain technical and positional elements.

I also feel like 'early-onset roboticism' rears its ugly head in young goalies when they don't spend enough time learning, failing, and trying things *on their own*. Once the youngster does receive his first structured goalie-specific coaching, I also feel that not enough time is spent strengthening and reinforcing the most important principles and basic fundamentals of goaltending, such as skating, catching, stick usage, and puck-handling. This also holds true for all facets of mental and off-ice training.

Clearly this doesn't happen with every young goalie in every region in North America, but generally speaking, I feel the problem lies in a faulty skill progression timeline. We're teaching young goalies how to do certain things well before they have the ability to process and understand the why and when. We show them how to do the cool things NHL goalies are doing, because we are so eager to learn and we're so eager to teach. We want to keep young kids moving. We want to make sure they sweat. We want to impress their parents. We want to show why we're worth $100 an hour.

But by doing these things, it does not guarantee that the young goalie will properly process and understand what we're teaching. He may be able to repeat the movements and engage his body to do it properly a few times, but from a cognitive standpoint, the learning process is such a fragile and complicated thing. And due to biochemical individuality, there's no way to truly know if the young goalie grasps what you teach with full situational awareness.

Furthermore, technique is only one piston in the engine of tactics, and tactics can't run without the fuel of proper reads and execution. It takes time to develop the areas of the brain needed to successfully select the right tools in the toolbox. Without a good understanding of this paradigm at the grassroots levels of volunteer and youth association goalie training, I believe the roots of roboticism are free to dig in and dig deep.

Many people agree that robotic goaltenders process the game without a free mind. And when you're eight or nine years old, you are not thinking with consciously competent awareness. Your mind is not yet free to determine what does and doesn't work best for your body. Instead, you only recognize what's on the surface; your pads are heavy and you're trying to stay balanced long enough to stop the puck. You do this without any true understanding of how to do it the most efficient or consistent way possible.

My *Automatonophobia* is always triggered when I see a tiny goalie who can barely stand on his skates getting coached by an over-aggressive goalie coach or over-enthusiastic father. Again, this is a cultural thing, and it's not like I'm trying to stop kids from spending time with a guy who just wants to train goalies, or a father who just wants to spend time with their son or daughter.

But I think this is a discussion we need to have more often. We need to invest more time in researching the impact this has on the way young athletes develop. Early-onset roboticism is a serious problem, and almost every coach with a deeper understanding of how to teach the position recognizes it as a very detrimental one to the future of goalies all over the world.

All of this being said, after some lengthy research over the past few years, and thanks to some brilliant minds I met over the summer, I've come to the conclusion that goalie coaches can strangle the weeds of roboticism by learning how to allow and guide goalies to better teach themselves.

In terms of developing the self-awareness needed to stave off roboticism, the best thing that ever happened to me was not having a goalie coach until I was 16 years old. Of course I would have jumped at the chance to get some guidance and goalie-specific training at an earlier age, but environmental factors (growing up in rural Texas) limited those opportunities. As a result of being a self-taught goalie throughout my younger years, although I was mechanically sloppy, I developed brilliant creativity skills.

Day after day, miserable fail after miserable fail, I slowly honed the biomechanics and muscle memory needed to stop pucks proficiently. I was forced to do this by simply figuring it out on my own. I had a great understanding of my own body's capabilities and postural patterns. I knew what I needed to do and how I needed to move in certain situations, because I had learned it on my own through repetitive organic trial and error. After doing something wrong so many times, eventually, you figure out how to do it right.

Psychologically speaking, I pushed through the obstacles of burnout and dejection, because my failures were never reprimanded by someone of authority. I was never scolded for making mistakes or allowing goals. Nobody scolded me or made me feel bad about myself when I fell flat on my face. Just the fact I could skate in all of that gear was cause for applause from my friends and family.

Conversely, and maybe more importantly, nobody lauded or glorified my minor successes. It was just me and my own cognizance, working harmoniously with a big imagination and an unquenchable passion for puck-stopping. If a technical or tactical problem arose that needed a solution, I relied on the instincts of a growing boy to come up with my own answer. After playing enough drop-in and street hockey games, I started to see patterns. More importantly, once I hit 13 or 14, I started to understand what these patterns meant, and how I could use something like pattern recognition to enhance natural instincts like anticipation, reaction speed, and hand dexterity.

Like every other athletic kid in the world, I unknowingly relied on my natural creativity skills to gradually improve. And due to this unaltered and uninhibited stage of learning, I began to move my body in more effective ways. I started to develop a kinesthetic sense, and I became familiar with what it was like to have a comfortable 'feel' for the game. The puck, my rhythm, and the concept of being 'in the zone' turned into identifiable and more definable 'personified' characteristics of playing the great game of hockey.

The kicker? Nobody told me how to do this. I figured it out by watching other goalies on TV and then emulating their movements in a free-reigned environment. I was not a budding genius or an overly-gifted athlete, either. I was just a regular boy who could care less if I sucked, because I was just out there having fun with my friends.

There's so much power that comes from doing something difficult all on your own at that age. Like when your dad lets you take the wheel of his riding tractor for the first time, you experience a liberating euphoria. Everything is so new and monumental, and you release certain chemicals that trigger the reward system of your brain. This also happens when you make a big glove save, when you stop a breakaway, and when you pull off a buttery smooth two-pad jammer.

When random, uncomfortable movements suddenly transform into successful and strategic problem solving, you're motivated to keep going until you repeat that sensation. You stop at nothing to do it again and again. Your self-motivating, self-rewarding neurological systems help reinforce the mental skills needed to stay dynamic and to remedy potential roboticism.

What's so amazing about this process is that anyone with the athletic ability to play the position for fun at an early age is going to have a similar experience. Even if you're from Texas and grew up on a horse ranch like I did, if you stick with it and have the passion to learn, you're going to organically develop the proper free-minded skills and intelligence. You may be flawed in some areas, like skating or butterfly sliding, and you will definitely still need coaching to reach the higher levels, but at least your mind is properly programmed.

At the end of the day, I truly believe goalie coaches and parents at the Atom, Mite, Squirt, and PeeWee levels should do way less coaching and way more observing. I think the volunteers and amateur coaches out there need to let more young goalies learn more things on their own. I think they should mainly be there to guide goalies and show them certain basics and fundamentals, but we should not spoon-feed them all of the answers. It's simply too soon to do this. And while I don't have the scientific knowledge to prove it, I think doing this when a kid is in that age range (6 to 12) is very crucial to a goalie's long-term *mental and emotional* development. They greatly benefit from spending more time engaging their minds by tinkering with skill-sets needed to self-learn certain aspects of the position. A coach also develops a more flexible friendship with a goalie when he or she spend more time watching, observing, and collaborating together.

At the end of the day, that imaginary switch from sentient to robotic is found on a certain control panel in the goalie's growing mind, and it needs to be left alone. Goalies will slowly develop the strength needed to flip their own switches when they develop better muscle memory and a conscious competence for playing the position. But if you go in and try to mess with these wires and flip these switches before the circuitry can handle the fragile flow of information, you'll be a catalyst for roboticism.

Even though I'm mostly speaking in opinionated metaphors regarding the plague of roboticism, we likely all agree that we're seeing way too many robots. I believe strongly that this is happening because *creativity is becoming a lost art*.

A Deeper Understanding of Creativity

Before digging deeper, I first want to state a caveat. Possessing and displaying creativity is not exclusively confined to a game. It's also found in the way a goalie practices, in the way they manage their state of mind in new environments, and the most fun aspect of all, how they wear and modify their gear. I define in-game creativity like this:

> *When presented with a problem in a sequence or situation – for example, a bad kick off the boards, a lost assignment in front of the net, a bouncing puck in the slot, or having to come up with a save after losing a stick or an edge – the goalie has the ability to solve that problem in an unorthodox*

> *or mentally flexible manner. They come up with solutions without defaulting to an automatic movement. They don't guess, they process. In-game creativity involves a structured or planned thought pattern or biomechanical process that helps them contort and react unconventionally or athletically in order to make the save.*

I also define in-game creativity as the ability to anticipate plays to the point that you can manipulate a player's intentions and dictate actions. Examples of this includes baiting or forcing a player to shoot in a certain spot, predicting how a deke will unfold and intentionally getting to the puck early, or any other number of similar aspects of properly and intelligently reading plays.

Forming my own definitions of creativity was just one of the many activities that filled my days and nights over the past 10 months. From there, I took the core principles of athletic creativity and found different ways to apply it to new realms of goalie development. Just like roboticism might be triggered at a young age, I figured the same could be said for creativity in all people, so I started my research in that area.

This led me to Michele Root-Bernstein's book, *Inventing Imaginary Worlds: From Childhood Play to Adult Creativity Across the Arts and Sciences*. Root-Bernstein, an artist and creativity scholar, focused her latest work on the imaginary worlds of young children. An intricate mix of personal revelations as a mother, history on the subject, and healthy doses of digestible science, it was coined as one of the most comprehensive accounts of childhood imagination and the creation of fictional worlds.

Root-Bernstein begins by introducing readers to a term called *Worldplay.*

Worldplay is defined as the invention of an imaginary world, often called a *Paracosm.* It's further defined as a part of the normally developing imagination in childhood and youth, often associated with play in secret, found, or constructed places. A form of "self-generated make-believe and mental modeling", one key notion by the author reinforced my idea that creativity in young goalies was dying:

> *"Over the last several decades, changes in lifestyle, child rearing, and education have, in fact, pushed aside pretend play in favor of commercial entertainments and test-driven learning. Since the 1970's, children have lost 12 hours of free time per week, which translates to 50-percent less time in unstructured outdoor activity and 25-percent less time in play overall. Should this cause us concern? Bet on it." –Root-Bernstein, Pg. 3*

After reading her introduction, I was hooked. I finished the book in less than a week and was in awe of her ability to interweave childhood development with many different types of successful creative adults. In summation of Root-Bernstein's book, there were three tenets that proved to me how Worldplay could lead to an opulence of creativity in athletes of any sport, including goalies.

First of all, Worldplay evokes the imagination through a process of forming conscious ideas or mental images of something that has never been perceived before. Apply this to goalies and it makes sense.

Secondly, a child's imagination is explorative, creative, compositional, and conceptual. From creating new secret languages to coming up with new names for creatures and towns in their Paracosm, the mind's construction of these things beckons a power to marry the known with the unknown in a manner that brings forth meaning to an otherwise meaningless moment or experience.

Thirdly, complex make-believe during childhood can have lifelong benefits for people in a variety of fields, including writers, artists, scientists, and yes, even athletes, because it stimulates the development of creative adult strategies in a variety of business and sports-oriented realms.

Ultimately, the key message I absorbed from Root-Bernstein's book was the impact a young athlete's ability to develop and embrace an imaginary world had on developing key creativity skills and behaviors that are scientifically proven to enrich and enhance their lives, no matter what they choose to do.

I can remember some of the imaginary worlds I created during my childhood. It was easy since I grew up on a horse ranch, surrounded by majestic beasts and monstrous thunderstorms, and the twisting, winding, snaking curves of a county-wide creek. I was always outside, so my mind was always wandering and imagining things I wanted to do, people I wanted to be, beasts I wanted to defeat.

I feel that this is the root of where creativity in a goalie begins to grow.

When it comes to hockey, imagination is an easy connection to make. We have all gone outside and imagined a world where we are suddenly transformed into our idols. We do it with our friends all the time, in a variety of different ways. It sounds funny, but when I was growing up, I was always a hybrid of my favorite goalies. I would call myself "Osvin" and "Potgood" in honor of being an imaginary mix of Osgood and Potvin, two of my idols.

If my friends and I were playing street hockey prior to a Stars game, I was always the opposing goalie. I don't know why, but I loved the idea of being the goalie everyone loved to hate. I also did this because I think I enjoyed acting like I was the goalie I hardly ever saw. Belfour and the rest of the Stars goalies were always on my TV, but seeing Cujo or Hasek or Jocelyn Thibault was a rare treat.

Our personal experiences within these Paracosms while playing hockey become a very valuable thing. Even into our 30's, they act as residue that greatly influences a goalie's interaction with their real-life playing environments. It's an interaction within their mind that influences their identity, their confidence, and even their view of their future.

Whether a young goalie's imagination and worldplay in hockey is fantastic (magical or unrealistic hockey visions), natural (following the laws of nature and reality, like playing a regular game), idealistic (success, like hoisting the Stanley Cup) or realistic (failure, losing a game in overtime), this part of becoming a goalie lays the foundation for future seeds of creativity and self-confidence to be planted.

Young goalies that willingly participate in hockey Paracosms are unfailingly led to emulate their heroes. This discovery – one that proves they can achieve anything – is so valuable that it influences their decision-making for years and years. This goes back to the Science of Shadowing, so there's no need to rehash the impact mimicry and idolization can have on a young goalie's potential and upside.

As time goes on and the goalie begins to play at a higher and more competitive level, drifting in and out of hockey-related Paracosms shifts the young athlete's mode of thinking from imaginary to applicatory. The two begin to mesh together to design a new offspring of something that is slightly familiar. This combination of divergent and convergent thinking brings new creativity skills to the surface, and as body awareness and technical competence rises, so too do the problem solving skills.

Goaltending Paracosms are as deep as they are beautiful. They fall into so many different categories of the neuroscience behind athletic self-development. This includes enacted make-believe (playing street hockey and choosing to be your favorite goalie), inactive reveries (daydreaming during class, and normal nighttime dreams), or constructed make-believe.

The impact of the constructed make-believe really resonates with a goalie's imagination, because they are using props (goalie gear) while enacting make-believe scenes in a setting where you are going through similar movements and real-life hockey and goalie sequences.

Altogether, Root-Bernstein's book tugged at a tiny idea in my mind and pulled out the knot that was keeping it bound in the region of the unknown. She taught me so many things that could be applied to young goalies and creativity, and for her work, I am forever grateful.

Most importantly, she proved that there is a strong link between childhood worldplay and eventual creativity in a wide range of disciplines, including the unspoken one – goaltending. Furthermore, she helped me establish a correlation between childhood and adult creativity; at times, they're quite similar to each other. Both flex the muscles of imagination. Both develop intelligent behaviors. Both improve the capacity to find and solve problems within the mind. Both nurture the ability to construct new thought patterns, new methods of learning, and new ways to stimulate improved ideas.

Although Root-Bernstein's book focused on the professions of art and science, in my mind, all of this was easily applicable to the goaltender. But the lack of research on creativity and athletes left me unfulfilled. I needed to be able to find some sort of concrete explanation for why I felt like the death of creativity in goaltending was breathing down my neck.

Fortunately, I found a way to cross paths with the right guy at the right time.

Connecting the Creativity Dots with Dr. Scott Barry Kaufman

At the forefront in the field of current creativity research is a man named Scott Barry Kaufman. The Scientific

Director of the Imagination Institute in the Positive Psychology Center at the University of Pennsylvania, Kaufman is a cutting-edge curator for many deep discussions on the wide world of intelligence and the philosophy of creativity. He also excels at making complex scientific research easy for the lay man like myself to understand.

Twitter is to thank for our introduction. While perusing the pale blue micro-blogging social media universe for the latest research on the topic, Scott's name popped up right away. One click later, I was following his timeline and trying to correlate his research and discussions directly to goalie development.

Turns out, the science behind creativity in not just hockey but in all sports has mostly gone untouched. As you could imagine, this opened up a whole new world of ideas when it came to better understanding the way young goalies learn some of those "core" movement and skating skills on their own.

In a blog titled "Beautiful Minds" on ScientificAmerican.com, Kaufman wrote an article called *The Real Neuroscience of Creativity* (published August 19, 2013). In it, he explained how creativity does not involve a single brain region or just one side of the brain. The whole process, from the moment a new idea enters the mind until the moment it is verified, consists of many different cognitive processes. The entire brain is engaged, different neurons firing and sparking and traveling down millions of different paths.

Kaufman goes on to list some of the different "brain networks" that are working together in the creativity process. For example, when you mentally rotate an object in your mind – like anticipating where the puck on a cross-body, cross-ice pass may end up, or determining how you need to rotate and position your arms and body to block a short little chip shot on the back door – the "Dorsal Attention / Visuospatial Network" is likely to be activated.

Meanwhile, Kaufman explains how the "Executive Attention Network" is activated when a task requires extreme focus and attention. In goaltending terms, that would be like extending a toe or a stick at the last moment on a penalty shot when you're falling forward, lunging out, and intensely focused on tracking the puck coming off the stick blade. Reading this part reminded me of those great Scorpion "heel-kick" saves that Kiprusoff made so many times during his NHL career. It reminded me of the amazing behind-the-back glove saves that Drew MacIntyre and Kasimir Kaskisuo (UMD Bulldogs) recently made.

Goaltending creativity at its finest. Finding unique ways – in the moment – to solve serious problems.

So creativity, Kaufman says, at least in terms of basic neuroscience, is not just a left-brain, right-brain notion. It's much more dynamic and complex than that; a cacophony of different brain regions are engaged and working together to solve problems and execute different processes related to intelligence.

Another one of Kaufman's articles, this one titled *Openness to Experience and Creative Achievement* (published November 25, 2013 on ScientificAmerican.com), discusses personality traits linked to creativity. According to recent research, he says, the personality trait most commonly associated with creativity is an openness to experience, otherwise known as cognitive exploration.

Scott goes into great detail about the many different forms of cognitive exploration, including a drive for intellectual curiosity, problem solving, reasoning, imagination, and emotional or fantasy richness.

It was after reading those two articles that I started to connect the dots to what I explained earlier in this chapter regarding self-taught goalies. The curiosity of figuring out how to play goal without any guidance. The absorption of being wrapped up in the glory and bright lights of a sublime goaltending Paracosm. Those experiences stimulate the mind in ways that simply can't be replaced.

I also thought back to all of the kids and pro goalies I worked with in Finland over the summer. As you will read in the next chapter, it's the combination of the Finnish person's environment and personality that make them so viable to having an expanded capacity for creativity. Dig deeper into Finland's education system, its structure and overwhelming benefits compared to the education system in the United States, and more dots connected in my mind. There's merit to the idea that Finnish goalies, generally speaking, are more creative than North Americans. Maybe research will shed more light on this someday.

As you could imagine, I was completely fascinated with everything Kaufman was teaching me about creativity. A pipe dream at the time, I found myself sending him an e-mail in the hopes of speaking with me for a few minutes. I figured, at the very least, he would respond and say thanks, but no thanks. I wondered if there was value in discussing creativity in hockey players, wondered if it was something that didn't really make sense, or maybe I was way off regarding my opinions and fledgling thoughts.

But then I found a podcast Scott recorded with David Epstein, a senior writer for Sports Illustrated and the author of the must-read book *The Sports Gene: Inside the Science of Extraordinary Athletic Performance*.

Propped up by body pillows in my dim candlelit bedroom, I listened to the podcast that same night and took notes. Inundated with ideas, I felt like I had to write everything down. Each statement and morsel of information built upon the last. It was rich with content, rich with expertise, and a stimulating conversation that I suggest you fill your ears with as soon as possible. In the end, it further strengthened my newfound passion for linking sports and creativity. Although the podcast mainly focused on skill, it made me feel like my request to discuss creativity in athletics with Kaufman was not so unfounded or strange.

A few weeks later, to my pleasant surprise, Scott made time for a phone call. So excited to finally talk to him, I was not surprised to find that, despite the fact my questions were uncommon, he was able to easily and eloquently discuss creativity skills and goaltending. After brief introductions and spending a few minutes explaining this chapter and my thoughts regarding the death of creativity in goalies, he dove right in with some amazing insights.

"People in sports are so obsessed with talent, talent, talent. Talent is not the same thing as creativity. Intelligence is not the same thing as talent. All of these things are different overlapping and non-overlapping skill sets," Kaufman said. "So in that regard, it seems like there's a great opportunity for creativity within the goaltending position that might not exist in other sports. For example, if you're trying to run a 500-meter dash, you don't want to be too creative, you just want to be really competent and fast."

It was at this moment that I became fully confident that I was on to something here. Like the pitcher in baseball and the quarterback in football, we know that goalies see the game from a completely different perspective. Goalies are on a proverbial island; we think the game alone, we act alone. Therefore, I feel creativity is an identifiable, unmistakable, and necessary skill.

"This is a whole new world that you've opened up to me; the opportunity to be in a position where you're in a game and you're simultaneously the observer and the participant," Kaufman said. "So how can you influence your teammates? How can you influence, in a creative way, the things that are going on in front of your eyes as the goalie?"

I answered him in the back of my mind by saying the skills and key elements of "pattern recognition" and "reading the play" and "communication".

"Creativity is not all about acquiring knowledge or acquiring information. It's also about breaking free of the tradition, or shedding some of that [tradition] and being very flexible," he continued. "A lot of it has to do with the flexibility and adaptability aspect, so maybe really creative goalies are incredibly adept at, first of all, making connections between things or seeing patterns in the game. A lot of it probably comes down to pattern detection and flexibility, or a combination of the two."

Bingo! Validation. It's as if he had already spoken to goalie gurus like Mitch Korn and Bill Ranford before.

"It's amazing to hear you use those words from your perspective," I said, my mind set aflame with ideas. "You nailed it, man. Elite goaltending is all about pattern recognition. Hockey is so superfluous, the game is chaotic and constantly changing. Different guys are on the ice at different times and the puck is pretty unpredictable. It can bounce or change direction at any time, or guys are whizzing by you and you momentarily lose sight of the puck, and then you have to relocate it and refocus as quickly as possible. So being able to recognize those patterns, and understand how to be in the right position at the right time to make saves as efficiently as possible, is goaltending in a nutshell."

I continued to explain how elite goaltending is also a lot about feel. You have to "feel" a certain way to be comfortable, you have to "feel" the rhythm and flow of the game. Like Scott said, in terms of pattern recognition and adaptability, those two key traits are found in all elite goaltenders. Those that can lean on years of experience gained from muscle memory, an improving visual system, and enhanced kinesthetic sense will have harmony between intuition, physiology, and brain science that leads to elite skill.

"I guess what I was trying to learn from you was, like you spoke about earlier: the dynamic or difference between talent, intelligence, and creativity. I think that's awesome insight for a lot of my readers, because that distinguishes the ways that young goalies can be developed," I said. "I just want coaches to realize what I learned many years ago – that we need to do a better job of stoking the flames of their creativity. We need to find new ways to allow kids to develop their creative habits in a manner that doesn't stymie their development or their ability to think freely at later ages. Does that make any scientific sense at all?"

"It absolutely does," Scott said emphatically. "It sounds like there needs to be, as part of the talent search, as well as part of the coach's role in development, a lot more different perspectives and methods where you infuse creativity into the process. So at the talent-search level, the coaching level, and the training level, you can apply some principles from the creativity field about what we call mental flexibility."

Again in the back of my mind, I tried to define mental flexibility. I guessed this had to do with what I said earlier in the chapter; it is problem solving in the moment when something goes wrong, or when a goalie is presented with a problem. Scott continued.

"This is a skill that is associated with insightful problem solving, with breaking free of impasses. So you might have goalies who experience being in a rut; they're getting scored on three or four times in a row. Instead of their self-esteem dropping so low, they problem solve and are adaptable to changing their habits," he said.

This made such perfect sense. Worlds were opening with every illuminating word Scott shared.

"A creative goalie, to me, is someone who becomes aware of what they're doing wrong, is really flexible to reflect on that, and then is flexible enough to change what they're doing that is causing the downward spiral. Another strong key aspect of creativity is called the flow state, which is very relevant to sports."

The 'feel' of the game, I thought. The eternal and never-ending soul journey of the steel-piped sojourner.

"Goalies would be well to learn how to not overthink at all times – to learn how to be flexible enough to 'feel' like you said earlier – and to allow yourself to feel the game and not get too stuck in the head game of the position," Kaufman said. "I see all of these different various elements heavily influencing the adaptability aspect – things that I think can be trained and emphasized by coaches. I also think some people might be more talented, I daresay. So from a talented standpoint, don't just look out for the standard talent, also look for creative talent."

Not that Kaufman's words were of the earth-shattering variety, but they were extremely poignant and scientifically based in a realm of sports performance and psychology that, up to this point, had never really been studied. It was a liberating feeling to hear him speak on this niche topic.

It reinforced the importance of facilitating this element of adaptability and problem solving into young goalies. We need to find ways to help our goalies 'feel' the answers, to create them on their own. They can't just be told the answers. It's not the same learning process. It's not as stimulating.

"Your advice and expertise is reiterating and proving something I wrote about in my first book," I stated. "The importance of a goalie having a stronger balance between their emotional and mental pillars, because it's through this harmony that a goalie becomes more self-aware. They can reach out and grab that elusive 'feel' for the game more easily. They can feel what they're doing and how they're doing it."

"And being able to regulate your emotional and mental state. For optimal mental flexibility, you have to be able to regulate both," he said.

In terms of regulating emotional and mental states, I thought about a concept that transcends all sports and all types of athletic performance – the optimal arousal level. There's a "sweet spot" all athletes try to achieve that constitutes the feeling of being in the zone. You're not too high, but you're not too low. Every element of your body's and mind's interaction with your playing environment works together. It's an amazing feeling, but it's foreign in young goalies and frustratingly elusive in adult goalies.

"So from a coaching perspective, what advice would you give to coaches in terms of being able to stimulate this mental flexibility and creativity, or at least to help facilitate it in younger goalies?"

"Well, I imagine that a coach could come up with some neat exercises that would parallel the kind of creativity exercises you would do in a classroom or a boardroom," he said. "You train the goalie to never at any one moment in time get too comfortable with a particular habit or style of drill. This is a kind of strategy we use in education. It's called the *Einstellung Effect*."

"Wait," I said, embarrassingly cutting him off. "Einstella---what?"

"The Einstellung Effect," he repeated. "Basically, a lot of people have to complete a task that follows a particular rule, and you find people that aren't able to flexibly switch the rule. Even when the rule changes, they still apply the old rule that doesn't work as well. Creative people are able to adjust really quickly to the new rule. So I wonder if you could apply some of those well-known techniques in other fields of creativity within the goalie field. I think that could actually work.

I was so positively charged by his words, I had to take a moment to publically reflect and thank him, while I had the chance.

"You have no idea how great it is to hear this," I said. "My passion right now in the realm of goalie development is all about finding new ways to solve old problems. All my life I've pretty much had to learn everything for myself. I had to be creative in my training methods and coaching methods. So learning about the science behind it from a guy like yourself really reinforces the purpose of some of my ideas."

"If you could apply the principle of *the Einstellung Effect* to goalies, I that would be..." He paused for a split second. "I bet you nobody in the history of sports has ever done that before. This is a really unique, dare I say creative, combination."

Scott Barry Kaufman, you cheeky, glorious man. This was the first time we had a chance to speak, but it most certainly won't be the last.

I thanked him repeatedly, hung up the phone, and without hesitation researched *The Einstellung Effect.*

The Einstellung Effect and Goaltending

According to numerous sources, the Einstellung Effect is defined as a person's predisposition to solve a given problem in a specific manner, even though better or more appropriate methods of solving the problem exist. It goes on to say that it is the negative effect of previous experience when having to solve new problems.

Rooted in the term "Aufgabe" in German, which translates to the word "Task", an example of the Einstellung Effect is when someone executes a task that is a tendency, or the result of a previously applicable behavior. Sometimes called Functional Fixedness, the Einstellung Effect is often connected to the impaired ability to discover a new use for a familiar object.

I am sure your mind is working through this exactly like mine did. Clearly this is very much applicable to goaltending. Trying to catch shots to the glove side the same way every single time. Dropping into the same narrow or wide butterfly on every single shot. The list of examples is totally endless.

Many studies have been produced regarding the impact of the Einstellung Effect on people of different ages, intelligence levels, and backgrounds. Studies and experiments have also put people through a series of different tests, environments, and learning situations. Most notably, research has been recorded on the effect that different stressful situations had on the Einstellung Effect. This intrigued me, since we know that goaltending is one of the most stressful positions in all of sports.

Sure enough, as you would expect, stressful situations increased the prevalence of the Einstellung Effect. Stress is a very lethal "performance killer" for goalies. It also happens to be one of the most prevalent and debilitating mental and emotional issues a goalie will face during their playing years. It's something we all feel at different times when we're playing, and it's a big reason why more goalies are now incorporating breathing techniques, Yoga, and meditation into their off-ice conditioning regimes. The less pressure we feel in a game, the more controlled and comfortable we feel in our environment, and therefore the less robotic and more creative we're likely to be.

I don't believe this is an exclusive rule, however. Sometimes it is when we are under the most pressure that we're forced into doing something unconventional or completely outside of our normal movement patterns. Nevertheless, scientific experiments have proven that anxiety-induced situations increases the likelihood that a person will fall victim to the Einstellung Effect.

I'd love for you to take a few minutes and reflect on this component of neuroscience and problem solving in your own goaltending experiences. In what type of situation do you fall victim to taking the path of least resistance when confronted with a "sticky" or uncomfortable situation that could threaten your success? At what times do you default into the solution you've used a million times before?

My first answer – puck tracking. When I don't track the puck very well, I end up dropping early, or just trying to seal the ice and hope I can control the puck off my pad. When my eye attachment is cut off for a moment due to a screen or a stick blade crossing my line of sight, I fall victim to the Einstellung Effect. It also happens when I'm mentally or physically tired, distracted or stressed out by other things happening in my life, or I'm not fully engaged or focused.

Goalies and goalie coaches around the world are hard-wired and obsessed with achieving the highest level of technical efficiency possible. This is not a flaw or error in our way of thinking. We want to find the path of least resistance and the shortest distance between two points in order to beat passes, arrive early to angles, and be fully 'set and ready' for a shot.

Similarly, the Einstellung Effect is one way a goalie creates the most "efficient" or the simplest solution to a problem. Unfortunately, even if a goalie considers his current solution to be the best because it feels the most comfortable, it still may not be the most effective one out there. There could be a better way.

This poses a very interesting conundrum in the neuroscience of creative problem solving and skill development for goalies. Does a goalie benefit more from discovering the most efficient "feel" in executing a movement or technique, or do they benefit more from an outside observer providing feedback and altering their muscle memory in order to refine a movement or technique? More simply put, do we allow goalies to develop movement patterns and muscle memory that feels the best, or that looks the best?

It looks like there are a lot of different answers out there, all of which lie somewhere in between.

I'm really excited about the discovery of the Einstellung Effect. I can't thank Scott enough for introducing me to this concept, and helping me understand its influence on goaltending and creativity. It's very eye-opening and fun to pontificate as we continue to search for newer, better training methods.

Although this section is a tiny sliver of my fingernail scratching the surface of a new and essentially untouched world regarding the way we understand creativity and goalie development, it's a start. It gets us thinking, and I hope it opens some doors for you to come up with new ways to solve old problems.

Ultimately, reviving the dying culture of creativity may rely on goalie coaches that can *cultivate* creativity. And this begs a key question: How do we cultivate creativity in young and old goalies alike?

A Few Ways to Cultivate Creativity in Goalies

There are a few ways I stimulate and cultivate a goalie's creativity. I am sure you have some of your own, and if you do, I hope you will find a way to contact me on Facebook or Twitter and share those with me, so I can share them with everyone else. Lord knows we need as many ideas out there as possible.

I'll begin by sharing a simple yet revealing fact: *Creativity can become a habit.*

Through our ability as coaches to help facilitate the development of good training and practice habits, the first way I cultivate creativity in goalies is through what I call the *FIO Method*. FIO simply stands for "Figure It Out" and forces the goalie to methodically problem solve. No matter how tired, frustrated, bored, or stubborn the goalie may be, this key phrase should motivate him or her to create new solutions, and therefore new thinking patterns that enhance their mind-body relationship.

I ask just as many questions as they do, and we share that learning process together.

I recently executed this method with a 15-year-old goalie. He had average skills, but for an in-house goalie playing

Bantam-AA, I knew he was smart enough to learn how to back-side push. He was determined to learn this skill, so I had him work on a simple pendulum rotation warm-up drill. Here's my re-created transcript of that portion of the session:

James: "I don't get why I'm struggling to backside push going to my blocker side."

Justin: "Well, try to figure it out."

James: "That's the problem…I can't. I've tried."

At this point, I took a moment to think back. Did he try the same way every time? Did he consider alternative solutions? Did he take the time to think and process and troubleshoot?

Justin: "Well, tell me this. How does it *feel* when you back-side push to your strong side?"

James: "It feels like I have perfect balance and I'm really stable and I can recover a lot faster."

Justin: "Okay, well that's good. That's what you want. How does it feel when you go to your weak side?"

James: "I dunno. It's like I'm dragging or not getting all of my blade on the ice when I push off."

Justin: "Okay. That makes sense. I see the same thing. But I'm curious about something. Do you feel like you are trying to move the same exact way when you go to the blocker side? Maybe you can't move exactly the same way on both sides of your body."

I wanted to get him to think about that. Maybe he needed a different mechanical solution when he moved to the blocker side, as opposed to how he was moving to his strong side, the glove side.

James: "Yeah, I'm just trying to move as consistently as possible both sides. That's what I should be doing, right?"

Justin: "You have to figure that out. Keep trying. Nailing this doesn't happen overnight. It's a 'feel' thing."

James tries a few more times, but to no avail. He was still slipping out and struggling going to his glove side. At this point, he was starting to over-think it. His brain was in his skates. He was trying to push off the toe, the heel, the mid-point. He was definitely processing, though. I decided at this point to give him a little more guidance, since I knew frustration was starting to settle in.

Justin: "Ok hold up. Don't get frustrated. Let's think about this. Maybe we should think about what your hands are doing. They might be part of the equation. Maybe it has something to do with the way you're setting your hands when you push off."

James: "Do you mean I should swing my hands more when I rotate?"

Justin: "Maybe. Try it. Or maybe your glove is falling behind your body when you rotate and push off and it's acting like an anchor. It's dragging and slowing you down. Do you feel like that's happening?"

I injected a little bit of Ideokinesis into the mix. I knew that the image of an anchor holding back a speed boat, or some similar idea, would materialize in his mind. I wanted him to transform that into the idea that the glove should be more like a rudder or a sail. James tried again. Smooth to the glove side, as usual. But this time, going to the blocker side, instead of letting the glove hand fall behind his body when he pushed off, which was in fact slowing him down, he moved the glove slightly forward and both hands led his body evenly. He nailed it.

Justin: "Nailed it, bud! See, your hands act as stabilizers for your body. If your hands are falling behind you, you're counteracting that balance. When you push to your blocker side and your glove falls behind you, it mangles your movement. But when you push to your glove side, your hand is already leading, so you don't suffer from the same issue going that way."

The smile on his face was a cool moment. He had figured it out. I merely guided him, and the endorphin rush he felt from problem solving on his own elevated his mood, elevated his energy levels, and motivated him to finish the practice on an emotional high. He was lights out the rest of the day.

Clearly not every goalie is going to have this exact type of revelation, but clearly there is great benefit to not spoon-feeding a goalie the answers. Guide and facilitate that type of learning, and you'll do more for the kid then you ever imagined.

Another way I facilitate creativity on the ice is the way in which I structure my drills.

I split drills into two platforms. The first one is the "Mechanics & Technique" platform. Drills on this platform are very methodical, slow, controlled, and structured. They often take place in very small areas, with small movements, and numerous repetitions. When it comes to refining or improving certain techniques and body mechanics, slow is smooth and smooth is fast. Before you can increase speed and power, you have to master the technique and the accuracy in which you execute it.

"Tactics & Strategy" is the second platform. These drills are the opposite; they're supposed to make you feel a little uncomfortable. They often include uncontrolled, chaotic, fast, or unstructured game-like sequences. Rebounds are played out. Players are given liberties with their shot selections.

The key with this platform is to try and stimulate creativity through unguided situational awareness. Maybe that's one way to really generate some creative thinking in a goalie during a practice session – by simply not telling him what the next drill will bring. Inform the shooters away from the goalie, run the first rep in the drill, and force the goalie to – you guessed it – figure it out.

Closing Thoughts on Creativity

You can guide young goalies to develop a creative mindset and you can point them in that direction, but sometimes the best way to develop creativity is to do nothing at all. Just let the goalie figure it out for themselves while their bodies and minds are still developing.

I wish I had the chance to spend more time speaking with Kaufman. I would have asked him if, in terms of coaching, observation can trump instruction in these impressionable years. If we do more observing, maybe we can better understand how they respond to specific situations. Not everything needs to be corrected right away, because goalies can be empowered if you allow them the time and give them the tools and guidance they need to learn how to fix their own mistakes, or solve their own problems.

I'm not trying to say our current culture of coaching is a path of destruction. I'm just tired of seeing goalies that look like mind-numbed slaves. I can't handle seeing young goalies going through the motions having never been given a chance to engage their own true kinesthetic capability, or a chance to tap into their biomechanical capacity. You can't just show up and tell them what to do all the time. I go to youth hockey practices and goalie coaches are yelling at them on exactly where to hold their hands, where to stand, where to position their skates. That's not to say that they are constantly being forced into playing or standing or positioning themselves in certain ways, but over-coaching at too early of an age is clearly a major concern in North America right now, and I've been seeing it first-hand for nearly a decade.

It's scary, to be honest. There's a whole generation of goalies potentially being raised in proverbial darkness. Their methods and strategies are being decided and implemented by someone else, by someone who, in too many cases, knows nothing about the development or maturation process of a goaltender. Remember, goalie coaching is still a fairly new field. It has only been around for 35 to 40 years, even less in North America.

Think of all the things we haven't learned yet because we haven't come to the realization that we may have been doing things the wrong way. This is something that only comes with time, but in my experience, being in so many places and seeing so many goalies, there is a very significant, deeply-rooted issue with the way things are evolving. It's not a simple solution, but there is a solution to be found, or at least a way to curtail the issues. We're polluting athletic ability by implanting technique before instincts can evolve, and before creativity is cultivated and nurtured.

There's a way to achieve consistent success for many different types of goalies out there, but they must learn it for themselves. They need their own daring visions and dreams, they need to study their own mistakes and determine their own solutions and consider their own methods.

It reminds me that there are only two truths in this world. One is found in nature, science, and math. The other is found in your heart. Only a goalie knows what a goalie needs to do to be successful, and it's the goalie coach's job to help his student discover the answers and refine their game to incorporate the solutions. The only truth is inside you, it's what you feel, not what someone tells you.

The "feel" of proper goaltending is different for each and every one of us, and even more importantly, the perception of having that comfortable "feel" in the crease is something independently individual. We all want that good feeling, but we all discover, achieve, and get there in different ways.

Creativity in goaltending is dying. This has to be reversed. But the only way to do this is by getting goalie coaches at the grassroots levels to do more observing and guiding, and a little less instructing. As I have learned in my own life, and throughout the summer, sometimes we simply need to get away from what we know in order to discover what we don't.

A narrow-minded view of what you think you know, combined with an inability to realize or discover what you don't know, stymies your creativity as a goalie and a coach. Don't let it die inside of you. Discover, uncover, and try new things. Break free from the chains that bind your intuition and unleash the true hidden power of your mind!

5

JOSH TUCKER ON VISION TRAINING AND CREATIVITY

A few months before my summer expedition commenced, I had already discovered and benefitted from a hidden realm of goalie development: Vision Training. Aside from a few great stories regarding NHL goalies like Dwayne Roloson, Pekka Rinne, Magnus Hellberg, and Frederik Andersen utilizing it, vision training has yet to be fully unleashed on the wide world of goaltending. But I know of at least one company in the United States fully committed to changing that.

Envision Sports is based in Edina, Minnesota, which is a mere 15 minutes away from Burnsville, the town where I was living when I first started my summer expedition. One of the preeminent places in the world for hockey players to train their eyes, the primary goal of Envision Sports is to build the fundamental visual skills needed to enhance athletic ability.

But in this facility, you will find no puck-shooting machines or synthetic ice. Instead, athletes of all ages strategically train their eyes through a series of carefully-planned exercises. It is not until goalies graduate from a 40-session program that they take their training to the turf and do more goalie-specific reactionary drills. Behind this rock-solid philosophy, Envision Sports has achieved amazing success with a number of elite goalies, and it all takes place inside a small office nestled in the corner of a much larger sports training center.

Josh Tucker, a former Minnesota high school goalie and current local goalie coach, is the proud owner of Envision Sports. He and I initially crossed paths in March of 2014 at the Let's Play Hockey Expo in St. Paul. While wading through the masses and reveling in the intoxicatingly pure atmosphere of the 2014 High School State Tournament, I came across Tucker's booth and watched him give a presentation to some kids and parents on their vision training program.

"This is so perfect for goalies," I said. It was the first time I had seen anything like this in person. As such, I was instantly drawn to their program and wanted to try it out and help spread the word. I snagged Tucker's card off the table and called him the very next day.

A week later, I met with Josh and agreed to pay him for some vision training while I was still in town. I knew it would become excellent material for the book, so during the month of April and leading up to my departure for the Warren Strelow Goalie Camp in early-May, I went through an expedited program with Tucker, and to my pleasant surprise, former Colorado College goalie Joe Howe.

The training experience was amazing. My initial visual system assessment was also quite revealing and informative, and it was something I wish I had done when I was 16. No pun intended, this program literally opened my eyes to a new realm of goalie development that I had only briefly considered in the past. With every one-hour session I took, I could feel my eyes getting stronger and more disciplined. I even noticed that I was able to read longer than usual late at night, which was a godsend for a guy like me. The results spoke for themselves on the ice as well; I felt like I didn't have to work as hard to focus on the puck. It was such an enjoyable training experience that I verbally expressed my frustration numerous times about not being able to go through the entire program. It was seriously that good.

I, like many goalies out there, sometimes forget that the eyes are controlled by muscles. As such, they can be trained to do some amazing things, like better track pucks traveling at faster speeds, or to see more on the outside edges of your regular field of vision. Most goalies, even those that have been drafted by NHL teams, will go through most of their lives without ever getting their athletic vision tested or assessed, which is clearly a major problem in a country where goalies need every developmental advantage they can possibly get.

When I first dove into the realm of goalie analysis years ago, I knew the importance of vision and being able to read plays and track pucks. Just like any other set of muscles, I also knew we were all born with varied visual abilities. I love using a term I call visual discipline, which is simply how well we control what we look at and how we look at it. But even as a guy with 20/20 vision, I never really knew I could train my eye muscles to see things more clearly and with more consistency.

That's where a company like Envision Sports can and will unleash a lot of power in terms of goalie development and training. It's pretty much a 'must-have' for any goalie that is looking to improve their skills, so I suggest you take some time to visit their website at *www.sportsvisiontraining.net* and learn more about them. Get informed on the benefits of vision training. If you have the chance to partake in their program, whatever you do, don't pass it up. No pill or gadget or goalie coach can replace what they provide.

Now that I've been through a slimmed down version of their program, I'm of the emphatic belief that vision is the most important tool a goalie can have and hone. Therefore, I'm working towards making vision training more accessible to goalies of all ages, because without it, you're not as good as you could be. This insightful interview with Josh tells us why.

Goldman: Why don't we start with a little bit of background info. How did you get involved in vision training as a goalie coach?

Tucker: "I've been a sports vision trainer for over 10 years. In that time, I've worked with NHL goalies, Olympians, lots of NCAA and World Juniors goalies, and all the way down to youth goalies. I went through vision training myself when I was a high school goalie and was amazed at what it did for me. I always just assumed that since I had 20/20 vision, that score was as far as I could go with my eyes. But I learned that we are all born with very different visual abilities, and that you can train the muscles of your eyes for faster reactions, better hand-eye coordination, wider peripheral awareness, and sharper focus. I was introduced to the program by an NHL goalie at a goalie camp, and my assessment showed that I had poor peripheral abilities. Basically, my inner eye muscles were very dominant, so my eyes preferred to pull inward, which was great for plays in close. But the negative effect was having a limited peripheral field, because my eyes wouldn't relax outward; I liken it to a race horse wearing blinders so he can't see what's going on around him. I always did great on plays in close, but longer shots were tougher than they should've been, and I also struggled to see players on the backdoor. So for me, the training opened up more of the ice and I was able to see more of the play, which was huge. I also noticed huge improvements in my reading speed, which helped me better balance school with hockey. I remember that the goalie who introduced me to the training had gone through it and was blown away at what it did for his game. He was a Hobey Baker winner in college, but in the NHL, he just couldn't crack that backup role. After doing the vision training, he finally cracked that threshold and earned a starting role, and that story has always stood out to me. You and I have discussed before that there's no one 'end-all be-all' answer to being a successful goalie. But when you're talking about pro goalies, they're as strong as they'll get and they have worked as much as they can on their skating and other physical skills. So something like vision training can push them over the edge, and that shows just how impactful it can be."

Goldman: I know my experience was extremely positive, but what other kind of feedback have you been getting from goalies that go through this program?

Tucker: "Of all the feedback we get, goalies are typically most excited about their faster reactions, improved peripheral awareness, and better tracking abilities. Again, a goalie's experience varies based on where he or she needs the most work. There was a pro goalie who had the opposite visual system that I did. He could always see everything peripherally, but his eyes wouldn't turn inward, which made tracking the last bit of the shot, and plays in close, harder for him. He was known to charge guys if they had their head down on a breakaway, and he told me later that the reason he did it was because he had no visual confidence on plays in tight. He knew that the closer they got, the harder it would be for him to make a save. He didn't really understand why until he got exposed to what was going on with his eyes. He trained his eyes for plays in tight and got rid of the problem, and his confidence skyrocketed as a result. Again, it's all about having the best tools for the job. It's like a kid who is struggling with his recovery slides, then you realize he is 180 pounds and sharpening his skates at a 7/8" radius. You give him a 3/8" radius and now he has sharper skates, better tools, and he's just zipping around out there. Visual skills are tools, and improving them will improve your game, plain and simple."

Goldman: After your assessment in high school, what kind of benefits did you notice in college and how did you end up here at Envision Sports?

Tucker: "Well, I went through the training with Envision Sports and absolutely loved it. When I got to college, I noticed huge improvements on the ice as well as much better efficiency in my reading. That is a big part of our philosophy – that duel benefit of the program. We work with professional and Olympic goalies, but ideally we tell people 'the younger the better'. Most of our clientele are going to be student-athletes for most or all of their careers, and part of success as a high school or college goalie is being able to balance all of the demands of your life. If you're getting your homework done quickly and easily, as opposed to being on the verge of being ineligible, just by proxy, that stress level will or will not carry over to the rink. My work as a trainer, and eventually as owner of Envision Sports, began after college. After graduating, I started working as a private goalie trainer. I didn't have enough hours there, so Jim Nelson, the originator and creator of Envision Sports, asked if I wanted to work for him, so I came on board and worked half with him and half coaching on the ice. That just kept going and I took more of a leadership role with Envision. The more time I spent as a trainer, the more I realized how much this program could help people, both on and off the ice. I loved coaching goalies, and continue to do so in Minnesota, but I knew I wanted to make vision training my career. I had undergone an apprenticeship under the man who created our program and learned so much from him, but as successful as we've been, most people are still not aware of this form of training. So my mission in life has become to raise awareness on the power of vision training. In my lifetime, I want to see our assessment integrated into the school's screening process so kids can identify these issues right away and not have to struggle or think they're bad athletes or not as smart as their peers. I have literally seen lives changed and careers extended and enhanced after going through our program. It is so powerful. I am beyond thankful to have the potential to reach people and to help them improve their quality of life. The biggest challenge right now is just letting people know this is out there, that they can do this!"

Goldman: On that note, let me start by asking you this simple question – how important is it for goalies to train their vision?

Tucker: "Extremely. We also worked with NFL and Major League Baseball athletes and they all have their own visual demands. But of all the positions in all of sports, hockey goalies have the hardest visual demands, and that's why they typically get the most excited about what they see in the results. Our head optometrist, Dr. Nathan Langemo [O.D.] explains it this way: 'Most athletes are content with 20/20 vision and do not understand there are other visual skills that can be trained. I try to express to all athletes the importance of maximizing their visual skills, no matter what age. You can train to be strong and fast, but if your vision system is not functioning at 100-percent, your on-ice reactions and decisions will be slower. Our training is unique in many ways. While goalies often picture us shooting pucks at them, our training is all done in our office, and involves intense eye exercises. Everything we do is quantifiable so goalies see how they're improving on a daily basis. Once goalies graduate from our training, which typically takes 40 sessions, then we move on to more action-based drills like catching tennis balls and other hand-eye drills. If we went straight to these drills, which is tempting because they can be more exciting, we would be ignoring the foundation of the visual system. Goalies would resort back to compensating for hitches in their tracking, overusing their dominant eye, et cetera.' Every goalie coach can relate to the philosophy that you must get a goalie to master the basic foundation of footwork and movement before moving on to advanced techniques. The degree to which goalies will improve through training depends on their starting scores. The kids on the lowest end quite often end up leaving team sports in general, because if your eyes can't track accurately, your coordination in all activities suffers, and you're not going to make it very far to start with. I often get athletes who come to me and say, 'I think I have great vision. I have great reactions.' My response is, 'I'm sure you do, but if you can be even better, wouldn't you want to? If you were a really fast sprinter, and I could make you even faster, would you want that, or would just be satisfied going pretty fast?' So, in summary, vision training is extremely important. Each goalie will see a varied degree of improvement, but every goalie can improve their game by improving their visual skills. And again, that goes way beyond just the 20/20 measure, so that's something I definitely want to stress. We have kids who have 20/20 vision, but their eyes can't track smoothly, or they have trouble changing focus, or their left eye is doing all the work."

Goldman: When you assess a goalie's vision, can you explain exactly what you're testing?

Tucker: "We look at a number of visual skills that aren't typically measured anywhere else. We measure reaction time, hand-eye coordination, peripheral abilities, speed of focus, endurance of the eye muscles, and how well the eyes are working together as a team. We show visual examples on video and we relate it to how it impacts their game. One nice thing is that with most of my trainers and I being former goalies, a lot of the promotional and educational materials we've put together are goalie-focused. Goalies, in my experience, are the quickest to grasp this program and they get the most excited about it, because it just makes sense to them. I think they inherently know, with the speed of the game, how important this is. Regardless, before we do a test, we sit down with each client and explain exactly what we are training and how it relates to their game. We explain Convergence, Divergence, Accommodation, and Tracking to them. It is important for us to educate them on the visual system and how it related to their game."

Goldman: Can you give basic definitions of those four traits you just mentioned?

Tucker: "Reaction time and eye-hand coordination are paramount for goalies, and I believe they are self-explanatory. Faster is better, and we make goalies faster. Tracking is a skill that is absolutely essential, yet most athletes have no idea whether or not they have tracking issues with their visual system. Tracking refers to how fluidly and smoothly the eyes move when following moving objects. We want to see eyes move as fluidly as possible. Sometimes we see eyes that are smooth for the most part, but jump like the second hand on a clock in certain areas. We even see their eyes skip as much as 25-percent of their range of motion. For example, the eyes won't look to the right, or they bounce around like a lottery ball. In these cases, it's very common for the athlete to comment that they have always struggled with shots in that area. No matter how much you practice shots to that area, you will always be battling these jumps that your eyes make. We videotape every athlete following objects in different paths – around in a circle, side to side, and diagonally. We then have the athlete watch the video. When an athlete with tracking difficulties sees their eyes jump, their jaw drops. To use a bad pun, it is very eye-opening. 'Convergence' and 'Divergence' fall together into a term called Fusion, which is basically how well the eyes are able to work together when the puck is moving toward or away from the goalie."

Goldman: Can you explain convergence and divergence in a little more detail?

Tucker: "If you visualize the area by your nose on the inside of your eyes, those muscles are going to be responsible for convergence. If you hold a pen out in front of you and slowly move it towards you, you're going to feel your eyes move inward, almost like they're going to cross. If you imagine a high glove shot, as that puck comes towards you, your eyes need to converge. When goalie coaches send me guys who are having trouble catching the puck cleanly, we often find that they are struggling with convergence. NHL forward Nick Bjugstad is a recent client of ours, and is a great example of how improving convergence can help on the ice. He came to us in hopes of improving his tips and rebounds, as most of his goals were coming off regular shots. But being 6-foot-5, his team needed more from him around the front of the net. We did some work on tips and immediately noticed that he would track the puck until it was about eight feet away, but then he would lose it. We worked hard on convergence and he has seen a huge improvement. He is currently in the top-25 goal scorers in the league, with most of his goals coming from tips and rebounds. Divergence is the opposing skill, where the eye muscles relax as they drift outward. I tell kids to think of a Hammerhead shark with the eyes on the outside of its head; that shark is going to be able to see everything around him. By teaching the eyes to relax as the puck moves further away, goalies can increase their field of view. An example I always use is on a 2-on-1. You're looking at the puck-carrier, but the wider your field of vision, the better you'll be able to see where the far-side threat is at. Our aim is to reduce the need to have that rapid head turning back and forth from shooter to the back-door threat and just see more of the ice at once. I would say divergence and tracking are typically the two skills where, when we work with elite goalies, those are most typically the ones that they're most excited about when they say they see changes on the ice. They see more of the ice and they track the puck quicker off the stick blade and all the way into their pads or gloves."

Goldman: And then you have accommodation, right?

Tucker: "Yes. Accommodation refers to the ability of the eyes to shift focus at different distances. Readers should try this: Turn on your phone's camera. Hold a piece of paper with text on it six inches in front of the camera lens, and then wait until it focuses. Now quickly turn the camera to a poster on your wall across the room. Alternate back and forth and notice how you have to tap on the screen and wait a second for things to come into focus. Our eyes operate in a similar way. Tiny muscles manipulate the lenses in our eyes to make things clear as we shift from close to far or vice-versa. When a goalie saves a shot from the point and the rebound drops two feet in front of them, their eyes must refocus in a fraction of a second. Any delay and the shooter will beat them to the puck and knock in the rebound. We train accommodation so that the eyes do a better job of refocusing at high speeds over and over again."

Goldman: When you start working with a goalie and you find that he doesn't test very well in a certain area, can you explain the training process? How do your goalies actually improve their skills?

Tucker: "At the end of the assessment, we look at the player's scores and identify areas of need. We then write out a personalized program that is different for each athlete. Much like a good workout program, each subsequent session is based on the previous session's results. If the athlete struggles, we stay where we are. When they are ready, we push them to a higher, more difficult level. The training takes an average of 35-40 sessions to complete. Our goal is to make each visual skill automatic. This requires muscle memory, which takes time to achieve. A session lasts about an hour and consists of going through about 10 different exercises. We will focus more heavily on certain areas depending on the athlete's unique needs. Every session provides immediate quantifiable feedback so we know when to push the athlete harder. Early on, it is not uncommon for the athlete to feel fatigue in the eyes, so we ride that line of pushing and patience. Athletes typically train with us two to three times per week, whereas our pro clients will do four to five, as their off season is very short and it is their best chance to get the training in. We have a large database of norms and averages based on past athletes and studies. We work closely with a team of optometrists and ophthalmologists who guide each athlete's program. Each test provides very exact quantifiable scores. None of the results come from our observation or our opinion. The tests and programs provide scores based on the athlete's responses."

Goldman: Once you've done some initial sessions, how do things progress from there?

Tucker: "The first step is getting them to learn how to activate the muscles we are training, but once they've done that, then it's just a matter of doing repetitions and pushing them to do more reps or work on more difficult tasks. As far as skill mastery and muscle memory goes, the number 10,000 jumps out, and it's quite well documented that, by the end of the training, goalies have done that, usually more than 10,000 repetitions. We have different stations, so most likely we'll start with convergence and divergence. It's just doing reps, taking a rest, doing sets, taking a rest, going to do a different station. We have a station where all we do is tracking, so they're following moving objects where we vary the speed of rotation or the distance traveled. We can isolate either eye or work them both together. We have a station for accommodation. That's where the lenses in our eyes is much like the camera on our phone, where you take a picture and you tap the screen and have to wait a second for it to find its focus. This is a really good one for goalies. Or vice-versa with a shot from the point and the rebound drops right in front, your eyes have to focus from far to near. Again if you're using a $20 camera from Walgreens, it might take a few seconds. But if you have a $1,000 Nikon, it will happen instantly. So we have a station where we use lenses to work those muscles that manipulate the lens of the eye. They have to really work your brain to make the target clear. We switch from something close to something far away and we're switching back and forth, making you read tiny words on a notecard and then you look up and read a bigger font at 20-30 feet way. So it's just a matter of training those muscles that control the lenses to snap back and forth for longer periods of time and for speed, so endurance is an important piece as well. If there's a really explosive athlete, but he tires out by the start of the third period and his legs fatigue, that won't cut it either. So we need that combination of speed fluidity and endurance for repeatability. So to summarize, we have a series of stations where we do multiple repetitions of the desired skill. We record how they did and then the goalie leaves, and just like other workouts, we have certain guidelines because the muscles do need to rest in order to recover. They'll come back for another session, and the process repeats. It's really a day-by-day monitoring, knowing we may need to push him in one area, back off in another, or focus more energy on a certain skill. Every goalie's experience is going to be a bit unique to another's. The tools we use and the goals we have are the same, but the path we take to get there is going to vary from goalie to goalie."

Goldman: Can you talk about a client's experience that had achieved excellent results in their training with clear-cut improvements in their vision?

Tucker: "Mike Lee, who is in the Arizona Coyotes organization. He was one who, if you look at our scores, he had a good solid visual system. He had no glaring weaknesses and his scores were good. But for him, good is fine, but great and excellent is better. Mike is a very hard worker, all business all the time. One of the challenges, especially with high-end guys, is that they're used to being good at everything. He really hit a plateau pretty quickly, where there was one target that he was having a hard time getting through. But once he finally cracked it, everything kind of opened up for him. His description for what his experience was is probably my favorite. The way he described it was, before training, he used to have to focus on focusing. And now, all the visual requirements during a game just happened naturally, so he was better able to pay attention to what was going on around him. Two things with that. One is we talk about things being automatic, so things happen without thought. It's fine if you're able to do something and perform something, but unless it's automatic, it won't happen in a game. When a puck is screaming at you, you don't have time to say, 'Okay I need to converge right now, and I'm going to focus.' The other thing with that is what fits into what we have talked about before, which is the ability to be creative. For Mike, when he plays now, we've removed one of the restrictive qualities that could prevent him from succeeding or being creative in the sense that he was consciously aware that we only have X amount of energy or focus to devote on any task. When our eyes are having to work and think about what they're doing, or he has to remind himself to focus, that is taking away from that limited and finite amount of energy and focus that he has, which he could be putting into what's going on around him. Just like an up-and-coming goalie has learned how to do recovery slides and he doesn't have to think about the mechanics of it anymore, all he has to do is just pay attention to where the puck is going and his body is going to know what to do. And so that, in a nutshell, is our goal. For someone like Mike, who has a good visual system with good reaction times, smooth tracking skills, balance between convergence and divergence, for him, it was a good-to-great thing, as opposed to bad-to-great. I just love the way he phrased it; 'Now I don't have to think about focusing, my eyes just do it, and all I do is pay attention to what's going on around me and use my energy better that way'."

Goldman: During my training with you, I've discussed with you my ideas regarding this issue of a lack of creativity in youth goaltending. How does vision training actually increase a goalie's creativity skills?

Tucker: "My view of creativity is that one cannot be creative until they've mastered the basic and fundamental skills. There was a basketball coach that said, 'Only when you mastered all of those can you become an artist on the court.' Once you have all the tools at your disposal, there's no limit to what you can do. I couldn't agree more. Having coached for 17 years now, I have also seen a sharp decline in the creativity of goalies. Especially right before the gear changes and J-S Giguere led the charge of the percentage-based blocking revolution. If you watched goalies in the late-80's, it was just street hockey all the time, like Grant Fuhr jumping on high shots and guys kicking their legs out with their toes up. I'm not saying goalies were better back then, but they certainly showed more diversity and creativity. Ten years ago, goaltending was becoming big gear and just block, block, block. With that, guys weren't taking as many risks and it really turned into a game of percentages. I think to a degree that's fine, but if you're dropping into a reverse-VH on the post every time the puck goes behind the net, regardless of where the other threats are, I think that can get you in trouble. I saw one of my goalies do it to a fault, and I would say it was a rule rather than a reaction for him, so he was getting burned. I encourage him to read the play and move based on what the play is doing, rather than doing the same thing every time. I still see NHL goalies getting burned on this play quite a bit. Shooters know what the goalie will do and they exploit it. If that goalie could be more creative on the post, it would keep the shooters guessing. The relationship between our training and creativity is therefore similar. Having better visual tools allows a goalie to be more confident in his or her reactions, and that means they do not have to rely solely on blocking, which leaves more room for risks and creativity. I think reactivity is a precursor to creativity. If a goalie has more confidence in his or her reactions, they can come a bit further out of the net, or try plays that other goalies are afraid to do. The goalie that I like watching the most without question is Alex Stalock. To me, he defines creativity, reactivity, and risk management. For him to be able to do that, a lot of things have to happen. Being a Minnesota guy, I was able to see him play growing up in South St. Paul and I've watched him train before. He works extremely, extremely hard on his footwork and puck handling. For him, these tools allow him to be more creative on the ice. If we think back to what Mike Lee said about how improving his vision freed his mind to pay closer attention to what was going on around him, that puts him in a better position to be creative, as compared to someone who has to consciously tell themselves to focus. He's in a better position now to be more creative with his play."

Goldman: That's exactly right, and it's something I really believe we need to try and re-inject into young goalies. They need to be able to balance the learning of fundamentals with the ability to use their imagination in a free and non-restrictive manner in order to come

up with new ideas and solutions to problems they face in the crease. But in terms of your vision training, how else does creativity get cultivated?

Tucker: "Let's say for someone with my visual system and a limited peripheral vision, I would be a lot less likely to leave the crease or go make a play with the puck, because I'm limited with what I can see around me. Someone with poor tracking will have to inevitably rely more on blocking pucks, because they don't have the tools needed to put themselves in a position where they force the shooter to do something else and the goalie knows he's okay because he has the reactions to back it up. Visually speaking, if I have a limitation as a goalie due to a visual deficiency or issue, I'm going to have to compensate for it, and most likely that's going to come in the form of 'playing it safe'. If you watch an Alex Stalock or Jon Quick, you're going to see them execute much more dynamic moves, and part of the reason why I think they're able to do that is because they have mastery of the fundamental visual and technical tools to back it up. There was a kid I coached who just drove me bananas; any shot to his right side, he'd over-slide and the puck would bounce off him like a grenade. We brought him in and tested his vision, and sure enough his left eye was doing all of the work, I mean everything. For him, any sort of creativity to his right side was hindered, because his right eye wasn't working. Once we trained him – and he took like 60 sessions, it was a really long process – we got to the point where, now to the right, he's not acting out of fear or uncertainty. He had total control over his visual system. So we're giving the goalie more tools for their toolbox so they have nothing they need to compensate anymore for visually. Just like a strength trainer would balance out muscles, visually speaking, we do the same thing in order to develop the complete player."

Goldman: That's awesome insight, and it really reinforces my belief that vision training is a must-have for developing goalies of all ages and skill levels. My last question would be about the future of your company. What is on the horizon in terms of making your program more effective for goalies or athletes in general?

Tucker: "We have just launched a 2nd phase to our training. Once a goalie completes our training, we work all off-season on the turf or synthetic ice, doing hand-eye, reaction, and peripheral awareness drills. People can see a few of the drills we do with our pro goalies on our website in a new section we've created called 'Goalie Corner'. We have also started offering in-home training to those who don't live in Minnesota. We set the athlete up with equipment in their home and do sessions via Skype. The biggest announcement we have is the launch of an online version of our training program. This has been years in the works, and we'll finally be able to provide sports vision training to students and athletes around the world! People can watch our website for launch details. I cannot express how excited I am about this big step towards helping more people gain access to our training."

6

DISCOVERING THE WORLD OF FINNISH GOALTENDING

"That a country with a profound understanding of isolation would develop a system to support and elevate what may be its loneliest calling makes perfect sense." –Chris Koentges, The Oracle of Ice Hockey

On the morning of April 2, 2014, I received an e-mail titled *Last Additions to GoaliePro 2014 Mentoring Program.* Click, click, boom.

Gentlemen,

Congratulations. You are the last ones we have officially accepted to this summer's mentoring program. Selection process took some time, as we got way more applications than we could accept.

Plan on being at Espoo, Finland for full days from June 1 to June 6. I do also recommend that you take some extra time also for other things than our camp.

Please confirm to me ASAP that you can make it to Finland in June and your travel schedule once you have it.

I will be sending additional information during the next few weeks along with full coaches list for 2014. You also need to start working on your white papers. If you have agreed on the topic with me, go ahead and get first draft done. If not, you can send me proposals for your topic along with reason why you want to write about that particular topic.

Terveisin / Best regards,

Jukka Ropponen
GoaliePro Consulting Oy
FINLAND

I had to read this through a few times, and as you could imagine, it took a few days to sink in. I was *finally* going to Finland. It was actually happening. I was accepted to the prestigious tenth-annual GoaliePro Coach Mentor Program by the founder and Finnish goalie coach legend, Jukka Ropponen.

Invitation accepted. Two days later, flights booked and tickets purchased. Time to hurry up and wait.

Behind nearly a decade of burning desire and public longing to visit Finland, a foreign land became such a vivid place in my mind. In so many of my lucid and lingering dreams, I had already been there. But geographical maps and overhead landscape photos filled in the gaps where imagination met real-life expectations, so a few days later, I purchased a little Thomas Cook traveler guide book on Finland.

As I leafed through it over the next few weeks, a couple of facts really stood out.

First of all, Finland is sparsely populated compared to not only North America, but all of Europe. Only 5.4 million people fill 130,524 square miles, which averages out to about 26 people per square mile. "Jeez," I thought. "I think I bump into 25 other people in one *square foot* when I'm in downtown Denver."

Secondly, the majority of Finland's population is located in the southernmost third of the country, while the north remains largely uninhabited. That being said, Helsinki is considered a perfect place to enjoy the Finnish nightlife. It's not necessarily a party town, but their club and music scene is world renowned.

The more I read about Finland's climate, landscape, history, politics, and culture, the more I came to realize that goaltending, a lonely and isolated calling for the few and far between, meshed so harmoniously with the lifestyle of the Finnish people.

Of all the things I learned on my trip, in terms of the general population, I loved seeing how in tune they were with nature. In the United States, the people often clash with nature. But in Finland, the wilderness, whether it was the myriad islands dotting the Gulf of Finland or the linear eskers in Ukko-Koli, integrated the entire population in a blue and white blanket of serene scenery. While there, whether you're a visitor or a native, you can't help but to retreat into the woods and reflect on life amongst the fallen limbs of a million different branches.

Without the usual daily distractions that inundate the typical American, it makes logical sense that the Finnish person is so much more connected with themselves and their surroundings. Heightened awareness and intelligent minds are as clear as the Karelian air, their synergy to nature as strong and as complex as their language.

No wonder Finland is the world's finest goalie factory. The position takes a special connection to nature to truly overcome the emotional pressures and mental obstacles that plague a goalie throughout their life.

To this very day, and every day until my final one arrives, I'm deeply breathing in those vivid memories of Finland. Barricaded by groves of frosty glazed grass and swaying Betulas trees, I'm still wandering the shore of Lake Bodom, lost amongst so many of those tall, skinny, pale wooden finger bones protruding high into the phthalo blue sky. Timeless, seamless transitions between day and night faded together like white turning into grey. The fishy smells of the salty sea mixed with the tasty aromas of coffee and fresh bread. It was so familiar in my mind, yet so fresh to my five senses.

American born and proud of it, I can't deny the fact that, for this nature lover, Finland will always be calling my name. I can't wait to go back there in the summer of 2015. I would totally live there, too. I would totally belong. Everyone speaks English, everyone loves goalies.

After immersing myself in Finland for nearly two weeks, I can say with full confidence that their goalies are a different breed. Amongst such a diverse group of native Finns, on so many different levels, from their unique personalities to their rather simple lifestyles, they are genetically designed to be elite goalies.

This was such an eye-opening learning experience that I returned home slightly embarrassed. Compared to Finland, the lack of structure and financial support for youth goalie development in the United States was yawning and vast. In my eyes, it was so extreme that I came away quite overwhelmed with the gap between the two worlds. We're nowhere close to each other. We're not even in the same realm or galaxy.

Of course this is not exclusive to the fault of anything in the USA. With the sheer size of the country, from Anaheim to Albany and every pocket of youth hockey in between, our ability to formalize and implement a goalie development and coaching certification program is being stymied. It's simply a cultural thing.

No matter how poignant or influential the written word, the frustrating ultimatum I face is forever the same. Unless you visit this country for yourself, and unless you take the time to experience Finnish goalie development first-hand, you will never truly grasp exactly what I (or anyone else) attempts to portray. You simply have to feel it.

Nevertheless, when the summer ended, not only was I beyond inspired to share some of my stories, but I knew I wanted to do whatever I could to initiate a change in the United States – to try and 'bridge the gap' so to speak. But before I could determine how to walk down that daunting path, I had to let my mind process everything I had learned. I had to somehow organize my newfound understanding of what Finnish goalie development was all about, what it had to offer, and what cultural differences were creating such a wide gap between the two worlds.

Ultimately, that's the focus of this chapter. While I could have written an entire book on my time in Helsinki, it's a fun and informative memoir of my trip, as well as a precursor to my interviews with two of today's most influential Finnish goalie coaches.

Finland's Club Hockey System

The rich soil from where Finland's phenomenal goalie development model grows is found within their club system. Combined with a stable and refined goalie coaching certification program and a very manageable hockey population, the country dominates in nearly all areas of youth and pro goalie development.

The club system flows through major cities like Espoo, Jyväskylä, Tampere, Oulu, Rauma, Turku, Pori, and more. Centralized almost exclusively in the southern half of the country, each club is structured to incorporate goalie coaches on every team at every level, from the Mites all the way up to the Finnish Elite League (SM-liiga). That also includes U-14, U-16, U-18, U-20, and the Mestis league (second-tier pro).

Their development program is managed and maintained by the Finnish Hockey Federation's director of goalie development, Hannu Nykvist. As you will learn in his interview, Hannu is the proverbial 'Alpha and Omega' of Finnish goaltending. He's the main man in charge of making sure every club has access to the information and resources they need to properly develop their goalies. It's a pretty straightforward gig, but even for a smaller country like Finland, it's an exhausting full-time job.

I was so fortunate to have the opportunity to meet, befriend, and interview the top guys on both sides of the Finnish goalie development ledger. Nykvist represents the National side, while the aforementioned Ropponen represents the private coaching side. Here, it's important to note that not only did Ropponen create the first goalie development handbook in Finland way back in 1985, but he also acts as a pro consultant for the development of these modules in other countries, such as Estonia and Canada to name a few (and hopefully USA in the near future).

These two guys reflect just a sliver of the sheer wealth and opulence Finland has had in terms of the history of great goalie minds, and their insights and willingness to share their ideas with me further reflected one of the most substantial cultural differences existing between Europe and North America.

Due to the hard work over the past 30 years from Nykvist, Ropponen, Ylonen, and many other top Finnish goalie coaches, each hockey club in Finland has a certified head goalie coach that not only works with the SM-liiga goalies, but with all of the goalies and goalie coaches at every level within that club. The less-experienced goalie coaches involved in a club will obviously work at the lower levels, but they are guided and mentored to higher levels by the head goalie coaches in that same club.

They can also call upon Nykvist for advice, feedback, or even just for an annual visit, if so needed.

With a goalie coaching certification program in place, not only does Nykvist work hard to keep all of the goalie coaches on the same page, but he nurtures a strong culture of sharing within his National network. Furthermore, he still gives individual coaches the creative license to tweak and implement some of their own training drills. The framework is solid, but it's not rigid. There is still a place for new ideas and growth.

Imagine the size and depth of the American goaltending talent pool if we had nearly 30 years of similar structure acting as a platform for their development. That fundamental difference, without question, is the most visible component creating the massive gap between two worlds.

That's not to say that America has been unable to develop goalies and goalie coaches, it's just that they have done so without an actual nationalized or regionalized development platform for the thousands upon thousands of grassroots goalies and volunteer amateur goalie coaches.

Instead of goalies training under a cloud of privatization and financial exclusivity, Finland's system is mainly built around a National and Federation model. The Finnish Hockey Federation also continues to invest in resources that are committed to keeping their country ahead of the curve. Still, Finland is not completely devoid of the privatized coaching industry that we see saturating and dominating the culture in North America. Aside from GoaliePro, I discovered at least five other smaller companies that train goalies independently. This is neither frowned upon nor disallowed in Finland, but it's not as prevalent due to the fact that so many youth goalies already receive in-season training within their clubs.

These companies are also run by goalie coaches that still follow the basic framework found in the national goalie coaching curriculum maintained and updated by Nykvist. It's so readily available and easily accessible that there's no reason not to use it. Plus, almost all of those coaches have already been certified, or have at least participated in goalie coaching clinics within a club at various times in the past.

That's another significant difference between the two worlds. Even the coaches that work outside of the club system in Finland have likely gone through a national coaching certification program at some point in time. The same can't be said for USA Hockey, since the only goalie coaching guidance anyone receives comes in small, short presentations at the Level 1 through Level 4 head coaching clinics. It is miniscule, if anything.

This is just a brief and very basic introduction to the club system network that currently exists in Finland, but it doesn't take long to learn that so many young goalies throughout the country's clubs are being positively influenced and properly developed by numerous quality, certified goalie coaches.

Reminiscing on my time in Helsinki, of all the goalies I met and worked with, I was most attracted to a kid named Oskar Autio. Playing for the U-16 Espoo Blues at the time, Oskar and I became good friends very quickly. I was so excited about his pro upside and long-term potential; he was such a hard-working kid that spoke excellent English and displayed tons of competitiveness. His style also reminded me of Sami Aittokallio, one of my favorite Finnish prospects currently playing in North America (Colorado Avalanche).

During one of our on-ice sessions at the GoaliePro camp, I asked Oskar about his development path in the club system. He told me how great it was, and I gave him a glimpse of the different setup in the USA.

He mentioned how he could have easily been on the ice with the Blues' Mestis team if a few injuries occurred, or if an opportunity to practice at the same time presented itself. This amazed me, because it simply would never happen in the USA. I also learned from him that this sort of thing happens on a fairly regular basis, and it's not uncommon for a U-16 goalie to train with pro level goalies from time to time, nor was it uncommon for a kid like him to meet and talk with guys like Nykvist or Ropponen.

Clearly a smaller country like Finland is conducive to this type of situation being more prevalent, but the more influential aspect to ponder is that a 16-year-old goalie can potentially train and learn from a pro goalie and a pro goalie coach at the same time. Since everything is interconnected due to the club system, a tremendous prospect like Autio further benefits from this immersion. He gains such valuable learning experiences and on-ice insights that goalies his age in North America rarely ever get.

On the flip side, after I told him about the development landscape in the USA, he told me how, sometimes, Finland's club system can be detrimental to a goalie. If that goalie isn't getting ample playing time, or if there are conflicts of interest between the goalie and the head coach, it's very difficult to change clubs.

In the USA, goalies can move from one youth organization to the next pretty much whenever they'd like.

I think that's an important, although fairly obvious note to make here. As pure and idyllic as Finland's club program may seem to be for goalie development, it is not without its own obstacles and political pitfalls. No matter who you are or where you're developing, those are aspects of hockey culture you simply can't escape.

Just for fun, let's imagine what it would look like if a club system existed in the United States. It would be like the Los Angeles Kings having a working player affiliation with the LA Junior Kings youth association.

So a goalie like Boba Jacobson, a pretty skilled bantam goalie that I scouted last year through my role with the NTDP, would be affiliated with the Jr. Kings program up through the U-20 level, the Ontario Reign (ECHL), the Manchester Monarchs (AHL), and then the NHL club. With the close proximity between Ontario (CA) and Los Angeles, Jacobson likely gets the chance to practice or shadow the Reign goalies, or sit down and learn from Bill Ranford and Kim Dillabaugh, the two goalie coaches for the Kings.

As you can imagine, a system like this would bring a trove of benefits to goalie development in North America. At the same time, with the size of the country and the scope of hockey within each state, this is unrealistic. The culture is too different and the budgets are too stretched for this to be a viable solution.

It's pretty overwhelming to even try and reconsider re-building such a massive network of youth hockey, so you simply have to find solutions within the framework already in place. And that's not going to be an easy thing to do.

Finland's Goalie Development Handbook

With the advent of their club system, Finland's framework for a structured goalie development model was able to thrive. The information and methods comprising their model was then able to flow through the pipelines due to a power cell – a handbook that acts as a manual for everything a goalie coach needs to properly train his or her students.

I visualize Finland's ideal goalie development model with a simple infinity sign. All of the information included in their model locks together to produce certified coaches and properly trained goalies. As long as goalies want to play and coaches want to teach, the infinite flow of information and the continual results will never stop.

On one side of the infinity sign is the goalie coach, which is strengthened by the information that flows through the coaching certification program. As more coaches become certified, they fuel the flow of that information through refined and updated training methods. It passes through the pipelines of the club system and crosses into the realm that rests on the other side of the infinity sign, the goaltender. Here, the student builds off of that information and develops in a manner that further strengthens the links.

The more talented goalies become as a whole, the more coaches can learn. The more they learn, the stronger the entire system becomes; new concepts are introduced and old concepts are refined. The information that flows within the infinity sign never stops flowing. Progress never comes to a halt. It's actually quite a beautiful and simple thing to behold.

Seeing Finland's latest goalie development handbook for the first time was a pretty surreal experience. I had heard about it before, but never expected to actually feel it in my hands and flip through its pages. This happened when Nykvist came to visit the GoaliePro camp and meet the coaches that had come in from overseas. In between the morning and afternoon sessions, I was introduced to Hannu. A few minutes later, he invited me and a few other coaches out to lunch at a strip mall a few miles away from the camp. It was there that he kindly showed me a copy of the goalie development handbook.

At first, it was a really strange interaction. I seriously thought I was doing something wrong, especially when I pulled out my phone and asked to take a photo of the cover. It was like I was spying right out in the open. Maybe Hannu was going to yell at me? Or maybe he would suddenly cover it up and stuff it back into his leather attaché case?

Nope. He was more than willing to allow it. In fact, he smiled, let me take pictures of at least half a dozen pages, and seemed fully aware of how I was basking in this surreal moment. He knew of my role with USA Hockey at the time, yet he had no problem sharing this type of information with me. Amazing.

Of course it didn't help that the entire thing was written in Finnish.

"Good luck trying to translate this," I thought.

So as much as I wanted to break down every single page and section in the handbook, I simply couldn't. To be honest, even if I had that opportunity, I wouldn't have done it. What works for Finland will not work for North America, and you can't just translate a goalie development handbook and expect all of the answers to magically fall into place.

It will never be that easy. Things between Finland and the USA will never be that compatible. It will take years to catch up.

Giving my head a good shake, I came back to reality, studied the guide closely, and listened closely to Hannu. Not only did this handbook explain all the basic and advanced aspects of technique, but it also included a very beefy and in-depth section on off-ice training. Pre-game warmups, hip-specific stretches, flexibility exercises, eye-hand warmups with tennis balls; all of these components were broken down with pictures, diagrams, written explanations, and step-by-step instructions on how to teach these methods.

The manual also included breakdowns of the half-butterfly save, the two-pad stack (yes, they still teach this in Finland), and drill progressions for the butterfly save. There was an entire section dedicated to active hands and how to catch properly, which is considered as the most prevalent staple of the Finnish goaltending style. There was also a section on leaning and shifting into pucks, blocking, managing depth, and more. There was even a section on puck trajectory, complete with diagrams and pictures showing aerial angles and colored shadows to visualize net coverage from different spots in the crease.

The handbook didn't end there. It also had diagrams reinforcing the importance of squaring up to pucks instead of players, as well as diagrams on how gaining proximity with the hands is a big benefit to maximizing net coverage. It also included a training grid in the back of the handbook for goalie coaches to use with their goalies all season long, so they can check off areas of technique and positioning they cover on a week-to-week and game-by-game basis.

To no surprise, I also found a few pages dedicated to mental conditioning, including how the Federation wants goalies to act. They want goalies to have a strong work ethic. They want goalies to understand what it means to be the last line of defense, what responsibilities come with being a team's goalie. They want goalies to have good practice habits, good body language, and to be coachable, ready for anything.

The entire thing also included age-specific training, complete with topics like avoiding burnout, proper nutrition, pre-game routines, and most importantly, the dangers of early-age over-specialization.

Over-specialization in goaltending is not a cultural issue in Finland like it has become in the United States for a few reasons. First of all, as I explained earlier, since goalies receive proper training during the season, it leaves their summers wide open to play other sports, do other things, or simply get away from hockey for a few months. But most American goalies rarely receive proper or adequate in-season goalie coaching in team practices, so they're forced to participate in summer goalie camps and private clinics.

Secondly, since the current handbook specifically warns coaches and goalies of this issue, more emphasis is placed on off-ice conditioning, which rounds out the athletic development of the individual.

The big lesson with everything I learned regarding the current Finnish goalie development handbook is that Finland does not have any magical secrets to goalie training hidden within these sacred pages.

As I've said before, there are very few on-ice training secrets out there anymore. Instead, I became aware that their program was considered the pinnacle of such, because it includes so much information on off-ice training, and it is the culmination of nearly three decades of continual refinement by influential goalie coaching leaders within the Federation. This not only allows for cultural and educational progression within the numerous goalie development subgenres, but also allows for an ability to implement 'keystone' extra-curricular elements at all ages, including but not limited to hip flexibility, progressive mental conditioning, and explanations of the goalie's humanity and emotions.

A few days after this enlightening lunch-time hour with Nykvist teaching me about the current state of the Finnish goalie development handbook, I experienced another one with Ropponen. Except this time, it was a look back at the past.

It came on an afternoon where Jukka invited the entire GoaliePro coaching staff over to his house for a traditional backyard Finnish barbeque. The succulent food and tasty libations combined with the amiable company created a blissful and memorable atmosphere. Soaking it in with all five senses engaged, I became eternally grateful for the opportunity. I made sure my gracious hosts were aware of this fact.

After we finished eating, with a simple smile and a nod in the direction of his patio doorways, Ropponen invited me into the lower level of his cozy home. Reaching further into my divine state of mind, the next 30 minutes was like stepping back into the Garden of Finnish Goalie Eden.

Inside a cluttered but neatly organized lower level of a vintage two-story home, nestled peacefully in a quiet neighborhood in the heart of a Helsinki suburb, I found the ancient roots of Finnish goaltending history. For, on the many stuffed shelves full of goalie masks, jerseys, and signed photographs of Ropponen and his most successful pro students, there rested an unassuming shelf with a couple of navy blue three-ring binders.

Within these two binders, I found the keys that eventually unlocked the doors to what is now the most successful plan for a country's national goalie development. The hard-covered binders instantly captured my attention, as a relaxing afternoon transformed into the focus of my current mission of uncovering the past and the genesis of Finnish goalie development.

One of the binders was Ropponen's very own custom-made goalie development manual, complete with old-school overhead transparent projector sleeves, rudimentary goalie pictures, and tons of diagrams with hand-written notes on angle play and positioning. The other binder was a goalie coaching program, as well as a manager's section for scouting and tracking a goalie's progress.

For this American-born goalie, those two binders were like long lost artifacts from the Knights Templar; things you knew existed, but considered to be lost in time. They were ghosts of the past. You felt their presence but never expected to see them in person. But when I finally uncovered them, when the artifact was actually resting in my hands, I could feel the power and the presence as I flipped through the pages.

Within these binders came the realization that I was looking at the beginning of an advancement in worldwide goalie development. It generated a new wave of training. It totally changed the world I had been living in for over 20 years.

When Jukka was done showing me these books and explaining how they came to be, I felt like I had stumbled upon them purposefully, like I had somehow been guided to reach this point in time. This feeling was not hard to grasp or fathom, but it was shocking to actually feel its immense influence of power. It was as if the entire purpose of the trip was woven into a million small actions, all of which tied into this exact moment. For, more glorious than I had even dreamed, I had discovered the answer to a lifelong question – where do good Finnish goalies come from?

Later that night, on the drive back to my apartment in downtown Helsinki, I came to an important realization regarding the culture of goalie development in Finland. The best gift I got from Jukka during my time in Finland wasn't my sleek red and black GoaliePro warmup suit. It wasn't the free ferry ticket to Estonia, nor was it the endless flow of traditional Finnish food and Jägermeister at the GoaliePro camp appreciation party. It was the gift of his unconditional sharing.

It was his genuine willingness to help me discover the world and history of Finnish goalie development. It was the fact that he cared enough to bring me into his home and show me the world he has lived in for so many years. I'm forever thankful for this moment, for his capacity to share allowed me to learn, and the learning led to tremendous growth as both a professional and a human being.

I experienced this gift of sharing not only from Ropponen, but also from Nykvist and every single Finnish goalie coach I met during my time in Helsinki.

The Finnish Coaching Style

Similar to the same thing I saw in the youth and pro goalies I worked with in Finland, the coaches had all of the same stoic, poised, quiet personality traits. They were more observant and less verbal. They acted more introverted. They were genuinely willing to share ideas and discuss technique, it never felt forced. When I would tell them about something we normally do here in the States, they didn't poo-poo the idea or scoff or smirk or make fun of it. They accepted it, pondered what they had heard, and smiled. It was almost eerie compared to the resistance and friction I had found in many previous coaching experiences.

The club setup in Finland is a remarkable specimen for coaches. When a kid decides at age seven or eight that he wants to be a full-time goalie, the club accepts him and Nykvist is informed. From there, the kid will train and develop in that same system for as long as he can, and the kid's growth is closely tracked and truly nurtured as time goes on.

The same goes for goalie coaches. There are just so many avenues for success and growth. Even the IIHF offers a two-year course in Vierumäki that trains accepted students how to coach not only hockey, but all sports. Within the available program for hockey, there's a special concentration on goaltending. And within goaltending, a big chunk of the syllabus is dedicated to mental training. I also learned that Finland is running a program to increase the number of female coaches in all sports, including hockey.

Nykvist has even had the support of his federation to hire a trained Martial Artist to teach flexibility for the National program. He explained to me how he learned about the importance of opening up the hips and getting out of a deep crouch – it can help reduce injury proneness and make a goalie more effective with his movements, including lateral weight transfers, recoveries, and even basic movements. So Nykvist is not only knowledgeable about these key components of development, but he continually learns new things and adds it into the program, injecting it into the virtual infinity sign I described earlier.

Nykvist also travels throughout Finland and visits each program at least twice a season. At that time, he meets with the goalie coaches in each program, ensuring that everyone is doing their job and is on the same page with the basic program. He also does quite a bit of scouting, discusses the progression of each club's top goalies, and then moves on to the next club.

Advantage, Finland.

When it comes to the Diffusionary comparative analysis of goalie coaching styles and methods in Finland and the USA, I think the most obvious place to start is with the time and importance placed on catching pucks. A much stronger emphasis is placed on this skill from the moment a Finnish goalie tosses on the pads, which goes a long way in improving their muscle memory for catching with the glove. That includes the ability to catch pucks low in front of the pad, across their body, and even over-hand with pucks coming directly at their face.

It's not a tough equation to solve. Since Finns spend more time working on these skills at a younger age, their mechanics are more inclined to become pure instincts sooner. In North America, the instincts to catch are there, but since less time is spent emphasizing the ability to catch pucks in front of the pads and face, it is not as mechanically fluid at key development stages. It just takes longer for many (not for all). For many Finns, generally speaking, it's an unconscious competent skill. For many Americans, it's something we still have to consciously engage while training or playing.

During the GoaliePro camp, I estimated that, compared to a similar camp held in the USA (of which I have been to many over the past five years), there was a 30-percent increase in the amount of time and emphasis placed on active hands and catching pucks in Finland. This obviously varies from camp to camp, and from program to program, so it's just an estimate.

Seeing this first-hand, I started to come up with potential solutions for how Americans could narrow the gap. Clearly it would help if we had standardized active-hand drills for goalies in all grassroots programs and forced goalies to work their hands on a more consistent basis. But what else could we do?

Maybe we could make youth goalie gloves just a little bit lighter and more flexible. I notice a rising number of younger goalies wearing pro-level gear, so the stiff, heavy gloves cause them to struggle catching pucks cleanly, or closing their glove like a smooth, buttery baseball mitt. If they're made soft on purpose, they become easier to close and developing the hand and wrist mechanics needed to catch at all angles and on all planes is much easier to develop.

Speaking of gloves, one very revealing difference between North America and Finland had to do with their construction.

If you're familiar with Niklas Backstrom, Kari Lehtonen, or Miikka Kiprusoff and their gear modifications, you'll notice they all wear the same type of glove. But the typical North American's glove is made to close a little differently. The Finnish-style glove closes more at the base of the fingers (just above the palm), whereas North Americans usually wear gloves that close more towards the top-third of the fingers (just below the tips).

Erno Suomalainen, who was one of the four pro goalies participating in the GoaliePro camp, taught me about this significant cultural difference. He explained how catching pucks with a glove that closed using the bottom part of the fingers provided more stability and strength. But when trying to catch pucks with the tips of the fingers, it was tougher.

Obviously this is still very much a personal preference thing, but generally speaking, he said that is why the "Kipper" or "Backstrom" glove spec is so popular in Finland, but not often used in North America.

As soon as I tried on his glove, I fell in love. My current Vaughn V6 glove has the "Pavelec" spec, which is constructed in this typical Finnish manner, where it closes using the base of the fingers. I'll never wear another model again. If you get the chance, try it out sometime, and get a feel for the different closures.

The main difference in goalie coaching when it came to skating fundamentals in Finland was the lack of a t-push. Instead, Finns teach their goalies to use the shuffle and c-cut almost exclusively to get around the crease. This isn't to say that the Finns don't teach the t-push at all, but it's rarely used, mainly when traveling very long distances on their feet across the crease, or when you need to open your hips in order to make a desperation save or an aggressive open extension.

When hearing the reason why Finnish goalie coaches mainly teach the shuffle, it made obvious sense. It was all about the economy of movement. The t-push takes more time and energy to execute, because you're turning the leg, flexing the hip in a different manner, turning the skate, then bringing it back underneath you. The shuffle, however, is just one step, one push, and the ankle or hip doesn't rotate as much as with a t-push. The shuffle takes just one step, while the t-push takes three steps.

Another major coaching difference in Finland is how they teach goalies to push off and stop with the same leg. It's always the outside leg if the puck is on either side of the center of the body. Since I already knew shuffles were emphasized more in Finland before the trip, in terms of coaching and outside of active hands, pushing and stopping with the same foot so that the proper leg is loaded is not something traditionally taught in the United States.

The Finnish goalie coaches I worked with also talked less during a goalie's reps and more when he was waiting for his next turn. They did more observing than usual and had less verbal feedback as well. They gave goalies the opportunity to figure out solutions to problems before chiming in, and they threw out less gimmicky terms (at least from what I could tell when they spoke in English). They mainly just reinforced basics and good pushes into appropriate spaces.

Yet another coaching difference was the way reps were handled in a station-based practice session. In Finland, a group of four goalies will spend a longer time rotating within a station, and they will also take many more reps on average compared to what you see at a camp in the States. Instead of taking six to eight reps before switching, I saw some goalies taking upward to 16 or 18 reps before switching.

When asking Ropponen and other coaches about this difference, their reasoning was simple. Finnish goalies will take more reps on average at a station because coaches want the goalie to get a really good feeling of how drills are to be executed. The more reps they take, the more familiar they become with the proper movements. If a goalie realizes he is struggling to make saves properly, they will stick with it and keep trying to improve their mechanics before they stop and switch with the next goalie.

With that in mind, one of the coolest coaching interactions that took place during the GoaliePro mentoring experience occurred on the final day of the camp. I was paired with Mikko Ramo, a 34-year-old pro Finnish goalie playing in the Mestis. He was not only one of the four goalies participating in the pro group, but he was also one of the main coaches for the youth camp.

Although he was clearly exhausted from his on and off-ice session earlier in the day, I was so impressed with the way he interacted and worked with the young goalies. I have never seen a coach have so much patience in my life. There were a few sequences in particular where Mikko must have spent nearly 10 minutes on his knees to methodically explain and teach one key tactic.

I saw him spend nearly 10 minutes explaining and demonstrating the proper angling of the stick and body while rotating and recovering back to the skates on a lateral adjustment. The kid continued to struggle and make the same mistake, but Mikko exhibited unbelievable poise and positive body language. Eventually, the kid figured it out.

In North America, I don't see that type of patience very often in a youth goalie camp. This is not to say coaches don't have that capacity, but drills are often rushed in order to conserve time and execute more reps. Even though the other goalies in his group were a little inactive during this time, Ramo put so much visible energy into helping the kid that, when he did execute the movement correctly, they had instantly formed a new bond and friendship. It is this dynamic and interaction that I feel really reflects the culture and personality of the typical Finnish goalie coach and youth goaltender.

As it goes with everything in the realm of goaltending, an idea or concept may work for some but not for others. In this situation, the positive of increased reps is that it allows the goalie to tinker and tweak and collect feedback on their mechanics. The negative is that it may tire them out more quickly or cause the other goalies to lose their focus since they are standing around for a longer amount of time.

Clearly these are only a handful of the many differences that exist between Finnish goalie coaches and American goalie coaches. At the same time, those differences and similarities are a matter of perspective. On a wider scale, at the end of the day, what we teach in our respective countries are essentially the same things. Efficiency. Economy of movement. Competing for every puck. Rebound control. Those key principles of goaltending are without borders, and they're shared globally.

Still, the comparative analysis I've briefly broached here should illuminate some of the most basic differences, and give you a solid introduction to what I learned during my time in Helsinki. These differences in coaching styles had a major influence on the training environment of the youth Finnish goalie, an environment that, in my opinion, is way more conducive to the long-term success of your typical youth goalie.

The Finnish Youth Goalie

Due to the goalie development and coaching certification programs in place over the past three decades, during my time spent in Finland, I worked with 11 and 12-year-old goalies that had more maturity, better on and off-ice habits, and more emotional control than many 15 and 16-year-old North Americans.

It is due to this structure that I felt the training environment in Finland was so conducive to creating young goalies with exceptional foundations in terms of skill and attitudes.

I was amazed at many exceptional aspects of the Finnish goalie's personality on the ice. They were all very receptive to criticism and feedback. They respected every coach on the ice, and not once did they reject or display negative or ungrateful body language while they were being told to make adjustments. They all had very strong work ethics. There was no complaining or excessive horseplay or inattentiveness when coaches were explaining drills. Everyone was astute. It was almost eerie.

Furthermore, whenever they weren't in the net for a station, I saw every single goalie at some point during the week, without any forced direction from a coach, skate off into a corner and work on footwork drills. They didn't do this because they were asked to do it, they did it because they wanted to do it. They had the natural discipline and the natural work ethic to continually refine and rework any problem areas. They did not sour themselves due to the dejection of struggling in an area. The struggle was part of the development process – they accepted it and did something about it.

If I were a 16-year-old American goalie and I was a part of this camp, it would have been a huge, rude awakening.

"Holy shit," I'd imagine myself saying. "Every single kid here works their bag off. I am one lazy bum."

I know the big caveat with all of this is the sample size; I'm going off less than two weeks of experience with about 40 different goalies of different ages and backgrounds. But when I asked the Finnish coaches if this was the norm, they agreed it was. This hard-working and disciplined atmosphere was not just what you find in the elite goalie camps in Finland, it's what you find in *every* goalie camp in Finland.

This reminded of an article I read online in Canada's The Star. It discussed goalie development with Rick Wamsley, who is part of Hockey Canada's goaltending leadership group.

> *"In general, from what I've seen, guys I've dealt with coming from junior to the pros, is they lack the ability to read the play, and they lack hand and foot skills. Finland is producing more good goalies per capita than anyone right now, and their goalies all seem to have good feet and good hands, like they've been taught skill first, positioning second. In Canada, it looks like our younger goalies are taught backwards: positioning first and then skill second."*

Reflecting on this quote, I realized that it's not that we may be teaching our goalies backwards in North America, but rather that we are not creating the proper training environment for the kids we teach at the grassroots levels. That environment is a product of the culture, and that culture is something that takes a very long time to change.

Ultimately, in my opinion, it's not *what* we're teaching our goalies in North America compared to Finland, it is *how* we're teaching them, and in what *environment* that teaching and coaching takes place.

While many years of this consistent training environment has successfully streamlined and 'smoothed out' things such as technical terminology, age-specific skill development progressions, off-ice training, and the many folds of the mental game, youth goaltending hasn't lost its smaller regional differences, either.

For example, one goalie I worked with during my time in Helsinki was from the northern part of Finland, a region called Lapland. Within the same program as clubs in the south, he was taught by his goalie coach to have a slightly different ready stance, with more emphasis on narrower feet. He also seemed to use the half butterfly on a more consistent basis. He looked slightly more 'old school' than his southern counterparts.

As the days went on, I started to see first-hand more of these regional style differences within the country. So they're clearly much more pure in terms of stylistic bloodlines, but just like we see in North America, plenty of distinct blends and mixtures still exist. I figured a big part of this was due to the fact that Finland's population is sparse in the north and denser in the south.

Once I got past the amazing utilization of active hands and the lack of an emphasis on t-pushes, I was really surprised to find that the Finnish goalies in the GoaliePro camp knew very little about the reverse-VH technique. But that opened the door for an awesome experience during my time there.

It took place on the second day of the camp. Ropponen gave me control of the ice and allowed me to teach the reverse-VH to the goalies. So after doing a mass teach on one end of the ice, we split into our regular stations, and each group that came to my station went through the same mini drill progression.

This was by far the coolest on-ice experience for me during the GoaliePro camp. Being able to introduce a relatively 'foreign' technique to a group of Finnish goalies was like a real-life alchemic experiment. I did my thing on Tuesday, then saw how goalies of different ages and sizes implemented it into their games on Wednesday, Thursday, and Friday.

After my initial mass teaching session on Tuesday, Jack Hartigan took over from there and added progressions on Wednesday. He also worked with the group of four pro goalies (Suomalainen, Ramo, Rasmus Tirronen and Rasmus Reijola), on this technique as well. He taught body angle changes through the utilization of a c-cut with the anchor leg, which allowed the goalie to rotate forward or backward depending on the puck's location. To rotate out, you push with the heel of the blade. To rotate back in and flatten your body along the goal line, you push with the toe of the blade.

This was great to see on the ice, as Jack discussed how the Swedes had mastered this reverse-VH progression, for as we know, they were the first to implement the technique on a regular basis. In Sweden, this is called SMS, which loosely translates in English to skate-on-post.

On Tuesday's session, as every goalie rotated through my station, I made sure to ask each and every goalie which variation of the reverse-VH they preferred. Nearly 80-percent of them felt more comfortable going shin-on-post. That led me to question whether or not there was an anatomical or physiological reason for this. It reminded me that Tuukka Rask almost always prefers to go shin-on-post, whereas almost every Swedish goalie goes skate-on-post.

Knowing that Ropponen and Nykvist are gleaning information about the advantages and disadvantages of all the variations out there, it will be very interesting to see how this gets implemented on a national scale over the next few years. Will Finland include literature in their development handbook that is a slight alteration to the Swedish SMS? If so, will it steer goalies towards going shin-on-post? If so, and I do believe this could be a possibility, they have the active hands to gain proximity on pucks despite the fact their body would rest slightly deeper in the crease compared to going skate on post.

Either way, it's nice to know that Finland has the system in place to implement changes and refinements on a national level, and those changes are easily and strategically capable of filtering throughout all of the country's youth hockey clubs. No wonder their coaching culture and teaching environment is so strong.

I have said it so many times already, but I have to say it again. Maybe it is a lack of being able to explain the complexities of what I saw, or maybe it's just the need to emphatically reinforce what I learned, but this was so much a cultural thing.

Right now, it's a pipe dream to believe Finland's level of structure could one day exist in North America. But I came to the realization that there are at least a few simple components that would loosely translate, and from there, solutions specific to our developmental obstacles would eventually rise to the surface.

More Memories from the GoaliePro Camp

It is when you willingly cast yourself into a sea of new life that you can emerge completely reborn.

My time spent in Helsinki was just that. Full of so many memorable meals, conversations, and interactions with a new type of people, in a totally new environment and culture, this trip was the pinnacle summer experience that set off a chain reaction for my future goals and visions.

As much as I wanted to write about every experience I had in Finland, I pinpointed just a few that stood out as perfect reflections of the concept of sharing. These experiences stimulated new paths in my life.

Ironically, the moments I'll remember the most in terms of goaltending were the discussions and meals I shared with all of the new coaching friends and Finnish goalies I worked with during the GoaliePro camp.

But that doesn't mean I didn't take some time to live it up and have some fun.

There was that surreal night I had partying with the boys at *Namu,* a popular dance club in Helsinki. Surrounded by absolutely gorgeous Finnish girls all night long, I was caught inside a dream within a dream. When you let yourself go and don't worry about the future or the past, you take everything for what it is and truly appreciate the sights, sounds, and tastes right in front of you. This was not hard to do at such a popular and packed place like *Namu*; I stayed there all night long talking to a handful of local Helsinki girls that spoke perfect English. They knew I was part of a group of guys that were pro and college-level goalies, so they flocked towards me with visible interest. That sort of thing simply doesn't happen to me when I go out in the States.

Being invited into the VIP lounge at *Namu* was really cool as well. In there, it was so funny to see Antti Niemi in there, just as casual as could be, wearing a t-shirt and a hat. He was with one friend, but was not surrounded by a flock of ladies. That's not his style I guess, and I respected his privacy by not going up to him to try and introduce myself.

That entire night was a taste of the high life in Finland, an intoxicating international partying experience I'll never forget. If you're American and you're a goalie, you are basically irresistible to the ladies over there. Oh, and it's no secret that Tinder works pretty well over there as well.

There's also the absolutely hilarious story that Tirronen, one of the goalies training in the pro group, told me about an interesting cultural difference between Finland and North America. Over an early dinner one afternoon, he told me how kids in Finland do not grow facial hair at the same rate of American kids. They grow facial hair much slower and later on, and even then, it's very little. But when a Finnish teen comes over to the States for his freshman year of college, it only takes a few months for their facial hair to explode in growth. A few months after that, they come back to Finland for summer vacation and their families are shocked, curious as to how this could have happened. Finnish kids go from being baby-faced to looking like lumberjacks.

Turns out, American food is so saturated with growth hormones, and fast-food joints like McDonald's are so prevalent, that it causes a more severe facial hair growth reaction in Finnish people. Scientists have studied this effect and it has been pinpointed to this interesting interaction with hormones in our food.

If that's not an example of an environmental and social factor influencing the genetics of a developing goaltender, I don't know what is. This story, as hilarious as it was (Rasmus even showed us some pictures to prove his story), was actually a key teaching point and really opened my eyes to the differences between the two worlds. Finnish kids are so much healthier compared to American kids.

Speaking of health, a few days into camp, I'll never forget the sudden realization I had when I found out there was probably not a single pudgy or obese kid to be found in Finland. The GoaliePro camp was held at a facility called *Konalan Jäähalli*, but connected to the two ice rinks were soccer fields and more dryland fields, so a figure skating camp and a soccer camp was also being held that same week. Being surrounded by over 100 young Finnish athletes, amazingly, there was not a single kid that looked even remotely out of shape. They were all skinny, athletic, and extremely disciplined when it came to their training. It was really remarkable.

I'm being partially facetious about not seeing a single fat kid in Finland. I swear to you though, with the obesity issues we're having in the USA, this experience I had further proved Ras' story regarding the amount of hormones you will find in American food compared to Finnish food. The food we eat literally has the power to change our genetics and our DNA.

Then there was the GoaliePro coach's appreciation party, hosted by Ropponen at a private plot of land on the shore of the Gulf of Helsinki. Complete with a massive traditional wooden sauna that fit 10 or 12 people, we had a huge dinner meal and some traditional brews as we enjoyed the long night. It was there that we were joined by Minnesota Wild goalie Niklas Backstrom and former Flyers prospect Niko Hovinen, who stopped by for a short time to catch up with Ropponen and the rest of us.

It was really cool to see Backstrom again. A year earlier, I had met him for the first time while writing *The Power Within*. He agreed to meet with me in person for a lunch interview at the Galleria in Edina. That was an awesome experience in and of itself, but nothing compared to seeing him again in Helsinki. I made sure to thank him personally for taking the time to meet with me for that interview, and he was happy to see the book had been so successful. Another cool, memorable moment amidst the rest.

Erno's hilarious transformation from a quiet guy to a "colorful" personality was another great moment, truly enjoyed by all. I was also ceremoniously inducted into the GoaliePro program through the ritual of downing a shot of vodka, biting into a piece of sausage, and then licking off a dab of spicy mustard off the side of my hand. As disgusting as that sounds, it was strangely tasty.

Those were just a few of the memories I had that stuck out to me as being truly entertaining outside of the camp experience. But some of the most influential in terms of how I see the world of goalie development as a whole happened during meals and walks through Helsinki.

Sharing New Ideas in New Lands

Ale Jääskeläinen was the first Finnish goalie coach I met after arriving in Helsinki. I was so excited to meet this guy because we had connected on Twitter a few years prior. Sharing the same passion for metal music, I instantly considered him the all-encompassing figure of my "model" Finnish citizen. He loves metal and goaltending, and his personality is a subtle symbiosis of the two. In fact, our mutual passion for metal music made us instant lifelong friends.

Ale had an aggressive appearance, complete with a thuggish motorcycle beard and tattoos. But his personality was the polar opposite. Quiet, shy, and reflective of the typical stoic Finn, he was more observant than outspoken, yet you could clearly see he was genuinely excited to have North Americans participating in the GoaliePro program.

Shortly after Larry, Ted, and I had settled into our apartment, Ale swung by and took us out to lunch. He drove us through a part of downtown Helsinki and pointed out a few clubs, bars, and areas of interest along the way. Once we arrived at the restaurant, the ice broke quickly between the four of us and we instantly started comparing and contrasting goaltending cultures between Finland, Canada, and the USA.

This lunch was memorable to me, because I believe that sharing a meal together is the best way to establish strong bonds with new friends.

After placing our order, Ale asked me what I thought the biggest difference was between Finnish and North American goalies. I said Finns seemed much more attentive and aware and alert on plays in close. I also felt that they had better hand dexterity, better skating skills, and better poise in chaotic situations.

I went on to explain how I really had no idea what to expect for my first trip to Finland, and that the premise of my book was to create a comparative analysis of goal-tending styles. I told him how I felt American goalies were mutts, but Swedish and Finnish goalies were much more purebred, with easily recognizable and identifiable styles. I also mentioned how I knew Finland put a lot more emphasis on off-ice training and dryland, because they understood the importance of having very well-rounded athletes.

Sadler chimed in and explained how the club system was the biggest difference between the two worlds, and how, in Canada, there was no incentive for it to be club-oriented, because no development programs were currently in place. But he quickly countered himself by explaining to Ale how Canadians were finally in the process of starting to develop a more streamlined 'identity' with the creation of their new goalie coaching certification program. Combined with their decision to ban international goalies in the CHL, Sadler pointed out how this was a really interesting and exciting time for them; they have the opportunity to take what Sweden and Finland already had in place and then build upon it.

"If they do it the right way, Canada could be a combination of both styles in a real effective way," he said.

At the time, I was really surprised to hear that Ale wanted us to show him and the GoaliePro students the Reverse-VH. As I mentioned earlier, I didn't know this technique was foreign or unfamiliar to the Finns. Ale explained that it wasn't totally new since the top goalies in the Finnish pro leagues were using it, but rather it was a technique that many coaches weren't fully comfortable teaching to the younger goalies.

After many more topics were broached, lunch ended, Ale took us back to our apartment, and then we continued to soak in the new world. A few hours later, Larry, Ted, and I took to the streets of Helsinki. During our walk, more stimulating discussions on comparative goaltending covered a plethora of topics. Buzzing from a splendid day of sightseeing and preparing for the GoaliePro camp, this conversation also resonated with me, because we were all mutually open to soaking in the sights and sounds surrounding us. We were completely immersed in a new environment, working together to process how things could be applied in North America. It wasn't Larry's first time in Finland, but his excitement matched Ted's and mine.

We first started with a discussion about some of the more progressive training "techniques" that may be coming after the Reverse-VH. Ted mentioned that he believed the most important wouldn't be a movement, but the method of mental conditioning, because he had learned that 60-percent of the position was determined by having such skills in place.

From there, we started to discuss vision skills. I relayed to them what I had learned from Josh Tucker at Envision Sports about a goalie's visual acuity system. Ted taught me about *Momentary Vision,* which is being able to gather information on a glance, and how you can't just notice where the player is standing, or that a player is there, but you have to know the entire target zone for a potential release.

From there, he said, a goalie needs to be able to process or evaluate what that potential release and result looks like.

After that, the discussion moved towards tracking the progress of a goalie's in-season performances. Larry mentioned how it was Thomas Magnusson (Sweden's director of goalie development, who you will be introduced to later in the book) who had the great idea that we should have a two-man tracking system for goalies. One guy's job is to enter and input the data, while the other's job is to observe and provide the data entry guy with the proper information. To do all of this as an individual has proven to be too difficult in a live setting, because it's when you look down to enter data that you're likely to miss another event.

Within this micro-discussion on scouting and evaluation, the three of us surmised that coaches could break down the fields of shot quality into three or four categories (beyond the obvious ones):

> ***Prevention:*** *Forcing a shooter to aim wide due to perfect angles and positioning*
> ***Retention:*** *Absorbing initial shots and not allowing any rebounds at all*
> ***Placement:*** *Gaining possession of the puck after a rebound is allowed*
> ***Dispersal:*** *The ability to break up potential shots due to tactics and responses*

We discussed how these categories should be tracked and converted into useable data, because they are vitally important to a goalie's success, regardless of the sequence. Another key component of progressive or advanced scouting we discussed was being able to pick up on trends. This is something that Double Blue Analytics and guys like Steve Valiquette are capable of doing quite well, especially if you have the video to back up the analysis. You'll learn a bit more about this in the chapter on Vulcan Vision.

We also discussed home-vs-road shot count disparity, which is a major issue right now in the world of goalie analytics. Not only is there a severe lack of consistency from rink to rink, but I can tell you that it does get into the heads of NHL goalies and goalie coaches. We consoled each other by realizing that it was only a matter of time before tracking chips would be added to pucks and players.

From there, I opined on one of my main goaltending philosophies; everything is eventually reduced down to movement, and movement is the 'ultimate truth' of all things goalie analytics. In agreement, Monnich went off on a passionate talk about this topic, teaching me many new things about the way the body works in harmony with the mind.

Everybody, he explained, has three energy systems that they use throughout their lives. These systems kick in sequentially, and the broadest of these is the aerobic system. A typical hockey shift engages the anaerobic lactic system, but a goalie doesn't perform at top speed for three minutes, only for 10 seconds, or in even shorter bursts. Therefore, the first system that a goalie initiates is the anaerobic alactic system.

"So for a goalie to do line sprints off the ice, well, it does nothing for his game," Ted said. "To optimize his development, you have to train differently."

This was the moment when I really became drawn to Ted's personality. He's such an old-school guy, a little quirky in a good way, but so genuinely passionate and caring. I can also safely say that he's probably the only goalie coach that also loves Turkish music. In fact, it was his understanding of the psychology of playing music that helped him gain notoriety as a goalie coach in the United States. His research on playing the guitar and its benefits for goalies (Henrik Lundqvist is the poster boy) stretched all the way back to 2003.

Monnich, a musician in his spare time, started to notice an improvement in his glove hand skills after practicing the guitar. Through the science of *cross-task facilitation*, Monnich found ways to prove how the neural pathways we create when practicing the guitar and making a glove save were the same. When you practice guitar, you stimulate the same area of the brain that memorizes the patterns of making a glove save. So when you learn a new chord or a new melody, those same nerves get triggered and, over time, they help hone your ability to improve your glove hand mechanics.

Sharing his energy for discovering new links between science and goaltending, Monnich furthered his point in ways that in turn stimulated some new ideas in my mind. As he told me more about his past and his passion for Turkish folk music, he brought up the science of flow theory, and how pieces of music build on each other without the musician even having to learn anything.

The discussions finally tapered off as we returned to our apartment. During that lengthy stroll, it felt like time stood perfectly still in the late afternoon of a Finnish midsummer day. In a totally foreign environment, three goalie coaches with three extremely different backgrounds shared new ideas that forever changed our perspectives on training methods, advanced techniques, and new analytics.

Evolutionary progress at its finest, whether intellectually or genetically, seems intimately tied to one's environment.

Closing Reflections on Finland

During my two-week stay in Helsinki, I don't think there was ever a point in time where I saw a complete absence of light or the full onset of darkness. The sun certainly dropped below the horizon, but the sky never faded to pitch black. Instead, the sky reached a deep ocean blue, lingered for a few hours, then quickly retreated back to the pale blue of a normal daytime sky.

It was really hard to adjust to this. I did not sleep much at all. But I didn't really care. I was already dreading my departure, an emotion I had to force out of the back of my mind.

Just live in the moment and soak it all in. The Finnish summer presented me with a gift to experience more hours in a day. Pure, blissful twilight pushed away the luminescent moon and the surrounding darkness. As I blissfully discovered, my idea of daylight lasted nearly 18 hours in the month of June.

Beyond the long days and obsolete nights, Helsinki was a collision of Eastern European cultures and somewhat clandestine archaeology. The city was wrapped in a natural landscape that combined the pithy air of an ocean harbor with the softer, dew-scented freshness of the hardwood forests.

Finland is literally one big giant forest. With an average of just over 16 times more forest per capita, it's the most heavily-wooded country in Europe. To put this in perspective, according to *BorealForest.org*, the total volume of Finnish timber amounts to nearly two billion cubic meters of stock. This amount would be equivalent to making a 10-by-5 meter wooden wall around the entire globe.

Since my time was primarily spent in the city of Helsinki, I was duly impressed by the combination of old weathered buildings and post-modern art museums, all of which were condensed into a few square miles just beyond the harbors and ports. There were tons of pale-skinned locals filling the cobblestone streets, but I loved how I never got that smothered and suffocating feeling. People moved a little slower, they were way more laid back, leisurely, and relaxed. It was a welcome change to the fast-paced chaotic blur of bustling cities in the United States.

It was also a stark reminder that Finland and everything it encases was as welcoming as the skin wrapped around my bones. After imagining what it would be like to visit this land for so many years, as you could imagine, I simply didn't want to leave.

When that final day arrived, I seriously considered missing my flight back to Minnesota. But it was not meant to be. I had other cities to visit, more coaches to meet, and a very hefty book project to complete.

Without a doubt, Finland is my favorite place in the world. The life and mindset of goaltenders are cherished here – respected, revered, and admired. It's the richest sports subculture the country has to offer, and that's the type of world I hope to live in. But that is not an opportunity simply given away. It has to be earned.

Heaven's gates don't suddenly fly open for anyone that wishes to enter.

Coded in the perpetual twilight of a Finnish night, I loved how so many of my new ideas sparked and spiraled between the minds of my coaching companions. Despite my physical exhaustion, I was spiritually at peace with my surroundings. I was so energized that I could literally feel the grey matter in my brain, the red blood in my veins, the blue marrow in my bones, and the fresh air flowing through the open chambers in my lungs.

In perfect matrimony with my idyllic vision of heaven on earth, Finland was magically carved straight out of my mental clay from so many past dreams of what I envisioned this place to be. It was the type of place where I could take a leisurely nighttime stroll to a little bar on the corner of two narrow Helsinki streets and shoot the shit with none other than Finland's director of goalie development.

7

HANNU NYKVIST ON FINNISH GOALIE DEVELOPMENT

Shortly after returning from our lengthy stroll through the heart of Helsinki, Larry announced that we were invited to head back into town later that same night to meet up with Hannu Nykvist. Keep in mind this transpired before Nykvist visited us at the GoaliePro camp, so I had no idea this would be happening, and I was not in the least bit prepared. For a moment, I was equal parts ecstatic and pissed off.

Getting the chance to meet this distinguished gentleman was as rare as seeing the Aurora Borealis in Texas, so I was quite anxious for a few minutes. I wanted to make a good first impression and I wanted a chance to tell him how excited I was to be here. I didn't want to miss out on the opportunity.

Little did I know that just a few months later, the two of us would be working together on the ice with eight NHL goalies and then putting our minds together to form a new organization called NetWork Goaltending. It was another one of the many synchronicities that made this entire summer experience so damn special. But more on that later.

Around 10:00 o'clock that night, despite the fact I was still dragging from the time change and our busy first day in Helsinki, Larry and I were joined by our fourth and final roommate Aljosa Pilko, a goalie coach from Slovenia who had arrived earlier in the afternoon.

Sharing a much-needed second wind, Larry, Aljosa, and I slipped into the city, until we reached the edge of downtown Helsinki and a local bar called *Storytime.*

Once inside, we descended down a narrow winding cast-iron staircase and paid a bouncer the 10-Euro cover charge. We squeezed past the stout bouncer, then slithered and snaked through a maze of drunk and dancing older locals, and then around the front of the stage to a set of small dinner tables. We took our seat and spent the next three hours drinking beers and shouting loudly at each other.

Nykvist was not yet at the table when we got there. Instead, he was found on the dance floor of this little local jazz and blues club, swaying to and fro with his wife. After a few songs, he casually sauntered back to our table with a beer in hand and a pinch of snuff in his upper lip.

Nykvist, who was clearly very relaxed, carried himself with a quiet sense of intelligence. A calming face with deep-set eyes, thick eyebrows, and slightly tousled dark brown hair, he had the demeanor of a man that had zero worries in the world.

Hakuna matata, buddy.

As soon as he sat down at our table, he hunched over in his chair and introduced himself. Having met Larry before, the two of them spent a few minutes catching up before he turned to me – a total stranger – and welcomed me to Finland with a handshake, a smile, and a monotone voice.

Much to my surprise, I didn't need to introduce myself. He somehow already knew who I was, and the first thing he said was how much he loved reading my first book. With a returning smile, I giggled like a schoolgirl and expressed my gratitude. I just wanted to tell him how happy I was to be there.

The blues music was obnoxiously loud. It frustrated me at the time, because I didn't want to miss a single word Hannu was saying. But he didn't say much. He was too busy soaking up the rhythms as if he was listening to headphones in a hammock on a hidden Costa Rican beach. He even played a little air guitar and drums, closing his eyes, nodding his head, and then casually glancing over at me with another smile.

"What in the *fuck* is going on here?" I screamed to Aljosa, laughing. We both shrugged, smiled, and clinked glasses. I could tell he was also pretty bewildered at the scene. We were the two youngest guys in the building, but we were loving it. I mean, when in the hell will I ever find myself in a small local Finnish blues club again? Hi-larious.

After a few more songs, the local band finally took a break, giving us a chance to talk some goaltending. Again, Nykvist didn't say much, but he did briefly explain his role as the director of goalie development for Finland. He also explained how he was in charge of selecting all of the goalie coaches within each club, managing the goalie training program, tracking all of the country's top prospects, and doing whatever he could to keep Finland ahead of the development curve.

The whole time he was talking, I was praying the band would stay silent for a little while longer. The only thing I was able to get in was a little bit about why I was here, what I was doing, and the basic premise of this book. His eyes showed me that he was truly attentive and supportive, but I could tell there was only one thing on his mind at the current moment – shaking his groove thing with his wife on the dance floor. Off he went, and there we sat.

A few hours later, we finally headed back to our apartment. Part of me was sad I didn't get the chance to talk to him more, but part of me was just happy to have made the connection. That was a great night.

Sure enough, as you read earlier, Nykvist showed up at the GoaliePro camp a few days later. I had an inkling that this was going to happen, but knowing his schedule was really hectic, I wasn't expecting to actually have time to sit down and interview him for the book. But when he appeared at the rink in order to take some of the North American coaches out to lunch, I was so ecstatic.

During that lunch, Jack, Larry, Ted, and I sat down in a nearby strip mall and shared lunch at a fast-food joint, and that's where this interview took place. Below you'll find two parts – one where I speak with him alone at a separate table while the other guys are eating, and one where all five of us are discussing Finnish goalie development together.

Goldman: I know you briefly explained this to me the first time we met at *Story time*, but can you explain to readers what your role is with the Finnish Hockey Federation?

Nykvist: "My role within the federation is that I'm in charge of the whole Finnish goalie program. I'm not creating everything myself since we already have 40 years of history behind us, but I'm one part of the chain that keeps things new. Since the beginning of when we started our goalie coaching, the core has always been there. When we started, the core was very technical. Then later on we've been adding and refining some stuff. One of my jobs is to be the junior national team goalie coach. My job is also to make sure that we have good youth training programs all over Finland. I have under me nine regional goalie coaches. Finland is divided into eight districts, and the Helsinki region is the biggest, so I have two guys working here. So these guys are responsible in their region for organizing a basic level of goalie coaching clinics, plus scouting the regional goalies for the first national team camps, plus they make visits to their clubs and organize federation goalie schools in their region."

Goldman: How do you go through selecting the goalie coaches for each region and club?

Nykvist: "Actually, it's basically finding someone who wants to be involved. They're part-time workers and we're so much smaller than Canada, so a lot of it here is based on the personal network. You get to know almost everyone here in Finland. The clubs work independently, but we're there to support and help them. But I choose who is in charge of each region, and they have to renew contracts every year. I think the longest guy has been around for almost 20 years. There are some changes on average every two or three years."

Goldman: Besides the fact that you guys are such a tight-knit operation, what would you say is the biggest advantage that young goalies have when it comes to developing into professionals?

Nykvist: "I think it's our influence and policy program in the club since Day 1 when they choose they want to be a goalie. We feel every goalie in the club, same as players, have a right to receive proper goalie coaching in their club. We feel that they shouldn't be paying an extra fee for that. They are a part of the team and they should have quality, certified goalie coaching. Whenever they choose to be a goalie, they have quality support on a daily basis."

Goldman: The biggest thing that Americans notice when it comes to the strength of Finnish goalies is their active hands. Can you briefly talk about how you instill this trait in the younger goalies and why it is recognized as one of the Finnish goalie's best traits?

Nykvist: "It's a funny story actually, because I've had a few American coaches ask me this question. But in the beginning, I didn't exactly know what this term 'active hands' meant, because in our program, from the beginning, when you go on the ice at eight years old, you start to teach those most basic saves, and if there's a high shot, you are taught to catch it. I think we prefer to teach catching first, then blocking the puck. I think the blocking is for the close-attack situations, when you can't control the fact that you don't have any more reaction time. But as long as possible, you try to catch the puck."

Goldman: When I was out on the ice with the older and the younger group, right away, it was the first thing I noticed. Regardless of age, their catching instincts were clearly engrained in their minds and bodies from a young age, and it was really awesome to see. Shifting gears, with this coaching certification program you have, what is your goal over the next few years?

Nykvist: "I think now we have to build up a good program for ages 14-to-19. We've made a very solid program for the younger ages. I think a huge goal and role for the Finnish Hockey Federation is to support the clubs and the club goalie coaches, because that's where the success comes from. You could say our national teams are a result of the work the clubs are doing."

Goldman: What do you think is the best path for Finnish goalies that want to play pro in North America? Should they stay in Finland and stay in their program as long as possible?

Nykvist: "I think generally, because it takes longer for goalies to develop compared to players, they just need to find their games and make their mistakes, and if you have a solid technical and athletic base, you have the chance to be a good goalie as time goes on, no matter where you play. I believe that European goalies shouldn't rush over, because it takes time to develop. I also think it's a question of personality. A more independent goalie who can carry the responsibilities of what he's doing can go over there a little earlier. But I think as long as you have a good club where you can play and get proper coaching, then the environment guarantees you can be successful in the future."

Goldman: If I were to ask you to define a Finnish goalie, how would you do it? I know it's a tough question, but I'm always curious how guys like you answer this question.

Nykvist: "Well, I can tell you what we're looking for. We want our goalies to be really top athletes with a solid technical base. We also want them to have good game-reading skills and strong mental character."

Goldman: I'm really humbled that you took the time to read _The Power Within_, which is what I had been working on for the past few years of my life. So in terms of the mental game and having that whole balanced approach, what are your thoughts on having that instilled in your Finnish goalies?

Nykvist: "I was actually very happy to read that book, because you and Mike Valley and I, and basically the whole Finnish federation, we are all on the same page. I think that's where everything starts; how you coach as a human. That makes up who you are as a coach. Then it's how you approach another human and coach the humanity of a player. That's something that you can really build on. But my philosophy is that your mind, your body, and your spirit, they are always there. You can discuss those values like independence and responsibility, but still at the same time discuss the weight training and technical training, so they are all together at the same time, and that was the good message from the book. I'd like to get rid of this old view of seeing a player only as a biomechanical tool. I think that's really old-fashioned."

Goldman: Many goalie coaches out there are so narrowly focused on technique and winning that they never realize how important it is to instill some of these core values in their goalies.

Nykvist: "I also think when you talk about this mental side, when you start to coach a kid who let's say is 16 years old, he already has maybe nine or 10 years behind him. I think as a coach, my responsibility is to study what he has done before, his background. Then start to walk with him in one direction where I'm guiding him. We always carry our history with us, and I think that's one huge part of what the goalie coach needs to take into consideration. Because what you're doing now is always a buildup of something we have done in the past. If we can open some new horizons and new ideas for the kids, then we can advance the history, but from this foundation we're going somewhere together."

Goldman: The thing that bothers me in the USA is that kids don't learn how to manage their own mental game until it's too late, so the book was a way for me to help goalies learn how to process and understand a lot of the mental pressures on their own.

Nykvist: "I think the main question is, should the goalie coach increase independence or dependence? There's an idiosyncrasy. In my mind, my job as a coach is to make myself feel unnecessary. If you think about the goalie, you have to practice so much moving and basic saves that, in a game, you have to do minimal thinking."

Goldman: Yes, and I also want to teach goalies how to be creative and think for themselves and figure out how to problem solve when situations occur.

Nykvist: "I also think it's really interesting how you explained things in the book. The Finnish language is so unique, it has nothing to do with Russian or German languages. These terms – how we think of these things compared to Americans – are very different. You've already seen in some discussions how we use so many words to describe the same things, and I think that sometimes creates a misunderstanding when North American goalie coaches are speaking with Finnish coaches."

Author's Note: *In the second part of my interview, I picked back up when we were all looking through the Finnish Goalie Development handbook together and Nykvist was breaking down certain sections. The earliest parts of this interview, unfortunately, were too noisy to transcribe, so they've been omitted.*

Hartigan: "They don't do full t-pushes in Finland, it's so cool."

Nykvist: "But that's basically the whole technical package, including drills you can do [he is pointing to a page in the handbook]. That's a classic all over the world, we call it 'Iron Cross' now. Actually, the first time I saw it was in the 1970's in the IIHF manual. So we include some drill ideas on how you can develop these skills, then we get into playing the angle, but we call it positioning here. So we include the ideology of the whole thing."

Monnich: "In the school I work with, we have two terms. One is Angle, which is the line from the puck through the center of my body, to the center of the net. That's the most important thing. And then how far out you come, we call Depth. How deep you are. And we say angle before depth."

Nykvist: "We call it sometimes Gap Control also. If I can translate it correctly, first you have to get the right positioning on that angle line, then by the game situation, you choose your depth. Then we have the basic saves, that's where what you call active hands and puck control comes from, because from Day 1, we start with all these basic saves."

Hartigan: "That's one question I asked you about before, because remember we were looking at the half-butterfly? That was one thing I was trying to teach back home, the basic half-butterfly, which is right here [pointing to manual]. On the video, it was really good."

Nykvist: "That's maybe a strong part of our culture, because from Day 1 we started with high shots with little kids, and basically you can have all these shots taken both in the butterfly and the goalie standing up, so there's a lot of variety. So there are some ideas about the basic saves, a little bit on puck control. Tuukka Rask uses this half-butterfly sometimes, and a lot of North American goalies use it, but maybe a little bit by accident in the right situation when they are trying to make a desperate save."

Hartigan: "We're always going down, but we don't extend, so our small goalies have too narrow of a butterfly, and they get beat in the low corners."

Nykvist: "I believe the more multi-dimensional you are, that's where the creativity is based around. So we have more drills for the basic saves, movements, how to handle rebounds, and we have some progressions for the beginners. Then we have a small chapter for stick handling, and things like that. Then we get through how goals are scored in game, how to handle game situations using technical abilities, like the shuffle and the C-Cut, in certain situations. There are some simple drills for those game situations. You also have to identify the situation, and then anticipate the play, and then use your tools within movement and positioning. Next we have a section on hockey sense, which is basically an understanding of how to play certain situations like wraparounds and breakaways correctly in relation to the individual's body. You understand the principles of the situation and reading the game means reading the direction, speed, and positioning of the puck and the players. But I think everything in terms of reading game situations and having rehearsed skills should be about getting tons of repetitions. Then I created programs and models for how to rehearse those skills. So until 14 years old, it's very detailed what techniques you should learn in those phases. I put everything into two-year phases, because I think it has to be that way. Then we have a section on how coaches can give their goalies attention during practices, and then I have a bunch of post integration variations for goalies at different ages. So when they have special goalie sections in the clubs, the coaches know what to work on with the more complex stuff. Now I'm adding something about coordination skills, reaction skills, balance, a combination of all those things and how you can adapt and improve agility and anticipation, including tools how to improve them. Then there's something here about motor skills, power, the hips and core. I'm really building a strong program for them to improve core stability and mobility and all of the necessary things you need to take care of your hips. But to protect these hips, I think it's a combination of your physical features, your technical features, and how you take care of your body off the ice. That's the whole picture, and that's why we recommend in practices to do more standing-up movements, maybe a 60-40 split, that's a rough recommendation out here."

Hartigan: "That's not very usual for Canada. It's all down-up, down-up, down and slide."

Nykvist: "Because we live in a different world, we have goalie coaches working in clubs, so I have a chapter how to organize your goalie coaches within each club. This includes job descriptions for each role within the club, including a little something about the planning for the season."

Hartigan: "I'd love to have that in English. That's awesome."

Nykvist: "Then we actually include something for when players come for their first National Team training camp. We have three categories of evaluation, including game, character, and skating. Game is to play the most correct situations as possible. Character is how you can see your character in the game, like how independent you are, how you carry the responsibilities of what you're doing, and then how you find your flow in the game. Skating is your puck control, all of the basic techniques, the outcome should be good puck control."

Monnich: "Have you ever considered leadership within the aspects of character category?"

Nykvist: "A little bit, but we don't actually demand it. But if you have it, then we encourage and support it. Niklas Backstrom has never been in charge of the room. So I think we have to go by the terms of each personality, then get the best out of them. I think you can't go against someone's basic human existence. But you still have to be able to communicate with your players, and that's something we expect and demand. Some players learn it on the way, but I think it's something like a natural born character. You can't really push somebody."

Monnich: "We simply try to encourage it. We don't want someone to feel like they can't speak up, but if it's in their nature, we encourage it."

Nykvist: "So then I have a season planner in the back. Basically all of the terms and main headlines depending on their age and maturity. You can add drills and build up your program and you can see what things you're doing. So that's, in a nutshell, our goalie manual."

Goldman: Do you guys have a specific scouting form for evaluating goalies?

Nykvist: "We use only one, and it's this one. Game, Character, Skating. We grade on a 1-to-5 scale. The scale is that if you go to an international tournament. So a 5 is if you're capable of being a top keeper in that tournament. If you're a 4, you're a winning goalie, if you're rated a 3, you're an average goalie in that tournament. So it's always related to the tournament you're playing in. If we're scouting regionally, we use the same 1-to-5 scale, but the 5 is that you're the best goalie in that regional area. Then we have an area for the coach to produce some text about how they read the game and perform. So this is our heritage, and we've had this in place for some time for kids, more or less, up to age 14. The next thing is to come up with another manual for the older and more talented goalies in Finland. We haven't decided how to do that yet, but we'll see. I just want to make sure our clubs need to realize that the first priority is the younger goalies, in order to create the solid foundation all over the country. But I don't think there's really that big of a difference. You have the same skills in Sweden and Canada. A high shot to the corner is still a high shot to the corner, doesn't matter where you are. But we've been able to create really good structure and we can spread it all over Finland easily. Like I said earlier, we can't compete with the quantity in North America, the only thing we can compete with is the good cooperation and sharing."

Goldman: For our NTDP, there's only three regional goalie scouts under Kevin Reiter, who is the head goalie coach for USA Hockey. That's it. So we're missing so many goalies in so many other areas and regions when we're scouting. We're looking for the top 15-year-olds in the country, we'll locate talent somewhere like California, but we see him two or three times all year. So we're trying to project character and upside and potential off an extremely small sample size. So what you said about quantity and the size of our country is so true. It's really tough to see everyone with the limited number of goalie scouts we have involved in the NTDP.

Sadler: "We're having a similar situation and going to go through a very interesting situation with the U-17 Program in Canada now. It's going to be completely based on the junior scouts, the scouts that are doing work for the three major leagues. So my question is how many of those guys have goalie experience?"

Goldman: "For a lot of programs in the USA, I think coaches are just looking for the best talent at that age at that moment in time. We're not even capable of knowing if he's a student of the position, if he applies techniques quickly, or if he's willing to improve his work ethic or character, except when we do research and learn from coaches and family members, most of who are very biased towards that goalie."

Sadler: "The only time that potential comes up when we're talking about 15 and 16-year-olds is if they're a tall goalie. If a goalie is big, and I'm speaking about Ontario, and I don't think I'm saying anything that's not true, is when they see a big goalie."

Nykvist: "The bigger and taller goalies at that age have even more challenges to get their physical game honed, I think the huge goalies maybe develop one year later compared to average goalies because their growing phases are so different. The bones are one size and the muscles are another size."

Author's Note: *The recognizable parts of this lunch discussion ended here. We continued to discuss aspects of body composition and variances in development between North America and Finland before we had to abruptly take off and head back to the facility for the afternoon on-ice sessions.*

8

VULCAN VISION, FINLAND'S NEW GOALIE TRAINING FRONTIER

"Always design a thing by considering it in its next larger context - a chair in a room, a room in a house, a house in an environment, an environment in a city plan." –Eliel Saarinen

Finland is well-known for its global and historical impact on design, architecture, and music. From their use of bold colors and contrasting themes to their painstakingly precise post-modern principles, you will find these influences folded into the fabric of the country's society, culture, and environment.

Some of you know that I've been a huge fan of Finnish metal ever since I was in college. Native bands run the gamut of subgenres, including black, death, and atmospheric, making the music scene a perfect example of those social and environmental contrasts. The dueling electric guitars and earth-shaking double-bass drums can be a tour-de-force on the eardrums, but listen to some of my favorite bands like Mors Principium Est, Insomnium, and Amorphis for long enough, and you'll quickly discover the beauty.

If the formulated sounds act as one side of the equation, the lyrics act as the other side. Often covering themes such as personal loss and darkened hardships, macabre apparitions and twisted visions, or the struggle between dreams and reality, Finnish metal is recognized for its powerful nature writing themes.

My concentration within my technical journalism major at Colorado State University was nature writing, and this was the main catalyst behind my instant love affair with European metal. In fact, if there's one part of one song that perfectly encapsulates nature writing's influence on Finnish metal, it's in found in the final stanza of Insomnium's song, *Mortal Share.*

> *"Like water flung from the highest cliff, we fall,*
> *lunge, swirl, dissolve, and fade away down into*
> *the unknown."*

Somber yet realistic lyrics, they're a combination of a stark truth mixed with a smidge of mystical imagery.

Beyond the music, I also experienced the "cohesiveness of contrasts" through the environment. I found myself appreciating the feel and smell of being cooked alive in a traditional Finnish wooden sauna, only to quickly run outside and have the chance to jump into the frigid Baltic Sea. To go from the sweltering, suffocating heat to the piercing, bone-jarring cold in mere seconds was a perfect example of the severe juxtaposition of Finnish design and landscapes.

Wandering through the city of Helsinki, the contrasts were even more noticeable; the steel framework of a downtown building just a few hundred yards from the rounded dome of a medieval church. The shadowy pale walls of a small sidewalk café shared with a neighboring new-age chic salon.

I also found this paradigm in Finland's traditional and wildly popular *Salmiakki* candy. The company's packaging and advertising has been considered well ahead of its time since the 1920s, so just like those small morsels of sweet and salty liquorish goodness, Finland's sleek design is truly an acquired taste.

The intelligent efficiency of Finnish architecture and design has extended well beyond classrooms and churches and chairs. Linux, the computer operating system, was created by a Finn. And those cute and strangely addictive Angry Birds games were developed by a Finnish-based computer game developer called Rovio Entertainment.

But now there's another new frontier being blazed by the Finns, and this one could be the dawn of a new age in how we examine a moving target. In our realm, this will change the way we evaluate and scout goaltenders.

Based in Helsinki, a new company called Vulcan Vision Corp. is currently developing what they call "floating viewpoint video technology", which allows a coach or trainer to see his or her students in a complete "multidimensional floating viewpoint" environment. Imagine a dome placed around the student and the ability to examine that student from practically everywhere on the dome surface. You know, like, every movement from every possible angle, using *live video.*

Let that sink in for a second.

To my pleasant surprise, Hannu Eronen, the CEO of Vulcan Vision, visited the coaching staff at the GoaliePro camp in order to do some solid market research. Not so surprisingly, Ropponen was already involved with the company as a board member and investor, so we got an exclusive look at this new technology when Eronen sat down with us to share the company's mission.

"There are two main things Vulcan Vision is trying to do to help you guys," Eronen said. "You know that when you coach or record video of a person, you only see them from one point of view – your own. So what we are doing is building a floating viewpoint image, picture and video, of who you are coaching."

He pulled out a laptop, flipped on the screen, and promptly played a YouTube video. My jaw hit the floor. I had just watched a ballerina execute a pirouette, and in mid-flight, the video stopped, rotated 180 degrees, and showed the other side of the dancer's body.

"The other challenge is that there is already technology that can measure an athlete's heart rate and muscle activity. But one of the challenges with those applications is that it's not so simple to read what they are actually saying, or to understand what it really means. We are trying to change that on a visual front through floating viewpoint illustrations."

"Wait. What? Oh shit," I said out loud. I laughed. Two parts sinister, two parts awe, that laugh was like I had just discovered a hidden Egyptian tomb and got to keep all of the artifacts for myself. Mind. Blown.

"The general issue we find with coaching goalies is that we only have a limited time to practice," Eronen said with a smile. "There's only 24 hours in a day, so you need to concentrate on quality practice. What we are developing is a solution through Vulcan Vision. We are designing a rig with multiple cameras. We place anywhere from 20 to 30 cameras in a rig, but that might be too many, we don't yet know. The idea is that we have cameras viewing the subject from many different angles, all of which are working together to provide video feed to a server. Then with our magic software, we generate a floating viewpoint video of that action."

After watching the example of Vulcan Vision's technology and answering some of Eronen's questions, it became very clear that this sort of product would be a massive game-changer. "Visuality" was of utmost importance to them, and then next came data integration. That's why Ropponen quickly got involved, and why he had already made arrangements to have the system permanently installed in his home rink.

"Permanent installation in the GoaliePro training center, with computers and everything, will give us another huge competitive advantage, so you can go in and train and get the floating viewpoint analysis any time," Ropponen said.

Soon, Ropponen will be the first goalie coach to use Vulcan Vision and its accompanying computer program to manage and collect data from floating viewpoint video. The video can be stopped at any time, then swiftly moved around, almost like what you saw in the Matrix. You can also change the viewpoint when the video is rolling, too. The floating viewpoint video illustrates and visualizes the action from all angles, giving you an unparalleled holistic view of what the goalie is doing with his body.

Vulcan Vision is also trying to visualize the body's health and performance parameters as well. For example, if a goalie is wearing smart pants with a monitoring device, Vulcan Vision would be able to illustrate the muscles that are being activated in certain areas, not just spit out numbers. So if a goalie were to have imbalances with their core or leg muscles, you would see different colors in the video and be able to easily evaluate and correct those imbalances in ways, until now, we've only dreamed of doing.

"One of the key advantages is that, with the integration of smart clothing, the Vulcan Vision system will allow us to drill down to the root cause of a problem very quickly," Ropponen said. "We really want to focus on correcting the right things, whether it's correcting technique, or a problem in the physical characteristics that don't allow a goalie to perform certain moves properly."

With a mission to integrate their newly designed software with tools that allows the coach to clearly visualize information with live floating viewpoint video, this technology is a new frontier, and Finland is at the root of it all.

"This is pretty much what I have to show you right now, as we are still in the beginning of the development," Eronen said. "Now we are getting the money and initial feedback from goalie coaches like yourselves, in order to know what would be useful in your environment. Our software development team is quite far along with coding already."

Take my money, Hannu, just take it. This stuff is food for the goalie coaching gods.

Advanced Stats and the Monumental Divide

There's a monumental divide right now in the world of hockey and advanced analytics. On one side, the floodgates for progress have opened with the mainstream acceptance of statistics that track all of the minor actions taking place in a game. Shots directed towards the net (Corsi and Fenwick) and other forms of puck possession have allowed scouts and fans alike to qualify and quantify the value of a player beyond their actual scoring production. WOWY (with or without you) stats are bringing new realms of analysis to players that find different ways to contribute, depending on their linemates and shifts.

You can even look at some of the "microstatistics" coming out of the woodworks – like score-adjusted Fenwick, or shot differentials following offensive zone faceoff wins and losses. In fact, new websites based around complex algorithms that scrub official NHL game sheets are popping up everywhere. You also have small symposiums being held to further cultivate the progress being made within the analytics community. Baseball analysts that are considered pioneers in sabermetrics are starting to lend a voice to the same revolution starting to take place within hockey.

On the other side of the divide, you still have a substantial lack of accurate or useful advanced analytics for goaltenders. Shot quality leads the way in this regard, as thousands upon thousands of shots have been tracked and neatly organized into categories such as rebounds, shots off the rush, deflections, clean shots, and more. Shot distance is calculable due to NHL game sheets, and even things like situational shots ("close", for example, means up or down by one goal) are bringing immense depth to how we analyze goaltending performances.

But even with the surge of progress that has been made in terms of evaluating and analyzing a goalie, shot quality has its limits. A shot is just a shot unless you can qualify and break down the situation around it. Starting in late-2014, former New York Rangers and New York Islanders goalie Steve Valiquette has taken massive strides in getting mainstream hockey media and thousands of fans to understand this aspect of goaltending evaluation.

Using his idea known as the *Royal Road,* which is an imaginary line running through the middle of the goal and intersecting another imaginary line that extends from the top of each faceoff circle, thus splitting the offensive zone in two halves, Valiquette has come up with a system that helps you better understand the potency of a shot that results from a specific sequence. With "Green" and "Red" shots as another qualifier, he has revealed that a team's chances of scoring are greatly increased when the puck (whether it's a pass or a developing play prior to a shot) crosses the Royal Road.

Combined with the work being done by Double Blue Analytics, which is a tracking system that allows a user to "tag" every shot a goalie faces and then qualify it situationally, all while collecting this information over the course of an entire season, evaluating goalie performance is reaching new heights. Together, the two analytical functions are increasing sample size, thus making it easier to have confidence in the results extracted from the information gathered.

If a goalie gives up 50 goals on 1,000 shots to the glove side over the course of a season, using Double Blue Analytics' technology, you could sit there and watch every single goal and shot to the glove side. And that's a lot more to work with if that goalie only allowed five goals on 100 shots to the glove side.

Now imagine if you had the Vulcan Vision technology to further support what Valiquette is doing. Not only is the world of sequence-based goalie analytics on the rise, but the video needed to accompany that analysis could also soon exponentially unfold before our very eyes.

Vulcan Vision's Infinite Uses

Listening to Hannu explain Vulcan Vision's technology led to an explosion of ideas, feedback, and awesome conversation. Personally speaking, as a guy whose career focused on scouting and evaluating goalies, I could hardly contain my excitement.

"I'd literally just sit there and watch goalies run through drills in floating viewpoint all day and night. I'd never leave my desk," I half-jokingly said to everyone.

Imagine being able to pull up a video of a goalie cutting off a pass from behind the net with an active stick while in the Reverse-VH on his glove side. Not only could you see this video from behind the net, but you could rotate the video and watch the puck try and cross the goal line from in front of the goalie's body. You could freeze and rotate the video and then see how the goalie's hands and stick is angled from along the goal line. The teaching points become an endless supply of information and insights.

One idea I had for Vulcan Vision was to offer Shadowcasting, which is where you overlay one rep or video sequence on top of another with different transparency settings. This allows the coach to see a previous sequence on top of a current sequence, allowing you to see exact differences in body angles, mechanics, and execution. You can see the differences between a goalie moving one way, and how they move after you've given feedback or the goalie has had a chance to watch his movements in floating viewpoint.

"We've thought about the same thing in terms of injuries," Eronen responded. "Like, if you record many times your action, then you had some sort of injury, we can compare earlier movements with new movements and notice if you're not putting weight or stresses in certain areas."

The next idea we came up with was Benchmarking, or showing floating viewpoint video of an elite athlete making a specific movement or reaction, then overlaying the student's video on top of it. You have this technology already in place with programs like Dartfish, but with this floating viewpoint technology, it opens up a whole new world.

Beyond the actual video, there is a plethora of uses that could make this technology revolutionary. For example, imagine being able to access a growing Vulcan Vision database, grab video of a Finnish goalie doing certain drills, and then show your own students that video using a Shadowcast. Or how about the idea that you could virtually fly your goalie to anywhere in the world and compare their mechanics with a goalie in another country. That's the future of video analysis, and it's here in 2015.

Vulcan Vision could also create a different user interface for each sport, including a library or a databank where hundreds of video clips are stored and categorized. You could have a video of goals against, various saves, drills and exercises, all while tagging everything and building a network for customers.

Within this new world, one must remain grounded in reality. For example, how would this technology integrate into a rink? For now, it looks like they are limited to permanent installations in training facilities or rinks. That means this isn't the type of system where you can just carry it rink-to-rink as a portable device. Furthermore, with so many cameras needed to create the floating viewpoint video, you're looking at a pretty expensive system.

If a team invested in a permanent installation, it would be great for home games, but even more valuable for practices. It would instantly become one of the premier goalie development facilities in the world.

As our small-group meeting continued, Clint Elberts brought up the good point that floating viewpoint video may not be so valuable on the ice due to all of the equipment a goalie is wearing, but in the gym, the value rises tremendously due to the fact you could see so much more in terms of biomechanics. We all agreed.

From there, we started to discuss that, while off-ice training would provide more valuable floating viewpoint feedback, there is still a lot of information we can obtain from seeing the backs of a goalie's legs, their ankles, their skates, how they engage their inside edges from different angles, and much more.

I also considered the benefits Vulcan Vision would bring beyond visualizing the body.

In Sweden, for example, a good chunk of their video analysis is done from visualizing the puck's perspective. Imagine being able to break down angles and positioning and net coverage with a 360-degree view of the puck's perspective, or its position in relation to the goalie and the shot release. So if the puck is shot through traffic and the aerial angle is severe, seeing a 360-degree view of the puck's trajectory from the moment it reads the stick blade becomes really valuable information. The goalie can see just how much net he fills, as well as having a much better understanding of his angle through the puck. Even seeing a 360-degree image of a stick blade acts as incredible information for a goalie. You could collect video of a player releasing a variety of shots – snap, wrist, slap, backhander – and then evaluate how the blade engages with the puck and how the wrists of the shooter impacts the puck's ultimate trajectory.

Most private goalie coaches are considered nomads these days, so creating a portable system, something that can be easily transferred from rink to rink, would be a major bonus in regards to sales. Regardless, there are a handful of well-known goalie training facilities that would make a perfect home for a full-blown installation, including a few of GDI's training centers, Stauber's GoalCrease in Edina, and Elberts' training center in Kansas City, MO.

At the end of the day, I truly believe the best value in terms of functionality across all levels of goaltending, is showing the student where the puck is going from a bunch of different angles. Imagine how this would enhance a goalie's ability to anticipate the trajectory of a shot. With cameras all around him, including over his head, the video feedback for things like eye attachment and head trajectory within game situations would be, for a lack of better words, unreal.

As our discussion came to a close, we agreed that 1080 HD video quality was of utmost importance with the final video product. Without the highest quality, motion blur could hinder the program's effectiveness. Being able to manipulate the frame rate would also be a huge advantage, as super 'slow-mo' takes the floating viewpoint analysis to an even higher realm. We also mentioned the importance of being able to access live updates to the system and programs, instead of having to re-purchase the whole thing every time successive improvements and new versions of the technology came along.

Our final pressing question, one that mainly went unanswered, was a good one. Which is more important? Just having the basic floating viewpoint video, or the additional information you can build in, like muscle activity and heart rate? The external information coming in from other data ports is truly important. But when you're looking at elite training, you can't put a price on having it all integrated together. The body's responses plus the video is the best of both worlds, and I am sure it's something Vulcan Vision will be able to one day provide.

Linus Torvalds, the man who created Linux, once said, "Intelligence is the ability to avoid doing work, yet getting the work done."

Vulcan Vision is not only a perfect example of new intelligence allowing goalie coaches to avoid extra work, it's an awesome reminder that Finland continues to set the trend for various aspects of advanced goalie development. When you have brilliant minds like Eronen and Ropponen and the rest of Vulcan Vision's board members working together, you don't just pull ahead of the curve, you stay ahead.

9

GETTING TO KNOW GOALIEPRO FOUNDER JUKKA ROPPONEN

Born on February 13 of 1959, Jukka Ropponen carries an illustrious career of coaching goalies at the highest levels for over 30 years. Whether it be in his native land of Finland, or in Canada, Switzerland, Estonia, Russia, or the United States, Jukka's reach and endless network of contacts is unparalleled in the world of goaltending.

Much could be written about Ropponen's coaching and training endeavors, along with the success he has had through GoaliePro, the private training company he founded back in 2002. But since you've already gotten to know him a little bit in a few of the previous chapters, I thought it would be of interest to document some of his successes in the business world.

For it his combination of business and goaltending IQ that makes him such an interesting and integral character in the world of progressive goalie development. Like you learned in the chapter on Vulcan Vision, his "behind the scenes" business savvy is at the forefront of the global evolution of goalie training.

Currently the CEO at Roima Intelligence, Ropponen brings them many years of international business expertise, both in the internationalization of business models and in the realm of corporate growth. Roima Intelligence is a high-tech service company with over 25 years of experience in creating solutions for production efficiency.

Prior to joining Roima Intelligence, Jukka was the COO for Ductor Corp. As stated on their LinkedIn profile, Ductor Corp is, "A Finnish biotechnology company with a unique portfolio of proprietary and patented technology for biologically producing ammonia and phosphates from recycled materials through a process that can be integrated into many applications, such as algae farming to provide nutrients and energy."

Eronen, the CEO at Vulcan Vision, worked with Ropponen at Ductor Corp and posted a glowing recommendation on the LinkedIn website.

"I've had a pleasure to work with Jukka at Ductor for over a year now," he said in April of 2013. "During that time, Jukka has demonstrated true leadership and operative excellence. Jukka's wide international contact network has already worked for Ductor in several occasions and his skills and experience in building international business will be absolutely pivotal for Ductor's success."

Prior to his time with Ductor, Ropponen spent many years working for Kodak as their Director of E-Business, Director of international business operations, and a top Channel Business Manager.

In 2004, a few years after he founded GoaliePro, Jukka established the Coach Mentor Program. Being a part of the 10-year anniversary of this camp was quite special for me, and thanks to him, this life-altering experience has been shared by countless goalie coaches in North America.

During my time in Finland, I learned a lot about Ropponen's coaching career, his methods, and the importance he places on dynamic off-ice training. But the one thing that I'll always remember about Jukka was his silent solitude. When speaking to him or working with him on the ice, the wheels are always turning in his mind, but he's usually just watching and smiling with a quiet and content look on his face.

With all the obsessing I've been doing regarding the science of creativity, I can safely say that Ropponen is one of the best at taking a creative idea and forming it into a full-blown strategic and efficient solution for the growth and development of a goaltender.

Goldman: So I guess let's start by talking about the development of the GoaliePro Program. Why did you create this program, and why did you decide to bring goalie coaches from other countries over here? Why are you doing this?

Ropponen: "To answer simply, we like sharing. Things don't get better unless you share the knowledge you have. We've always been very open-minded and wanting to share things. It really started because we would run this camp for many years and we had coaches contacting us asking us how they could help out or come and watch or video tape drills, so we thought why not make it more official and have people join the program through our Coach Mentor camp. We like sharing. It's not an issue of who has better drills or anything like that. It's really about who has the eye to see things and correct things. We like to share that and things don't get better if you don't share. It's great because it's not about the money or being the best, it's about the passion for hockey and goaltending."

Goldman: Can you give readers a bit of background on yourself and your coaching resume?

Ropponen: "I've coached for over 30 years and played goal myself for over 40 years. Since I started coaching in the 1980's in the junior ranks, then quickly I was up in the Finnish Division-1 league, which is one level below the SM-Liiga. Then I moved to the States and started coaching college goalies. My first US coaching position was with Hobart College, a small D-III school in Geneva, New York. My whole program has grown from there, and when I moved back to Finland after my first two years in the USA, I was invited in the middle of the season to work with the new Elite league team in Espoo. They were struggling during their first years in the league. Ever since then I've worked with Finns, Russians, I spent nine years in the Swiss league, and I don't know, maybe the best way to describe it is that I've been lucky to work with good teams and good goalies, including several NHL'ers that have come over from Finland. I've been blessed to work with goalies that are really talented like Niklas Backstrom, Ari Sulander, and Kari Lehtonen.

I worked with Lehtonen after he signed a contract with Atlanta, but was still playing in Finland. During his time in Jokerit, we really worked together to prepare him for North America. So this variety has been a great experience. It's a different world in Switzerland and we had a lot of success. As an example, Ari Sulander was my goalie there and we had a lot of good juniors like Reto Berra, Leo Genoni, and others that were underneath us."

Goldman: What was your experience like coaching in the United States and what did you learn about American goaltenders back then?

Ropponen: "The biggest thing I noticed is that they don't look at the athletes as a whole. I don't understand why they would only work on something on the ice, then they don't look at the other side. Being a professional athlete requires a lot more; you have to understand the strength and conditioning and all of those other things. What you do on the ice is only one part of a goalie's development. So I think that's the biggest difference – we pay more attention to the other side. As a coach you have to understand it and you have to work on that side."

Goldman: Can you talk about the off-ice component of development with the goalies you work with now and how you stress this side to them?

Ropponen: "We build and program every goalie's off-ice workout every day. We look at their results with the tracking system from OmegaWave. We look at their readings on a computer after their morning measurements, which allows us to see how their body, nervous system and cardiovascular system is recovering, if their body is ready for another full day of training or not. The program we write for each goalie is optimized in response to what their readings are telling us, so if a goalie hasn't recovered, we know to call them and discuss it and alter the program on the fly just to make sure they're doing the right things at the right time and to optimize their off-ice training. It's not about working as hard as you can, but as smart as you can, and OmegaWave allows us to monitor this and that is our responsibility – to make the most of their training and to do the right things on and off the ice."

Goldman: If you had to give someone your coaching philosophy, what would it be? I feel like a lot of goalie coaches in North America just want a basic understanding of how an elite Finnish goalie coach thinks and what they try to instill in their students.

Ropponen: "Throw the cookie-cutter away; that's the first thing. Then I think there are some basic bylaws that really apply to this. Like I really hate to see people doing some of these elegant, extra moves. The T-Push is one of them. When I see people doing short-distance T-Pushes in the crease, I wonder why on earth would you do three moves when you can just do a simple shuffle move and be in a save-ready position all the time? Also, why do you pull your hands back to close holes? That's a faulty philosophy. You can bring the hands out in front of your body and actually cover a lot more space, and you can also control the puck instead of giving up rebounds. These might be the biggest differences."

Goldman: Besides those bylaws you just spoke about, what else do you think separates your coaching philosophy from those in North America, or even other coaches here in Finland?

Ropponen: "I think it's more about the individualism. There are a lot of goalie coaches that do a good job, but it only goes so far unless you have the ability to really apply it to each individual and find what's best for them. We really try to be a tailor shop; the way we find what works for each goalie in terms of their age, their conditioning, and their unique body proportions. Do they have a shorter legs, a longer back, longer arms, or whatever? We find what works for the individual and create a complete package for their development. We don't coach one goalie the same way as the next one. We find a way for each goalie to be the most effective they can be. So it's really a tailor-made approach."

Goldman: In terms of your drill progressions for this five-day camp, can you talk about how you structure these? I know goalie coaches in North America will be very interested to hear how you set this up. I noticed that you created drills for the camp on a day-by-day basis. They weren't pre-determined, which I think is something that will begin to catch on in the States as time goes on.

Ropponen: "We have the first two days written out before the camp starts. The first day is pretty much set all the time, and the second day is written, but not published. The second day, I'm already starting to change some of the drills depending on the goalies we have and what they really need. The third day I'm writing drills from scratch just to tailor them to the group of kids we have in each camp. So one day is cast in stone in order to see what they're capable of doing, the second day we're already changing maybe 30-percent of the drills, and for the last three days of the camp, we write the drills on the previous night, including what things we want to repeat or reinforce. We usually do these in order to emphasize not over-doing something. So this continues our tailor-made approach to a group of kids."

Goldman: Can you talk about the success of the Coach Mentor program? Now that I've been through it, I know how valuable this experience has been, but maybe give your thoughts on the growth of North American coaches that have been part of this program for numerous years, like Clint Elberts and Jack Hartigan.

Ropponen: "I think the whole goalie program Jack is starting in Nova Scotia is a great example because it started due to his experience here in Finland. He was able to sell it to Hockey Nova Scotia and it all started with his attendance in the GoaliePro Mentoring Program. Clint is another great example because he's been with us many years, I believe six times now. His whole teaching style has changed compared to when he started with us. Ten years ago, he was teaching all goalies a certain specific way, but now every year he's learning more and starting to read his goalies and actually teaching what works for each individual goalie. But I see a lot of Americans that really have a cookie-cutter approach and teach different goalies the same ways. The more people spend time with us, the more they learn how to adapt to each individual, instead of trying to fit everyone into the same form."

Goldman: Jack is a little bit different since he's more on the structural side of goalie development. But he played in Finland and has been with you for a few years. He's restructuring all of Hockey Nova Scotia, which is an amazing endeavor. It's more interesting to me since I'm more on the scouting side of things.

Ropponen: "I think Jack had a huge awakening when the CHL banned European goalies. That summer, his white paper for our program was really on how to structure goalie educational programs. I think he saw the light and got an awakening and realized things were really bad back home. He wanted to take what we have here in Finland and bring it back to Nova Scotia. He started to approach Hockey Canada and I give him a lot of credit for his ability to push this agenda to them and getting them to buy into the idea that restructuring was needed. He might be one of the top future goalie coaches in Canada with the approach he has taken over the past few years."

Goldman: Can you think of any other coaches from North America that has been a model coach for your program?

Ropponen: "Well I think guys like Travis Harrington from Mind The Net in Saskatchewan is a good example. He really had an eye-opening experience in 2012 when he was with us. He really understood the concept of not just blocking the puck and giving up rebounds, but controlling the puck. You see their goalie school starting to do great things and we're continuing to cooperate with them."

Goldman: Let's shift gears now and instead of talking about the technical side of goaltending and your program, let's talk about the cultural side of Finnish goalies and their personality, as this has been the biggest eye-opener for me. In your own words, what is it that separates them from American goalies?

Ropponen: "Well I think you have to look at something that's not really an actual comparison, but something like how Finns are generally very good at individual sports. Like I told you during the week, we have world champions in racing, Formula 1's, javelin, skiing, and then we have a lot of elite goalies. It's kind of a situation where Finns thrive in individual sports because we are more introverted. If you give a good goalie prospect to a good coach, they'll do anything you ask. It's really in the Finnish nature of doing it that way. They'll go through a brick wall if you ask them to. It's great to coach Finnish goalies. I've coached in Canada and the USA and Finns are so much easier to coach. If you gain they're trust, they'll do anything for you. So it's really the coach-goalie relationship that is important."

Goldman: Why do you think that is? Why do I come here to a local camp and see 12-13-14-year old goalies with more emotional control and discipline compared to 18-year-olds in North America? Is it just the Finnish human nature, the way they were raised?

Ropponen: "It's just a combination of all those things. It's the way they've been brought up, and also the character and nature of Finnish people. Hockey goaltending just really suits Finns well. So combine that with our strong educational program and our goalie coaching program and that is driving the success."

Goldman: I learned a few ways you're staying ahead of the goalie development curve in relation to the rest of the world with OmegaWave and Vulcan Vision. But besides those things, what do you think is the key for you in staying ahead of the curve?

Ropponen: "Game analysis. I don't need to think two seconds about that answer. If you come out here next summer, you'll see all different drills and things we're working on. During the season, the game analysis is really growing and really important to our program. If you have a really good grasp of what the game of hockey and goaltending is all about today, you know it won't be the same next year. Continual game analysis allows you to discover new techniques, new drills. Whatever changes there are in the game, we have to stay ahead of it. You see too many North Americans learn one thing and then teach and coach it year after year. We'll change every year, every time all the time."

Goldman: So what do you think is next in terms of game analysis? Is it breaking down shot location? What will give you a better edge in this department?

Ropponen: "Well there's always several things in the works, but it's important to understand it's a different type of game analysis in North America and a different type in Europe. The games are very different and even in Europe it varies by country. The Swiss game is different from the Finnish game and depending on where the goalie plays, we coach differently. I can't teach a goalie playing in Switzerland to play the angles the same way a goalie in North America, so I can't pinpoint anything, but I can tell you it's the next big thing for goalie coaches all over the world. I see maybe 20 games a week, including highlights and then the video guys send me monthly summaries of scoring chances. Then I look through it all and make sure I'm ahead of the curve in terms of what's happening on the ice and how goals are being scored and what we can do to stop them."

Goldman: In terms of the mental approach to goaltending, what is your philosophy there? What are your thoughts in terms of what you try to instill in your goalies?

Ropponen: "That also varies by each person I work with. They're all different in their confidences and mental structures. Goalie coaching is as much mental coaching as it is technique coaching. You have to have a close relationship with the goalie. One of the biggest things you can do as a goalie coach is to share the pressure they have, and work with them so they don't have to do it all on their own shoulders and he knows you're there to do it with him. The biggest thing is maybe teaching them that they can't worry about the things they can't change. They can't worry about everyone else on the team, or how they're defensemen handle assignments. Do your own part and expect others to do their own part. You have to focus on your own play."

Goldman: Was there ever a point in time when you realized Finnish goalies were going to be successful at the highest levels in North America?

Ropponen: "I think it happened the moment I knew the first Finnish bona-fide number-one goalie in the NHL was going to be Pasi Nurminen. I was coaching him when he got the job in Atlanta and I already knew that we had more talented, better-sized goalies coming up, so I knew Pasi was going to be the first one to break the ice and open the door for more Finnish goalies to establish themselves in the NHL. I worked with Pasi on his technique and on-ice stuff, but he did his own dryland stuff, which wasn't good. I actually warned him two years before his career was over that he was destroying his future because he wasn't really working out the way he should have. But that's when I knew we were going to have a lot more Finnish goalies starting in the NHL."

Goldman: Let's take a guy like Tirronen, who has very clear-cut pro upside. What is your advice for a guy like him in terms of the path he should take to play pro hockey in North America? I know every goalie is different, but

how would you generally advise young Finnish prospects to take

Ropponen: "We're pushing our kids to take care of school properly, because only so many people can get a good job and make good money playing hockey. We want to make sure they get a good education. The best path is for kids to play Junior-A hockey in Finland and then get a scholarship to play NCAA D-I hockey. A lot of kids we're also starting to put into the USHL and NAHL (Tier-I and Tier-II USA junior hockey) so they get noticed by the colleges. So we're really pushing the US college route because we think that's really good to get a four-year stint in college. Sometimes in Finland, the Junior-A level is really competitive and you may not play for a year, then you fall off the map and get forgotten. But with a four-year collegiate career, if you don't play one year it's not a big deal, because you can still get noticed the following year, and a lot of current goalies are late bloomers. This is the path we want a lot of our guys to go through."

Goldman: What are one or two key pitfalls you see within the Finnish club structure?

Ropponen: "Too many guys are ranked and are put into certain brackets too early. There are a lot of late-bloomers, especially goalies. Tirronen [Merrimack] and Reijola [St. Cloud] are good examples. They weren't highly ranked in Finland, and now they're D-I college goalies that have good chances to be pro goalies. Some guys could have puberty hit later and have muscle growth two years later than another goalie. So it's bad when you rank and label goalies too early."

Goldman: What about in terms of the development model that's currently in place? I had a chance to see it when I met with Hannu Nykvist, but what obstacles does he face with his role right now?

Ropponen: "Well Hannu is a great guy and it's a funny coincidence that we were born and raised in the same suburb, Kontula, in eastern Helsinki. He is a good organizer and he has a great skill of structuring the levels and training for youth goalies and goalie coaches. But he's a one-man show, and with a big federation like Finland, and with hockey being the national sport of this country, I think it's a shame we only have one full-time guy trying to do everything. It's just not possible."

Goldman: I think you said there were like 10 people working in the women's hockey department, but only one in goaltending?

Ropponen: "I think there's even more than 10. Nothing against women's hockey, but if you look at the amount of NHL goalies we're producing, and the whole federation only has one full-time person working in goaltending, but you having more people employed to work in other areas, something's not right. It doesn't do any justice for what goalies truly deserve. We have a great goalie development program, but we could produce even more goalies if we put more emphasis on that program."

Goldman: I guess to wrap this up, what would be your advice for a guy like myself? An American trying to help out USA Hockey's lack of structure? What can I take back to the states with me?

Ropponen: "Try to push USA Hockey so that they can put an official structure to educating goalie coaches. When I worked 29 years ago for the Finnish Hockey Federation as the head goalie coach for the Helsinki area, I trained between 60-to-100 new goalie coaches every year. We marketed the program and you put a lot of the foundation for success right there. A lot of the current Finnish NHL goalies were coached in the early years of their career by guys that we trained 29 years ago. So you really have to have an educational program for goalie coaches in place, and it starts growing from there. I would do two or three classes with 20 to 30 people every year and they were always full. We had no problem filling the classes as long as you did a good enough job. So educating goalie coaches is the key."

Goldman: What would be your advice for goalies in North America that will learn what I'm learning and will want to start to train in Finland and join programs like yours?

Ropponen: "Great question. I would say don't be afraid to try and get on a European team that has a good goalie coach and play a few years there to begin your pro career after you play in college or juniors. It might be a good career path because having a good goalie coach will really help you. But it's hard to say what's good for North Americans because the traffic generally goes the other way. And if you look at the number of high-level Finnish goalies compared to US goalies, it's ridiculous. I mean there should be 10 times more US-born goalies [in the NHL] compared to Finland, but it doesn't work that way today. So it's really hard to say – you don't see a lot of Americans coming to Europe unless it's near the end of their career."

10

DISCOVERING THE WORLD OF ESTONIAN HOCKEY

On the final day of my Finland adventure, Jukka graciously presented Clint, Ted, and I with a special gift – a daytime trip to Tallinn, Estonia. Not only did he treat us to a first-class ferry ride to the mysterious country's capital, but once we arrived, he also surprised us with a guided tour of the Estonian Ice Hockey Association's official headquarters.

Despite being the second-smallest hockey federation in the world, Estonia's membership in the International Ice Hockey Federation (IIHF) dates all the way back to 1935. Their involvement had initially expired when Estonia was annexed by the Soviet Union, but when their independence was re-established in the 1990's, they re-joined. Since then, the association has unfortunately battled through numerous pitfalls, including some nasty unwelcomed corruption, ensuing bad press, a lack of talent and numbers, limited resources, minimal financial support from their jaded government, and blatant mismanagement.

Due to Estonia's struggles with player development and a cloud of corruption muddying their history, when I dug for additional research, I stayed away from information I found online. As it turns out, because trusted and accurate information is so hard to find regarding this topic, the only way to learn about the current state of Estonian hockey was by talking directly to the guys at the top.

This made Jukka's surprise trip to Tallinn a really educational adventure. As a result, the interviews below act as one of the only trusted pieces of information on the subject on Estonian hockey.

After my experience in Estonia, I realized I had no reason to ever complain about goalie development in the United States. Never had I experienced such an extreme shift in my perception of the global hockey landscape. Our wealth in numbers in the USA compared to Estonia was almost nauseating, and if there was ever something to complain about, it was the severe lack of gratitude I felt leading up to this moment.

We are so fortunate to have the funds and support and structure that we have, and it only took a few hours in Estonia to realize it first-hand.

If I ever complain or seem ungrateful about the misappropriation of services, funds, or structure in the way goalies are developed in the United States, I only have to close my eyes and remember my day in Estonia, and it all goes away. I simply couldn't imagine what it would be like to try and work through a tumultuous relationship between USA Hockey and the American government.

Fortunately, it appears as if Estonia Hockey's story will eventually have a happy ending.

Over the past few years, *Eesti Jäähoki Liit* has been run by a pair of gentleman that have nothing but the purest of intentions for the growth of hockey at all ages and skill levels in Estonia.

Ahti-Kullervo Jogi is one of the two men working full-time, for very little pay, to transform Estonia's hockey association into a legitimate, thriving club. Jogi's son was one of the students in the GoaliePro camp, so knowing that a small contingency of North American goalie coaches would be in Finland for the Coach Mentoring Program, he worked very hard to set up this tour of their small, fledgling operation.

Jaan Molder is the current president of Hockey Estonia. His background, as you will learn below, is as interesting as they come. His virtuous work is commendable, and I am happy to give him and Jogi any support I possibly can. They desperately need it.

I can't say enough about the tremendous dedication these guys have. It's one thing to be a part of a large operation like Hockey Canada and USA Hockey, but it's quite another to be a lone wolf in a small country with no support from anyone, only to have to weed out corruption and completely change and re-establish the culture of a nation's hockey association. Without the tools, how can one paint a clear picture of future success? They have to carve the tools out of the ground with their bare hands, and that takes time.

Full compliments to both Jogi and Molder for their work. They were two of the most interesting men I have ever met in my life, and I wish them nothing but good luck and good fortune as they continue to fight the good fight for the betterment of hockey in Estonia.

Author's Note: *After we arrived in Tallinn and worked our way through the crowds filtering into the old town, we came to a parking lot where a small white bus was waiting. It was there that we were greeted by an eager and visibly excited Jogi, and during our 10-minute ride to his office, I had a chance to interview him and learn a little bit about this tiny country and their hockey background.*

Goldman: Can you explain the basic structure of hockey in Estonia?

Jogi: "Estonia is a tiny hockey country. South of us is Latvia, north from us is Finland, west from us is Sweden, east from us is Russia, and they're all top hockey nations. Estonia is a country in between them all with no hockey, in a true hockey sense. We only have seven rinks in five locations, so it's a tiny hockey country."

Goldman: Do you know what your current numbers are for actual registered players?

Jogi: "These numbers are pretty small, around 500 actual players. From 500, maybe 450 are full amateurs. So we really only have approximately 50 players that play in a competitive pro sense."

Goldman: Do you know how many goaltenders you have?

Jogi: "Probably at any level, around 10. Besides my son, there's another Estonian native in the GoaliePro camp, a coach named Christian Adami. But Estonian hockey and goaltending is as bumpy as this bus ride [laughing], so there's a lot of work to be done."

Goldman: So what has your goal been over the past year and what is the future goal in terms of developing Estonian goaltenders?

Jogi: "Actually, we try to get our young guys to play in good leagues around the world, especially in Finland. Through that, we hope to develop their skills, promote our hockey, and develop national team goalies. There's one kid born in 1999 [Conrad Molder] that is a number one goalie in Helsinki. The first negative however is that he's been offered Finnish citizenship, so he's kind of deciding whether or not to stay in Estonia. My kid [Christopher Jogi] is a 2000 [birth year] playing in Finland as well, and we have others playing in Finland, so many guys have had opportunities to develop elsewhere."

Goldman: How have you leaned on Jukka to help your cause?

Jogi: "Jukka has been helping our cause not a little bit, but a lot. He has even been our National Team coach and we won a Division-II championships with him at the helm. Besides that, he's been helping guys by including them in his camps, and training other guys tied to our program as well, so he's helped a lot."

Goldman: Despite the lack of numbers being an obvious obstacle, what else would you like to see improve here in Estonia?

Jogi: "Actually, everything. Starting from our competitiveness all the way to the National Team. Just everything. Developing hockey is tough because we have such few options. We are practically in need of everything at this point."

Author's Note: *Our interview stopped here, as we had arrived at the head offices. Once inside a slate and matted grey building, we were brought through a few dark hallways into a very small office, comprised of only two small rooms. The reception room had nothing but a small round table in one corner, a secretary desk, and a few bookshelves with some old VHS tapes, a couple of boxes of documents and files, and some hanging jerseys. The room behind this was only big enough for three small cubicles and a few chairs for visitors. That was the extent of Estonia Hockey's headquarters. At this time, we were introduced to Molder, the president of Hockey Estonia. We all sat down and had a great conversation, most of which I was able to record. A few minutes went by where we had general introductions and we all gave a brief background on our coaching experience and endeavors, so that part was omitted. This is a fascinating look into one of the smallest hockey nations in the world, and it just goes to show you how extremely lucky we are to have a competent government in North America that supports our hockey federations, especially with the immense numbers we have. Could you imagine growing up in Estonia and wanting to be a competitive hockey player?*

Molder: "I'm not a hockey person at all. I have never played hockey [laughing]. I was for the first time in an ice rink four years ago when I was in Kiev. My background is medical; I am also a member of a medical committee. My sport background is more rally. My family is all drivers. My father is a champion racer and I have won some championships and my son has as well. Suddenly, I was invited to get involved in hockey, and it has been a headache for the past three years. I'm trying to get help through Europe and we'll see what happens. And like Jukka said, we're the second smallest hockey country in the world after Iceland, but we have a year-round hockey championship. But in Iceland, they are supported by the government and the president personally. In Estonia, all sports are not very friendly for government and the politics. We are in big trouble, because we have very few ice rinks. We only have seven rinks, but only four places where we can play our championships. Last year, we had six teams playing, which was maybe a little bit too much for us, so we are thinking of having only four teams this year."

Jogi: "Something that Jukka told you on the bus about Jaan is that, despite not being a hockey person, he has done a huge thing for Estonian hockey by getting rid of all this rotten and corrupt management. Maybe not being a hockey person himself, his heart is definitely in the hockey. He has been doing a lot of things to cure the field, and to bring real structure to the table for Estonian hockey. It's a hard thing for politicians here, so Jaan said his next plan and step is to find a new president for Estonia hockey. We have been working with some guys to get more hockey in this room, and to get all the 'dirt' away and that has been taking I would say at least 70-percent of the time, but it's a good thing."

Ropponen: "Bring the game back to the players."

Jogi: "Exactly. And not many people understand it, but I would say everyone in hockey out here feels that these are all things we need 100-percent, so Jaan has been very good for the game."

Molder: "We are also looking up to our Finnish friends to continue helping our coaches and we have done some good things in the past year."

Jogi: "Exactly. There are so many steps to be taken and so much to do, but we are on the right path. Personally I believe in this. These are the two smaller rooms where Estonia hockey is run [laughing]. The main thing our association is doing is running a local championship for our U-16's this season. Our youth championships are held in every age group, then we have a U-18, U-20, and a Men's national team that are involved internationally and that's the main thing. We try to introduce summer camps with an initiative of having some players from here to help run them. We have a few Estonians playing in the Finnish SM-liiga and we will be getting behind their invitational camps for boys playing here. There's another Estonian that will try to bring some summer camps next year as well. These are the things we do, and these are the rooms we do it in, and that's about it."

Molder: "We are very small [laughing]. We have one person who gets paid, and she is our secretary. She runs everything in Estonian hockey."

Jogi: "She is the only person who gets paid. The rest is all voluntary work and giving our time. It's sometimes crazy, but also a lot of fun."

Molder: "There's a lot of mornings where I am shaving and I look in the mirror and I see 'idiot' written here [points to chest and laughs]."

Ropponen: "You guys see, we complain in Finland because we only have one full-time person for goaltending. Estonia only has one-full time person for their entire hockey federation. So it's a different scale of things. And you guys coming from a big country, it's good to see how small it is here."

Jogi: "Like I said in the bus, my kid was in Jukka's camp a fifth year, so in terms of GoaliePro, we've been in the picture all along, and we love every second of it. For me personally, this year was more difficult for me financially, but my son was so persistent, he went to Jukka's house and said 'I need to be there!' and Jukka had no problem accepting him. That's the way it should be and it's really helpful.

Molder: "Internationally, we are also aware that our teams are not quite good enough level for us to be in the top level. It's nonsense because we can't afford it, but now we have men's team in 1st division Group B."

Jogi: "We're like 26th in the world. We're around the same place with our kids. There's really only a population of 1.3 million in Estonia and we're the second-smallest hockey nation in the world, but on the other hand, we're competing against other big nations…so it's kind of mixed feelings."

Molder: "It's coming from the 1950's last century when our politicians decided we were not going to play hockey, we were going to play basketball mainly. Latvia is more of an ice hockey country and Lithuania is more of a basketball country as well."

Jogi: "It was kind of a forced bureaucracy that was very, very organized during Soviet times. Estonians decided there would be no hockey and soccer in this country. So building it up from actually from nothing is quite a bit of work."

Molder: "We have also every year to organize some world championship tournaments. This season we already have two tournaments to organize for our U-20 teams and U-18 teams, and next year I hope to get a men's tournament here."

Jogi: "They think of us and our efforts as doing really well, and Jan has been invited into the medical community with the IIHF. As small as we are, we're actually quite busy. Each world championship we have at least two things. Frontier goalie sticks, which are made in Estonia. And there is one hockey referee linesman that lives in Tallinn that works at the top level. All nations, even Canadian, wears Tackla. Their factories are here in Estonia as well. But they do many jobs from here in Estonia."

Elberts: "How long has it been going in the right direction?"

Molder: "I came to be president three years ago. It took one year for me to understand what was going on and what was happening. Now over the past two years, I kicked off the previous general secretary and last year I kicked off all of our council and now for one year I have done all of what I think is needed and must be done."

Elberts: "So you think you still have another 9-10 years left until it turns, you think?"

Molder: "It's already turned. When I came three years ago, everyone in Estonia was talking about how bad it was here, how guys were stealing money and so on. In the first year, it was 95-percent negative for me and 5-percent positive. Now it's about 60-percent positive and 40-percent negative. So everyone is saying our association is OK economically and this allows us to make deals and money to pay for things. We are expecting things to grow."

Ropponen: "There's a great new facility coming here in town with three sheets of ice and good new stands for the spectators on the main rink. It's going to be a huge boost to the country."

Elberts: "I feel like it's such a small country that this could be a hotbed for future talent because the population is so controllable. USA Hockey is so large that it's uncontrollable."

Ropponen: "We could do a lot of things here through GoaliePro, but Estonia has to propose what they want. Now these guys have seen what we can do in Finland and we could do a lot more for Estonia hockey to help, but you need to propose what you want so we can move forward."

Author's Note: *I want to take a moment to say thanks to Molder, Jogi, and Ropponen for taking their time to speak with us regarding Estonia Hockey. I was honored when they gifted me a game-worn Estonia jersey from one of their recent world championships. It's something I hang in my room with great pride. Best of luck to you in the future and please reach out if there's anything I can do to help support the growth of hockey in Estonia!*

11

DISCUSSING MENTAL CONDITIONING WITH TED MONNICH

One of the most intriguing fellows I met over the summer was an American goalie coach named Ted Monnich. Also accepted into the GoaliePro coach mentor camp, Ted joined Larry Sadler and myself in Helsinki, where all three of us stayed together in the same downtown apartment.

As I quickly discovered, Monnich was a kindred heart. His character and mannerisms displayed a quiet serenity. His voice was gentle, like someone you would hear narrating a guided meditation DVD. He walked slowly during our time off, appreciating every step. He spoke to every goalie coach with respect and pure uninhibited curiosity, truly embracing the opportunity laid out before him. I was enthralled with all of the facts he dropped about the history of the world and the science of sports psychology.

We had some great in-depth conversations together while walking through the narrowed streets of downtown

Helsinki, and you could tell just how grateful he was for the opportunity to share his philosophies with the rest of us. I considered him to be an old soul, someone who saw beauty in everything. And there was plenty of beauty to behold on the southernmost shores of Finland.

Maybe the most interesting thing about Ted was his affinity for Turkish people and their culture. I've never met anyone so enthralled by their music, either. In fact, Ted plays an instrument called the Saz in a band called TURKU, Nomads of the Silk Road.

If you haven't already, look this guy up and send him a message. Get to know him a little bit, and you'll quickly learn what I learned – this is the type of guy we need working with goalies of all ages and levels. His ideas and his knowledge on the mental conditioning of a goaltender is a rare trait to find in a high-level goalie coach, and his future work will pave the way for more goalie coaches to feel comfortable earning degrees in sports psychology and sharing their work with the rest of the goalie community.

Visibly passionate about what he does and how he mentors goalies, Ted also learned a lot about the cultural and philosophical differences between Finland and North America during his time in Helsinki. As such, he turned into a great interview for this book, and I'm very happy to now call him a good friend.

Goldman: Let's start by getting a brief background on your goalie coaching endeavors.

Monnich: "I've been involved in goaltending for over 40 years and I've been an active goalie coach for the past

12 years. I started coaching with the PuckStoppers goaltending school in London, Ontario. While working there, our head coach was Jukka Ropponen, and that is how I got to know him. I continued to work for PuckStoppers for almost 10 years, and during that time, I started looking for what was next; how coaching and the game was developing. I really like innovation and I like change. I don't like to be looking to the past, I like looking to the future. So at that time, I found Ian Clark's writings and I believed it to be very innovative and extremely technical, and it really excited me. I thought, 'boy, I would love to work with this program and with this school.' In the 2007-08 season, I was the assistant coach with the ECHL's Columbia Inferno and we had a goaltending coach come in, a guy named Ryan Honick with GDI. Our starting goaltender, Todd Ford, was from Calgary and was a GDI trained goalie, so he was the one that brought Ryan in. I got to meet him and I told him how I was excited about what they were doing. As a result of that, Ryan brought me into the fold. So I started working at GDI events and at regional and national development camps at Shattuck St. Mary's. I've been working with GDI USA for the past seven or eight years now, and I've enjoyed contributing to the evolution and continued innovation in the teaching that we're doing there."

Goldman: Can you briefly explain your international coaching experience? I had no idea when I met you that you had such extensive experience and that you were so well-traveled.

Monnich: "Well, I've coached in Turkey quite a bit. Through my life I've had some interest in Turkish culture, and I've spent some time there for that purpose, you know, just traveling. When some friends there found out about my hockey experience, they put me in touch with the Turkish Ice Hockey Federation, who in turn asked me to coach there. So I've worked with the goalies on the Turkish National Team in Ankara, and I've also worked with a club in Istanbul – that was in the 2012-13 season – as their goaltending and assistant coach. In 2008, I coached at a school in Weiden, Germany called the ACE Goaltending School, which is run by a retired pro goalie from that area. From there I went on to Slovakia, where I consulted with two teams in the Slovak Extraliiga. One was a team called Dukla Trencin, and Trencin is really like the hockey factory of Slovakia. This is where Marian Gaborik is from, and where Zdeno Chara is from, as well as a lot of other Slovakian NHL players. So I worked with goaltenders there, including a guy that is a Slovak legend named Miroslav Hala. He once held the international shutout minutes record, until it was broken by Brian Boucher a few years back. Another team I consulted with there was named HKM Zvolen. Then of course our time in Finland this past summer working with Jukka and his great program, and then of course Canada and the USA."

Goldman: How did mental conditioning become your main area of work in goaltending?

Monnich: "Towards the end of my playing career, I had some issues with my own mental game. Mostly focus issues, some confidence issues. And I worked with a sports psychologist named Dr. Eva Monsma at the University of South Carolina. I spent some time working with her on my issues and I really became excited about all of the insights and skills that she was sharing with me. I started using this more and more, and reading and researching this on my own, so that I could use it with my own goalies. From my playing experiences and from my own issues, I seemed to have some insight into the mental struggles and weaknesses that goalies were dealing with in their game. The more I worked with goalies on this, the more coaches seemed to want to send me their goalies. I finally decided about four years ago to formalize my education in this realm, so I returned to school at the University of North Carolina in Greensboro to pursue a graduate degree, and now eventually a doctoral degree in sports psychology. In the past two seasons, I've been lecturing at camps and for teams on mental conditioning, as well as working with professional and amateur clients. I'm really seeing a lot of good results; students have really embraced it and have given good testimonials. This season, I'm working with the South Carolina Stingrays in the ECHL as the team's mental conditioning coach."

Goldman: So when did the title of Mental Conditioning Coach really come into play for you?

Monnich: "I had an interesting experience where, two seasons ago, I was coaching for a club in Turkey, which has a rapidly-growing hockey program. They're system is a club system like in Germany and Finland, so they have all levels of hockey within that club, up to the professional team. I told the president I wanted to meet with the coaches, and he said, "To talk about sports psychology?" And I answered yes. He said, "We don't have those kind of problems," and I suddenly realized that I was battling the misinterpretation of this word psychology. I was doing an independent study with my advisor at that time, so I told her how I wasn't going to use that title anymore and I'm not going to say I'm a sports psychologist. Rather, I'm going to say I'm a mental conditioning coach. We have to condition the mind as well as we condition the body. We understand physiology and we understand technique, now we have to condition the mind. And that's how I've been dedicating my time as a goalie coach."

Goldman: In regards to our recent experience in Finland, what initially led you to apply for the program, and what did you learn that really resonated with you during our time there?

Monnich: "You can't be involved in goaltending in North America and not be aware of the Finnish school. So many elite goaltenders have been coming out of Finland for quite a while, and we've all taken note of this as coaches. I've known, mainly through reading other articles by coaches who have worked there, what the general differences were. Skating technique, glove usage – I knew that this was the core of it. When Jukka invited me to come to the GoaliePro mentorship program, I saw it as an opportunity to go and look at specifically what is being done differently. Not just these techniques, but how are coaches approaching their work, and how they're working with their students and clients. How does this stand out differently from North America? I'm a very strong believer and advocate with the programs I've been working with for the past five years. Although we continue to innovate, you tend to believe fully in your core doctrine, and I do. So going to Finland and knowing that they don't tend to use a long, powerful T-Push the way the North American school tends to use it, I was a bit skeptical. But on the first day on the ice, I'm watching these drills and my mind was just spinning. I wasn't of the point of view that they were wrong, I just wanted to see and understand it better, so I was asking tons of questions why, to find out specifically the purpose, the philosophy, and the idea behind it. Talking to Jukka off the ice and talking to the goalies that were on the ice with us, it was worthy of consideration. After a week, my mind was turned, and I came back to North America and went into GDI USA East's National Camp at Quinnipiac and I thought I was spreading a virus. I'd go up behind one of our pro goalies and ask them to try this, and they said wow I like this, and I'd say, "Yep, you just got infected." So I see the virtue in the technical difference that they're applying. We had a lot of discussion at our camp about this. The GDI coaches knew I was going to Finland to figure out what they were doing. For this and all of goaltending, it's reducing physical stress, reducing injuries, and simplifying the game. Simplification equals economy equals speed equals success, and that's the simple logic I see [in Finland] and apply to this."

Goldman: I had a similar experience and remember how exciting it was to understand why Finnish goalies shuffle instead of T-Push. It just made so much sense.

But what else did you learn beyond the basic skating differences?

Monnich: "Beyond that, of course the glove usage was a big one. However, I didn't see that as foreign, because I worked with Jukka 12 years ago at PuckStoppers. And what did we teach there under his guidance? Active hands. Your hands are out in front of your body so you can see them. This was just second-nature to me now. But beyond these technical differences, what really stood out to me was the attitudes. This really plays to my interests in the goaltender's mental state. The goalies that were being trained in the Finnish camp were so focused, so motivated, and so trusting of the coaches that you never had to convince anyone to try something. They immediately dove in, and they performed with such application, such interest, and such passion of their own, it was so motivating to me. Later, I spoke with Jukka's wife, who is a schoolteacher. I said, 'There's something different in the way these people are raised and these children are taught.' They have different values at the core, not just in ice hockey, but in how they regard their teachers, in how they regard their studies, and how they apply themselves. It turns out that education in Finland is much different than education in North America. I looked into this further and I found out that in the public schools in Finland, students will have 40 minutes of class time followed by 15 minutes of recess outdoors, and this happens immediately after every class period. I thought that was amazing. When I was in Nova Scotia in July, Jukka and his wife were there, so I asked her about this again. She said, 'Always, it's always this way.' So I think their attention is so much better, their retention of information and knowledge is so much better, and this, at the core, I believe really influences these young people's ability to perform in other things that they pursue, like goaltending. They approach learning how to be a goalie with the same focus and attentiveness as they do in their studies. And when you lay on top of that Hannu Nykvist's national goalie development program, which is so systemized that it gives them an easy pattern and course to follow, this is what is growing successful goalies in Finland. So you're bringing in this state of mind that these children are raised with, and then you're giving them a good program to follow, then they're motivated with good coaches that are of course certified, so it's great success for a program."

Goldman: It's great to hear you say all of this with so much passion, because I pretty much learned the same thing as you, and it was remarkable to see how respectful the kids were to the goalie coaches. Especially for someone like myself, I was amazed how receptive they were to what I had to say, and it's not something that I see as part of the culture in youth goaltending in the USA. Knowing that you're a mental conditioning coach, what did you learn about how you teach those topics when you were in Finland?

Monnich: "In talking with a veteran pro goalie in Finland about what I teach in terms of the mental game, I learned very quickly that he faces the same issues that my goalies in North America face. He has the same challenges. The game isn't different. How a goalie dedicates himself to learning and performing might be different, but he's still going to perceive everything through his mind. The learning system in Finland does not necessarily condition these athletes any better than it does in North America. So they're facing the same issues and they're confronted with the same potential weaknesses and pitfalls from a mental point of view. You face the same uncertainties and as a result you might have confidence issues. You might have issues with focus and concentration in the same way, because perhaps an injury or perhaps a goal against becomes a distraction you can't move past. These are issues that are simply common to the human experience. That was what was confirmed to me in discussion with these pro goalies in Finland. Some of them are playing the game in North America, so although they have come to respect training a little better or differently compared to North Americans, it doesn't change the pressures, or how they might react to those pressures or stresses of the position."

Goldman: Because the culture is so different in Finland, what do you think are one or two things that goalies in North America can do to improve their mental game?

Monnich: "Stop thinking. And that is so hard, so hard. I say that with a chuckle, because we perceive everything in our world through our mind. However, our minds are like an untamed wild animal that does whatever it wants. We think we control it, but it controls us. In fact, because it has a wild state, it almost has a wild animal's preservation instinct. In this highly developed state of being a human, this preservation state, which we call our ego, is still trying to protect us and is looking out for every possible threat, even to the point that it manufactures them. Is there a problem? Is that a threat? Is something going wrong? A seed of doubt, once planted, grows into a vicious mind weed. When we say to ourselves in a game after allowing a goal, 'What's wrong with me', then that is a seed of doubt, and it is going to run wild in our mind, and that's when goalies have the meltdown. So thinking is really the root of these key problems. What mental conditioning does – and the skills and the exercises that I teach – is help us start to control and tame this wild animal. It also starts to control our thinking so that the mind starts to work on our terms; it starts to work for us and we develop something called mindfulness, where we're aware of how our mind works. We're aware to recognize when we're thinking on the ice, and all of a sudden we will catch ourselves thinking or getting frustrated or angry, experiencing emotions that are going to distract us from our focus and our attention. Ideally, we want to perform with no thoughts. Hockey is much too fast to think, and we can't think fast enough to stop a puck. So my job as a mental conditioning coach is, first of all, to make the goaltender aware of what's going on in their head. As I do this, I see people open up about issues they're experiencing, so I help them become aware of it. I teach them how the mind works, and then I teach them simple skills to identify the thinking and stop it. We want to keep things simple. The analogy is that we have to condition our mind as well as we condition our body. I can teach these athletes how to condition their mind so that's not the weak link. However, the game that we play is all predicated on the fact that we're going to be scored on. The game doesn't exist if we don't fail or get scored on. So we have to accept that fact and we can't beat ourselves up and call ourselves failures. We have to look closely at why we failed at that moment. I teach goaltenders to embrace their weaknesses, because if we can identify and embrace our weaknesses, then we can go to the coaches and state them openly and without fear. From there, we can eliminate it, and when we eliminate it, we become stronger. At the core, what I'm teaching goalies is how to identify and embrace weaknesses so that they can eliminate them and constantly improve. In doing this, we're building up something called intrinsic motivation."

Goldman: What are the biggest obstacles that North American goalies face when it comes to learning this concept of intrinsic motivation?

Monnich: "First let me give you two comparisons of different European goalies. When I coached in Slovakia, I got on the ice at a team practice and all of the players were doing skating drills. But the goalies were standing over at the boards, just talking. I was coming from the ECHL, so I didn't recognize this. I go to the head coach and say, 'The goalies don't skate?' and the coach says, 'Do they skate in America?' I said, 'Yes' and so the coach blows his whistle and yells at his goalies to skate. Well, they're giving me a dirty look and I realize it's going to be a tough week [laughing]. So there's one cultural difference. This was one of the top teams in Slovakia and the goalies weren't doing the same skating drills as the players in practice. In Finland, a general personality characteristic of their population, especially men, is that they tend to be stoic. There's not a lot of emotions expressed, and this is how they're raised. This is going to affect how they react, perform, and think. So that's two examples of European approaches, and these are mental things, they're attitudes. But to address your question about North American goalies, I think one problem is how big geographically each country is; these are vast areas. Goalies are coming from all over, but there's also no systematized program of development like there is in smaller countries like Finland and Sweden. They have these programs that generally all goalies start with, but the US doesn't. They might have a dream of it, but it would be so hard to apply in such a vast country. There is no standard for coaching over here. Dads step in and they're the goalie coach. Some dads turn into good goalie coaches, but there's an inconsistency in coaching and development. Also, in North America, it becomes more and more expensive to play hockey at a higher level and to attend some of these camps where the good coaching exists. The coaches need to pay their bills, and they charge appropriately, but they still don't make a lot of money. So not everyone can afford that, which causes an inconsistency in training. So what characterizes North America to me in terms of obstacles is the inconsistency."

Goldman: Knowing that inconsistency is a challenge for everyone over here, and knowing it's harder today to get goalies turned on to having a mental conditioning coach, what do you feel like the next step is for you?

Monnich: "I think the two most critical points right now in further developing a North American goaltender's mental conditioning is awareness and acceptance. Once a coach and a player understands it and becomes aware of it, then they accept it and have the resources to improve, the battle is won. We can't see the mind. We can lift weights and see muscle develop and feel those changes. But we can't see our minds. And when we put the spotlight on it, we might react defensively. I'm not saying we have clinical problems, but we don't want to have mental weaknesses, we don't want the stresses to reveal a weak link or a breakdown. We want to be prepared for each stage of the season, which is different mentally. So just as we condition our bodies for the beginning of the season, then the middle of the season and the grind and then to peak for the playoffs, we have to condition our minds as well."

Goldman: When I was in Madison, Mike Valley had a chance to talk with eight NHL goalies about the mental game. I want to tell you this analogy and get your thoughts on it. He said, "Now we understand the importance of the food we eat, and how everything we eat affects every cell in our body. Thoughts are just like food. Every thought you put into your mind affects every cell in your body." How does that analogy resonate with you and how you teach goalies across the globe?

Monnich: "I agree with it 100 percent. If you say, 'I am not good,' then you are not good. If you say, 'I am full of potential,' then you are full of potential. The old adage goes, 'Set your limitations and they are yours,' and this is the truth. If we maintain a good positive space with good self-talk, we're not permitting bad thoughts to exist. When one occurs, we learn to identify it and dismiss it. So yes, good thoughts are like good food for the mind. You don't want to be around negative people, either. You start to feel drained physically, like there's no hope. But being around positive people is so great and optimistic, and you're filled with life. But I am not a motivational speaker; my job is not to make a goalie feel good and play better. Part of my coaching is to get you to acknowledge and accept your weaknesses so we can eliminate them, and that may not be comfortable, but it's going to make you better."

Goldman: Is there anything else you learned this summer that you think readers would want to know about your experience coaching in North America and Europe.

Monnich: "What is so wonderful about the North American culture is how optimistic our mindset has been. This is something that is over a century old. We're always looking ahead, looking at possibilities. This is something cultural, part of our society. So athletes over here are more willing to accept the possibility. It's not a negative bunch at all. So that helps quite a bit."

12

BOBBY GOEPFERT ON TRAINING WITH DOMINIK HASEK

Author's Note: *Bobby Goepfert is an All-American pro goalie currently playing in Germany. His winding journey through the college and minor league ranks perfectly fits the description of my idea that most American goalies are "mutts" in terms of style and developmental influences. He's also one of the most hilarious goalies you'll find. With writing skills that are as unique as his goaltending skills, his willingness to write this chapter for the book was greatly appreciated. This chapter gives you an inside look at an American goalie's personal training experience in Europe with one of the best goalies to ever play the game. A special thanks to Bobby for sharing his memories and thoughts with us!*

First thing's first. I will never be confused with the likes of a typical professional athlete. I am not "big". I am not "strong". I am not the most physically intimidating specimen you will ever see in your life.

What I do have, however, are a very particular set of skills. Skills I have acquired over a very long career. Skills that make me a nightmare for frozen vulcanized rubber puck-ers like you.

Well, at least I tell myself that. And I tell pucks that. But that does not deter them from the physical and mental beating they have placed upon me over the years.

Skill.

What is skill? Are you born with it? Do you develop it? Can you teach it? Hell if I know. The only thing I really know about the goaltending position is that you have to keep the puck in front of the goal line and those four-by-six iron "best friends" draped in triple coiled cotton twine.

I never truly had a goalie coach or goalie-specific training, so the aforementioned belief in a goalie's job is all I know. Through the years though, I have been fortunate enough to briefly train with great minds in North America and in Europe; goaltending minds that think different than your average puck stopper.

Playing alongside many goalies from many different backgrounds has also allowed me to take a peek into different cultures, styles, and philosophies I had never conceived before, especially being a brash ignorant tender of goals from the borough of Queens, New York.

Take the ice away. Growing up as a goalie, through youth hockey, juniors, and college, the focus was always on getting bigger and stronger. Sure, sounds right. But my gut was always saying, "Is this making me a better goalie?" or "Would this make me stop pucks better?"

I would often be partnered with a 6-foot-3, 215-pound bruising defenseman, lifting weights Olympic style. I curled a brow to this during the initial pick.

"But it will make you explosive," they said.

Perhaps. And I am not discounting the fact that fast-twitch muscles and building those muscles are needed for your body to achieve maximum puck repellence. But where was the innovation? Where was the specificity to the goaltending position, the one that is unlike so many others in sports?

It was not until 2009 that the nagging voice in the back of my head was vindicated.

I was playing in Austria at the time, and was invited to train for one week in a remote town in the Czech Republic with the one and only Dominik Hasek. This was at the same time he was making a comeback from his (first) retirement.

Small town, Litvinov is.

Looking back on walking into the hotel the night before our first training session, it seemed like a movie. It was dark. A 40-watt lightbulb strained itself in a chandelier that begged for a 90. I grabbed my key and went to my room to unwind from the anxieties of a five-hour trip on the Autobahn, a real-life modern day Mario Kart experience. And this coming from a guy who spent most of his life praying for safety on the Belt parkway.

I knew of Hasek obviously. I heard of the stories of his awkwardness in personality and in training and thought I would fit right in. But nevertheless, excitement and fear set in. I barely got a lick of sleep.

The next day, as the cock crowed on ol' Litvinov, I awoke with bright eyes and a bushy tail. Driving my car through the town, following the GPS step-by-step, I turned off the main road onto a dirt one and found myself in tall grass meadows with nothing but a house. A blazed trailed maze lay behind the two story "house" I pulled into.

A house it was not. From the outside, yes. But inside, it was a pure goalie factory. It was one of those experiences when you walk in, you know that when you leave you will be better. Hasek or not, this place catered to the position, and even though I didn't speak Czech, we all spoke Goalie.

The first floor looked like a sauna. All wood everywhere. That was our off-ice training room. Filled with stabilization balls, wood boxes, hula hoops, an array of balls from reaction to tennis to medicine to soccer (I mean Futbol) to racquet and so on. Slide boards were drilled into the hardwood. A Ninja warrior-esque setup was in the back. It truly seemed to capture the vision the voice in the back of my head had while questioning why I was trying to squat 400 pounds.

Upstairs was even sweeter. A lounge area with sofas and a coffee/juice bar piggybacked by a locker room, and to the side of the sitting area was a big Plexiglas window peering into a small rink with one of those motorized puck shooters, mouth yawned wide, yearning to shoot pucks. The black puck marks on the walls and glass told me I wasn't the first to be here, and sure enough wouldn't be the last.

I sat there in awe. All the meanwhile, taking in this goalie haven, I neglected to see the bicycle parked out front with a "Dominator" label all over it. As I walked up that second floor taking in my surroundings, I also neglected the gray-haired man lacing his skates getting ready for his ice session.

Through a translator, he had been there for two hours already. It was only 8:00 in the morning. "Apparently the cock crows a lot earlier where he's from," I thought.

"He already rode his bike 10 kilometers and then he did his usual morning workout," the translator said. I was 25 at the time. He was 44.

That's when I realized why I wasn't riding around on a "Bobby-nator" bike.

They told me I could start in 20 minutes, so have a coffee or a juice and stretch if I liked.

"Hell yeah. Stretching. My specialty. I'll show them something they've never seen before."

While I sat there, over compensating my stretches in between espresso sips, the Dominator took to the ice and started stretching on his own. In pure "middle child" syndrome, I tried to up my ante, neglecting my coffee cup and really going after it, only to be the opening act to the "Dominator" and his on-ice warm up.

Gumby, rubber band, slinky spine. Say anything relative to the sort and it does not do the man justice. I sat there, totally enamored. In awe. He was 44. I was 25.

He warmed up by taking shots to the head. Well, the pucks were flying at his head, and he proceeded to duck the incoming forehead-labeled flying discs of fury with impeccable quickness. I know what you're thinking. I was too. The translator said, "It helps warm up eyes."

Can you warm up eyes?!

Then he laid on his back. His head was facing the smiling puck shooting machine. His eyes upside down, he stared into the face of the puck shooter as it shot pucks above him and he tried to kick the pucks by tracking.

"More eye warmup, but with body," the translator said.

My jaw touching what seemed to be a rarely vacuumed carpet, the trainer tapped me on my shoulder parlayed with the singular word, "Time."

I was to head downstairs and start my training, but I could not take my eyes off of what I was seeing. So out of the tractor beam I was forced, and into the wooden goalie-gilded sauna room. Hot it was, and warm-ups was not what I was used to. Your run-of-the-mill dynamic warmup it was not, as we started with the timeless jumping jack. Piece of cake.

Two hundred. Saying it and reading it does not do 200 jumping jacks justice.

"Stretch," my trainer said.

Head first. Through a translator, he explained that the best method for "us" and he used "us", which was awesome, was to stretch from head to toe. Head being first.

Twenty minutes later, ladled with sweat thinking that was the workout, he threw me a hula hoop and three tennis balls.

"Juggle," my one-worded trainer commanded.

My mind went straight to when I was six years old in Brooklyn with my family. A performer on the Coney Island pier was teaching everyone to juggle. My parents encouraged me to learn, but I declined. How I regretted that at that present moment. Ball after ball fell as the hula hoop laid at my feet. I could see the disappointment in my trainer's eyes. I managed to get better and his face forced a smile.

"Hoop. Leg." Whoa. Two words. Wait, what?

I was to juggle the three balls while hula hooping the cursed plastic ring around one leg and balancing on the other. It was the only moment in my life that I longed for a squat rack.

More drills similar to the coordination, eye-enriched, full-body athleticism ensued until the Dominator came down. Slide board time.

My father and I made a slide board when I was younger. From humble beginnings, our family made every penny count, so after a trip to Home Depot and a purchase of some Canola Oil, I became one with the slide board as a youth. No problem, I thought.

The Dominator went first.

With knee pads I had never seen before, the 44-year-old picked up the oft-dropped tennis balls that were in my hand not even 10 minutes ago. He began to butterfly slide on his knees juggling them. Then to a command in Czech I didn't understand, he started juggling them off the wall while he slid. Left to right, right to left. And not the laboring slide, but the skillful, elegant, angelic, graceful, and fluid slides.

In awe once again, I was deaf to the realization that it was now my turn. Oh, how I wanted to impress the Dominator! But stumbling and bumbling and fumbling about, I just couldn't. I should have taken that juggling lesson at Coney Island. But I didn't. And there I was, getting everything I wanted in a goalie training experience, and failing miserably.

We finished the session with the Ninja Warrior-esque obstacle course, and then some extraneous core exercises. Topping it all off was the 5-K high grass run outside, which induced a healthy heaping plate of claustrophobia and a hearty side of exhaustion.

When I was finished running, I thought I was done for the day. But it turns out I also had an ice session similar to the Dominator's. A solo 45-minute session in which I never felt so alone. That smiling puck shooting machine seemed to have a bigger smile accompanied with a laugh when I tried to replicate the drills Hasek was doing only two hours earlier.

Warmup shots to the head, in which I was not ducking for eye movement, but out of sheer fear as the chuckling machine spit black tar right at me. My legs flopped without Hasek's ambition or control. My arms waved without a purpose. Feeling defeated, I thought my day was finally over. It wasn't.

Instead, we trudged to the nearby public swimming pool, where my bathing suit was actually considered as being over-dressed. Even Adam and his biblical fig leaf might have been over-dressed in this place. But Hasek's legendary goalie coach Josef Bruk had a speedo and a stop watch as we swam in the deep.

"Swam" isn't the correct word, though. It's more like we "goalied" in the deep, as we mimicked goalie movements for a set amount of time designated by Mr. Bruk's stopwatch. Anything from an anaerobic kick movement with your hands in the air, to 45 seconds of pretend pad stacks, left then right, violently kicking from one side to the next. Flutter kicks, mimic kick saves, and then similar sequences with our arms.

I buoyed on the water after the last interval. A mouth full of dirty chlorine water, Dominator to my right in his signature voice, "Good verk, keep goving".

I remember thinking, "Now *this* is Goalie Heaven."

All of us were working for a common goal, and we were all working hard with a purpose. Drills and exercises were specific, or at least very close to, some of the situations and scenarios we would face during a game. Whether that be movement of our puck-stopping limbs, cardio exertion like the nights filled of peppered pucks, or reactions when that devilish demon of rubber deflects off stick, legs, or the unknown, everything had a purpose. It was everything that voice in the back of my head desired while lifting weights with my bruising d-man in school many years ago.

As I looked around, nobody paid us any mind. Growing up in North America, and more particularly in the USA, there were people constantly giving me statistics about how hard it was to make it. Or they gave me reasons why I couldn't make it.

Back home, when people see you training, there's a quizzical look of "what for?" on their face. An insecure judgmental chuckle of "what are they doing?"

But in that small town in the Czech Republic, nobody paid us any mind. And the ones who did stare at these random goalies doing random goalie things in that public pool had a look on their faces that was one part admiration and one part envy. "Why not them?"

The feeling I would have training in the United States, especially with goalie-specific exercises, felt almost like I had to vindicate myself. In Europe, it felt like I was training with a purposeful pursuit toward a goal. And in the irony of it all, I was training with a purposeful pursuit to repel goals. Such is the duality of the goaltender; stopping goals in order to achieve them.

The existentialistic thought quickly came to a halt. We left the pool and I got ready for my second off-ice and on-ice session. Afterwards, I spent my evening in agonizing elation on my small European hotel bed, on the phone with my father talking about the experience that seemed like a dream. There would be six more days of that grueling, yet inspiring experience, each day harder than the next.

In the following weeks and now years after that unforgettable experience, I look back with a smile. There are many things I'm fortunate for in my career, but that experience alone is at the top of the list.

Not only did it allow me to see what it was like on the other side of the pond, how different the training was, the philosophy behind it, and the euphoric sensation while doing it, but it showed me that no matter the nationality, the culture, the stature of a goalie, whether you were a 16-year-old project, a 25-year-old minor leaguer, or a 44-year-old future Hall of Famer, there is a respect and appreciation associated with the position. We try to help each other, encourage each other, we bring out the best in one another.

Only goalies can understand goalies.

Our mailing addresses could be separated by miles (or kilometers) or oceans, but in the end, we all call that blue semi-circle crease home. That's the beauty of the position that nobody else can see.

13

CANADIAN GOALIE DEVELOPMENT WITH LARRY SADLER

If you've ever met *SmartGoalie* founder Larry Sadler before, then I'll be shocked if you weren't instantly reminded of the famous actor Richard Dreyfuss. They look exactly the same, with that prominent pure white beard, and they both had very similar mannerisms.

One part comedian, one part sophisticated world traveler, and one part fatherly figure, Sadler is one of the most passionate and caring Canadian goalie coaches I've ever met.

We had exchanged emails and shared articles together a few years ago, but we met face-to-face for the first time in Helsinki. Not only was he kind enough to pick me up from the Helsinki airport, but he instantly became both my tour guide and my personal assistant. He informed me on just about everything I needed to know about the layout of the camp and what to expect during my time in Finland.

Compared to my free-spirited wandering nature, I thought Sadler was like the over-prepared, somewhat paranoid planner. Everything was mapped out almost down to the minute, and he would constantly remind me if I had everything I needed for the day. He was always making sure things were in place and people were in the right spot. He was always double-checking bus schedules and restaurant reservations.

If he was your father on this type of trip, your eyes would have exploded from the number of times you'd roll them into the back of your head. But for me, I considered all of his quirks and planning to be endearing. You could tell this man was extremely passionate about his place in the goalie world, and even though he may be initially judged due to his age, he is the type of coach and teacher that Canada is lucky to have on their side.

Experience always breeds wisdom when it comes to working with goalies, so I was truly grateful for the time I got to spend with Larry. His stories, background, world travels, and ability to explain what he has learned over the decades was irreplaceable information, so I'm happy to add this interview in the book.

Goldman: Why don't you start by telling us what your role is up in Ontario?

Sadler: "It's a new position for me, but I've been asked to assist with the goalie development program initially. I am also assisting the Ontario Minor Hockey Association in instituting the Hockey Canada goalie coaching certification program, which has just been introduced. So my job right now will be to assist in getting the program into the communities. How we're going to do that, however, is what I'm going to be doing next. I have to sit down and come up with a structure and so forth."

Goldman: For those reading this that don't have prior knowledge of you, can you give a brief background on how you got to this part

Sadler: "I've been working with goaltenders for over 40 years. I was initially with one of Toronto's original goaltending schools, which I was also a part-organizer for. Since then, I've been involved as a university and junior goalie coach, I've been a consultant and general consultant for four different Ontario Hockey League major-junior teams, I've been a goalie coach for several minor youth hockey teams in the greater Toronto area, and presently I'm working as a full-time goaltending instructor for my own company, Smart Goalie. I'm working with kids of all ages and even some adults."

Goldman: With your experiences traveling all over the world, what are some of the countries you've visited besides Finland?

Sadler: "Besides Finland, I've visited Sweden and the United States. I'm looking at major hockey powers, so I've also had conversations and consultations with people coaching in Russia, the Czech Republic, Austria, Estonia, Germany, and Italy. So I have a rough image of what they're doing in those countries in terms of goaltending development."

Goldman: Can you give a brief synopsis of how Canada is structured in terms of goalie development?

Sadler: "Canadian hockey is run by Hockey Canada. Each of the 11 Canadian provinces has a hockey branch which is an organization that takes care of hockey administration and development. One province is different, however, and that's Ontario. It's such a large province that it actually has three branches, and the largest branch is the Ontario Hockey Federation. This is made up of the Northern Ontario Hockey Association [NOHA], the Ontario Minor Hockey Association [OMHA], the Greater Toronto Hockey League [GTHL], the Ontario Women's Hockey Association [OWHA[, the Minor Hockey Alliance of Ontario [MHAO], which all deal with minor hockey, and the Ontario Hockey League, which controls major-junior hockey. As far as minor hockey development, it is recognized as an activity for kids from ages of five or six on up, although they don't encourage competition until individuals are eight or nine years of age, although some are pushing for a little younger than that. The age groups are broken up predominantly into major categories. Novice is for seven or eight year olds. Novice Atom, Peewee is for 11 and 12 year olds, Bantam is for 13 and 14-year olds, then Midgets [15-17] and Junior [18-22]. Kids play in their own communities and are hopefully progressing through their communities. Each branch is different; some allow kids to move around, others don't. An area that is highly populated, like in the GTHL in Toronto, allows players to move from organization to organization. In fact, there are some kids I know of – not necessarily goalies – that have played on nine different teams in nine different years. There are very few kids that actually stay with an organization from novice all the way up to midget. But when you take a look at the OMHA, the MHAO, the NOHA, and the rest of the province, it's pretty much based on a residency rule that requires kids to play where they live, and that's defined by where their parents live. Other provinces and organizations across Canada, like Saskatchewan for example, do allow a little bit freer movement, but it depends on how old the kid is, and for what reason the family is moving, and so on and so forth."

Goldman: Compared to Finland, we know that North America is very different because Finland has the club system structure. So what obstacles arise with Canada's current structure and system? What is the biggest obstacle for goalies?

Sadler: "I don't know if it's an obstacle so much as it is just a situation. The first part is that hockey coaching in Canada is primarily volunteer up until major-junior. Other countries do allow for partially paid or fully-paid coaches, but what I've been finding in Canada is that since it is a volunteer basis, some of the biggest drawbacks and concerns come from parents coaching their kids. There are some organizations that have been extremely successful in Canada – including Bedford Minor Hockey which is based just outside of Halifax – which doesn't allow parents to coach in their organization. But that's very rare rather than a common rule, and parents are sometimes biased, whether intentionally or unintentionally. So that's the first thing. Secondly, Canada is so large and our population is so spread out that, in some ways, we're not like one country, but like 13 or 14 mini countries. When Hockey Canada meets, the branches and members decide what the policies and procedures will be. So in many cases, whenever ideas are going to be presented, it's like presenting them to 13 or 14 independent entities."

Goldman: Do you have a recent example of this issue playing out?

Sadler: "The best example I can give you is through the organization I'm working with. The Ontario Minor Hockey Association is the world's largest minor hockey organization with over 110,000 registered players. That's four times the registered hockey population of Finland. And we're like close to three times the size of Sweden. So that gives you an indication of where we are. My perception is that those countries have a slightly easier time developing goalies because they're smaller, more manageable, less spread out, so it's easier to institute change. In Canada, it's much harder because it has to be pressed through all the branches. So in many ways, for us to have taken 30 years to finally come up with a goalie coaching certification program, when all that time Finland has already had one, gives you an indication of how slow sometimes things happen. So I think the size of the country, the size of our registered numbers, and the structure of the branches makes development issues of any kind harder to change. Not impossible, but just harder to implement."

Goldman: Speaking of not impossible, it seems like Canada is starting to undergo a real positive transition period, and even a potential renaissance in the sense that you guys are starting to create a new goalie coaching certification program. So in terms of all the questions I've been asking about how you define a goalie in your country, it sounds like what makes a Canadian goalie is currently being determined.

Sadler: "At the Hockey Canada meeting we had a few weeks ago, I was glad to see we actually grabbed the bull by the horns and decided to identify and teach the Canadian goaltender not by nationality, but by style. I think that was interesting. Of course in many ways, the identification of who you are starts off by determining who you aren't. So in our particular situation, we are starting to identify that the Canadian goaltender is no longer the blocking style. The Canadian goaltender has active hands, tighter post positioning with the arm outside the post and the body against the post. I think we're better with our stick and with puck-handling and playmaking compared to Europeans. And in many cases, a lot of this stuff isn't by design, it has come about by happenstance. Now what we've done, we're trying to filter what makes sense from what doesn't make sense to come up with a much better idea of what a Canadian goalie is. Temperament is also a big thing. General perception amongst scouts is that the Canadian goaltender is mentally tough. Other countries are looked upon as not being as mentally tough, or more entitled possibly, or 'soft' is one word. I don't think we're tough to the exclusion of others, but we have a toughness that permeates all levels of hockey in Canada."

Goldman: What got you interested in the Finnish style of goaltending and the GoaliePro methods? How did that come about and how did that inspire you to get more involved in coaching goalies here in Canada?

Sadler: "Well about six or seven years ago, I had a major situation occur in my life, one that caused me to be able to reassess what I wanted to do with the rest of it. I then identified that I wanted to get more seriously involved in goaltending development. One of the reasons for this was that I didn't think, at the time, that we had the proper approach to development; nothing was consistent. So when I did some research, I realized that in a 10-year period, from 1999 to 2009, Finnish goaltending had gone from zero representation in the NHL at the 20-game or more mark, and Canada having 65-percent of the goalies, to the Finns having 17-percent and Canada slipping to 45-percent in that time period. So we've actually declined in terms of representation in the NHL. And since that is considered to be the top hockey league in the world, that's what you kind of look upon as an indicator for success. When I then took a look at the number of registered hockey players, we had 10 times the number of registered players as Finland, yet we didn't have the same numbers reflected in terms of goalies. So it obviously came to me very quickly that they were doing something different. The more research I did, the more I realized that a big part of their success was due to their goalie coaching certification program. I decided at that time to reach out to anyone I could find in Finland who would be interested in talking to me, and that ended up being the guys at GoaliePro. Once I submitted my resume, they were quite open to inviting me over, and I've been coming to their camp for the past six years, with this being my fourth time over here."

Goldman: So what has been the biggest revelation for you in regards to this six-year experience?

Sadler: "I guess the analogy I tell people all too often is that, if you want to find out how to be good at something, you go to somebody who is good at it. If you want to make a million dollars, you look up to someone who has made a million dollars. This is what I equate the Finnish approach to. You don't sit there and talk to the person who is behind you in a lottery line, which is what I believe we have been doing in Canada. We seem to be reluctant to accept ideas that come in from outside. So with that in mind, I decided to take this step. I haven't regretted it, and with the contacts I've made here and in Sweden, I guess the big revelation is that the Scandinavian approach to goaltending is something that's well worth looking at and possibly adopting in some small way, both in terms of technique and structure."

Goldman: Let's talk about those two aspects. In regards to overall structure, I'm reinforcing in the book many times that Finland's club system is of great benefit to overall goalie development because of the country's size and consistency throughout all of their programs.

But beyond that, what about the club system here have you learned is of such huge benefit for developing goalies?

Sadler: "Well, with Finland's goalie coaching certification program, they've made it very apparent that nobody can work with a rep-team goalie unless they've taken the program. The Level-1 program is 16 hours long, and the Level-2 program is the same length of time, and then it goes up from there with Level-3 and Level-4 at the junior and national ranks. So an individual working with a 10-year-old goalie playing rep hockey may be a father, but he has still gone through the program. So there's a real consistency in the way in which they approach certain things. Now some people are a little concerned that this gets in the way of innovation, but it doesn't. It actually enhances innovation, because it gives people a foundation from which they can move forward. When looking at their structure, it's also centrally based, so it does allow for regional representation with individuals in the fields whom are working quite closely with the individual teams and organizations to enhance their goaltending coaching and the goalies themselves. By doing that, not only are they enhancing skills, but they're better identifying the goalies they have. So when kids get into the elite programs, it's easier to funnel them along, and there's very few kids that are being missed. If some are missed, there's even a 'recheck' program to make sure they don't miss as many."

Goldman: Technically speaking, what do you feel like you've learned from being over here in terms of

what separates successful Finnish goalies from North American goalies?

Sadler: "My degree is in history and political science, so I try and put a historical perspective on this. It became an important question for me since Day 1 when I came to Finland, and it has become an important question now that I'm visiting Sweden as well: 'What is it that is in the Finnish culture and identity that makes them more effective as goaltenders?' They're not born goalies, but it's obvious they're streamed towards that. It became apparent from a historical perspective and also from an assessment of what's going on in their society today that they are a very sturdy individual, they're very stoic in some cases. They have had major economic and major cultural shifts within their country that have almost destroyed them in the past, but they have come out of it much, much stronger. They're a country that is based on the importance of universality and equal opportunity. So in their education system and their health system, more people are being allowed to get an education and more people are allowed to be healthy. With their education system, one of the things I've felt over the past few years is that it's very apparent to me that not only are the Finns well-educated, but they have a very strong appreciation for education. So for everything they do, there's a certification process or an education program that is required. They don't have any qualms about taking a course that will make them a better coach, while in Canada and in some cases in the United States, people are reluctant to take things because they figure past experience is equal to a formal education, when in fact it isn't necessarily. So I think there's an acceptance on that part, and an acceptance too within the Finnish psyche and culture that they approach the whole issue of defeat or turmoil as an opportunity to learn, which is why Finnish goaltenders are able to shut down what doesn't work and focus on what has to be done to succeed. They make ideal goalies in that respect because they don't allow past failures to weigh them down."

Goldman: You mentioned you've been to Sweden as well. How would you answer the same question for Swedish goalies? I was personally blown away by seeing a lot of young Finnish goalies managing their own game and doing some self-correcting without a coach having to verbally command them to do it.

Sadler: "Interestingly enough, I did hear a comment from one of the Swedes this year that, when I mentioned this to them about Finnish culture and goalies, they felt that some of those same traits were also attributable to Swedish athletes and goalies as well. So they felt it was more of an overall Scandinavian approach in terms of the influence of things like their universal health culture, which is quite similar to the Finns. But I'd also mention too that it's very clear to me from Finland's education system that children are coming up with a very strong sense of self-discipline, self-awareness, and self-sufficiency. Whenever I see a gathering of Finnish athletes in the 10-12 age group, I'm absolutely amazed at how a lot of their work is based on self-training. I will see a 10-year-old girl doing a high-jump all by herself, over and over and over again, because she realized repetition is so important. And she's doing this without any adult or parent there to supervise her or push her along. So I think it's a major, major strong point with their approach."

Goldman: So if you were to take this same paradigm and compare it to Canadian goalies, what about their approach or identity influences how their goalies develop? I know you touched on this a little bit earlier, but maybe you can include some more details with your historical background.

Sadler: "First of all, the perception that we've invented the game. I don't mean that as a derogatory statement, it's just something we strongly feel. The sense that we invented the game, I mean there's an entire campaign based around a beer company saying hockey is Canada's game. Hockey is such an integral part of the culture, and yet surprisingly, enrollment in Canadian hockey is on the decline. Soccer's registration figures are larger and kids that can actually play the sport is a low percentage. That gives you an indication right there that our perception of the sport versus the reality is two different things. Taking that aside, the one thing that's really interesting about Canadian kids growing up interested in becoming goaltenders is that they identify with success. They also identify with a little bit of celebrity, so kids, as they grow up, have an affinity for a goaltender. Surprisingly, kids won't differentiate between a Canadian or a European goaltender, they like just the goalie, and they'll pattern themselves after one they really like. We have regional differences in Canada, so there are different approaches to goaltending and hockey itself. We try and state that we have a general Canadian approach, but it's very different."

Goldman: Can you briefly describe some of those regional differences?

Sadler: "I'd say generally speaking, Quebec likes to focus their players on speed. The west is usually perceived as being tough, aggressive, and good checking players. Ontario is perceived as somewhere in between. The Quebec approach to goaltending is still very much based on Francois Allaire. In fact, if you take a look at Quebec, they've had a goalie coaching certification for a few years, and if you look at it, it's predominantly based on Allaire's materials and all of the research he has done in the past. As far as the west is concerned, there's an excellent program in Saskatchewan right now, which has identified what is a Canadian goaltender. It's predominantly from a western viewpoint, because their interactions are strictly within their region. So if I was to identify the good points of a Canadian goaltender, one would be pride in execution. I would say the next one is the perception of toughness, whether it's real or not, and the ability to identify with that toughness. Then there's also the perception that we have a strong work ethic."

Goldman: I just want to clarify to readers that you don't mean 'perception' as a bad thing, but rather how the rest of the world likely sees Canadian goalies. But what are some of the 'realities' as you see them?

Sadler: "One reality is that predominantly our goaltending development is all on-ice based, as opposed to having an off-ice component. Goaltending is becoming more and more a rich or richer person's position because the general costs of hockey are going up. When you look at Sweden or Finland, they're paying less for an hour of ice than what we're paying in Canada even though we have more rinks per player. And it's because of how they perceive the importance of physical activity. We're not as fit as we should be. In my personal opinion, we are running into a danger of entitlement, whereby the perception of play is based on the fact that we're there and therefore should be playing, when in fact we're not owning that. We're trying to come to grips with fair play at the younger groups versus the best playing the best when they get to high school. That transition from what I'll call the 'elementary school' approach to the 'high school' approach is something I think a lot of us are trying coming to grips with right now. So I think there's that, and I think the last thing is that there's a general feeling in the country that goaltenders aren't getting the instruction they need. Most of the successful or existing goalie instruction in Canada is based on privatization rather than a branch or organization-based goalie development."

Goldman: So shifting gears now, we all had to create a white-paper essay for the GoaliePro coach mentoring program. What is your white-paper topic?

Sadler: "My goal is to compare the Swedish, Finnish, U.S., and Canadian U-17, U-18, and U-20 development programs for goaltenders, in lieu of what we call in

Canada the Program of Excellence approach. So I've attended the Swedish U-17 to U-20 camps, I attended the Finnish U-17 and U-20 Elite camps, and I'll be attending the Hockey Canada U-17 camp in Calgary next week. After that, I'll have a much better idea how to compare what's actually going on with structure and execution. Hopefully through you and a couple other people, I'll get a good overview of what's going on in the USA. So my topic is comparing those programs in those countries compare to each other."

Goldman: What did you learn from attending Sweden's camp?

Sadler: "Not meaning to sound egotistical, but I was thinking to myself during a random early morning was that if I had a small population and wanted to develop hockey at an accelerated rate, so as to stay competitive or to surpass USA and Canada, then the Swedish and Finnish structures would be what I'd do. Regional identification, club development, identification of the elites using the individuals you have in the field, and then promoting those individuals to improve at their own rate so as to provide them with the opportunity to play at the elite level. So that's what I've noticed with them. I think they're extremely well-structured. It's not a perfect system but nothing is. But it's pretty close."

Goldman: You also attended Finland's camps. What did you learn there?

Sadler: "The same appreciation for their approach to structure and their main objectives. I think the one thing that is really interesting for both countries, and I have to speak generally about both for a minute. But the thing that interests me is that they're well-structured now, but they're not satisfied with where they are, they want to get better. Both the goaltending program of Sweden, which is approximately 12 years old, and the goaltending development program for Finland, which is 30 years old, are both going through a massive re-write right now. So while the rest of us are trying to get started [Canada and USA], they're refining and moving on to the next step. That dedication to growth is really what is propelling them forward and keeping them ahead, as well as recognizing that they can be better. The other thing I'll mention too is that both organizations are extremely willing to share. I find that admirable, because I have been in situations where individuals who are supposedly at the top of their field are less willing to share. I think that's why they will always stay ahead for quite a few years, I should think."

Goldman: Generally speaking, what's one thing about Finnish goaltenders you've coached that you'd like to see in the Canadian goalie? It doesn't have to be personality, it could be technical.

Sadler: "What I'd like to see Canadian youth goalies adopt is a much stronger dedication to fitness. Let's face it, we all know that obesity is a big problem in North America, and that's something we talked about before.

So it's not that Finland is not suffering from some of these things with older people, but Finland's approach to fitness at the younger ages is very important. I think they have more of a respect for fitness and a willingness to work at being fit. Secondly, work ethic. It's not just blind work ethic, it's an intelligent work ethic. They understand if something works, then they do it. If they identify with something that makes technical sense, they'll understand it, accept why it works, and use it intelligently. We have that capability in Canada, but we haven't been using it. We teach kids to do things without giving them proper explanations as to why, and that hurts us. I think the involvement of the parents in the overall plan for the goaltenders is much better thought out here than it is in Canada. My perception with what the problem may be in Canada is that we teach, but we don't evaluate afterwards to see if it's being executed. That's not an issue here. Both goaltending development directors in Sweden [Magnusson] and Finland [Nykvist] told me that they're not only teaching, but they're trying to get a good handle of the evaluation portion of the field. The last thing too is this: the proper approach to challenging our kids so that they learn from the experience to better themselves and not become discouraged. I don't think in Canada we challenge appropriately, I think we do it in an improper manner, but I do believe this is starting to change. So I think those are the things I'd like to pass along to more of my goaltenders, and I think I have been."

Goldman: What do you feel will be the short-term impact for the new goalie coaching certification program being built in Canada? What are your hopes for the long-term impact?

Sadler: "I think a lot of people will be excited when they hear it's done. As I will be saying to my instructors, most of the people that I will encourage to become involved as goalie instructors in the OMHA presentation of the goalie certification program have all been voices crying in the wilderness up to now. Because we have seen ourselves in this way, we're separate entities unto ourselves, and we may be a little reluctant to share. We have to cast that aside now and change that. So in the short term, the people who know nothing about goaltending will appreciate what's being presented. The people who believe they know something about goaltending may not even take advantage of the opportunity and therefore not add to it. Long-term, when I see the people who are seated around the table having input on the program, I'm really impressed with not just their technical expertise, but with their teaching knowledge to such an extent that I can see this program, as it exists now, may go through two or three revisions over the next four or five years. During that time, each time will be a refinement that will lead to more development. So I'm quite excited with it. I think it's a step in the right direction and in the short-term it might seem like pouring a glass of water on a raging forest fire, but I think in the long-term, as Confucius once said, the longest journey begins with the first step, I think this is the first step. I think it will assist with the overall betterment of goaltending development in Canada."

Goldman: And probably around the world as well.

Sadler: "Oh yes, that's true. The one thing you have to remember is that Canada's development programs in other fields have been adopted by other countries for quite some time. If anything, our shortfall has been our reluctance to accept input as readily as we should from other countries because we think we invented the game. We had a discussion a few nights ago with someone who said that one of the things they do in Finland is take programs that Canada offers and refine them, change them, and alter them and made them quite successful to their own environment, so that's not unusual, and that's the goal here in Canada."

14

CLARE AUSTIN ON EUROPEAN GOALIES IN THE NHL

Author's Note: *Clare Austin is a passionate goalie enthusiast with a penchant and talent for advanced statistical analysis. As a teacher, she is quite skilled at gathering, organizing, and explaining complex information. She has been a big supporter of mine for many years, and I believe her analysis and musings on goaltending is pretty spot on. She deserves to have her voice be heard, so I invited her to publish some of her findings regarding European goalies for this book. Be sure to follow her on Twitter @Puckologist and give her a shout out!*

Writer's Note: *The following is based on a sample of 491 pro goalies who played in the top pro leagues in Europe and North America between 2007-08 and 2012-13. These goalies represent 20 nationalities and they played their amateur hockey in 17 different countries. They were born between 1965 and 1995. The 42-percent who were picked in the NHL Draft were selected between 1991 and 2014. In terms of pro experience, they have played anywhere from one to 1,291 games in those nine leagues.*

The question Justin posed to me was whether goaltenders who wait to come to North America do better than those who don't. Does staying in your home system (or close to it) give a goalie a benefit in terms of NHL success?

This is a question I've grappled with before, albeit in a limited way – using only drafted goaltenders. Earlier evidence seemed to point to the idea that the two groups who did the best in terms of NHL games played were, firstly, those goalies who are exceptionally talented and who get noticed at a young age. Secondly, evidence pointed to those goalies who might be considered late-bloomers – those who got noticed in their early-20s. The former are players like, for instance, Olaf Kolzig and Martin Brodeur, who were drafted high and played a lot of games from a very young age. The latter are players like Pekka Rinne and Cristobal Huet, who were drafted after age 21. The former group tended to be more successful, for obvious reasons. But the latter group tended to have fewer players who fail to make at least some impact in the NHL.

With this new set of data I collected, I was able to look more closely at the age question, including free agents and comparing European goalies with North American goalies. In isolating Europeans, I am concerned with two separate but overlapping subsets of data:

1. *European goalies who play in North American amateur leagues (such as the Canadian Hockey League or the NCAA)*

2. *European goalies who play in North America as young pros*

Overall, the evidence was mixed on whether age had any effect on NHL success levels. While there was a very, very slight correlation between young starts and NHL success, that was mostly due to the talent of a few individuals getting NHL games at an early age and then building long and successful NHL careers. For other European players, the indication was that beginning in North America at a later time led to fewer low-end outcomes and better mid-range outcomes, if not as many high-end outcomes.

Goalies Arriving Before Age 20

Within my sample, there are 36 European goalies who played in Canadian juniors, the NCAA, or high school leagues in the United States. Most of them (24) chose the Canadian juniors route.

Eleven of these players (30.6 percent) have played NHL games; all 11 were drafted by NHL teams. Thirty percent was a much higher rate of entry than those who played amateur hockey in Europe. Only goalies who played amateur hockey in Sweden had a comparable rate. The following table compares Europeans who played at least some junior/amateur hockey in North America with Europeans who stayed in their home country (Swedes who played in Sweden, for instance).

Amateur country	Rate of entry into NHL
Euro goalies in NA amateur hockey (n=36)	30.6 %
CZE (n=38)	7.9 %
FIN (n=45)	15.6%
GER (n=26)	3.8%
RUS (n=46)	15.2%
SUI (n=32)	12.5%
SWE (n=47)	27.7%
Total European	14.96%

Overall, however, players from North American amateur leagues – in particular, Canadian juniors – did far better at this measure than anyone else. They met this benchmark far beyond their representation in the overall population. So far beyond, in fact, that it suggests something other than a skill difference is at play. Exposure is almost certainly a factor in the success rates, as is draft status.

Most of the Europeans who came to play in Canadian juniors, for instance, did so after they were drafted. All of the players who made the NHL were drafted. In that sense, this is a group selected for their apparent skill at age 18-20, and can thus be expected to have higher NHL entry rates on that basis alone. To the extent that NHL drafting is able to identify goaltender talent, it is likely that talent or skill differences account for a significant part of their ability to meet that benchmark, as opposed to age or differences in the training a league can provide. However, North American goalies tend to be drafted at higher rates than Europeans, even when accounting for population differences.

In any event, the Canadian amateur route is no longer accessible to European goalies now that the CHL has banned import goaltenders. There will be fewer opportunities for Europeans to play amateur hockey in North America in the future, whether they are drafted or not. If talent is the determinant, European amateur leagues should see an increase in the rates of NHL entry over time. If exposure or training is the determinant, they will not—or at least not much.

Goalies Arriving After Age 20

The next question is whether goalies who arrive as young professionals see an age benefit. Do those who begin playing in North America before age 23 do better, worse, or the same as those who make the transition as 23 to 27 year olds? That depends on how you slice the data.

Among all European goalies with NHL experience, those who played their first North American game (not necessarily an NHL game) at age 20 or above had a very slight tendency to do better (measured in Games Played) when starting younger, but the correlation was very, very small ($R^2 = .027$).

As with any arbitrary measurement of success, using Games Played as the benchmark does have its problems. The biggest one is that the spread of results is extremely large. A small percentage of players have very high numbers of games played, while a larger percentage of players have a very low number of games played. The most common result, regardless of where a goalie played amateur hockey, was to have fewer than 100 games played.

Another concern is that players who start earlier have more opportunity to play games, which is indicative not only of ability, but also of league structure. A goalie playing in Finland can't be called up to the NHL, but one playing in the AHL can, regardless of talent or age. The longer a goalie is available to NHL teams, the more opportunity he will have to play an NHL game. Thus, it would be surprising if goalies who started younger did not, to some extent, have higher numbers of games played than those who started later.

To account for this I also examined "failure" rates. How many players never caught on in the NHL in any significant way? How many played only very few games? To control for the necessary development time, I looked only at goalies born before 1989.

Goalies who came to North America later (age 23 or older) had much lower rates of failure (fewer than 10 NHL games) compared to those who came to North America before that. The 23-to-27 age group was more tightly clustered as well.

Age at 1st N. American Game	<10 GP	<100 GP	>500 GP
Under 23	29.41%	70.59%	11.76%
23-27	6.67%	46.67%	20.00%

It's a similar story for age at first NHL game: a very slight tendency to do better when starting younger (in terms of number of GP) but a very small correlation (R^2 = .026). In other words, age at NHL entry had very little direct effect on the number of games a goalie played. Again, however, a greater percentage of younger players have very few games than older players.

Age @ 1st NHL Gm (European players)	<10 GP	<100 GP	>500 GP
Under 23	26.7%	53.3%	13.3%
23-27	6.7%	40%	26.7%

These results are independent of draft status, except to the extent that high drafted players tend to be younger and to get NHL games younger than lower drafted or undrafted players.

The interesting part was that this pattern did not hold for North American-born players. While on the individual level the R^2 was a little better, it was still very small, at 0.088. This indicates that for an individual, age at entry to the NHL was not a good predictor of success. But as a group, Canadian and American goalies had less success when they entered the league later.

Age at 1st NHL Game (N.A. players)	<10 GP	<100 GP	>500 GP
Under 23	19.61%	37.25%	13.73%
23-27	43.48%	82.61%	0.00%

One reason for this relates to league structures in North America. Players in minor pro hockey (AHL and ECHL) in North America are eligible to get NHL games, regardless of age or nationality. However, pro goaltenders overwhelmingly play their early professional years in their home systems or close to it. Thus North American goaltenders are highly likely to play in the leagues from which they can enter the NHL at a young age.

In other words, young pros from North America benefit from a structural advantage in getting NHL games regardless of talent level or draft status. A higher proportion of young North American players are getting several shots at the NHL simply because there are more of them available to NHL teams, and once a player has NHL experience he is more likely to be called on again. This is no more and no less than a factor of the opportunity afforded by starting your pro career in the ECHL or AHL.

It is striking, however, that the most successful North American goalies tended to get started very young – all by age 22, most by age 19 – while the most successful European goalies tended to get started between age 22 and 24. Combined with the greater likelihood of a North American (especially Canadian) goaltender getting drafted, it again suggests that exposure to these players has been more prolonged and thorough.

Conclusions

In the final analysis there's mixed evidence about the relationship between age and success. As individuals, there is no real indication that NHL success has anything to do with age at entry, except for those elite players who get noticed very young, start playing NHL games very young and go on to play a very large number of NHL games.

In other words, for individuals, playing in North America at a younger age is very slightly better, but that is largely a function of the number of games that very talented elite goaltenders get when they are 18 or 19 years old. However, for European goalies looking out for their own interests, getting NHL games at a young age is one way to get a shot – but a player must be in the AHL to do that. Therefore, on the individual level, getting into the AHL – even when young – has to be seriously considered, but should be weighed against the benefits of staying at home to develop between the ages of 18 and 22 or 23.

For teams, however, there is strong evidence that there has been a gap in knowledge and evaluation of European goaltenders as opposed to North American goaltenders. Getting better and more thorough information about European goalies can pay good dividends. If the best European goalies can be identified at a younger age, an NHL team will get better return on the investment they make in them. As long as development practices are roughly equivalent, finding these goaltenders at age 19 (like the best North American goalies) could only benefit a franchise. In the meantime, it appears that there could be a competitive advantage in looking at older European goaltenders as free agents.

At this point, there is a clear increase in value among European goalies (as a group) between ages 18 and 23, but not among North American goalies (as a group). It appears that outside of exceptional cases, the best North Americans are identified at a younger age than the best Europeans. Whether that is a function of differences in training is beyond the scope of this data. It is quite possible that it's a function simply of time, a process that is visible for North American players but not for European players. In other words, in these cases, teams have been locating goaltenders who have already survived a European development process instead of relying on their North American process.

So I ask, is a later North American debut better for European goalies? For many, there's some evidence that this is likely true. For a few extraordinary individuals, however, it's not true. For a team looking for goaltending talent, older European goalies tend to be as good an investment as younger North American goaltenders, suggesting that, ultimately, waiting until age 22 or 23 to make a determination about a goalie's potential is often not a bad strategy.

15

ELI WILSON ON CANADIAN GOALTENDING

Eli Wilson, founder of *Eli Wilson Goaltending,* had some special hockey opportunities during his childhood. He grew up in Maple Ridge, British Columbia, an environment where he was able to get into NHL practices on a pretty consistent basis. Because of this, watching and meeting all of his childhood idols laid a strong foundation for what has become a very prominent and successful pro goalie coaching career.

"I skipped a lot of school and had to take three buses in order to get to the PNE Coliseum and watch the Canucks and the visiting teams practice," Wilson said. "Even though the practices were closed to the public, I became friends with the security guard and could get into any skate I wanted."

Opportunity often knocks on the door of those who toil endlessly in the fields, and thanks to his fierce dedication to coaching goalies at a very young age, Eli eventually earned rare opportunities to coach some of the world's finest NHL goalies, including Carey Price, Tim Thomas, Ray Emery, and Tuukka Rask. Because of his star-studded pro clientele, it's no surprise that thousands of North American goalies are eager to attend one of his summer camps, or his prestigious invite-only Elite Prospects Camp.

I've been fortunate to attend two consecutive annual Elite Prospects Camps. The first was held in Edmonton in the summer of 2013, and then I attended the same program in Toronto this past summer. That camp included some great prospects, including Justin Fazio (Sarnia, OHL), Brendan Johnston (Windsor, OHL), and Matej Tomek, a draft-eligible Slovakian currently tearing up the NAHL.

A no-nonsense coach on the ice, Wilson is known for including an exhausting power-hour bag skate into his camps. This is an intense one-hour power skating session that leaves everyone gassed and borderline nauseous. But every kid, whether they like it or not, sees the value in this fierce training. It's all part of the pro-like atmosphere Wilson creates during this camp.

The kids get rewarded, though. He brings in a professional massage therapist, they stay at a four-star hotel, and they are supplied with all the BioSteel they could possibly handle.

When sitting down with Wilson to get his perspective on Canadian goalie development, I was not surprised to hear some of his candid opinions.

"I believe that the lack of a goaltending-specific environment in Canadian hockey is very sad and negative," Wilson said. "I think we have great goaltenders and great goaltending coaches. But when we are put into regular or pure hockey environments, we are treated and viewed as second-class citizens. Media, fans, parents, and coaches can be cruel to those who play the position. The young kids that love the position are working at their game as hard as they can."

After seeing how he works with goalies on the ice, I'd say unflappable determination and a no-nonsense approach to the position describes Wilson quite well. He's calm and relaxed off the ice, but once the door slams shut and the ice is dry, it's time to get to work.

At least that's one surefire way to get results, even if it almost makes you puke.

Goldman: I'd like to start by getting a bit of a personal background on yourself and how you got involved with coaching goalies at the highest level.

Wilson: "I was born in Mission, B.C. but grew up in Maple Ridge. I started playing hockey at a later age – second year PeeWee – and it became my life. At times, nothing else really mattered. I stuck with it long enough – obviously it didn't work as a player – and I got some great experiences as a kid. Not that I wasn't a very good goalie, but things didn't go the way I wanted, so it didn't work out, but probably for the best. I started becoming a coach at a really young age, and a real serious coach almost instantaneously. I was coaching goalies as a full-time job at the age of 22. Maybe the money wasn't enough for a full-time job, but I wasn't doing anything else at the time. I took it very seriously."

Goldman: If you look back at when you started to transition from being a player to a coach, who influenced you on both sides of the spectrum?

Wilson: "Probably the same people. I had two great coaches as a kid. One was Pete Fry, who is still a friend and mentor of mine. He was able to get the best out of a lot of people. He believed in people and in himself. Not only did he produce goalies, but when it was all said and done, three of the guys he worked with – Robb Tallas, Mike Valley, and myself – all become NHL goalie coaches at some time. Probably all of us were taking a lot out of what Pete showed us at a young age. Another goalie coach that I had was John De Jonge. It came full circle, as now his daughter is a student of mine. Even though the game technically changed, he was all about work ethic and he had the type of attitude that, if you didn't give it 110-percent, you'd let him down. I don't even know if it was something he said or did, it was just his personality that made you react and respond to him as a coach."

Goldman: What were a few of the things that Fry and De Jonge instilled in you that still acts as a staple for how you coach goalies today?

Wilson: "I think Pete was a no-excuse guy. I remember he would talk about a guy that had been burned in a house fire, and rather than the guy shutting down from the world, he ended up running and owning the biggest fireplace store in the history of the United States. He became a billionaire and he had 80-percent of his body burned by fire. So Pete had a story like that for you every single day. He was high energy and was super intense, but there was no excuse about anything. If you had an excuse about something, he'd put something right in front of your face that told you that you were wrong if you doubted yourself. He believed in good things and I remember that everything he did was positive. His approach, the music he listened to; he really believed in guys making huge leaps."

Goldman: Shifting gears and getting into technique and style, I want readers to know what your coaching philosophy is on the ice. What are some of your main teaching and stylistic points?

Wilson: "I think the number one thing is to be open-minded and understand that the game is like us; that's always improving and always changing. Adapt and build skill level rather than a particular style. Do the best thing that's available at the time to be successful. Sometimes you see a goalie that looks a certain way and another goalie a little different, but if you really break it down and look at the naked part of it, a lot of the stuff they're doing is the same. That goes back to simple fundamentals and that's moving, always being in position, and understanding the easiest way to be in position. I believe in taking things out of a guy's game rather than adding things to a guy's game, to make their game less complicated so that they have a higher chance of being successful, since there's less room for error. I'm a huge believer in being in the middle of the net, a huge believer in soft focus, in visual attachment, and I think that those are things that doesn't matter what style you're playing, those things still all matter and always will matter. Another big thing that is important to me is the determination to make saves and the will to not get scored on. This is totally different than work ethic. If getting scored on isn't pissing you off, then you can't be an elite goaltending. At the same time, you always need to be able to move forward. Hard work is nothing more than exercise, but pure determination is what makes a true puck-hungry goalie."

Goldman: Explain "soft focus" for readers. It's a term I don't hear often, but we usually call it shoulder checks.

Wilson: "It's basically identifying what's going to happen. If you're facing one side of the ice, you need to see what's happening on the other side of the ice. You're going to be on the post and the puck is down low, you need to look across your body and then look back to the puck. It goes back to hockey sense, and people talk about seeing the ice really well, but it's not a given thing. You can understand reading plays and I remember this was years ago working with Carey Price as a young goalie, I remember we were doing 2-on-1's, and before the whistle would go every time, he'd look to see who was next in line before they went. Well, that's awareness. If he doesn't look, he doesn't know. That's something you think about and you do it. You can talk about all of the things that are happening consciously, subconsciously, and mentally, but it's an actual physical thing that you're doing. It's the same thing as visual attachment. It's a physical thing that turns into a mental thing."

Goldman: Can you talk about how working with NHL goalies and elite teenagers often results in sharing and teaching the same things? A lot of the messages you're reinforcing are actually pretty consistent.

Wilson: "To me, the position is real simple. If I can see something that is going to work at the NHL level, there's no reason that a guy at a younger level or in minor hockey can't do the same thing. It's the same position, just at a different level. Yeah, things happen faster, but you're still going to make a glove save the same way, whether the puck is going 50 miles per hour or 80 miles per hour. The fundamentals are exactly the same, tactically it's the same, so a goalie that I work with at 10 years old is going to be doing the same thing as a goalie that's 30 years old. That's going to be my approach, anyways."

Goldman: Getting into some of the experiences you've had training goalies from different regions, my first question is, as a guy who has coached a lot of Canadians, how would you define the Canadian goaltender?

Wilson: "Well I think role modeling is huge in goaltending. In Canada, I'd think that basically for nine out of 10 guys, their favorite goalie is going to be Carey Price. So guys are going to try and emulate and copy that style. I think he's the current face of Canadian goaltending. You're seeing the top prospects, whether it's the Stuart Skinner's or the Eric Comrie's, they're all very similar to playing the way that Carey Price does. I could be wrong, because those are other guys that I work with. But if I had a goalie that wasn't doing anything, that's how I would teach him or her to be a goalie. So I think that's what a Canadian goalie strives to be and strives to look like. He's the top of the food chain now. It's debatable in the world, but it's not debatable in Canada."

Goldman: Where do you feel like Canada is at as a whole in terms of goalie development?

Wilson: "It's interesting in Canada. Goalie development is very privatized and people are running businesses to become goalie coaches. It's sort of sad to me that guys go against what the other guy is doing just to go against them and they don't really do what they believe in necessarily because they believe in it. Sometimes they do stuff for other reasons, but I think our goaltending at the top levels is in pretty good shape. I see games at every level of hockey and I think we have some really good athletic goalies playing at every level. I think we probably have the best goalies in the world still. I don't know if we have the most, but we probably have the best in pro. We probably have the best pros in junior, and I think we have the best young goalies. So I think people talk about it more than it's worth. I think if you look at someone like Malcolm Subban, if he gives up a few goals in the World Juniors, some think he's not a player. You'd be hard pressed to find anyone in the world at his age to be as good as him. Maybe you find someone as good as him, maybe. But you don't find anyone that's better than him, that's for sure. So our goalies are good. We've got some pretty good goalies playing at pretty good levels."

Goldman: What do you think Hockey Canada could do better with their goalie development? The raw talent is obviously there, but do you think they need more structure? Do you have any ideas you'd like to share in terms of goalie development models or programs in Canada?

Wilson: "I mean there's a number of things they could do. I think the CHL should allow older goalies to play. Increase over-age players on the team if there is a goalie. It would increase 20-year-olds in the CHL and not for the benefit necessarily of that 20-year-old, but to stop guys that are not ready and unprepared that are coming into the league. Major-junior hockey produces the greatest players in the world. At the same time, when you do that, you have real high standards all the time. So you eat guys up and spit them out before they ever have a chance. There's a lot of guys that are out there that could have been great goalies that didn't get a chance because they came along too early. Maybe on a weak team, maybe not in the right situation, maybe immature mentally, maybe immature physically, but we do definitely not give young goalies the best chance to succeed. It's sort of the cream rises to the top, and if you're not at the top at a certain time, you're junk."

Goldman: You've coached three elite goalies from three powerhouse countries in Tuukka Rask, Carey Price, and Tim Thomas. What has that experience been like for you in terms of working with three very different types of styles and personalities?

Wilson: "It's pretty interesting because I think Tuukka and Carey were somewhat very similar on the ice and with their attitudes. Tim had this really interesting thing about him. It didn't really matter how good other players were, he was better than them. He didn't really come out and say it, and he probably wasn't, but he still felt that he was. This may have been a sign of going through all this previous stuff to get to where he did at the end, but he never became frustrated at technical things that he didn't do. Although he believed that they would make him better, he still believed he was better without them anyhow, which was really interesting to me. He'd get beat in a drill pretty easily, and not that he wouldn't take responsibility for it, but it would just be like, 'well the guy would never score on me anyways in a game, so I'm not too worried about that drill.' So his mind was kind of free from practice in a way."

Goldman: Is there anything that you feel like is kind of a trademark of a Finnish goalie, or a guy like Rask, that gives him an advantage over goalies from other countries?

Wilson: "It's probably easier if I had the chance to work with more Finnish goalies, but when Tuukka and I worked together, I got to know him pretty well due to the way our camp was structured. He left the game at the rink. When it was done, it was over. Even though we were goalies and goalie coaches, obviously when you're around each other, the position comes up. It's not like he was disinterested in talking about it, but he was more interested in not talking about it. I feel like Carey is the same way in a lot of senses. Which is huge I think for being able to clear your mind and get away from it and not worry about it."

Goldman: I know that you mentioned earlier about seeing Price when he was much younger. Earlier in the day we talked about drafting goalies and their development. What do you see in a goalie, no matter where

he's from, that tells you he has the potential to be very special?

Wilson: "It's hard to tell by just seeing him on the ice. I think you need to have some interaction with the kid and be around him a little bit, not a lot. All the guys I've had or worked with or had a chance to be around that have played in the NHL that I was around pre-NHL years, they were going to play in the NHL. There wasn't more to it than that. There was no doubt, it was like, this is what I'm going to do. That's just what they're doing, you know? It's like tomorrow is Thursday, that's just it."

Goldman: To me, I think environment and your surroundings play a huge role in the way you develop and what you turn into. What are your thoughts on that with your experience coaching goalies at so many different levels?

Wilson: "Oh, 100-percent agree. We don't all have perfect attitudes, and your environment affects your attitude. And when your attitude is affected, then your mental game, your work ethic, everything is affected. It's huge. If you take a kid that doesn't have a chance to go to the gym, but sometimes. He doesn't have great food, but sometimes he does. He's not into his proteins and he's not into stuff like that, it's his environment. You take that exact same kid, you put him in a dorm situation with all the right things, he's on the ice with the goalie coach with major structure, that goalie basically becomes a different person. That becomes their life."

Goldman: Have you ever seen or worked with a goalie that had a bad environmental surrounding, then the environment changed and he exceeded his expectations?

Wilson: "I can go back and think of a guy who went the other way in Matt Keetley. He was as good as it as it comes as a goalie, period. I've always said that and always will. I've been around some of the best goalies that are playing hockey today, and he's every bit as good as the best goalie I've worked with. Skill, talent, work ethic, focus, size, everything was there, everything. Some parts even better than the best goalie in the world today. But he was a hometown kid. He had some of that in him. If he was a first-round pick and not a fourth-round pick, the organization would have had more patience with him and provided more for him. The organization that he did go to, for whatever reason, they didn't believe in him as much as the other guy they had, who was the same age but was drafted in the first round. So they had to try and make him into a goaltender. So Matt kind of got left behind, and when things started to not go how they had the previous four years, things got worse and worse and worse to the point where he's not even a goalie anymore. It was a bad environment for a player. So if that same goalie went to another team, he would have made $60 or $70 million dollars playing hockey and everyone would know his name."

Goldman: So while you're thinking of someone who went in the other direction, what would your message be to goalies or coaches that is similar to what we've heard a lot of this week, which is goalies managing their own

game and altering their environment in order to be in their favor?

Wilson: "You have to understand that when you're going through it, no matter how bad it gets, when you quit and it's over, it sucks worse than ever. It doesn't matter if you're in Syracuse riding the bus and you're sitting on the pine and you're not playing games and your coach hates you and you're not getting a chance and you're not getting called up, and you're this close to going to the ECHL, when that's gone out of your life, you would wish you were back sitting on that bench. So you know what? Enjoy it, embrace it, and keep working. Stay with it as long as you can, push as hard as you can, and keep going. It's amazing, my best experience in hockey as a player was a chance and an opportunity to be invited to the Vancouver Canucks as a free agent at their training camp in 1998. If I could live my entire life and repeat that entire week over and over, I'd be the happiest person ever. It's amazing doing what you love. It's simply that. When it's gone, it's finished. When you're there and you're riding the bus and it sucks, it's way better than what most people are doing, that's for sure."

Goldman: Is there anything that you've picked up on in terms of European culture, or their personality that makes them more viable for having success at the pro level?

Wilson: "Well, there's less pressure on the Europeans for sure. They don't hold the NHL at the same level we do. They don't grow up with the NHL being the be-all, end-all of their life every day. It's like a Canadian playing in the Swedish Elite League. How much pressure is on them? Not as much."

Goldman: What about Carey Price's personality separates him from another quality goalie?

Wilson: "They see themselves as better than the people they're playing against. I know that Carey went to the Olympics that he was going there for one reason, to win. There's no doubt in Carey's mind. I know he got frustrated and things were really bad in Montreal, it wasn't like his career was over. There's some wavering doubt about situation, but never about himself as a player."

Goldman: We know the game is constantly evolving and you have to continually learn new things. I saw you taking notes during my presentation, which was really cool to see considering you've been an NHL goalie coach and I'm way lower on the totem pole.

Wilson: "There is no totem pole. There are double standards in hockey and some people are treated better, but I still learn from 10-year-olds on the ice watching things happen. We're dealing with things, things that happen, things that don't happen. We're dealing with people, people that have ideas, good ideas. Sometimes things that happen for the wrong reason, you find a good reason to use it in a game."

Goldman: So what do you think is next when it comes to coaching a goalie?

Wilson: "I think it's going to be about building confidence in people, and realizing that you can't set a limitation on anybody. It's just helping them push as far as possible. Dealing with kids, you think a guy can only get so good. But what kind of shitty attitude is that? For one, that's not the point of what we should be doing. Two, who knows what someone's potential is. All your job is as a coach or mentor is to give him the best opportunity to be the best he can be. If you look at him and only work on his stance and his glove hand because you're narrow-minded, you need to throw that out the window and try to find out how to help him take a huge step forward. We shouldn't limit anything in anybody."

Goldman: We had a really good discussion earlier today about development patterns and drafting goalies. What do you think about drafting goalies? Are they overexposed at a younger age? What are your thoughts on the culture of drafting goalies at 17-18-19 years old?

Wilson: "It's a challenge. The scout has a hard job and they have to do it. You have to try and find the best guys you can at the time. But I agree with you, the focus should be huge on the development side. You hear scouts say how they drafted guys and they didn't pan out, or they're flops or busts, but at the end of the day, what did those guys do to help that goalie get better? The answer is probably nothing. If you measured it, it's probably nothing. You took him to a development camp and showed him where a fork was on a plate setting, told him how to speak to someone with manners, but you didn't really help him become the best player that he could be. What do guys do about helping kids with bad attitudes? The attitude that a goalie has a bad attitude, and writing that off is in fact a bad attitude."

Goldman: There's a clear-cut culture in the NHL, especially in the USA, where it's an ass-backwards mentality for what type of support and mentoring goalies get. What do you think needs to change in terms of that culture getting better for goalies, aside from paying more money for more goalie coaching?

Wilson: "Well, you've got to have someone that can help goalies that knows what they're doing. You've got to create a system and something that you put in place that you believe in, and make it work. There's a lot of different things that work, but none of it will work if you don't believe it. So if you look at other sports that are more advanced than hockey as far as developing athletes, and I always talk about Dominicans in baseball, they can turn regular people into ballplayers. But you can go into the American Hockey League, and I've been there a few times with Syracuse and Binghamton, and another team rolls into town and there's no goalie coach out there at all, and they're playing rebound game at the end of practice and they're not doing anything. We talk about guys going out for 20 minutes before practice and getting some work in, and you can do some pretty fun things in 20 minutes, but producing goalies isn't one of them. You have to put some time into it. You have to put a system in place, and it has to be a priority. Goalie development is still not a priority. If you want better goalies, develop better goalies. There's nothing else to it than that. If you can see a kid improve in half an hour on the ice, you can see a pro goalie improve a ton in a year. Even a little bit of improvement at the highest levels as a goalie is a lot of improvement. Roll up the sleeves, get to work, don't put any limits on anyone, and go as far as you can with him."

Goldman: Is there anything else on the topic of styles in different regions...

Wilson: "Give me a name of any NHL goalie, doesn't matter where he's from."

Goldman: Craig Anderson.

Wilson: "Now give me the exact opposite goalie of him in the NHL."

Goldman: Let's see, the complete opposite of Craig Anderson would be...hmm...Jhonas Enroth.

Wilson: "And really at the end of the day, if you took them on the ice and spent an hour with them doing simple drills; beat the pass, make a save, follow the rebound, get to the post, soft focus, step out, make another save, inside edge push back to the post to finish the drill. Could both of those guys do that?"

Goldman: Yeah, but they'd look a little different.

Wilson: "I didn't ask you that yet [smiling]."

Goldman: Yes, they'd both do that.

Wilson: "So how much different are they really? If you really look at it, overall, you gave me the two biggest different goalies in the NHL, and they would have both done the same things in that drill. So really, outside of you walking through that lobby and me walking through that lobby, and just seeing our silhouettes, you would look a little bit different, but we'd basically look the same. So how much different are guys? The style is different because your body is different. Your approach to catch a puck; Quick and Price catch the puck the same way. I don't know if there's a vast difference, and that's what I said before, a small difference in goaltending is a big difference, but really, how much different is it? It's not like you have Bill Ranford in one end and Felix Potvin on the other end, where everything they're doing is totally different."

Goldman: And that's where I find myself going in circles. I see things from a pretty analytical perspective, so I see all these little things equal out to big differences, but obviously they're trying to accomplish the same thing. So I struggle to explain that. Enroth is totally different from Anderson in my eyes, but from a big scale, they're pretty similar like you said. So at the end of the day, are there big differences in regards to styles

by region, like Finns and Canadiens? I guess it's all a matter of perspective.

Wilson: "Well, they're way more similar than they are different, that's not even a question. Like if you don't get up with your back leg when you recover, basically you do, it's a known thing, no matter where you came from. There's a few guys that look a little different, but a lot of stuff is happening the same way."

16

SPEAKING WITH HOCKEY CANADA'S COREY HIRSCH

As the winter of 2014 moved along, I started hearing more about Hockey Canada's newfound mission to advance and improve their goaltending development. Similar to what I had done on my own, Hockey Canada sent a small delegation to Finland and Sweden in order to shadow their directors of goalie development (Nykvist and Magnusson) and learn more about their systematic approach to training.

This group was comprised of former NHL goalies Corey Hirsch, Fred Brathwaite, and Sean Burke, but also included Hockey Canada's Joe Birch and Corey McNab. Sure enough, it turned out to be one of the biggest moves in worldwide goalie development in the past four years.

Because of this trip, Canada's top hockey development voices learned what I learned; structure breeds success, both for the athletes and the coaches. As a result of their trip, they also witnessed the vast gap between the two worlds, enough to instantly change their perspectives and ultimately make the necessary concessions to quickly develop and implement a new Level 1 goalie coaching certification program.

It was awesome to hear about this from not only Hirsch, but from Hartigan and Sadler as well. The fact I had created friendships with all of these guys really supported my own mission, because it gave me an opportunity to continue sharing and learning from them. And by discussing a lot of these developments in this book, my biggest hope is that it will eventually help thrust USA Hockey up the same mountain, a rocky crag we must be willing to climb as soon as possible.

The more important aspect of this, as I will explain in my chapter on goalie coaching culture, is the sharing. As you know by now, Canada and the USA are quite different countries, but we share a border, and that blurs the lines between some very key pockets of goalie development, including the Northeast, the Great Lakes, and the Pacific Northwest regions. Goalie coaches often travel across these borders and train goalies in both countries, so their influences exist on both sides, and it is because of this that Canada and the United States must share information and try to work together as much as possible to build similar programs that can still successfully manage their specific problem-solving agendas.

The Canada-USA rivalry is fierce, but the only way we develop stronger goalies and goalie coaches on both sides of the border is if we're willing to share ideas and concepts and strategies. I'm a firm believer in this, and you can guarantee that amazing things are going to come out of Hockey Canada's righteous efforts to initiate a change in their goaltending culture.

That being said, getting to know Hirsch better was a way to reinforce my mission of trying to bring some structure to USA Hockey goaltending, and I'm very appreciative of his time and willingness to share what he learned in Europe. His recent work as a broadcaster may limit his role with Hockey Canada in terms of research and development, but at the same time, it increases his reach and influence in the world of goaltending.

For that reason, he's a powerful influencer and a key player in this changing game.

Goldman: I know you recently visited Finland and Sweden and got to know both Hannu Nykvist and Thomas Magnusson. This entire book is based on what I learned from those two guys, as well as many others that are involved in goalie development across the globe. But specific to your recent trip, what were your impressions about what you learned in October?

Hirsch: "You know what, Justin? The biggest thing when we went over there is that it wasn't so much what they're teaching their goalies, because we're teaching a lot of the same things in terms of technique and save selection; there's no real secret in that. But what they had that was real eye-opening was exactly what you said and saw, the structure. They had structure all the way from the time the kid was eight years old until the time they played in their pro clubs. And we have none of that over here. What we have is that a kid may not see a goalie coach until they're 11 or 12 years old, and then it's on the parent's time, and they're trying to pick and choose who's going to give their kid the best chance at being a good goalie. And none of it's regulated. So a lot of these goalie coaches that we have in North America are just making money. They're not really teaching the kids properly, and you end up with studio goalies. You end up with guys that can play well in a structured area, but when the game is on, they're not really thriving in the game. They're just learning lessons. That's something that we need to change, and in Canada that's what we're doing now, but we're five-to-seven years out from developing that. You know what else I noticed too that I spoke to Hannu about? There seems to be in North America that there's a real lack of respect for goalie coaching. We're seen as the bottom-of-the-barrel nerds of hockey. We just don't get the respect that they get over there. If we ask for a few minutes, it's just not met with respect, or it's met with sarcasm or frustration. Do you understand what I'm saying when I talk like this?"

Goldman: Absolutely. My experience was similar. I'm not a big-time goalie coach, but when I went to work with these kids in Finland, the respect they gave me as a guy they had never met before was unbelievable. Even little things like their eye contact, their focus, their ability to retain information and apply it without having to repeat myself, it was just fascinating. And that to me is what I learned in terms of the Finnish culture, the Finnish person and their personality – it's so different over there. To be immersed in their culture and see how the kids are, what did you pick up on that impressed you or stuck with you?

Hirsch: "Yeah, you know, when working with the kids on the ice, they were just sponges. They were eager to learn and they were excited we were there. And I think when you talk about the culture of it, I think that's why over in Finland and Sweden they have created a culture where, you know it's not just like shuffling goalies off into a corner and let me know when you're done, it's a whole team atmosphere. Goalies are brought in as a bigger part of the team, but they are considered special and important. I think the kids really feed off that and they were having fun, enjoying themselves, and they were just sponges."

Goldman: When you got to know Hannu better, what did you learn from him, or what did you learn about his role in Finland that impressed you?

Hirsch: "He just has a really good grasp on who all of his goalie coaches are. Finland is like as big as the state of Texas, so it's a lot easier for them to have a good handle on their goalie coaches. He knows all of his regions and he instructs all of his head people. Whereas we would have more issues with that here in North America because it's such a larger country with such a vast area to cover. So you really need someone full-time that's going to watch over all of this. There's got to be someone who is on top of all their goalie guys. So Hannu was great at directing his guys, telling him what they needed, and meeting with them. It was a planned system with structure, whereas like you said in North America, it's kind of a free-for-all, right?"

Goldman: Did you get a chance to see and look through their goalie development handbook?

Hirsch: "I did, but I couldn't understand most of it [laughing]."

Goldman: Yeah, I had the same problem [laughing]. When I met with Hannu in Helsinki, he kind of leafed through it and explained each section and I was just blown away. I had never seen anything like it. What were your thoughts after you got a chance to see it?

Hirsch: "Well what I noticed is that they have a very – again we go back to this -- a solid structure. They seem to have the proper methods for teaching goalies from young ones all the way up. So what I mean by that, is that there are certain steps at each age that goalies should go through, what they should and shouldn't learn. Finland and Sweden seem to have it right. But we're teaching our seven-year-old goalies how to backside push or post lean. That's probably not the right direction. Those kids are too little and that's an advanced skill. So they seem to have structured it a lot better than we have. I noticed in the book that there's a progression, an excellent progression to the skill development."

Goldman: What about your experience in Sweden? That's something I didn't have a chance to do, unfortunately.

Hirsch: "My experience in Sweden was a little bit different. They like more of the technical aspect. They seem to really want to be up on the technical side, and always advancing things and finding new ways to stop the puck, which was awesome. Whereas the Finns with Hannu, he was more about playing the game and being a little more athletic in that direction. But Sweden had a good system, too. They have different philosophies but the structure around the country was the same. They had one head guy, Thomas, that knows all of his goalie coaches and all of his heads, and he had people he could trust that were underneath them that would be developing goalies the right way."

Goldman: I'm pretty curious because most recently you worked with Jaroslav Halak and Brian Elliott in St. Louis, so I'm curious what you may have learned about the European goalie versus the Canadian goalie?

Hirsch: "I'd say Halak was a bit more internal, whereas Brian was more outward. He was more of an athletic and hard-working goalie, where Jaro was more of a thinker, methodical about his stuff. But I think some of that comes with their upbringing. Jaro was from Slovakia and that probably wasn't easy, because that country went through a lot of changes and so did his parents. So Jaro was a little more guarded with his approach. But Brian was here in North America and it was all about how hard he could work. The one thing I will say about Brian Elliott; I have never worked with anybody that has worked harder, and I'm not sure there's a goalie in the NHL that works harder than him."

Goldman: What about for yourself as a player. What was that experience like for you playing internationally?

Hirsch: "That was the opportunity of a lifetime, to be honest. I recommend for any player that is on the bubble or are done with hockey in North America to go over there and play. It's a life experience and there are so many good leagues over there. The Swedish league was excellent, the Finnish league is excellent, and there are some great players. We're confined to our little bubble of the NHL over here in North America, but there are some leagues around the world that are developing good hockey players. I traveled the world and played hockey. How much better can life get than that?"

Goldman: Obviously I'm really curious about the trip you recently took with Hockey Canada over the Finland and Sweden. What do you think came out of that? What did you guys learn as a whole in terms of Hockey Canada working towards some structure with goalie development?

Hirsch: "Just that we need a lot more goaltending coaches that know at least the minimal basics. That's what we pulled out of this trip. So that our younger kids, whether it be a dad or a parent, that someone is always on the ice with these kids, that there's always a goalie coach. I understand that it can't be *every* day and that's difficult, but nine out of 10 days, we need somebody on the ice with these kids that is certified by Hockey Canada that knows what they're doing. In the USA and Canada, we don't allow head coaches on the ice without some form of Level 1, 2, 3, or 4 certification. However, we'll let anybody teach our goalies. That's ludicrous and it's completely wrong. So that's really what we learned and that's what Hockey Canada decided to do. We're going to create and develop a program that, if you're going to be on the ice with these goalies, you're going to have to have some type of knowledge."

Goldman: One of the biggest things I learned this summer was this culture of sharing information. I've seen it first-hand for a couple of years now going to all these different goalie camps in North America, and it's very legit in the sense that we don't share enough and we're not as willing to share over here nearly as much as in Europe. Is that something you've experienced in Canada? Is there any way that you can break those barriers down and change the culture of sharing?

Hirsch: "You know what? You hit it right on the head with the willingness to share. It's another aspect that is completely wrong in my book. We need to share information and we need to help each other to develop goalies. I've noticed that if you're not willing to share information, it makes you insecure about what you're doing. I think if you're good, you don't worry about that stuff. You just try to make as many kids as good as you can and develop goalies. The more information we all have, the better our goalies are going to be. You never know where you're going to learn something, too. That's kind of my life motto. So if you're not going to share with somebody else and they're not going to share with you, you're probably missing out."

Goldman: So what's next for you with Hockey Canada? I'm not exactly sure what your role is, but is this something you're excited to be a part of?

Hirsch: "Yeah, absolutely. My role is research and development. So my role with Hockey Canada is exactly what we're talking about and what you're writing about. It's researching so that we can put together the best program we can in Canada so that we can develop our goalies more effectively from age eight to the age of 20, when they're ready to take the step into pro hockey. So I'm a research and development guy and do a little broadcasting right now, so it's pretty exciting times right now."

Goldman: Alright, well I really appreciate your time, and it's really cool to be able to add you to the book after your experience in Europe. I'll be honest, last year was my first year as a goalie scout and mentor with USA Hockey, and it was just mind-blowing to me how little structure there is in North America as a whole. I'm really hoping that with you guys starting to make a change, it pushes us to actually move forward with a program of our own. Kevin Reiter is an unbelievable guy, but he's asked to do everything and he's a one-man show."

Hirsch: "That's way too much for one guy. You need a guy in every area. The country is way too big for one guy. We have 500,000 registered players and at least 80,000 goalies across the country. You have to have more than one guy."

Goldman: I'm not sure if you're familiar with our structure, but with USA Hockey, Reiter is focused on working with our U-17 and U-18 goalies. Then he has three regional goalie scouts across the whole country, that's it. One is out east, one is in Michigan, and then last year I was the guy based in Minnesota. So we don't have anyone in Texas or California or Florida, and so many kids get zero exposure or support, because we only have three regional goalie scouts under the head goalie coach.

Hirsch: "See and that's ridiculous. You have to have more goalie guys involved."

Goldman: I know, and after going to Finland and learning from Hannu and Thomas, it's almost scary how massive the gap is between the two worlds.

Hirsch: "Yeah, for sure. Well if we're five-to-seven years behind in Canada, if the USA doesn't get started, they're going to be even further behind."

Goldman: I think it's wonderful that you guys planned the trip, went over there, learned what you did, and you're already applying it. That's execution at its finest. I spent the whole summer traveling and learning this stuff, and ever since June, I've been trying to knock on USA Hockey's door just to get my voice heard. We have to do something because something is better than nothing, and that's where I've been stuck for almost six months. I

hope that what you guys are doing will push us to move forward sooner rather than later.

Hirsch: "What's happened is that you guys haven't been forced to worry about it yet. You have developed some goalies that will carry you for the next little while. We're starting to see at the World Junior level where we don't have the goaltending anymore. We really only have Carey Price right now, and that's kind of what has helped put the push on us, our goaltending just hasn't been good enough the past five or six years. The US hasn't quite hit that yet, but they will, and then they'll start to get nervous, and then they'll be like us. But they've got guys like Quick, and eventually it will come to a point where they need to catch up with other countries. As Canada's goaltending gets better, then that will make a difference because that's the big rivalry. So it'll happen."

17

GOALIE COACHING CULTURE IN THE UNITED STATES

"Children must be taught how to think, not what to think." – Margaret Mead

When I say goaltending constantly evolves, it's important to keep in mind that I mean so much more than just the technical and tactical aspects of the position. I'm also talking about the way in which goalies are coached and taught. In terms of coaching here in the United States, I simply pose to you this question:

What difference do new advancements in technique and tactics make if we don't even have the right type of people coaching our young goalies the right way?

Upon being hired by USA Hockey back in September of 2014, I've wanted to help the United States, a country that still lacks the type of goalie coaching structure found in Sweden and Finland, to develop a culture where volunteers, amateurs, and goalie parents had the information and support they needed to not only better train young goalies, but actually teach them how to better think and learn for themselves.

This is my biggest frustration with the current goalie coaching culture in the USA. The way I see it, the coaching at the junior, college, and pro level is absolutely fantastic; I couldn't be more impressed. But it's at the grassroots and youth levels where the coaching culture scares me. Not only do I feel like we're devoid of quality coaches in too many growing regions (like California, for example), but the number of adequately experienced coaches simply aren't there for the sheer size of this country. The lack of structure hurts our numbers and our chances to develop more quality American-born coaches.

I must say, however, that I've seen excellent progress at the highest levels over the past decade. Even with no coaching certification program in place, former pro goalies turned coaches and other various American-born gurus have created a strong privatized industry that is thriving and becoming a more potent force than ever before. The United States may be "way behind" Sweden and Finland, but at the highest levels, it's a slim margin.

It's also only fair to mention that there are a number of Canadian-born goalie coaches working in the United States right now. This doesn't anger the American purist in me; these guys should be recognized and appreciated for their work, and I welcome them with open arms. They actually mentor and guide a lot of American-born coaches and American-born goalies that could one day become goalie coaches.

I personally never really fit the traditional mold of a goalie coach. I grew up in rural Texas playing basketball before I ever dropped a mask onto my head, and I never played hockey beyond the ACHA. It was such a different way of life as a hockey player in Texas back then. It was more of a hobby and a late-afternoon energy expellant, but it was the only thing I wanted to do with my life. So while my path to becoming a goalie coach was quite unique, as I have learned, the same could be said for so many other quality American-born goalie coaches out there.

I honestly think this is the key driving force behind the successful development patterns we're slowly starting to establish in this country. We don't have the benefit of a 30-year system in place like Finland, but we do have the sheer passion and desire to teach and take goalies to the top. For most that I've interviewed and spoken with, it seems to be born from a desire to stay involved in the game, because when these coaches were growing up, the game didn't offer them as many opportunities as they'd like.

That's how it worked for me. I wanted to become a goalie coach in large part because I wanted to help kids that suffered from similar pitfalls. I wanted to help kids that didn't have the means or the money to learn on their own. Since I was forced to learn on my own, I wanted to make sure that the kids I did train didn't just develop technical skills and move on. I wanted them to develop the mental and cognitive tools needed to learn, problem solve, and improve skills in the absence of goalie coaching supervision.

Learning from my NTDP Counterparts

In March of 2014, a few months before my lengthy summer expedition commenced, I was on staff for the annual NTDP Tryout Camp in Ann Arbor, Michigan. This camp included the top 40 hockey players in the country born in 1998, all vying for a chance to make the NTDP's U-17 team.

As a member of the NTDP scouting staff, I was responsible for evaluating 1998-born goalies in the Minnesota region. Throughout the year, I attended hundreds of Tier-1 AAA, Prep, and High School hockey games in search of the best goalies from that age group. It was an honor and a great experience.

Surprisingly, three of the six goalies invited to the NTDP tryouts hailed from Minnesota. So I was quite a busy guy all of last season, as I worked very hard to learn as much as I possibly could about those three. Dayton Rasmussen (Holy Family Catholic) was my personal favorite of the three in terms of long-term potential, but Ryan Edquist (Shattuck St. Mary's) is a legitimate NHL prospect, and Jake Oettinger (Lakeville North) had this uncanny steely resolve for a freshman backstopping a varsity high school team.

There are only three regional goalie scouts on the entire NTDP scouting staff. Aside from myself, Adam Berkhoel covered the Michigan region and Jared Waimon covered the East region. During tryouts, although I didn't get any official interviews since the book was merely an idea at that time, I spoke at length with Berkhoel, Waimon, and

Reiter, the NTDP's head goalie coach (our boss), about the current state of American goalie coaching.

All three of them had nothing but great things to say. More importantly, their feedback was not sugarcoated, because I didn't pose any questions or stir up any discussions under the premise that it was for my book. I was just genuinely interested in learning from them. As a result, their unbiased answers taught me a lot about their backgrounds as coaches and as players. That created a much clearer vision in my mind of what has been transpiring in this country over the past few decades.

One key learning point that came out of these conversations was how relatively new goalie coaching still is in the United States. I wouldn't say the culture is in its infancy (although we could argue that point), but we're still building the foundation for a purer lineage and more successful legacy that will hopefully start to grow and evolve at a more rapid rate. Guys like Warren Strelow and Mitch Korn are basically seen as the forefathers and first ancestors, forever to be revered by every current and future American goalie coach.

Because I still feel our goalie coaching culture is relatively young, maybe the only way to really start closing the coaching gap with Finland and Sweden is by experiencing a cataclysmic amount of failure with our goaltending at the highest levels (Olympics, the NHL, or the World Juniors). That's what happened in Sweden about a decade ago, and while it was bad for them at the time, it turned out to be for the greater good for all of their youth goalies. (You will learn more about this in the chapter with

Thomas Magnusson, the director of goalie development for the Swedish Hockey Federation.)

If that doesn't happen, and it probably won't since the best US-born goalies are extremely talented, some other drastic shift in the current culture has to take place. But who knows what that is, or when it happens.

Kevin, Adam, and Jared also echoed my thoughts above regarding the passion and dedication that many "non-pro" experienced American goalie coaches have, and how that has been a catalyst to their success.

Later that night, as I reflected on these conversations I had with my NTDP goalie brothers, I started to realize that goalie coaching in the USA reflected the "Wild West" archetype. It seemed to me like there were no boundaries out there, nor was there any formal certification clinic; it was just kind of a free-for-all.

But, leading up to this point, has that necessarily been a bad thing? I'm not sure of the answer, but it's one we must certainly pose. A part of me actually thinks that's quite exciting, because the potential for growth in such a big country is so vast.

Not so coincidentally, that same archetype is a perfect reflection for the typical American-born goalie. So many kids are centaurs and chimeras, wild and competitive hybrid beasts with a mix of different styles found in different realms. This extends beyond hockey and exists in all facets of our society – we're a melting pot of people and cultures. We're all mutts. That so many American-born goalies and goalie coaches have been heavily influenced by those that were not indigenous to this country is quite special.

That's America in a nutshell. I mean, who knows where I'd be if I didn't have the total freedom to just go out there and start randomly coaching goalies in a youth summer camp in Denver, and then eventually with the University of Denver Junior Pioneers. A "free-for-all" opens the doors for anyone and everyone.

Training Amateurs to Coach Properly

Over the past few years, goalie coaching culture in the United States has visibly shifted.

Instead of the focus being primarily on developing better drills and technique, the goalie coaching community is starting to lean towards educating head coaches on how to better manage and teach their goalies in team practices. In fact, I guarantee you that, if there's one thing that every goalie coach in this country hates, it's when head coaches either micro-manage their goalies or completely ignore them.

Think of all the horror stories you've heard about, or seen first-hand, where head coaches mismanaged their goalies. Think about all the nauseating tales parents tell each other about their eight-year-old getting pulled and benched for an entire tournament, because he or she gave up a fluky goal from just inside the blue line. For the most part, I think goalie coaches would agree that most head coaches, even if their motives are pure and positive, end up doing more harm than good.

This doesn't happen occasionally, it happens regularly, all over the country. This is a deep-rooted problem with the culture of coaching goalies in the USA, and the only way it changes is if we can invest money in a nationalized program dedicated to providing education and training resources for head coaches, and eventually, a goalie coaching certification program.

In fact, it's such a plight on goalie development that it's not even worth trying to scratch the surface of that topic. Even thinking about it right now makes me want to punch something.

But at least I know there's a growing contingency of high-level goalie coaches out there working day and night to make sure the head coach doesn't blindly bark orders at their goalies, mindlessly blast pucks at their head, carelessly deride them, or publicly rip into them for making one little mistake in a game.

At the beginning of this chapter, I wondered what purpose grassroots goalie coaching would serve if those coaches aren't teaching the right things in the right manner. I posed this question in an effort to help you realize that something had to be done in order to show our parents, volunteers, and of course our head coaches, that it's important to understand the difference between coaching and mentoring.

At the youngest ages, let's say from six to 10, I believe that goalies need more guidance and less rigid coaching. Of course there should be a strong emphasis placed on teaching goalies the fundamentals and the most basic skills, like forward and backward skating, catching pucks, and those all-important practice and preparation habits, but that can't be the only thing they do.

Beyond the *things* we need to teach our grassroots goalie coaches to pass down to their students, we also need to spend a lot more time and energy on the *methods* of how they should teach. We have to make sure goalie parents and volunteer coaches know that it's fine if a goalie is struggling in a certain area for a while. We have to make sure they realize that it's fine if a goalie chooses to stand up and hug the post at these ages. It's okay if the goalie wants to do things a little differently than what you're seeing from an NHL goalie. These kids are so young. Their bodies and their brains need to grow and develop.

The biggest key to all of this? We have to teach the amateur goalie coach how to allow goalies to be a little creative in the way they stop the puck, and we have to incorporate some literature on the importance of allowing goalies to learn certain things for themselves. Key cognitive skills like self-assessment, self-discipline, problem solving, creativity, and coming up with little drills without a coach spoon-feeding a goalie the answers is a huge culture shift we need to have with our grassroots goalie training.

Goalie coaches for this age group, I believe, are *not* there to be the gatekeepers of technique. They're not supposed to let certain things that they personally like through and keep certain things that they don't like out. In my opinion, they should be more like mentors and guides for developing a higher state of self-learning.

I explained this before, but "robotic" goalies come from over-coaching technique at too young of an age. Knowing this, it is the duty of high-level coaches to make sure parents and volunteer coaches do not try to coach unnecessarily. The simpler their roles are on the ice, and the simpler their messages and drills are, the more it allows the goalie to learn on their own. It should be more about supervision and less about teaching. It should be more about developing a working friendship and less about the rigid and mundane drill-rep-drill-rep system.

At these young ages, when most goalies can't process or make adjustments with a lot of the advanced goaltending techniques, time should be put into allowing the goalie to teach themselves how to correct mistakes. Point them in the right direction, but let them figure it out for themselves. Do not coddle them every time something goes wrong. Give out clues and positive reinforcement, but let them figure some things out on their own.

I think this leads to another important discussion regarding the importance of a young goalie's internal reward system. When a goalie discovers a solution to a technical or tactical problem on his or her own, no matter what age they are, there's an important feeling of reward and gratification that acts as a catalyst for further growth and enlightenment. This key aspect of athletic biochemistry is something I've already discussed earlier in the book, but it's important to reinforce it here; we need to create as many situations as possible for young goalies to experience this feeling. Goalies often don't succeed until they have failed time and time again, but the glory of problem solving on their own has similar importance to future success. The more they get this feeling of creating solutions through their own dynamic and creative thinking, the more it benefits their growth as they physically and mentally mature.

I think this reveals itself in a very special way. In my experience, so many successful American-born pro goalies have told me that they mostly learned the basics all on their own.

A Brief Look at Privatization

One of the main vehicles pushing the American goalie coaching culture forward is privatization. Both good and bad for the future of our country's goalies, aside from those who play on prestigious AAA travel or junior-A teams with part-time goalie coaches, this is pretty much the main way in-house and grassroots goalies are being trained.

From top to bottom and coast to coast, you will find private goalie companies popping up everywhere. It's nice to see that the list is growing, but that doesn't necessarily mean the quality is rising. Without a national certification program in place, anyone can create an LLC in their home state, design a logo, suddenly call themselves a goalie coach, and start churning out camps and clinics. Some of these guys have more experience and natural coaching skills than others, but there's no way to weed them out or force them to go through any sort of nationalized training.

This free-wheeling format has benefits and negatives. On one hand, we need all the goalie coaches we can get, even if they're not the highest of quality. On the other hand, bad coaching destroys potential talent. Coaching is also becoming more important in the goalie industry than ever before, which means the costs associated with private coaching continues to rise, which limits the reach.

Because high-caliber goalie coaching is hard to find outside of the American hockey hotbeds, coaches can charge more. I've seen some guys charge up to $120 an hour, or charge outrageous rates for video analysis and coming out to work with a goalie at their team practice. Furthermore, the best goalie coaches in the country are so limited by their time that they don't get to work with many goalies during the course of a season.

In fact, after looking at American-born goalie coaching at the highest levels and studying their lineage, I learned that only six of the 50-plus NHL and AHL goalie coaches are American-born. That list includes Mitch Korn (Washington Capitals), Bob Mason (Minnesota Wild), Chris Terreri (New Jersey Devils), Bob Janosz (Buffalo Sabres), Mike Dunham (New York Islanders), and Mike Buckley (Pittsburgh Penguins).

From that list, Korn, Janosz, and Buckley all own private companies. From there, aside from Arturs Irbe (Sabres) and Olaf Kolzig (Capitals), the rest are Canadian. That statistic needs to change, but how will Americans take that next step?

This is a tough question to answer. I can easily rattle off five or six Americans that could coach at the AHL or NHL level (Dave Caruso was an assistant goalie coach with New Jersey until the start of the 2014-15 season), but that position may not be appealing to those individuals. With such a rigorous game and practice schedule, it takes a lot of dedication and hours to fulfill all of the tasks that pro-level goalie coaches are expected to handle, and the money is not that great. So it's a labor of love, and that can be a hindrance to those who can make more as private goalie coaches with other side-careers.

But again, faced with these issues, and knowing that high-level American-born goalies have done an outstanding job amidst those obstacles, I'm always pondering and piecing out potential solutions.

There's a laundry list of things we could do to help our current contingency of American-born goalie coaches get to the next level. But I think the most important thing this country could do falls within the NCAA rulebook. If the NCAA could find a way to allow goalie coaching to be a full-time paid position for all D-1 and D-3 programs, the face of American goalie coaching would greatly improve. Privatization would still dominate the landscape, but at least there would be a place for goalie coaches to be groomed for the pro level, while alleviating some of the financial pressures that come with being a volunteer goalie coach under the NCAA's current rules.

Speaking on the topic of privatization, I have put a lot of thought into this going beyond goalie coaching. Maybe there is a place for companies to offer goalie coach training.

Now that The Goalie Guild is officially a non-profit 501-c3, as opposed to a for-profit DBA under my old company (The Hockey Guild, LLC), I have a new mission statement. That mission is to support and guide under-educated and under-privileged goalies *and* goalie coaches. I added goalie coaches to the end of that mission statement because I believe I could make a difference by working with youth associations all over the country to train volunteers and parents to act as basic goalie coaches for their in-house teams.

In fact, I spent about a month working with Dave Rogalski on a program that would have accomplished this very thing. We laid out a plan where associations would hire us to come in and work with the head coaches and any volunteer goalie coaches to implement a plan that catered to the proper development of goalies. It included age-specific drills that could easily be run for 5-10 minutes at the start of a practice, as well as an Excel spreadsheet that helped team managers track their goalie's training progress. It included a section for game warmups, regular practices, and then an individualized pre-game routine. Every time a goalie accomplished their requirements for each section, the team manager would check it off on the spreadsheet. Once a certain number of checks were collected, goalies would earn some sort of reward.

By rewarding goalies for following through with their training requirements, it would not only force them to accomplish key elements of goalie development, but it would create and reinforce good habits. This is the culture we live in today; we may have to create a tangible rewards system for both goalies and coaches for doing things that should come naturally. But if it works, and if it's viable enough for youth associations to buy into the idea, it's good enough for me.

Maybe I'll be able to bring that type of program to life once this book is published. Maybe I can earn some grant money and invest it in programs that support goalie development for youth associations in non-traditional hockey markets like Phoenix, Tampa, Nashville, or Salt Lake City.

As the prominence of hockey grows across the USA and the importance of proper goalie training rises, so too will the costs. That is simple economics, and there's not much that can be done to change this. If USA Hockey is unable to establish or implement the proper protocols or basic coaching certification programs internally, they may need to rely on private companies to help create or install these programs for them.

Rogalski and I have already laid out a blueprint for this type of program, so it's just a matter of pushing forward and getting youth associations to buy in to the concept that they can stop outsourcing their goalie training to private coaches. Instead, they can integrate an all-encompassing development program into their association, which produces better results and alleviate some of these higher costs.

Privatization may always reign supreme in the USA, but if we can move beyond just offering high-priced private lessons and week-long summer camps and help associations help themselves, we can eliminate some of the pitfalls we face, including the reach of the top coaches and the size of the country.

A Look at Coaching in Different Regions

As you know, the sheer size and breadth of the United States brings a number of key obstacles to consistent goalie coaching and development. But just like you find in other countries, there are different regions and pockets of influence where goalie coaching is more plentiful than others.

I've looked at the numbers, both on a national scale and through my own research, and I believe the state of Minnesota is arguably the most saturated area for goalie coaching in the USA. Just in the Twin Cities area, you'll find Zach Sikich from ProHybrid Training, Justin Johnson from

Mega Goaltending, the entire Pro Goalie Development staff, Dave Rogalski, Steve Carroll, Robb Stauber and Jeff Hall from Stauber's GoalCrease, Des Christopher from The Goalie Club, Ryan Ess from Devenir Goaltending, Pete Samargia from Attitude Goaltending, and a countless number of high school, D-III and Minnesota-based junior goalie coaches like Elliot Hogue, Adam Houser, and others.

I lived in the Twin Cities for two years, (from August 2012 until the end of this past summer's expedition) so I can tell you from experience that the Minnesota region is extremely unique in terms of its goalie coaching culture. Having also lived in Texas for 18 years, I can honestly say that Minnesota high school hockey is the same as Texas high school football. In both states, their respective sports are life.

I'll never forget the time I spent soaked in the pure passion of Minnesota high school hockey. Lines out the doors of small high school rinks, packed to the rim with people that don't even have kids on the team or in the school. Scouts from the CHL, NCAA, and NHL at every game. Players getting interviewed by major newspaper reporters before and after games. Girls screaming for their boyfriends like they were at a Justin Bieber concert. Tons of potential and drama. Huge egos. Plenty of politics. Insane parents.

Even when I would go play drop-in hockey (sorry, it's called "pick-up" hockey in Minnesota...oh, and goalie pants are "breezers" up there, too), I was blown away when I would hear guys talking about midget or bantam AA tournaments. Forget the Wild, forget the Stanley Cup

Playoffs. In Minnesota, the average middle-aged rec hockey player is talking high school and midget AA hockey with the rest of the guys.

Only in Minnesota.

Another interesting aspect I learned regarding Minnesota is the "bubble" of goalie coaching. With so many goalie coaches in the region, very few goalie camps outside of the local ones are capable of thriving. Try as you might, you will find no GDI, no FuturePro, no Jon Elkins, no Elite Goalies. In fact, aside from a couple of smaller Canadian Pro Goalie Schools (CPGS) camps and one summer camp run by Mitch Korn in Duluth, you are not going to find any out-of-state goalie camps in Minnesota.

Even Korn's camp has met resistance in the Twin Cities. My first week living in Edina back in 2012 took place the same week Korn held his camp at Braemar Arena. But that would be the last year, as he was unable to get enough goalies to register to make it a viable location. In Duluth, however, Korn would draw as many as 40 goalies from as far west as Alaska and as far east as Florida.

Turns out, there are just too many goalies that already have their local in-season and summer goalie coaches or camps to make any out-of-state programs viable. So almost all of the goalie coaching in Minnesota is indigenous, native to the state and localized almost exclusively in the Twin Cities area.

I thought it was really interesting how a living legend like Korn could struggle to get numbers in Minnesota, yet there were so many less-qualified goalie coaches out there filling camps on a regular basis. Obviously there were a number of factors at play here, but the disproportionate allocation of numbers was more about the culture of Minnesota goaltending than anything else.

Up there, I don't think it's a stretch to say that more emphasis is placed on the experience a goalie coach had during his high school years than anything else. If you were a varsity goalie and became a coach in the area some years later, you were more likely to draw students from all over the state. I don't mean this in a bad way, but if you played varsity high school hockey in Minnesota, you're revered and respected regardless of where you played after that. If you didn't, or if you're a transplant from another state, even if you have more experience than the native, nobody seems to care who you are or how well you coach.

Minnesota is one end of the goalie coaching spectrum, but here in Colorado where I currently live again, you find the other end. Goalie coaching is at a premium in the Denver Metro Area, and outside of Denver, it's essentially non-existent. In Colorado, there is a very dim spotlight on high school hockey, there is no junior Tier I or Tier II hockey, and there are not enough rinks to support enough goalie camps or private companies. Good ice is very hard to find, and if you do find it, you have to charge more to cover costs.

In my entire time living in Denver after graduating from CSU in 2004, I may have come across three or four "legitimate" goalie coaches. Timm Lorenz and Mark Sample (In The Crease and GDI), Sean Savage (my personal goalie coach, but now retired), Joel Weeks (Big Bear Ice Arena) and a few others come to mind, but that is pretty much it. Maybe you had one or two guys up in the mountains, but it's such an isolated region that you can't rely on anything outside of the occasional camp in Vail, Aspen, and Breckenridge.

There's literally nothing west of the Continental Divide, either. You have Grand Junction, but that town has been without a rink for a few years due to mechanical and financial issues. So everything is centrally located in the Denver Metro area and Colorado Springs.

Sample is the most recognizable goalie coach in Colorado, but he's an extremely polarizing one. He represented GDI for a very long time and likely carries the torch for coaching the most goalies in the Denver Metro Area. Unfortunately, I have heard many stories about his methods and on-ice personality not meshing well with many parents and players. So I learned he is the type of coach you either love or hate, which was disappointing, because he had one of the biggest influences on goaltending in the state.

The other problem that faces goalie coaching culture in Colorado is the lack of junior hockey. Once a goalie coach reaches the AAA level with a team like the Pikes Peak Miners or Colorado Thunderbirds, they have nowhere to go in Colorado to play Junior-A hockey in the USHL or NAHL. I know that Colorado does have a WSHL team, but Tier-III junior hockey in the USA is not viable for the type of growth that could develop future pro goalie coaches.

And while a handful of more reputable goalie camps will hold satellite camps in Denver (Eli Wilson and Rick Heinz are two examples), it's simply not enough for sustained goaltending development in the same state that USA Hockey calls home.

If only Francois Allaire held his summer camps for the average youth goalie throughout the summer.

This dry well of goalie coaching in Colorado is actually how someone like myself was able to develop the skills to become a quality goalie coach. There were so many coaching opportunities at the youth level in Denver that, even without a Level 1 head coaching certification from USA Hockey, I was hired as a part-time employee of the University of Denver recreation center. I would spend 10-15 hours a week coaching goalies during team practices for the Junior Pioneers youth hockey association, despite only coaching goalies in a couple of summer hockey camps.

If not for the opportunity to work with goalies at DU, I may never have found the confidence or gained the experience needed to eventually become the organization's head goalie coach. Without spending all those hours on the ice for more than three years, I wouldn't have discovered my passion for mentoring and scouting. I may have never even considered starting The Goalie Guild.

From saturated states like Minnesota and Michigan, to barren states like Colorado and California, you basically end up finding the deepest pocket of goalie coaching in the Northeast. I've never lived there and have not had a chance to soak in that culture, but I have attended some camps in New York and Massachusetts. I did research a ton about the pockets of influence found in Boston and even more non-traditional areas like Charlotte and Maine, but for the most part, it's an area that is still pretty new to me.

I know that many quality coaches exist in that region, like Chris Economou in Philly, Shane Clifford in Pittsburgh, and Buckley as well. Martin Biron is the head goalie coach at HARBORCENTER in downtown Buffalo. Brian Daccord dominates Boston and surrounding areas, and his goalie coaches are all very solid, working with numerous college and high school prep teams.

Clearly, the East Coast is in a world of its own. A lot of the top goalies in the country develop into NCAA prospects out East. The prep hockey scene is as massive as it is strong, and there is a lot of quality junior hockey in that area as well. The goalie coaching is more plentiful and more connected than you will find in any other area of the country, especially due to the dense population in terms of hockey numbers and the distances between programs.

In fact, whenever a parent or goalie approaches me and wants advice on how to be recruited for a college scholarship, I tell them they need to go to Minnesota, Michigan, or somewhere on the East Coast. That's where the college programs do most of their recruiting, that's where the showcases are being held that have the most success, and that's where a college scout can drive a few hours and hit three or four junior or AAA programs in the same day if they wanted.

Another benefit of living in the northeast is the close proximity to Toronto and other areas in Ontario. This presents a much wider array of playing and coaching opportunities that obviously don't exist in the southern areas of the country. There is one perfect example of a goalie that grew up in the northeast as a duel citizen, but leapfrogged many other goalies in his age group thanks to an opportunity in Ontario.

Stephen Dhillon is a 1998-born prospect that was on our radar very late in the 2013-14 season for the NTDP. Although I never saw him play during the season since I was based in Minnesota, he had received some interest from Waimon and Reiter. With five goalies 'locked in' for an invite to the NTDP Tryouts in March, we needed one more goalie to round out the group of six. Dhillon was that sixth goalie.

With very little expectations for him to compete with the other five goalies in camp, the 6-foot-2 duel citizen lumbered his way into the mix, exciting scouts outside of USA Hockey. These scouts were invited to watch tryouts, which surprised me considering how much the NTDP covets the information we procure when viewing our native prospects.

Dhillon did not earn a spot on the NTDP, but he definitely raised eyebrows during tryouts. He did enough to get selected by Niagara in the third round of the OHL Draft later that spring. One door closed, but since he lived in close proximity to another high-end junior league, he was drafted, recruited, and ultimately placed in a position to succeed with Niagara.

That's simply part of the game. As much as it helps to know the right people, you have to either live or work your way into an area where those people can see you more than once. If you live in Florida, sign up for a camp in Minneapolis. If you live in Arizona, travel to Boston for a camp.

While this is certainly not an extensive in-depth look at scouting and exposure influences by region, it's safe to say that the densest areas in terms of goalie development can be found in the upper Midwest and the Northeast.

But as you continue to populate the United States with more and more goalie coaches, you start to notice that, without a goalie coaching certification program, every coach is isolated in their own realm. It's easier to network in areas like Minnesota and New York, but if you live in an isolated area, you're left to research everything on your own. Very few resources are provided for you, and there are very few shoulders to lean on for help and guidance in the realm of developing goalies.

It also must be noted that a lot of the goalie coaching you'll find in the United States is influenced by Canadian coaching. This is not a bad thing, because we don't have the volume or the quality of purebred American coaches to be picky. The lines are already quite blurry between Canadian and American styles, and since we're brother countries, there has to be open sharing on both sides.

I've spent so much time over the past five years building friendship bridges with goalie coaches all over Canada. From Eli Wilson in Vancouver to Marco Marciano in Montreal, there are goalie coaches who I love talking to and learning from, all while building a relationship in an open and free environment.

If you're researching goalie coaches in Anytown, USA, you don't have to go far until you find one with Canadian influence. Steve Briere from Canadian Professional Goaltending Schools was teaching in Alabama of all places before he moved to Minnesota and took over the head goalie coach position at Northern Educate in the Twin Cities.

Sean Savage, a Canadian who played professionally in Europe, was the goalie coach that taught me everything I know as a player from 1999 to 2001. He was living in

Colorado at the time, was a goalie coach at PuckStoppers, and helped me tremendously after moving away from Texas.

This train of thought could go on for pages and pages. Goalie coaches living in America that were raised with a Canadian influence, where goalie coaching has been much more prominent and substantial over the past few decades.

This part of the American goalie coaching culture will never change, and it's worth embracing due to the fact it incorporates and cultivates so many different types of coaching and training methods.

The Importance of Adaptability

Ultimately, I came to the realization that goaltending and goalie coaching in the USA is a true melting pot. Styles, coaches, influences, lineage, playing experience – we're all splashed on the map together like a Jackson Pollock painting, and because of this country's size, it's not going to change anytime soon.

This is why I feel one of the most important elements an American goalie and goalie coach can have is adaptability.

Adaptability is when a goalie can adjust or transform the way they play or learn whenever their situation or environment changes. And since goalies and coaches in America move around from program to program way more often than in European countries, this trait is a must-have. Furthermore, since so many coaches have so many different methods (some wildly outdated), American goalies must be willing to learn different ways of executing similar types of positional and technical strategies.

If you're developing with an open mind and you're willing to work with anyone at any time regardless of who they are or what their experience level is, I honestly believe you will go further than those who are close-minded, or those who only choose to work with elite-level goalie coaches a few times a year.

For me, being adaptable was easy, because I had no other choice. I was just lucky to have someone willing to work with me. I soaked up everything from everyone, because I never had the luxury of choices when I was younger. I couldn't afford to be picky. This alone made me more successful as a professional, and when I reflect on it further, I realize I have rarely been close-minded in the realm of goaltending.

As a whole, I've come to terms with the fact that American goalie coaching culture still lacks an established, clear-cut identity. We are not like the Finns, the Swedes, or even the Canadians. We are the amalgamation of everything, both in the way we learn and the way we play. We're amorphic matter. But at the same time, the beauty in all of this is that we are free to be whatever we want to be.

How is that for being truly American in shape and form?

So through all I have experienced and all I have learned in my many years researching goalie coaching culture in the United States, I've learned that this country is very much a true reflection of that "Wild West" archetype I mentioned earlier. Just about anyone with playing experience and a passion for goaltending can go out and find a youth organization and call it home, and that can open the door for the uncovering of hidden gems (both goalies and coaches).

As I made my final conclusions for this book, I came to the realization that, as much as I respect and appreciate this environment, this country still needs to institute a change at the lower levels. We must provide some sort of basic certification or training for our aspiring and volunteer coaches so that the youth goalies and organizations, the ones that need the most help, will receive it. And while it could eventually eradicate the "Wild West" approach that makes this country so unique, if we do things the right way, we can still allow passionate pioneers to blaze their own path.

Instead of doing it all on their own, we'll be able to provide them with the basic trailblazing tools needed to create their own coaching style. I want to live in a country that can inject confidence into parents and people that have a zest for goalie coaching, but have never done it before. I've been there; I know it is daunting. I know that you first start out wearing blinders – you don't know what the proper developmental process looks like. I know that it takes time for those blinders to come off. But I was able to remove mine thanks to an unquenchable thirst for learning, and thanks to some key American mentors and coaches that assisted me when I needed it the most.

Able-bodied goalie coaches with a passion for making kids better in the right manner is a very powerful weapon, but that weapon won't fire unless it's loaded correctly. You also have to make sure the safety is off, and that means breaking down barriers. That's what I hope we can begin to instill into the culture of goalie coaching in the United States. I want to breed more intelligent head coaches and volunteer goalie coaches early enough in the process that their students can eliminate bad habits and develop a dynamic mind that allows them to go off and teach themselves.

At the same time, I'm really excited to see that, as time goes on, we're slowly economizing, industrializing, and evolving in a way that will hopefully establish a purer, truly "American" identity.

I think that's the greatest joy that comes from imagining and potentially realizing a Level 1 goalie coaching certification program. There's a basic structure to be had, but it would still allow passionate goalies and parents to roam freely into the thick of the things, and over time, with some basic guidance, they can be steered in a direction where they are doing more good than harm for youth goalies across the country.

At this point in my life, there's no sweeter dream than this, and I hope USA Hockey will one day allow me to be a part of the solution.

18

JACK HARTIGAN ON GOALIE DEVELOPMENT MODELS

Jack Hartigan, founder of ***FinnGoalie*** in Nova Scotia, was born in 1988. He's almost six years younger than me, but for some reason, when I finally met him at the GoaliePro camp and spent a week with him in Helsinki, he quickly transformed into the older brother I never had.

I think a big part of this was due to his coaching and playing experience. Jack was a pro in Finland for a few seasons with Varkaus and Warkis, two teams in the *II-divisioona* league. Forced to retire prematurely due to injury, almost overnight, Hartigan established himself as one of Canada's top goalie coaches by infusing the progressive Finnish development methods into his own North American training styles.

Astute on the ice and a great teacher for both the young goalies and the NCAA and pro goalies at the GoaliePro camp, his real wisdom came with his understanding of goalie development models. His work in creating and formulating advanced goalie development models has, for more than a year, been followed and recognized by Hockey Canada. He's not only an integral member of the board of goalie directors responsible for producing the country's new Level 1 goalie coaching certification program, but he's also currently working on restructuring and regionalizing Hockey Nova Scotia's goaltending development.

From the moment we met, Jack's support and guidance has been nothing short of amazing. Not only does he reflect the true nature of an egoless goalie coach, but he has chosen to help me without any request for money, exposure, or any other self-glorifying perk. He sees beyond the veil of 'country versus country' and takes a global approach to the evolution of the goaltending community.

I've never met anyone that had made such an influence on goaltending at such a young age. Having followed him on Twitter for over a year prior to actually meeting him in person, I always thought he was an older guy, or someone in his 40's. If you were to speak to Jack, he'd be the first to say that much of his knowledge and success stems from, you guessed it, Ropponen and his GoaliePro coach mentoring program. Such is the bond that tie the two guys together, and how great it is to call both men friends!

It wasn't just Jack's goaltending IQ or his playing and coaching experience that made him seem well beyond his years, but it was his ability to strategically build his ideas piece-by-piece day-by-day, and then implement them in real-time. To have these ideas is one thing – to actually put them into place and bring them to life is quite another.

That's where I focused most of my time with Jack during the GoaliePro camp. It only took a few days for me to realize that, due in large part to how I admired and looked up to Hartigan, my passion was quickly moving towards developing ideas that would become a similar model for USA Hockey.

After the camp ended, I leaned heavily on Hartigan when I finally decided to start creating that imaginary model on my own time. For this support, I'm eternally in his debt.

Jack and I had an awesome time hanging out together away from the rink. We shared tons of stories, cracked a lot of jokes, and enjoyed many succulent meals together. The newfound friendship we created, and the ensuing manner in which we've been ping-ponging ideas off each other, was a microcosm of the most significant lesson in this "Between Two Worlds" adventure.

In the game of life and in goaltending, like I said in the book's introduction, it's not what you know and what you do with it – it's who you know, what you learn from them, and how you treat them. It's about relationships. Treat relationships well and your ideas and dreams can truly come to life.

Goldman: Before we discuss your proposal for restructuring and regionalizing goalie development in Nova Scotia, can you start by giving me an explanation of your current role and duties beyond running FinnGoalie Training?

Hartigan: "Basically, I'm looking at restructuring the entire minor hockey program for goaltending. Right now we don't have a program that exists. There's no structure in place for minor hockey that provides information to goalie coaches and goalies. So right now, I'm submitting a proposal for a brand new goaltending program that covers everything from developing goalie coaches within associations, to placement and structure of goalie camps within each region, to a high-performance goalie program where we track and develop our top goalies that were identified through our tryout camps. My current involvement with Hockey Nova Scotia right now is that I help the province with their high performance program alongside another goalie coach named Bob Mayo, on the male side. So we train the goalies when they're available at the high performance camps, which are the tryout camps in the spring time, and then a weekend HPP goaltender camp, and then a week-long training camp in August, where the teams are selected for the U-14, U-15, U-16, and Team Atlantic events. I also coach with Hockey Nova Scotia at their Spring development sessions, where the majority of the U-14 through U-16 goalies come to train two times a week for two months. I also volunteer with various HNS programs that involve goaltender coaching, like Atom development sessions, or Hockey Day in Canada's outdoor goalie sessions."

Goldman: What inspired you to put together this type of proposal? How did it come to be?

Hartigan: "I essentially put together a proposal after years of playing and studying in Finland. I saw first-hand the positive effects the established program in Finland had on grassroots and national-level goalies and thought there could be a way to bring a similar program to Canada. I've been looking really closely at how Finland has established regional goaltending leaders, minor hockey program leaders, and how they interact with the country's head of goaltending development. There are eight regions in Nova Scotia, but it's not that big of a province; Halifax has about 350,000 people, and then there are rural areas where the population really drops off. Goaltending in Halifax is really good right now, with a few really great goalie coaches, but the rural areas are getting left behind in terms of quantity and quality of the coaching. The structure I would like to see for most provinces would break down like this: three head goaltending leaders for the province, a 'Head of Goaltending Nova Scotia' for development programs, one male 'Head of Goaltending' for our high performance programs, and one female 'Head of Goaltending' for high performance, coaching the U-15, U-16, U-17, kind of like your National Team Development Program [NTDP]. Then you have your eight regional leaders, which forms a board of 11 trusted goalie development leaders. Now there's 34 associations in Nova Scotia, so I'd like to see 34 minor hockey head development goalie guys mandated, even if they have little goalie coaching backgrounds."

Goldman: Are most of those 34 associations based in Halifax?

Hartigan: "Probably one-third of them are in Halifax, maybe around 10. My association is the biggest one in Nova Scotia and I'm responsible for 100 goalies, so we have almost 40 teams in our association. I'm able to do this much work, because there are four rinks in the facility for the whole association. I go to work at three-o-clock in the afternoon and do a goalie clinic for each age group, then go around for each team's practices, watch games, do early-morning practices, go away for tournaments to scout, and so on. I have another volunteer goaltender coach named Alec Murphy helping me out, especially with our novice and rec programs. That's what I do during the season in terms of minor hockey development within one association. This was all made possible by Bedford Minor Hockey's coach technical director Shawn Mackenzie, who brought me in five years ago when my hockey career was done. He was a former NHL and AHL goaltender himself, so he knew the importance of having a goaltender development system in place."

Goldman: So you'd want one of these mandated head guys in each association in Nova Scotia?

Hartigan: "Yes, so there would be around 45 goalie leaders for the province of Nova Scotia. These leaders would be the first wave of coaches to be trained by Hockey Canada's new program, which is coming out soon. It would be a good starting point to have information passed on to any and all interested in goaltender development. In July [2014], we had a goaltending symposium, which was a three-day event that included top goalie coaches and keynote special guest presenters like Jukka [Ropponen], who helped create Finland's original goaltender program. We also had Ted [Monnich] speak on mental Training, Dan Kerluke from Double Blue Sports

Analytics, John Alexander from Alexander Goaltending in New Brunswick, and Kyle MacDonald from Hockey New Brunswick. It was held in conjunction with our high performance goaltender camp, so our top goalies were training all weekend. Our targeted attendees were all current goalie coaches in the Nova Scotia area, or anyone interested in becoming a goalie coaches. We had a total of 26 coaches attend, seven high-level goalie coaches who presented, six junior or pro goalie mentors, and 20 provincial level goalie coaches, male and female. And why? We're trying to educate goalie instructors, goalies, and hockey personnel on the position. We want to share resources, network, and discuss training methods and ways to improve the position throughout the province."

Goldman: That's awesome stuff. And you said during the symposium, you also held a camp. Was this part of your restructuring and regionalizing proposal?

Hartigan: "This was our development weekend, so it was in conjunction with the symposium. So it was also a three-day training event for kids that made it through the Spring combine. There were six goalies selected from our U-14, U-15, and U-16 camps, forming 18 goalies, which is a perfect number for a goalie camp in my opinion. They were all able to go on the ice at the same time and train together. I mirrored it off Hockey Canada's Program of Excellence camp, which is the equivalent to your Warren Strelow camp. Then, for the proposal, I was looking at year-round tracking and development of our top goalies. I want to track and guide them and keep up to date with them, see what they're up to every week, see how they're training, and making sure they're doing it properly. Summer development would include off-ice training and on-ice recommendation. So we'd get to see them four or five times over the summer. There's also an in-season development section to the proposal, where we talk about having the goalies come together for a weekend to make sure they're up to date on everything, maybe bring their goalie coaches along if they're around. The next part of the proposal is talking about doing clinics and camps under our own goaltending Nova Scotia program. The idea would be to have clinics in different regions, making it like a tour, and in each stop you link up with the regional leader. He puts the shooters and goalies together and then I come and help to reinforce our ideas and make sure the camp is being run correctly. We'd team up and come up with new ideas and we'd find ways to make it cost-effective so the association pays for it, making it as cheap as possible for the kids. Most of the time the associations are willing to put in the money to do this once a month, or once every few months."

Goldman: Would you or do you already have something available online as a resource? I know that's one area I'm working on with USA Hockey, trying to get their goaltending website updated.

Hartigan: "I actually created an online resource library, much like the IIHF's resources in Finland right now, with videos on goalie training, drill printouts, manuals, coaching tips, a goalie handbook. I have an example of the Swedish version, and then the coach's technical package, which is for your normal team head hockey coach, so he has some info on goaltending as well. I am just working out a few kinks right now and should have it all launched soon."

Goldman: This is very impressive work. So you really have created a program that is all-inclusive and gives a province or region like Nova Scotia everything they need to develop goalies at all levels.

Hartigan: "That's the goal. The proposal has everything in there, it is very detailed and includes the entire skeleton, including drills for both on-ice and off-ice training, equipment info, certification levels, goalie coaching development sessions and seminars, which is another thing we're looking at doing. That would include general annual meetings, which would be two-to-three times a year for all 45 goalie coaches in the Nova Scotia program. Implementing goalie coaching programs for in-season development, making sure a goalie coach is on the ice for one or two practices per-week, including one goalie-specific training clinic per week, one off-ice goalie training session per week. Goalie coach attendance at all home games with post-game feedback, in-season progress report cards, goalie-specific pre-game warmups, post-game stretching, video analysis and breakdowns. So every goalie at the minor hockey level gets that. It doesn't matter if they play A, B, or AAA-level, they all get it, so there's all an equal playing field each year. As a result, we've seen guys that have gone from like a Bantam-C level to playing Major-Midget, because they've been given this opportunity. Sometimes they just play very strong, because there was nobody placing the goalies properly, so I'm able to identify the potential and our team of evaluators at the beginning of the year know there's an equal playing ground and an equal chance to develop. This takes a lot of the politics out of the equation, and while there will always be politics, it definitely helps to have this system in place. It's better than having a goalie company come in and just pick their own kids."

Goldman: Since this program is so unbelievably comprehensive, can you think of anything else involved that we may have missed?

Hartigan: "Yeah, some other stuff we looked at was improving our novice program by getting kids at that age more excited to become goalies and trying to get the parents more turned on to it. We have a goalie gear swap-and-sell program, where we have a flea market twice a year where everyone brings their gear and swaps it, or buys and sells it. There are 150 goalies in the program and kids grow out of their gear, so we find ways to recycle and save the parents more money. We implemented Yoga into our off-ice program, focused on educating parents, and put more focus on year-round off-ice training. Those were goals we had last year when this came out, and we've checked off all of them, so they're all done."

Part 2: Catching Up with Hartigan, November 2104

Author's Note: *During my Thanksgiving holiday, I spent every minute of free time typing up the rest of the hand-written chapters*

I compiled over the summer. I also caught up with Jack again, because I knew he was deeply involved with Hockey Canada's new goalie coaching certification program. It was amazing to see the progress he and his counterparts had made in such a short amount of time, and while I was a tad bit jealous to see how quickly things had been happening, it was further proof of Hartigan's strong work ethic, solid experience, and the deep knowledge base needed to create solutions to some pretty big problems. Below is the conversation we had on November 30, just one week after he attended a key Hockey Canada goalie advisory board meeting in Toronto.

Goldman: So I know a lot has happened in a short amount of time with your new goalie coaching certification program. What can you say about the progress Hockey Canada has made since the summer came to a close?

Hartigan: "I think that weekend in Toronto was a religious experience for the goalie coaches involved. The advisory board that went over [to Finland and Sweden] is a great group of guys and they're all on the same page. They really saw the light when they were over there, so it was definitely a worthwhile trip for them. For guys like me and Travis Harrington from Behind The Net – guys who have been over to Jukka's camps, and where I've spent so many years already – it's definitely a different perspective for us. The hardest part will be properly implementing the programs in each and every region, because of all the private companies out there. The coolest part is that all of the branch members basically have goalie companies, so the networking we did there was a lot of fun. There's a great mix on the advisory board. Having guys like Pasco Valana is great, because he's involved a lot in minor hockey. Then there are coaches like Corey Hirsch, Freddie Brathwaite, and Rick Wamsley, guys who bring in their high level of goalie playing and coaching experience. They've got a good mix going on there."

Goldman: How do you plan on certifying and training the Level-1 goalie coaches? Are you providing the information online? Is it an in-person clinic?

Hartigan: "At this time I'm personally unsure of the start date of the program and its official release. But from my understanding, in order to be trained, you need to have an hour-and-a-half of on-ice instruction and an hour-and-a-half of classroom session instruction to be Level-1 trained. So we're looking at probably doing events where you sign up for the weekend, you come in, and you do your hour-and-a-half on the ice. We would be out there explaining everything with a couple other goalie coaches, like how to do everything, showing the content in the Level-1 session with demo goalies. And then the classroom session would basically be explaining and teaching them that content in the Level-1. We already had 20 volunteer goalie coaches from different associations come to the convention six months ago [see part 1], so that gave us a great platform to possibly deliver such a program down the road."

Goldman: Interesting.

Hartigan: "Another big thing that they're looking at doing is licensing goalie schools. When it comes out, a reputable goalie school will be able to get licensed as a certified Hockey Canada skills school, so people will know certain goalie schools are teaching the proper methods. They know we're teaching basic levels. This will allow Hockey Canada to recommend schools for kids to train at. You may have those knuckleheads out there that are running goalie schools that may refuse to support the National Program, but this will help get everyone on board. Kind of like your CoachTracker map on your website, schools could be up on the Hockey Canada website as recommended goalie schools to attend."

Goldman: That's great. I wish USA Hockey could get something going like this. And you mentioned that a Level-2 is already in the works?

Hartigan: "The Level-2 that we're doing is more for experienced goalie coaches. So it's kind of like for guys at our level, and it is way more advanced and more into the tactical and save selection side. The Level-3 is going to be really tough, more like a Master's. You have to do like an on-ice, year-round tracking system. There wouldn't be that many Level-3 goalie coaches across Canada. Kind of like your high-performance platform. So that's a basic overview of what we're up to."

Goldman: You said the experience in Toronto was kind of religious. What did you learn or what did you guys do that made it so special?

Hartigan: "I think the main thing was just having 20-plus goalie guys together. A lot of us had already interacted on social media before or coached at various camps and events, but to meet all of them and all be on the same page and literally talk goalies for three days straight was pretty cool. We all had our laptops out there, sharing videos and different things that we've been doing on the ice. Having some of those bigger goalie coaches there, like Hirsch and Brathwaite, was really awesome. To have a chance to pick their brains was awesome; it's not very often that you get to sit down with an ex-NHL goaltender and NHL goalie coaches. I really enjoyed when they were giving us some group tasks. For example, I was teamed up with a goalie coach named Anthony Stapleton from WhiteHorse [Hockey North]. He was in my group and our subject was clear shots. So there's 10 different scoring chances, and we were tasked with explaining how to get set. Then we swapped our task with the other smaller groups and they would add their two cents into the same task. So then we put it all together as a large group, looked at the results, and continued to do a ton of drill sharing and stuff like that."

Goldman: You guys have made so much progress in such a short amount of time and you guys are already pushing out the Level-1 and working on the Level-2. You kind of know where I'm at with USA Hockey and how I'm trying to get into the same room with guys making the decisions.

What would your recommendation be for USA Hockey in terms of trying to take the same steps you guys are taking?

Hartigan: "I think right now the biggest thing is that Corey McNabb is the guy facilitating the whole meeting, and he's not a goalie guy at all. He's the Senior Manager of coach and player development for Hockey Canada, so he was the key piece to the whole thing, because he was basically relaying everything we were doing back to Hockey Canada. He's so high up there that he was really involved with the whole thing, and so he knows exactly what is going on. So for him to push this program and help us launch it was the key part. So you're going to have to have somebody like him advocating whatever you create. Then you need to look at creating an advisory board and selecting your branch guys. So you need somebody in USA Hockey that is able to throw their weight around a bit in the office, get you some funding, and bring all of your goalie guys together for a weekend to start making plans. I think the biggest thing is just figuring out all of the different challenges. Like we have with our provinces, you guys will probably have that in all the states down there. Every state is going to have their different challenges in getting these programs set up. Some of the provinces in Canada just have logistical issues, like there's just some places that have many hours between towns. There are other places that have so many goalie schools in a small areas that everyone's on different pages instead of one unified system."

Goldman: Yeah, like your guys' Toronto is kind of like our Minneapolis. The area is so over-saturated with

goalies and goalie coaches with private companies. But you go west of Denver and east of Los Angeles, it's very, very sparse.

Hartigan: "Yeah. The biggest problem is that every province has their individual challenges, but there are provinces where guys are waking up and asking what they're doing with the long distances and guys are coming up with different ideas and that's why getting together is so important. So it's just getting a general idea of what areas need help where, what challenges you're facing, and understanding the differences within each area. You have the New England, Michigan and Minnesota with a lot of goalie coaches and guys getting good training, right?"

Goldman: Yeah. The Northeast, Minnesota, and Michigan. Also there are more and more goalies coming out of California even though the goalie coaching is pretty sparse and spread out. And we're trying to cover an entire country with one head goalie coach and three regional goalie scouts within the NTDP. So we have literally four goalie guys and a bunch of volunteers.

Hartigan: "Every province has their trusted goalie guys that they can send to these meetings, on both the male and female side. They send goalie coaches to our Canada Games, so all these goalie coaches in Canada are getting together and we're sharing ideas all the time. I was at the Atlantic Provincial Tournament two months ago, and there were three other reps there from Newfoundland, Prince Edward Island, and New Brunswick. We were all sitting together watching our goalies but we were giving each other pointers and helping each other with our goalies. So we already kind of have that network setup where I don't think in the United States you have the kind of unity we have within our provinces."

Goldman: We have great coaches, especially at the higher levels, but you're right. There's very little unity. I think for the most part, guys want to join forces and work together on a National scale, but there's nothing in place for us to get together and share ideas and build up a program.

Hartigan: "Basically what you have to look at are the big challenges that each state is going to face. We had this great weekend and we all got together and made all these great plans, but the hardest part is that some provinces are going to have a harder time getting that information out as easily as others. Getting it into every minor hockey system and getting enough goalie guys to go out and teach this stuff properly. So that's what I wanted to talk more about. I'm going into my fifth year with Bedford Minor Hockey, and that's how I've learned how to implement a goaltending system into a minor hockey association. If you can't do that, all of this is useless. If you can't actually get everyone to buy in to having one goalie guy working with all the teams year-after-year as these kids grow up, and teaching them this stuff in line with the manuals, it won't work. The problem with the private goalie companies is that they will go train one or two practices, but they won't see games because they're running around doing the same thing with a bunch of other associations. It's almost like you have to have the regional leaders. In Finland and Sweden, the regional leaders are reporting to the provincial leaders, and they report above. So you have to set it up and say, OK I'm the head of Colorado. Who is on my team? Who are my regional leaders? Who has the south side of Denver? Who has the north side? Who is covering the mountain areas? That's the whole idea, and that's when you have a team of guys that are involved in minor hockey in Colorado. It's like a pyramid. How are they going to pass information up the chain of command? The regional leaders is the biggest single thing in this whole concept."

Goldman: And you think this type of regionalization can work here in the United States?

Hartigan: "If you can get USA Hockey to name a head of goaltending in each state and then name your regional leaders, then yeah, you're definitely making progress."

Goldman: I'm doing everything I can. I have to start at the very beginning and try and get guys above Kevin to get into the same room as us, so we can just lay out and explain the whole situation to them. I know this book will help expose a lot of this stuff to anyone who reads it, but it's a totally different ballgame trying to get USA Hockey to invest in goalie development or goalie coaching development. The more I talk to guys like yourself and Hirsch and Ropponen, the bigger that mountain seems. But I have the support of all these goalie guys in Strelow and USA Hockey though, so I think it's just a matter of time. It might take a few years, though.

Hartigan: "It's probably going to take four or five years to really get things going. The biggest thing we were trying to stress at the meeting in Toronto is that we need to picture ourselves as if we didn't know anything about the position. Imagine if you were going to a clinic on Cricket, because I don't know anything about Cricket. I don't know the rules or how to hold the bat or anything. That's how we have to make this program – like goaltending for dummies. There are parents out there that could be from other countries or have never seen a hockey game before. Some will still want to go out there and try to help their kid be a goalie, so if they have a basic manual to help them with the basics, they're going to learn it before age 10. Then the Level-2 coaches can take over from there, and then the Level-3 guys can take over when the goalie gets to major-junior or the junior-A ranks. Then you just have to build a system of placing goalie coaches appropriately, just like they have in Finland and Sweden. So your Level-1 is simple stuff like angles and stance; you could probably build a Level-1 in a few weeks. It wouldn't take too long."

Goldman: Yeah, I get that. But for us, it's all about getting approval or funding to actually build and implement it across the country.

Hartigan: "If you look at Sweden, the biggest thing you can use is to look at their goalie summit after the Olympics with Tommy Salo. They held that summit and re-did their goalie program, in the past 10 years, they've had unbelievable results with the draft picks, and that's just within 10 to 12 years."

Goldman: Yeah, one of the coolest parts of my summer was meeting Thomas in Madison and getting to learn all about his work in revolutionizing Sweden's goaltending culture.

Hartigan: "Yeah, that's right. I forgot you were down there with Thomas and Hannu."

Goldman: I was very fortunate to be there. It was a great end to this crazy summer project, especially after everything I learned in Finland. I hope this book gives readers a much better understanding of the current landscape of goaltending development around the world, especially in the four big powerhouse countries. It should kind of show how North America is pretty far behind in some ways, and how Canada is currently taking the necessary steps to make the change like Sweden did. I hope it somehow sparks USA Hockey to start their own revolution.

Hartigan: "USA Hockey has a really good high-level program with the NTDP. Your best goalies are getting the proper training."

Goldman: Yeah, it's pretty amazing what the NTDP has been able to accomplish lately. We have great goalie coaches involved in the Warren Strelow program, and Reiter is doing a great job in his first year as USA Hockey's head goalie coach. But there's no system for the lower-level guys to thrive, prosper, or grow, because there's no national grassroots standards in place.

Hartigan: "That's the biggest thing – you need a program where everyone is teaching similar stuff. That's where USA Hockey is ahead at the highest levels. But over time, you need to invest in the youth programs. The other thing to remember is that these are cost-effective programs, because you're educating volunteer goalie coaches. That means parents and goalies won't feel the need to go to year-round goalie schools or camps and invest so much in private coaches, because they're getting the support they need through volunteers at the minor hockey levels. Or the youth associations are paying goalie coaches more often to come in and do the work, which saves parents a lot of money over the course of a few years. Training is the biggest expense for goalies right now, and you'll always spend money on that over the summer. But getting volunteer goalie coaches that teach the right things at the right time at the youth levels is the biggest advantage programs like this can bring to countries like ours."

19

GARRET SPARKS AND THE GGSU LEGENDS CAMP

I first crossed paths with Garret Sparks shortly after he was selected by the Toronto Maple Leafs in the final round of the 2011 NHL Draft.

Back then, aside from knowing that he fit the mold of a typical Francois Allaire pupil, I knew next to nothing about the lumbering and lanky kid from Elmhurst, Illinois. I had seen a few YouTube videos and had read a few articles about his tenure with the Chicago Mission program, but other than that, as it usually goes for players drafted 190th overall, he was pretty much an unknown entity.

For that reason, I was curious about him. Maybe it was the sudden and speedy rise from AAA hockey to playing with the Ontario Hockey League's Guelph Storm, or the fact he was an American playing juniors in Canada, or his hidden and fast-tracked path, but either way, he intrigued me.

So I reached out to him a few days after he was drafted for a profiler interview on The Goalie Guild. Turns out, there was an incredible amount of depth and intelligence to his answers. Not that I didn't think he was a bright kid, but I guess I just didn't expect it from someone who was still so young and impressionable.

Since that interview, which took place way back on June 30 of 2011, I have watched Sparks develop into a very keen professional athlete. He has faced numerous physical and emotional obstacles over the past few seasons, and despite all the pitfalls and setbacks and uncontrollable situations, I can tell you that he's one of the most approachable and happy-go-lucky pro goalies I've ever met. Even during times when I knew he was struggling, every time I talked to him, he was still very much a kid at heart. And that's not an easy demeanor to achieve in a rabid and cutthroat hockey market like Toronto.

When Sparks reached out to me last year and told me he was creating a goalie camp specifically for members of the GGSU Facebook group, I thought he was crazy.

"Dude, you're in the AHL, playing the biggest hockey games of your life. The last thing you should be doing right now is trying to run a goalie camp," I thought. "You need to focus on your game."

It was not my right nor my position to ever say something like that to his face, but that's what I thought at the time. Even if I did respectfully say something to him as a mentor, it wouldn't have mattered. It was something he had set out to accomplish, and nothing was stopping him. He wanted to give back, he wanted to support the strongest online goalie community in the world, and he wanted to open doors for tons of kids that had the same dreams and aspirations.

Sure enough, just a few months later, not only was I impressed that he was able to pull it off, but I was desperately trying to find a way to attend the GGSU Legends Goalie Camp. I didn't want to miss it.

The GGSU Legends Camp started the day after I returned from Finland, so even though I miraculously made it without collapsing, I was somewhat of a zombie for the days I was there. It was really important that I made it; I had actually worked with Sparks to raise money for a friend of ours, Ty Ulmer, to attend the camp. Ty is a cancer survivor who was forced to amputate his leg in order to survive. While recovering, Ty fell in love with hockey and goaltending thanks to the Idaho Steelheads and their goalie at the time, Tyler Beskorowany.

Even with a prosthetic leg, Ty never gave up on his dreams of being a goalie. That's how he first became a member of the GGSU community, and shortly after that, everyone in the group had rallied around his amazing story. It didn't take long for us to raise the money we needed to send him to the camp. I was so inspired by his story and his perseverance that I also took Ty under my wing a bit and befriended him. I paid for his hotel room, rented a fun car for us to drive to and from the rink in, and made sure he had the time of his life. Ty is just one of the many GGSU members that bring their passion for life and goaltending to the table on a daily basis, so it was impossible for me to not want to get involved and help out.

Like Ulmer's story, the GGSU Legends camp was anything but traditional. But as a result, it was extremely powerful. It proved without a shadow of doubt that perfection is not needed to obtain results. All you need is a welcoming environment where goalies can learn from each other in a free and friendly way. In terms of a camp's structure, however, it seemed like everything I had attended over the past few years was the typical "coach-student" setup, where an older guy with a specific idea of how he wants to train and develop talent brings in a bunch of goalies and puts them all through the same learning experience.

After Sparks wrote his piece below and sent it over to me, we reflected on his path and the influence the GGSU Legends camp had on the goalie community. I asked him to write something for the book, because I wanted people to learn what I did while I was at the Seven Bridges Ice Arena in Chicago. I wanted people to see that the coaching and training culture in America is quite an unbridled but very potent environment.

During our conversation, Sparks said something that really struck me. Amidst all of the complexities I had uncovered and researched regarding goalie development during the writing process, he unintentionally reminded me that free will was way more powerful than any revolutionary technique or training method.

"No one realizes that pro hockey players come from the same place that beer leaguers come from," Sparks said. "It's just the choices they make along the way that makes the difference. I was playing AAA hockey five seasons ago. What did I do during those five years to get to where I am, and why can't everyone do it? That's my message to kids who say it's out of reach. Like, oh yeah? Why?"

Whether it was a natural inclination or a conscientious decision to change his attitude, Sparks chose hard work.

And it was this unique quote that was spread through his actions during the GGSU Legends camp.

In a traditional goalie camp, if an older goalie coach says the same thing as Sparks, the message isn't as piercing or as poignant to a group of ambitious dreamers. But stick a popular 21-year-old AHL goalie in the room with no older chaperones overseeing the camp, and every camper listens. They hold each other accountable. They all want to be mature leaders, and that causes the bullying and cliquish defense mechanisms to disappear. It's a really positive learning environment.

At the beginning of this chapter, I mentioned how I knew nothing about this random seventh-round draft pick. But for some reason, I was still really drawn to him and his development path. Was it just the sense of the unknown that reeled me in? Probably a little bit.

After getting a glimpse of his playing style and background, I realized that the guy affectionately referred to as "Dictator Sparks" in the GGSU household was the prototypical American-born goalie. He was a self-made man that didn't have a goalie coach until he was a little older, so he thrived on bold ambition and creative intelligence. He was also willing to make sacrifices and commitments that most kids wouldn't.

Sparks and his two trusty pro goalie companions that helped him run the camp – Scott Darling (a man who I hope writes a book about his incredible story someday) and Mike Condon – proved to me that goalie community forms the most beautiful and eclectic subculture in sports. We not only play a very intimate position compared to skaters, but we have totally different perspectives, belief systems, and approaches to daily life.

It is this special subculture that has the capacity to create such a robust environment, one where pro goalies in their early to mid-20s can work with aspiring younger goalies without any older adult supervision and still produce amazing results in a week-long summer camp. Regardless of skill level or age, everyone was on the same level. I was one of the oldest guys there, but I did not have any more authority than anyone else. I was not there to teach technique, I was there to give feedback and to learn. I was there to share my experiences, to make sure the environment was as positive as possible, and to help out wherever it was needed. We were all students, we were all teachers, and for those few days, we were all loving brothers and sisters. We all had the best intentions for one another in mind.

Overall, despite the fact I was exhausted from my trip to Finland, the GGSU Legends Camp was an unbelievably fresh and revitalizing experience. It made me realize that so much freedom and creativity can flow when goalies are teaching goalies. Everything is accepted – playing styles, gear, ideas – and nothing is disregarded as being wrong, but rather as an alternative method.

As someone who is obsessed with creativity and development patterns in athletes, "goalies teaching goalies" is such a beautiful thing to behold. Not all camps can achieve what GGSU did, but I honestly believe the peer-to-peer dynamic may be more beneficial for a kid's development than the more traditional coach-to-student dynamic that dominates the current landscape.

The sheer empowerment that each goalie – the pros and the pupils – gained during the GGSU Legends camp was almost medicinal and mind-expanding in form.

I can't wait for the next GGSU Legends camp. I am dying to experience that same empowering feeling again. With the dynamic that Sparks, Darling, and Condon were able to create, I feel like their lure and youthful experience could establish a new lineage of peer-oriented camps. Furthermore, all three guys perfectly reflect that "Wild West" archetype of living the American dream, and it's impossible for young goalies to not be drawn to that same intoxicating and confidence-boosting energy.

A Personal Reflection by Garret Sparks

Author's Note: *Below is Garret's reflection on his development path, and why he created the GGSU Legends Camp. A special thanks to Sparks for taking time out of his busy schedule to write a few pages on his experience growing up outside of Chicago and playing junior hockey in Canada with the Guelph Storm. It is a really good example of what American goaltending is all about, and why the culture is more than capable of thriving despite the lack of an established goalie coaching certification program.*

My story starts during the winter of 2000 just outside of Chicago, Illinois in the learn-to-skate program at the Elmhurst YMCA. A little ice rink nestled next to a neighborhood gym, I had skated there all winter learning a game I already knew I loved.

My dad played men's league as a goalie and passed it on to me. I watched the powerhouses of the 1990s battle on ESPN and we made regular trips to the United Center and Jerry's Hockey Warehouse. I had sticks and pucks and jerseys all over the place, every night. I was fully immersed in the flashy side of the game from a young age, and I loved every bit of it.

As the final practice before the last days of the winter season ended, the coach called for two volunteers to play goalie at the following week's year-end scrimmage. Nobody answered. So he called again. You never think the decisions you make when you are seven years old are going to change your life forever. But from the first moment I volunteered, I haven't left the net.

To this day, I still don't know why I raised my hand. Maybe I was curious. Maybe I wanted my dad to be proud. Or maybe goaltending was just in my blood and like it or not, it was my destiny. Regardless of what it was, I'm now 15 years removed from that decision and I'm currently playing pro hockey as a prospect for an NHL team. I can't complain with how things have gone; there are good days and bad days, but for the most part, it has been a smooth ride. Looking back on my road here, compared to so many others, it hasn't been too hard.

I played for three minor hockey organizations in Chicago: the Blues, Team Illinois, and the Chicago Mission. I was fortunate enough to have played on exceptional teams in all three organizations. All but two seasons of minor hockey ended with an Illinois State Championship.

From a goaltending perspective, my minor hockey career was picturesque. Playing on high-end teams afforded me the opportunity to face the best players my age every day at practice, which made me a better goalie and taught me how to win from a young age.

As far as goalie-specific training goes, it was pretty hit-or-miss in Chicago. A lot of the AAA programs had people that would come out once a week if I was lucky, but there wasn't really an overload of instructors around. I used to take private lessons occasionally with Kelly Gee, who coached in the USHL for a bit, but outside of making an effort to find a capable coach, it wasn't a readily available resource compared to a city like Toronto.

When I started to get into my older years of minor hockey, I would go out with the younger teams and volunteer my time with the goalies, because I knew how exciting it was to have someone come teach you something when you're trying to figure out the game all by yourself. It was after being able to help other goalies with their game that I decided I really enjoyed the coaching aspect. Discussing things and simplifying them for someone trying to learn even helped me out with my game; it encouraged me to think critically about what I did in net.

While it was nice to win games and be on good teams, as I got older, I realized it became more about who was seeing you play. Kids my age were committing to high-end Division-1 colleges, and I watched from the sidelines. I always played hockey for fun and solely because I love it, but I did want to take hockey as far as my skills would let me. I always dreamed of playing college hockey, and that's why I couldn't help but be frustrated when my name wasn't called during the USHL Futures Draft.

Shortly after, I was taken in the OHL Draft and my mindset quickly changed. Guelph selected me and made me a priority. They frequently checked in on me, seeing how things were going while I finished out that last AAA season in Chicago. They sent scouts to watch me play and reported back to Mike Parson, who was Guelph's goalie coach at the time.

We ended up finishing that last minor hockey season with a National Championship on home ice.

I remember answering a phone call in high school a few days later from my head coach, Anders Sorensen. He told me that a lot of USHL teams were interested in drafting me, but I told them not to bother – I was signing with Guelph.

As soon as that happened, my hockey world changed. I was now officially playing hockey as a contracted player. I was a 6-foot-2 goalie weighing 230 pounds, yet none of it was muscle. Up until that point, I got by on skill and minimal effort. But that would never fly in the OHL.

So I got to work that summer and whittled my way down to 204 pounds before main camp, just to give myself a fighting chance. It was hard work, but hockey was all I had ever known and I wasn't ready for it to end. I was lucky enough that Guelph's goalie coach had seen a short clip of my play from the season prior to getting drafted and liked my playing style.

Finding a goalie coach that I meshed with was something I first experienced in Guelph with Mike. Without his support, I wouldn't have made it out of junior hockey. I showed up to camp as the third-string goalie to a 19-year-old returner and a Czech National team import selection, Matej Machovsky. I played three full games prior to Christmas, two of which came because the coach had no choice but to play me due to an injury in warm-ups and a one-game suspension for fighting to starter Brandon Foote.

My OHL intro was a baptism by fire, but Mike taught me a lot and went to battle for me often early in my first season, pointing to my hard work as evidence for an opportunity to prove myself. I treated practice and warm ups as my games, impressing just enough for Guelph to trade Machovsky in December. As a result, I started an additional 15 games after Christmas, which was enough to get selected in Round 7 of that year's NHL Draft. From there, I started another 120 OHL regular season games before making the jump to pro hockey with the Toronto Marlies and Orlando Solar Bears.

As I said, I can't complain with the way things have gone thus far. I'm a 21-year-old goalie prospect playing in a tough league against good players with a lot of good people looking over me. I get to start a lot of games, and in those games, I face a lot of high quality scoring chances. It is everything a goalie prospect could ask for. I also see a lot of goalies my age playing at higher levels, and while part of me is jealous of the success they're having, I'm really happy with the way my game is coming along.

There's no shame in taking your time to develop.

For the most part, I've been on the fast track, moving from AAA hockey to the AHL in just three seasons. Being able to play as often as I do is a luxury not many goalie prospects my age get. I have had a few injury setbacks this season, which contributed to my demotion to the ECHL, but as I continue to figure out the professional aspect of the game down here in Orlando, I honestly feel myself becoming a smarter goalie every day with the help of Toronto's goalie coach, Piero Greco.

Piero is the goalie coach I wish I would've had at age 15. His views on the position have changed my game dramatically. Being able to take what I learn to practice each day is a tool I'm not sure a lot of goalies know how to use, so it really makes me appreciate the benefit of having a quality goalie coach.

Being a pro goalie has also afforded me the opportunity to work with some of the most well-known goalie coaches in hockey. Being able to draw parts from all of the interesting ideologies of specific coaches and the things that they consider the most essential to the position is an opportunity not many goalies get.

For the most part, that is what inspires me to be so open about my career path. I'll talk about any aspect of it, because I am just a normal kid, all grown up, playing a game I love. I haven't had to do anything too crazy. It's been long hours and hard work, but if you truly love it, the work you put in isn't really work at all. There's injuries, and you miss things you want to do, and there's strained relationships with people you really care about, and it can be a bit of a circus sometimes, but if you can find a way to block all of that out, your love of the game will take you very far.

I took things to the point where I started my own goalie camp last summer. It was the brainchild of a Facebook group I'm involved with called *Goalie Gear Sluts United.* Our desire to become a bit more multi-dimensional in the goalie community has quickly led to it being the premier place to go for any and all goalie-related gossip on the internet. No matter what time it is, there's never a dull moment on GGSU.

The group is a collection of 15,000 like-minded goalies that love the position and the gear that comes with it. Because of this, we decided to put on a summer camp for our members to come together for quality goalie instruction. My goal was to give people who truly love the game, no matter their level of skill or age, an opportunity to maximize their potential.

From the 15-year-old AAA prospect – a kid I once was, just dreaming of a higher level of hockey – to the 40-year-old beer leaguer trying to work on his movement, goalies get coaching from some of the best young pro prospects in the game, including Scott Darling of the Chicago Blackhawks, Mike Condon of the Montreal Canadiens, and myself.

We then enlist the help of our offensive-minded buddies from the AHL, ECHL, OHL and NCAA to shoot on our goalies, a luxury most camps can't provide. While our camp is definitely more of a "country club" attitude than many of the other major goalie camps out there, we pride ourselves on the work we put in and the fun we have. The young kids get worked out hard every day on ice and in the gym, learning proper lifting techniques, key areas of focus for strength and stability, as well as nutritional seminars and daily warm up and recovery exercises. And while we wouldn't expect many recreational goalies to want to go through that routine for five straight days, we work heavily on warmup and recovery practices to help them play as long and as pain-free as possible.

In addition to the quality instruction, we also have a variety of interesting guests in the goalie community in attendance all week. We have a major retail sponsor in Total Hockey as well as gear reps sent to camp by CCM, Reebok,

Warrior, and this upcoming summer we will have Bauer as well as Passau. We try to provide resources to goalies that they may not otherwise have access to. We watched video cut from some of the NHL's top goalies best games last year. Being able to watch an NHL goalie under the microscope in a room with 20 other goalies and dissect it is something many have never gotten to do. We provide gear demos for goalies to try new things in on ice situations. Even facing pro shooters is a luxury for the students.

We had some big names out with us last year and I only anticipate better shooters showing up, especially this year in Pittsburgh. Last year, Justin was kind enough to join us for a couple days as well and spread his wealth of knowledge throughout the camp.

So the idea is to really continue to build the camp into a fun and educational environment that goalies everywhere know about. We always have a great week and I'm looking forward to two more great ones this summer in Chicago and Pittsburgh.

I try to instill good habits into all of the goalies I work with, and try to act as a mentor as well. But aside from the technical advice, I want to leave you all with an important lesson I learned when I was younger.

I want you to know that if you fall in love with the position – if you dream about it, if you design your dream pads in your free time, if you think about how much you'd love to be strapping them on as you sit on a boat in the middle of your lake on a 90-degrees summer day, if the position is in your blood and there's just no real explanation for it – you have what it takes to make it in hockey.

20

AMERICAN GOALIE DEVELOPMENT WITH DAVE ROGALSKI

I first met St. Cloud State goalie coach Dave Rogalski a few months after I moved to Minnesota back in 2012. Having known of my pursuits over the past five years, Dave graciously invited me out to breakfast one morning in order to talk goalies at a little place in St. Louis Park called Good Day Café. When I walked in, I suddenly felt like I was in a rustic north shore cabin. It was encased in authentic wooden panels dotted with paintings of picturesque lakes and birds flying across pale gray skies.

Instead of seeing a guy in a warmup jacket or a track suit, I found a guy that was close to my age, wearing a faded navy blue baseball cap, a sweater, and blue jeans. One part avid hunter and two parts family man, Rogalski seemed like just another one of those good ol' Minnesota boys.

Like most of the people I met during my two years in Minnesota, Rogalski was extremely friendly. He clearly had no ego, and he didn't look like the type of guy that felt like he had to show the world he was a high-level NCAA goalie coach. We quickly became friends during that breakfast meeting, and I think it was due in large part to the fact we had a mutual respect for one another. It didn't take long for me to realize he was in it for the right reasons, and vice-versa.

A few weeks later, Rogalski allowed me to come out and watch him work with Tampa Bay Lightning prospect Adam Wilcox and Boston Bruins prospect Zane McIntyre. Together, the two of them melted the ice, ripping through a bunch of drills on a small 3-on-3 rink. It took me less than five minutes to realize that these guys were pro-level goalies in the making, and as I watched Rogalski work with them on some key fundamentals, I came to realize that he had the making of a pro-level goalie coach.

I also appreciated his passion for new ideas. Over the next year, we would meet a number of times to discuss different plans for different goalie development programs. We even successfully ran The Goalie Guild's first-ever Scouting Clinic in the summer of 2013. This one-day event included six goalies working together with Dave and myself on that same 3-on-3 rink in St. Louis Park. We were also joined by Joe Howe, Alex Fons (University of Minnesota-Duluth) and Josh Robinson, who was in the ECHL at the time. These six goalies not only got high-level training from our awesome little coaching staff, but we brought a handful of iPads on the ice in order to give them instant video feedback. Following the event, I also wrote a full one-page scouting report on each goalie and posted it on my website, which helped them gain more exposure.

That event was unique and fun, and it really showed me just how committed Rogalski was to making goalies better. The ideas kept flowing, the admiration between each other grew, and that's why I chose to interview him about American goaltending way before most even knew I was writing my second book.

To me, Rogalski represents a lot of what currently defines the American goalie coach. Talented enough to be one of the top 100 in the world, but without a structured system in place, his voice is usually lost in chaotic mix with so many other intelligent, enthusiastic NCAA goalie coaches.

Still, he fights with fire in his eyes to develop the best goalies in the best way he knows how.

Goldman: Right off the bat, I want to know how you'd define an American goaltender.

Rogalski: "I would say if you look at every elite American goalie like Jimmy Howard, Jonathan Quick, or Ben Bishop, Ryan Miller, Alex Stalock, Craig Anderson, they're all different. You can't define them as one specific group of goalies, because they're unique in their own way. Even Bishop at 6-foot-7 stands up to make saves from time to time. Howard's hand positioning is different from Quick's, and their post integration is different as well. I think the number one thing about American goalies is that they're completely themselves and then they slowly refine their skills from there."

Goldman: So are you saying that they might take a longer time to get to the top of their game?

Rogalski: "Yes and no. It takes 99.99-percent of all goalies a long time to get to the top of their game. How many Carey Price's in the world are there? One, that's it. It is rare to see young NHL goalies become starters right out of juniors or college. It takes time and that's okay. I do think the American goalie has a different outlook. Their competitiveness is so different that they will do whatever it takes to stop the puck. That gets them to a level where they can develop their game further. If a pro scout sees they are competitive and a true athlete, American goalies will get chances to develop. It's just a matter of if they can or not. One thing that can hurt them is if they go to a goalie coach that tries to transform them into something that they're not, and not letting them actually reach their full potential through being their unique selves, which actually got them to that point. Let's not forget that the turtle wins the race, not the hare."

Goldman: So do you think it's good that American goalies, generally speaking, may work with a lot of different goalie coaches that likely teach different styles? That's what I notice, that a lot of American goalies cross paths with a variety of coaches, and while they're basically teaching the same things, they have different definitions and a different lexicon to explain the same thing.

Rogalski: "We've had this conversation before, and I'm not sold they work with that many different goalie coaches. I think there are a lot of claims in the goalie world. I wouldn't say two to three goalie coaches in a career is a lot. I don't consider a one-time, one-week camp as being that goalie's coach. It's just one week – not even 60 or 70 or more hours with a kid. This is a whole other book, an ugly side of the business. When it comes to teaching, I want to believe that 75-percent of the teaching done in America is very close. I don't want it to be all on the same page, but I want the approach to be the same. The difference in the elite goalie coach is that they don't hold their kids back, and that's the biggest difference. They give them tactics, hold them accountable, give them honest feedback, and show them video instead of giving them ultimatums. They just work within that kid's game."

Goldman: At St. Cloud, you've worked with many different goalies from many different countries, like Finland, Canada, and the USA. You've experienced working with these guys at the same time, too. Specific to those guys, what can you tell me about the similarities and differences in styles?

Rogalski: "Well, I hate to throw a wrench in it, but Mike Lee [Arizona Coyotes] is more of a Canadian goalie than Ryan Faragher [Anaheim Ducks], and Ryan was more of an American goalie than Mike."

Goldman: So why do you think that is?

Rogalski: "Well, Ryan didn't have a goalie coach until he got to the junior and college level. So he kind of throws a kink into things, but Mike had training for a while. Mike is tough because he's a very smart goalie and very fundamentally sound. Getting to Rasmus [Reijola], he still catches pucks and scoops up every puck. I don't know if it's from not playing baseball, but he scoops at pucks. So it just takes a while to understand what he's doing every time you see it, because it's the most unique way of catching pucks that I've ever seen. When I first saw it, I was like, why are you under-handing pucks like a Jai-Lai player? But I'd say Adam Wilcox, Zane McIntyre and John Gillies are prime examples of an American goalie. They all have the foundation of recovery, their post work is within their style, and even though they play very differently, they play their game."

Goldman: A casual hockey fan would probably watch Wilcox and say he plays like Jonathan Quick, which is a fair comparison in my mind, but there's very few goalies that have that type of athleticism and can play that way. So I don't think it's apt to say that American goalies are like Quick, because so few can actually play that way.

Rogalski: "I respectfully disagree. A lot of American goalies are like Quick. They're unique, none are the same. If I'm an NHL scout or coach, I personally wouldn't care where the goalie is from. I think we are producing some of the NHL's most elite goalies right now, but not all, and no one country will ever produce all of them. No one will dominate the league from just one country. Yes, per capita, kudos to Finland, it's amazing, but they have a league where they can really develop Finnish goalies. There should be more guys coming over from there, honestly. I believe most American coaches think staying on your feet is really important. But when it comes to the game, we understand that if the kid goes down, we just want to see proper seals and a proper butterfly. Yes, I am a butterfly guy and I love the Reverse-VH in certain situations, but you need to be patient and trust your feet. That's how you get from Point A to B with the most accuracy. But we always want them to work in practice and in training on footwork, whereas in some other countries, a lot of it is how you move on your knees, especially in Sweden. Every picture I see from a European goalie coach right now is teaching the RVH. Whether that's right or wrong, I don't know."

Goldman: This is what intrigues me. You start with a really broad view of what makes a goalie in a specific region unique, but then when you think about the goalies you actually work with, you notice that the generalities disappear at the individual level. So I think American goalies do not have a specific identity at all, which begs the question whether or not that's a good or bad thing. Should USA Hockey implement a coaching system like what Finland and Sweden has?

Rogalski: "It is 100-percent a must-have. I feel like we're going to fall behind if we don't work on incorporating a structured goalie coaching program. But, the fine line is not training or teaching a certain style. Instead, you're coaching and working with the goalies and giving them guidance and letting them know it's OK to fail. We're not pigeonholing them into one style, but giving them the attention they need to develop their own style. USA Hockey has done a phenomenal job with the Warren Strelow program, but if we want more, we need a goalie development program. That comes down to just standardizing very fundamental things we believe in, but also preaching to coaches to let the handcuffs off and just go out and play. So when we get a volunteer coach that doesn't know the position, tell him he's getting 15 minutes per practice solely on goalie training, then for the other 45 minutes, just let them go out and have fun. At the squirt, peewee and bantam level, this is super basic stuff that doesn't cost an arm and a leg, but stuff that helps coaches to develop fundamental awareness. It's not reverse-VH or back-side recoveries; we're focused on teaching coaches how to implement simple things like tracking pucks, catching pucks, or just having coaches take 150 shots to the hands each day and focus their attention on coaching some of the more simple and key basics of technique. It's the biggest hole we have right now. If it sounds crazy or elementary to just have 150 pucks shot at a kid's hands to get warmed up, believe me, I know. In Minnesota, there are ton of goalie coaches, yet I know there are a ton of kids that get absolutely zero attention. Our state needs to do better and we haven't done anything to improve it for many years."

Goldman: The way I explain it is that coaching has become a big business because they're trying to make a living in a situation where they shouldn't rely on coaching amateur goalies to be their sole income. So teaching technique becomes more of a marketing tool instead of guiding or mentoring young goalies for the sake of sheer

development. So goalies at a young age don't get the mentoring, they just get information thrown at them.

Rogalski: "I started coaching when I was 16 and I'm 34 now, so I've seen it all in the last 18 years. Our state has some great guys, but we don't work together, and that's ok. Where I have an issue is when the 'Post Load' or VH is tagged as one man's own business. Changing the names of a save selection to market that is amazing. Call it what it is. If you're a good goalie coach, you'll be fine. Clearly they are smarter at marketing than me, but I'm not selling that. Don't get me wrong, it's a business and a good one – we're helping young men reach their goals. I just wish there was more integrity. I don't see that ever happening in my lifetime. One camp cost $5,000 dollars. I'm sorry, but that's insane. Most of the coaches sell to associations to bring in their whole staff. We don't need to have the youth coaches out there on the ice. Here's the deal. If you want to make a difference, teach the volunteers. These guys have access to 45 practices, and over the course of a season, that can make a huge difference."

Goldman: Every coach's perspective is so different on what makes a goalie successful, how to develop a goalie correctly, and the patterns that go into developing kids to the next level. So the more you dig into it, the less consistency or the less established set groundwork I seem to find. There's no real legit foundation. Everything is completely unique to the individual because their bodies are different, they learn at different rates, they live in different regions and have different environmental factors influencing their progress.

Rogalski: "The body limitations for me is the number one thing people forget. They have to understand that your body can only take you so far. If you don't have the genetic DNA to get there, no goalie coach can turn you into a pro. But they will for sure tell you otherwise!"

Goldman: Beyond the body, there are just so many limiting factors here in the USA, and coaching is one of them. So it's a double-edged sword.

Rogalski: "It comes back to opportunity as well. We're not giving our kids enough opportunities, because a part of me believes we're bringing in too many goalies from other countries. European goalies are awesome goalies, but if you want to develop and compete with those guys, and if that's one of your goals, then you have to limit the amount that come over. On the flip side, we don't do a good enough job of promoting our goalies to other countries. We've made mistakes in the past by not getting the top goalies to the Select 15, 16, and 17 Festivals. Everyone just talks about the top one or two goalies, but nobody talks about the other 10 or 12 that can also play. We need to learn how to promote our goalies better to the USHL and NAHL teams, not just rely on a goalie coach emailing a head coach asking to take their top guy. Too often that ends up in the coach going out and finding an import instead."

Goldman: It's easy to compare styles in terms of technique, but when you look at development patterns, it's so tough to make sense of it all. As an American goalie from Texas, I didn't start skating until I was 11-12 years old,

so my first influences weren't even American because I grew up watching Felix Potvin, Dominik Hasek, Eddie Belfour, and even guys like Nikolai Khabibulin. But if you grew up around the same time in Finland or Sweden, you didn't have ESPN and NHL Center Ice, so you were primarily influenced by goalies from your homeland.

Rogalski: "Exactly. Most American-born goalies these days are mutts, in an awesome way."

Goldman: So is that a good thing or a bad thing?

Rogalski: "I think it's wonderful and I think it's the best thing we have going for us. However, I don't think American goalies are getting enough respect. Their technical flaws are over-analyzed and over-criticized, but really, at the end of the day we have winners."

Goldman: I think there's something to be said for goalies not having highly-specialized goalie coaching until they're 13 or 14.

Rogalski: "If you have the resources at an earlier age, then great, go for it. Just make sure you're playing one or two other sports, or skating out until they force you to only play goal. We all know that skating out is important for your development."

Goldman: I think American goalies who learn to coach themselves because they have no other way to get better always retain their natural instincts. The goalies

who rely on parents to get private instruction, and the goalie coach doesn't mentor, he just coaches technique, that goalie in turn loses his instincts as he gets older and reaches a plateau with his analytical and problem-solving skills.

Rogalski: "You're right, but you can still have a goalie coach. Just do your homework on who you are hiring. There are some beauties out there, promoting their pro hockey career, even though they played five games in four years. But they are pro and they played in leagues, ones that I'm not so sure are actually pro hockey. Just do your homework as a parent on who you are paying to coach your kid. You don't need to be a pro to be a great goalie coach, so when you do homework on guys, you will know who will have the best intentions for your children."

Goldman: One coach I asked said American goalies are lucky. Not in terms of skill, but in terms of their environmental factors.

Rogalski: "No, I don't think so. "I can't say it enough – it's DNA and you have put your hard hat on. If you're good enough, you will find a way. What could hurt us over the next five to 10 years is an inability to market our goalies. European countries market their goalies better, so they eventually all of a sudden get more opportunities to play in different leagues. For some reason, in the last two to three years, I have heard so much about European goalies and their coaches, but no one is talking about any of the top North American coaches or goalies. It's odd to me."

Goldman: There's also a lot to be said for this perception that the next great goalie is hiding in Finland or Sweden somewhere. Or the Pekka Rinne's and Niklas Backstrom's of the world are repeatable or sustainable occurrences, yet they overlook an American goalie that could be just as successful as that Finnish goalie, but is a little less talented at age 16. We sort of stab ourselves in the foot, and that's a cultural thing.

Rogalski: "I have a hard time with this. I don't believe they are better at 16. It's more about having the commitment to their development through their mid-20's that makes the difference. Then they get an NHL deal and teams work with them, so they get more chances. I mentioned to someone that we should start a program for 18 to 24-year-old American goalies. Their exact quote was, 'waste of money and time, we need to focus on 14 to 18-year-olds.' I disagreed, and this guy is a very well-respected goalie coach. We need to focus on all of them, I think that's important. Finland is way more committed to developing their goalies, and that makes a huge difference compared to here in America. The NCAA refuses to recognize goalie coaches as a paid or full-time position, so they're all volunteers unless hired as one of two assistant coaches. Highly rare, but it's starting to trend that way. This is a huge problem, because college is such a huge breeding ground for pro goalies. I don't regret coaching for St. Cloud for one minute and never will – it's the best thing I've ever done. But it's incredible that guys like myself, Karl Goehring [University of North Dakota] and Justin Johnson [University of Minnesota], and other guys that are volunteer goalie coaches around the county, aren't recognized financially. It limits the time and resources those goalies get. This needs to change and I hope College Hockey helps with that as time goes on."

21

THE 2014 WARREN STRELOW GOALIE MENTORSHIP CAMP

Two years ago, I never imagined I would be on the coaching staff for USA Hockey's most prestigious annual goaltending event. Even the idea of being hired by the NTDP was a faint and far-distant dream come true. So to say that attending the Warren Strelow Goalie Mentorship Camp was the culmination of my goalie coaching and scouting career (up to that point) would be a vast understatement.

I had been on the NTDP staff for an entire season, but I still felt like I didn't belong out there. When I saw the full list of the coaching staff, my name stuck out like a sore thumb. I was like the socially awkward 'third-wheel' on a proverbial hot date; I simply wanted to contribute in whatever way possible without getting in the way.

The seventh-annual Strelow camp was held from May 9-12, 2014 at the home of the NTDP, the Ann Arbor Ice Cube. It featured the top 36 American-born goaltenders

(24 boys, 12 girls) in a high-intensity training environment with the top US-born goalie coaches. The athletes' birth years were 1995 to 1998.

Each goaltender was evaluated and selected to attend the camp during the 2013-14 season by a network of coaches and scouts managed by Reiter, USA Hockey's Head Goaltending Coach. Assisting Reiter were the three NTDP regional goalie scouts and mentors (myself, Berkhoel, Waimon).

For those of you unfamiliar with the Strelow program, this annual camp is designed to recruit, develop, and produce elite US-born goaltenders. The program also aims to increase the depth of the talent pool from which all annual National and Olympic teams are selected. By bringing the top goalies and goalie coaches together once a year, USA Hockey continues to build upon the past and future success of these athletes by making them as multi-dimensional and fundamentally sound as possible.

Each year, the Strelow camp emphasizes the core physical principles of goaltending, as well as the mental skills necessary to handle the demanding pressures of the position. In turn, this helps produce elite goalies that rank among the best in the world for their specific age group. Some past participants of the Strelow Camp include Jack Campbell, John Gibson, Jon Gillies, Thatcher Demko, Alex Nedeljkovic, Evan Cowley, Ian Jenkins (may he rest in peace), and many more.

Although it's not a highly recognizable program in the wide world of hockey, it is considered to be one of the strongest national elite goalie camps in the world.

A Brief Background on Warren Strelow

Throughout the halls of USA Hockey's corporate offices in Colorado Springs and Ann Arbor, Strelow is immortalized as a true American hockey legend.

Born in 1934 in St. Paul, Minnesota, Strelow grew up playing hockey with his lifelong friend, Herb Brooks. After graduating from Johnson High School in 1951, Strelow's friendship with Brooks led both men to coach for the University of Minnesota and then later for the 1980 "Miracle on Ice" U.S. Men's Olympic Ice Hockey Team.

In 1983, the Washington Capitals made Strelow the first full-time goalie coach in the history of the NHL. He would then go on to coach for the New Jersey Devils and the San Jose Sharks before passing away in 2007 at the age of 73.

Strelow had a positive and everlasting influence on every goalie he worked with, including his most prized pupils Martin Brodeur, Evgeni Nabokov, Miikka Kiprusoff, and Johan Hedberg.

Strelow's vision, work ethic, dedication, and unyielding perseverance were traits that proved iconic for all American-born goaltenders, as they are consistently reinforced and passed down to young goaltenders through the Strelow staff. Not only was he a passionate coach, but also a true mentor that nurtured and guided athletes throughout their careers.

The On-Ice Component

The on-ice portion of the seventh-annual Strelow camp was comprised of six sessions, with each session including six different drills and stations. Each session focused on a different core principle, including: Angles/Positioning, Puck Retention and Rebound Control, Recoveries, Post Integrations, Reads, and Puck Handling/Traffic Play.

The six drills in each session built on one another so that the goalies could easily absorb the main teaching points while also displaying and showcasing their battle skills. Each session began with a basic movement drill to get warmed up and a basic fundamental drill to reinforce the most vital aspects of each principle. Drills were carefully selected from a vast library within the Strelow program, all of which are refined and updated on a yearly basis.

In terms of skill application and drill progressions, one of the most important aspects of this camp was the pre-camp coaches' meeting. Shortly after all of the coaches arrived on-site in Ann Arbor, Reiter led a meeting that went through each and every drill that would be used during the camp. From there, the floor was open for anyone to speak up about the grid that he created. During this time, he collected feedback from coaches on what would be the most effective and strategic way to implement the drill progressions.

During this meeting, I was really impressed with the flexibility and open-minded chemistry of the entire coaching staff. Everyone was open to suggestions and ideas, and we all worked together with the sole purpose of making the on-ice sessions as effective as possible.

As a result, some drills were moved around and tweaked in order to place a stronger emphasis on certain key elements, including tracking pucks into and off of the body, scanning and evaluating the open ice for potential back-door or far-side threats, and better understanding of progressive post integration tactics and techniques, including the Reverse-VH method.

With this productive meeting completed before the camp started, the entire coaching staff was on the same page about the drills and skills we would be teaching over the next four days.

My Role at Strelow Camp

As one of the three NTDP regional goalie scouts and mentors working under Reiter, I was automatically added to the Strelow coaching staff. Had I not been hired by the NTDP, I definitely would not have been part of this exclusive event. Knowing this, I made sure to give Reiter an opportunity to utilize my writing, video editing, and creativity skills in a manner that would benefit the camp and program in new ways. So I offered to capture video clips of every single goalie in the camp, then spend a few minutes with them in small group meetings in order to review video, and then provide them with a copy of *The Power Within*. Using my trusty Asus Transformer tablet, I took it upon myself to roam around each station during every on-ice session in order to record the goalies and give them instant feedback when they rotated out of the net. Each night after camp, I spent a few hours in my hotel room cutting and editing down excess video, and then I categorized them and uploaded them on Coach's Eye, an excellent app that I believe is simply the best when it comes to marking up video and providing feedback. If you haven't used it before, download it without any hesitation. You'll love it.

That was my main role during camp, but I didn't stop there. I also made sure to show my appreciation for being on the coaching staff by cleaning our meeting room a few times, logging information from group meetings on a dry-erase board, and doing smaller tasks in order to help the camp run more smoothly. Since I had the least amount of coaching experience there, I felt it was my duty to be the intern of sorts.

It is through our body language that we mentor young goalies, so I made sure to constantly show positive, enthusiastic body language. I made it clear to everyone involved, both goalies and coaches alike, that I was just happy to be there, just excited to be associated with the program.

In my opinion, no elite goalie camp is complete without a strong message. In that regard, I was excited to also offer up my creative skills to Reiter by developing a theme for the seventh-annual camp. After pondering this idea for a week, I went with a simple but poignant message: *"Preparation is Everything."*

The purpose of this theme was to reinforce a key mental principle that would allow each goalie to improve their identity by giving them a chance to discuss, refine, and focus on things like their pre-game routines, practice habits, and overall preparation skills.

During Reiter's camp-opening speech, he did an excellent job emphasizing the theme, ensuring that every goalie understood the opportunity they had to learn from an elite coaching staff. He also mentioned that this was the chance of a lifetime to improve their understanding of the position by being open and honest with the coaching staff. Most importantly, they had a chance to represent USA Hockey in a live and professional setting.

To further expand on the camp's theme, I had created a simple one-page questionnaire for each goalie, and it included specific questions regarding preparation. It asked for their own definition of preparation, what they do to prepare for a game and practice (both physically and mentally), and how they would like to improve their pre-game preparation techniques during the camp.

Aside from actually implementing an annual theme for each Strelow camp, I think the questionnaire, or any type of written assignment, is extremely important to have in a program such as this. Not only does it provide the coaching staff with excellent feedback, which is used for scouting purposes, but it gives the goalies a way to further reinforce the importance of the topic. By writing things down, goalies are subconsciously emphasizing the theme. They're placing it at the front of their mind and they're gaining wisdom without exerting much physical effort.

I'm such a huge believer in the power of the written word. Self-reflection and professing one's goals is an absolute must when goalies are in this type of training environment.

Aside from being on the ice logging video and giving goalies feedback, I actually volunteered to drive the goalies back and forth from the rink to the hotel every day. I did this because I knew it would be a great chance to spend some time bonding with them. It gave me some great insights into some of the personalities of these goalies off the ice, and friendships grew organically over the four days.

Of all the additions I was able to incorporate into this Strelow camp, none was more gratifying than being able to hand every goalie (and the coaching staff) a copy of *The Power Within*. I was humbled to have the book be so well-received by everyone, especially when I got to spend about 10 minutes with the goalies in small groups on the final day of camp.

During these small group meetings, I introduced the concepts behind the book and pointed to a few passages that reinforced the camp's theme on preparation. I also spent a few minutes breaking down some of the videos I snagged during camp. But instead of giving them direct feedback individually, I had the goalies watch certain clips together, and then give feedback to each other as a group.

I did this for a very specific reason – I think it's important that goalies of this caliber get comfortable evaluating themselves in an honest and open manner. It can be an ego check, and it can help them take off those 'rose-colored' glasses. If a goalie always self-evaluates in a private manner, it can sometimes lead to deflecting mistakes, or coming up with excuses for why goals were allowed. I think it's important that goalies break down their own video so they can further learn to manage their own game without over-relying on their goalie coach.

Since I rested at the bottom of the coaching staff Totem pole, I took great pride in knowing I was able to be an asset to the Strelow program and do my part in mentoring and coaching the goalies in the camp.

Along with the book, the goalies also received a binder complete with the camp schedule, a copy of the revised drill grid, and a printout of every on-ice drill being used. Thanks to Berkhoel, they also took home a Vaughn Hockey backpack that we filled with a reaction ball, a jump rope, an agility ladder, and a case of tennis balls.

Having each goalie receive a binder with all of the drills was a crucial component for obvious reasons, as it was a great resource for them to have. Reinforcing all of the technical content and the collection of drills would lead to some consistency in a country where the educational structure is somewhat lacking.

After everyone had arrived in Ann Arbor for camp, most of the coaching staff held a pre-camp meeting to prepare for the next day's opening session. I took diligent notes throughout this session in order to give readers a glimpse into what transpired. Below is a list of the main highlights:

1. *All of the coaches came together to discuss the layout of each session and the drill progressions. Beezer, Osaer, Berkhoel, Lassonde, Millar, Waimon, Exter, Goldman, Petraglia, Vetter, Clifford, and Reiter were in attendance.*

2. *We spent two hours tweaking drills and changing progressions so that goalies would have a better understanding of what's an attack sequence and what isn't. We want to make sure we're giving goalies the knowledge they need to go out and make the save the right way.*

3. *An entire camp session was re-vamped in order to put a stronger emphasis on post integrations. We*

changed the progression of those drills to expand on coming out of the Reverse-VH and setting yourself up to make the next save with balance and good posture.

4. *We spent time discussing stick placement in the reverse-VH on wraparounds and jams. We wanted to make sure and emphasize to goalies that they can't leave their stick behind the back-side knee, but rather keep it closer to the front-side knee. I actually got up to the front of the room and demonstrated some of the issues that arise when goalies extend their blocker-side arm too far out, which causes the heel of the stick blade to open up a window and a passing lane.*

5. *We also spent time discussing the ever-popular topic of skate-on-post versus pad-on-post in the reverse-VH. Exter appeared to be on the side of always having your skate on the post, but I am more of a proponent of going pad-on-post.*

6. *A lot of the guys were vocal about this topic, but a few stayed quiet. Most of the coaches agreed that it can be hard to continually execute skate-on-post and then lean back against the post. I personally don't consider it to be difficult when you're younger and more flexible, but I don't like it because it deactivates the glove and forces it to fill the space directly off the hip.*

7. *After listening to Exter explain some things about skate-on-post, I became a stronger advocate for it. He*

showed me how skate on post can actually fill passing lanes and lengthen lateral coverage. A lot of goalies, he said, get beat inside the far post, so having skate on post does a lot to aid in that extension for goalies.

8. *We agreed that it's good for goalies to go paddle down on a jam play (tight wrap), but if the puck is further than one foot away from the goalie, they need to lock the blocker thumb to the top of their pad. They also need to watch the angle of the anchor leg and make sure it's not moving unnecessarily. The lower the knee is to the ice, the easier and quicker he can create a seal. But that also makes it tougher to strengthen the upper body seal against the post. We are also looking for strong recoveries with the anchor leg by making a solid c-cut with good blade engagement.*

9. *Lassonde was pretty on point with a couple of drill tweaks, as he just wanted to make sure goalies were making certain movements in certain situations. We had one drill tweaked in order to force goalies to scan the ice by checking over his far-side shoulder, then looking back into the corner to re-attach his eyes to the puck.*

10. *Reiter emphasized making sure we are seeing goalies rotate their body and find the precise angle at which they arrive behind a potential rebound shot with full squareness to the puck.*

11. *We discussed the importance of making sure goalies are using all of the joints in their arm to make glove*

saves, not just the forearm, the bicep, or the shoulders. All three joints need to be engaged in order to achieve a relaxed and fluid glove reaction.

It only took a few hours of being in a room with most of the coaching staff to realize this was going to be an incredible learning experience.

The Strelow Coaching Staff

The amount of coaching and playing success in this precamp meeting was daunting. I couldn't even begin to list all of the accolades these guys have had as players and coaches, and some of them need no introduction. It just goes to show how many brilliant goaltending minds we actually have at the higher levels in this country. It also further proves just how well the country has done as a whole developing our top goalies, despite the lack of structure with a national development model.

As one top Canadian goalie coach told me, USA Hockey is actually considered to be ahead of Hockey Canada and the Finnish Hockey Federation in terms of top-end goalie development, due in large part to the Strelow program. I can't say I disagree with that statement, as there are plenty of success stories within the NTDP and the growing Strelow alumni circle.

The seventh-annual Strelow camp included the following coaches:

1. ***Kevin Reiter:*** *USA Hockey's Head Goalie Coach (NTDP)*

2. ***Mike Ayers:*** *Boston College's goalie coach, former USA Hockey head goalie coach*
3. ***Joe Exter:*** *Ohio State's assistant and goalie coach, godfather of the Warren Strelow program*
4. ***David Lassonde:*** *Senior Strelow staff member, assistant coach at Dartmouth, formerly with DU*
5. ***Shane Clifford:*** *Former NHL goalie coach, currently in Pittsburgh area, worked with Gibson, etc*
6. ***Jared Waimon:*** *East Regional goalie scout for NTDP, Quinnipiac's goalie coach*
7. ***Adam Berkhoel:*** *NCAA champion, former NHL and AHL goalie, Vaughn pro rep, NTDP scout*
8. ***Nick Petraglia:*** *Miami Ohio's goalie coach, seven-year veteran Strelow goalie coach*
9. ***Phil Osaer:*** *12-year pro career, goalie coach with Michigan State, former USHL goalie coach*
10. ***Matt Millar:*** *Former NTDP regional goalie scout, Dubuque's assistant GM and goalie coach*
11. ***Bob Janosz:*** *Buffalo Sabres assistant goalie coach*
12. ***John Vanbiesbrouck:*** *USA Hockey Hall of Fame, former NHL goaltender*
13. ***Jessie Vetter:*** *USA Hockey Women's Olympic goaltender*
14. ***Brianne McLaughlin:*** *USA Hockey Women's Olympic goaltender*
15. ***Alison Quandt:*** *Assistant and goalie coach, Boston College women's team*
16. ***Robb Stauber:*** *Former NHL goaltender, goalie coach for USA Hockey women's Olympic team*
17. ***Justin Goldman:*** *Minnesota Regional goalie scout for NTDP, founder of The Goalie Guild*

You should have seen me when Reiter was introducing the entire coaching staff to the goalies during the camp-opening meeting. Everyone had some sort of pro-level playing or coaching experience attached to their name. I had none of that. But I've dealt with the lack of pro experience all my life, so while I felt slightly out of place, that's what has always fueled me to never take any opportunity for granted. That is why I had the patience and fortitude to do all of the little things that the other coaches appreciated. More importantly, I never once felt unaccepted, ostracized, or looked down upon. Everyone respected me, and everyone was happy to have me there.

Since my goal was to do as many of the 'little things' as possible to prove I could be a valuable member of the coaching staff, I made numerous trips to the airport to pick up goalies when they arrived. I also pulled a 'solid' for my buddy Millar, one that actually turned out to have a major impact on my situation with USA Hockey.

When Reiter passed out everyone's hotel room assignments, there was one room with a single instead of a double bed. I landed it, but Millar wanted to change rooms with someone, so I nominated myself. I had no problem giving it up for him, it was something I wanted to do.

Turns out, my roommate was none other than Vanbiesbrouck. I was ecstatic. I mean, when would I ever get the chance to be roommates with one of the best American-born goalies of all time? It was a no-brainer, and I guess you could say I was in the right place at the right time.

That change in plans allowed me to spend some quality time developing a friendship with Beezer. Not only was he one of my favorite goalies growing up, but even at age 32, I was looking up to him as a mentor. I asked him questions, I reflected on some of the memories I had about his career, and he seemed to enjoy my enthusiasm and passion. I was just happy to have him around.

I have weird tendency to over-respect a lot of NHL players. Even though I know John would have had no problem being interviewed for the book, I didn't want to bother him with it. I didn't want to think he was in the spotlight or under the microscope. It was a rare chance for him to just chill out and talk hockey, so I stashed the digital voice recorder and kept his insights to myself.

A few months after Strelow camp ended, Reiter relayed to me that Beezer was impressed with my work and attitude. He told Reiter that the program needed to keep me involved, that USA Hockey needed guys like me around. It was an honor to know that I had a positive influence on Beezer during camp, and I'm really glad I nominated myself to change rooms with Millar. It was just one of those things that, regardless of what ultimately happens with USA Hockey, I feel like I was meant to room with him.

It wasn't hard to come away from the camp impressed with the whole coaching staff, but most of all, I was impressed with Reiter. For him to step in and manage everything as well as he did in his first year as the head goalie coach for USA Hockey said a lot about his work ethic and intelligence. It was even more admirable that he did this with Ayers and Exter in attendance. Exter is the founder of the whole program, and Ayers held Reiter's position last year. If I were in Reiter's shoes, I would have been pretty nervous, but he handled everything calmly, and he did all of this after putting in so many exhausting hours making sure everything would run smoothly.

Reiter's ability to lean on Ayers, Exter, and even myself for support and advice on how to plan the camp and drill progressions was great to see. He had zero ego. He was willing to compromise. He listened well but was no doormat, as he was authoritative when needed. Even after spending a lot of time creating the drill grid for the camp, he was flexible when it came to making changes. After that initial coach's meeting, he even took the time to update the drill grid, re-print them, and re-add them into everyone's binders.

Explaining Reiter's coaching style within this camp wasn't easy, because a lot of his time was spent managing all of the other components that went into running the camp. But I can tell you that he's a very straightforward coach that will not stand for laziness or for goalies that don't pay attention to detail. There is no reason why goalies should not be able to process what they are being told, and there's no reason why they can't apply things quickly and effectively. He is certainly a patient coach, but he will get on you if you make unnecessary mistakes. He really likes to verbally reinforce good habits and he stresses stick on puck and not shifting into pucks unless absolutely necessary.

"Just give yourself a chance," is his go-to line. I crack a smile and find myself laughing every time I hear it. It's so funny, but it's so true.

Even though he did less coaching and more overseeing on the ice, he held the off-ice classroom session in the middle of camp. This was a pretty basic rundown of everything we worked on during the most important on-ice session, which was post integrations. He broke down both the skate-on-post and pad-on-post technique. He showed examples of this with Jonathan Quick, Carey Price, and Semyon Varlamov. He kept all 32 goalies focused and attentive, and his explanations were easy to understand.

After his classroom session, Reiter also conducted the on-ice mass teach at the start of the ensuing on-ice session. This took about 10 minutes, and he did it twice in a row since there were two groups of 12 goalies (for the boys).

I was really surprised to hear that some goalies, including Garrett Nieto, had never used the reverse-VH before. That raised an interesting question; how do goalies that attend Strelow learn these new techniques beyond this one annual event? If only we had a website where Strelow alumni could continue their education with videos, drills, notes from the coaching staff, and updates on other goalies in the program, then maybe we would be able to have a stronger impact on their development.

If only.

Another coach on the Strelow staff that really impressed me was Waimon. His intelligence level is through the roof, and he's an excellent problem solver. He took initiative when Reiter was on the ice and ran an entire coach's meeting regarding age-specific goalie training. There, he did an excellent job dictating the flow of the meeting. He's computer savvy, he's good on the ice, and he's a coach that genuinely cares.

Waimon is another one of the many goalie coaches that fly under the radar out East. He's currently coaching at Quinnipiac and for his private company, but I could see him being a successful pro goalie coach someday.

Another lifelong memory I'll have from this camp was naturally gelling with Exter.

At the start of camp, I realized my last name was misspelled on a couple of printed materials. Instead of Goldman, it said Goodman. Exter picked up on this right away and affectionately started calling me "Goodie" instead of Goldie, which is my usual nickname.

I loved that so much. It put me at ease. In my lifetime, I rarely got to experience that type of coach-student dynamic since I grew up in such a non-traditional hockey market. Same goes for the bonding you get with a college or junior team that travels across the country for an entire season. Just being 'one of the guys' means everything to me, especially in this coaching environment, where my confidence was a little fragile, and I was just trying to fit in and not screw up.

I'll also never forget when Exter said he wanted to follow me around for a day, just to see what my life was like. I had a good laugh at that, because I'm the one that wants to be following him around at Ohio State University. Oh, and the little inside story regarding a tweet I accidentally sent regarding John Gibson starting a playoff game for the Ducks was classic. I had a borderline panic attack on that one.

I never knew this until the Strelow camp, but Exter has an absolutely incredible life story. This man has stared down death in a harrowing and haunting manner from a scary on-ice injury, and he came through stronger than most men I've ever met. This life experience played a key role in his ability to quickly transform into one of the world's top goalie coaches, and he's someone that I hope continues to stay involved with USA Hockey as time goes on. He's "The Godfather" of the Strelow camp. If it weren't for him, none of this would be possible.

Robb Stauber and I had a chance to chat at the airport before heading back to Minneapolis, so I got to know him better as well. He pretty much dominates the goalie coaching scene in the Twin Cities through Stauber's GoalCrease in Edina, so it was great to finally put a face to the name and build that relationship.

Lassonde was a great character as well, and I'll never forget the first thing he ever said to me.

"Hey Justin, can you text me Kevin's number? Thanks *brotha!*"

Hanging out with Jessie Vetter and Brianne McLaughlin at Applebee's and getting to know them throughout the camp was really awesome, too. They were like sisters to me, and since I have four older sisters already, I got along with them really well. The fact they were even a part of this camp was so awesome, and I know the 12 girls in camp loved having them around. Kudos to Reiter for inviting them and enhancing the girl's portion of the Strelow camp.

One coach that was really quiet when I was around him was Ayers. I was intimidated by this guy from the moment

I met him. Maybe not as intimidating as Peter Ward (I had some very interesting interactions with him during the NTDP scouting season), but intimidating nonetheless. He and I had never been formally introduced to each other before, but when he arrived for the camp, I could tell that he knew who I was.

I'll be honest, my first impression was that he was probably wondering why the hell I was there, but it could have just been my slight insecurity gnawing at the back of my skull. I get this all the time when I'm around the elite goalies and goalie coaches, so it doesn't bother me beyond that moment or few minutes I feel it for the first time. Once I'm around a pro goalie or goalie coach for a few days, they pick up on my positive vibes and they know I'm there for the right reasons.

This same thing happened with Ayers. I don't think we spoke directly to each other until the final two days of camp, but once we did, it was fine.

I remember we were in the locker room after one of the ice sessions and I was regaling in the awesome atmosphere that I had just experienced over the past 90 minutes. I told him what I found so impressive with this staff was how well everyone was able to pick up on even the slightest or most subtle inefficiencies in a goalie's technique or tactics. It's really quite remarkable. All of the coaches on staff had the ability to peel back more layers than I ever imagined, and they were doing it without having to go back and watch any video. They gave very detailed verbal feedback on the fly, whereas I was still at a level where I needed some time to process and calculate the feedback before I said anything.

Ayers, like the rest of the staff, treated me just like one of the other coaches. He smiled and mentioned how years of experience helps it to flow naturally, so giving instant feedback was more about just trusting your intuition and being open with the goalie you're working with. It was awesome to hear one of the country's best goalie coaches talk to me as if I was right on his level, and it definitely released any tension I felt around him leading up to that moment.

Overall, the dynamic of the entire coaching staff was unbelievable. Everyone was on the same page with just about everything you could imagine. Those that weren't were flexible enough to keep their emotions in check for the good of the camp. More importantly, I didn't see any excessive over-coaching on the ice, or any of the coaches trying to go rogue status by trying to explain something that didn't jive with what the staff was trying to reinforce as a whole.

Maybe the most impressive part for me was coming to the realization that nobody on the coaching staff considered their way was the absolute right way. Everyone was open to discussing alternatives. Whether it was a T-Push instead of a C-Cut here, or a reverse-VH instead of a traditional VH there, the terminology and the application of certain strategies was very consistent.

I was very pleased to see that everyone on the staff agreed that we had to stress less sliding and more footwork, blade engagements, and keeping their feet. There was not a single verbal disagreement or any noticeable tension between certain coaches, either. Everyone was respectful and friendly. The chemistry as the week went along between all of the coaches got stronger and stronger.

I'll also never forget the last thing Ayers said to me when camp ended and we parted ways.

"Reach out if there's anything I can do for you."

At the time, I couldn't think of anything I'd ever want from a guy like him, except for the opportunity to maybe shadow him someday.

But now there's something I definitely want.

I just want him (and the rest of the Strelow staff) to let me stay involved in the program. I just want to continue being the video guy. I want to hold a presentation on my books. I want to create more written materials and enhance the program in ways that fall into my wheelhouse. I want to be the civil and dutiful servant, chipping in and documenting the progress and the evolution of the program. I want to do more yeoman's work and be behind the scenes and take pressure off the rest of the staff so they can do their thing without having to worry about a bunch of little remedial tasks.

At the end of the day, just like I've learned in my year and a half with USA Hockey, the goalie coaches in this country are a true melting pot of styles, influences, and personalities. But we're a proud bunch, and our work ethic, competitiveness, and willingness to do whatever it takes to make the best young goalies in this country even better makes us an indivisible group, with liberty and justice for all.

What I Learned at Camp

Ironically, when I looked back at my Strelow experience, preparation was the one skill I leaned on heavily to help make this a successful coaching venture. Since I had never been a part of the program before, I had no idea of what to expect. I had so many questions that needed answering, and the whole thing was over as soon as it started. It was a blissful blur, but one that really boosted my confidence when it came to working with top young goalie prospects.

I approached the whole thing exactly like a player. That mindset is so innate – the way I process the pressure of a big game is truly a way of dealing with many aspects of life outside of hockey. So I just tried to show up as prepared as possible, knowing that you can only do so much to help your team. You try to learn as much as possible from the people who have more experience than you. You try to be a sponge.

Thanks to the extreme importance I placed on this camp, I learned how to better prepare myself in the moment. In fact, as I was learning these things during camp, I was reinforcing the same exact message to the goalies in the camp. I spoke to them about the importance of recognizing the situation they were in and appreciating the opportunity to learn. I told them how it would be good to try and disconnect from social media during camp and simply focus on the camp's theme and the interactions they would have on the ice with the rest of the goalies and the coaches. This was such an exclusive and rare learning environment; the top US-born goalie coaches working with the top US-born goalies means you're completely surrounded by high-caliber talent, elite coaching, and some very smart people. To be distracted by stuff happening away from the camp is to lose out on a key learning experience.

Repeating the same things I was learning during camp continued on the ice as well.

"Be willing to try new things," I said. "Experiment. Engage. Create new ways of thinking and preparing for a key practice or game. Create new friendships with the goalies and coaches in the camp. Be sure to thank everyone and carry yourself with a professional and positive attitude. Put yourself in a vulnerable state of mind, one where you can accept the fact you don't know as much as you think you know. Be willing to let someone tell you there's a better way to do things."

I said these things as if I had been teaching them for 50 years. But the lessons were being experienced in that moment, so verbalizing it was to accept the fact I was a coach learning the same as a student.

Sure enough, I stressed the importance of reflecting on the experience as it was happening. Taking five minutes to write out a few thoughts each night goes a long way, yet few goalies take the time to do this in such a daunting and exciting atmosphere. "What did you learn? What did you like about today's lessons? What will you take with you and try to implement once the camp is over?"

This chapter and this entire book is my way of reflecting on a whole summer's worth of amazing learning experiences, and the value of self-reflection will forever be of great importance to me.

I also learned that, while Strelow is most certainly a showcase of the country's top goaltending talent, first and foremost, it's a symposium. It's a living, breathing *Omnium Gatherum*. It is an interactive platform for top coaches and top talent to discuss and share ideas. The staff is here to teach, to instruct, to improve. Mainly there as volunteers, our mission is to cultivate the student's evolution in an environment where everyone is cared for and appreciated. There's no ill will or contempt or petty competition between students. Everyone is on the same page, everyone is working in a communal manner, and everyone walks away stronger, smarter, and more skilled than ever before.

This mixing of methods and ideas is essential to the future success of American goaltenders.

Simply put, goalies were invited to attend for one key unspoken purpose – to learn from each other and strengthen their confidence by reinforcing their skills through the country's best coaching staff. There were no scouts in the stands ranking goalies for future reference. There were no grades being handed out. This was not a win or lose situation. It was all about one thing and one thing only – development.

It was this lowering of win-loss expectations, this ability to remove the stress that comes with other prestigious goalie camps that made it so conducive to learning for the goalies. The goalies developed an amazing level of trust with the staff, because they knew the coaches didn't care about how many pucks would be stopped or how polished and perfect everyone looked. All we cared about was the learning process, building relationships with the goalies, and letting them know that it was OK to fail, it was OK to make mistakes, and it was OK to try new things.

As I've explained before, goalies in America deal with more pressure from social media now than any other time in history. It's our culture, our identity, and we're always being pulled in a million different directions because of that. We spend more and more time telling people where we are, what we're doing, and how we're feeling. This plays a huge role in an American goalie's development, because there's more pressure to make others like us, agree with us, or console us when we're down.

Mistakes become these vile, obtrusive things that flaw our online identity, and we feel like when we make a mistake, we're less appealing. But this is not the case when you're on the ice at Strelow. We want to see mistakes. We want to see flaws. For it is when we see these flaws that we have the opportunity to help a talented goalie correct them.

I think that's ultimately what makes the Strelow program so amazing. It gives every goalie the freedom to establish the confidence and experience needed to trust their path and their unique development process. Knowing we are there only to make them better, they can relax and appreciate the opportunity and focus on doing whatever they can to get better. Sure enough, I saw every single goalie interacting in a studious and efficient manner. Everyone was wanting to try new things and discuss their ideas and opinions, both on and off the ice.

More importantly, the positive vibes from all of the new friendships that were made act as special memories of a time where the goalies knew they were being nurtured and given special attention. From the meals that were shared, to the funny stories told in the locker rooms, to the goofing off that took place in the hotel, to the bus rides to and from the rink, the learning environment and the people involved created one of the best hockey experiences I ever had.

Expanding the Warren Strelow Program

After everything I learned about goalie development models in Europe and North America, I became even more confident in my ability to help USA Hockey potentially expand the Warren Strelow program. It is so damn successful and vital to this country's success that we must find a way to increase its reach. New coaches will always come and go as the years go on, but the Strelow mission will always remain the same. So why can't we make it bigger? Not only is this a benefit for the goalies, but it brings more coaches into the fold. Just like I experienced as a newcomer to the coaching staff, it can expose new minds to everyone involved and inject fresh ideas into the bloodstream.

In order for this event to be successful on a wider scale, we only need to keep recruiting and choosing passionate, intelligent coaches that have no agenda other than improving the country's top goalies.

In the eyes of an event manager, however, expanding an annual event always comes down to the almighty dollar. If more money was allocated to goaltending through USA Hockey, the event could easily be expanded. Instead of eight goalies per birth year, maybe we could have 16. Instead of grouping men and women together, maybe the women could host their own camp and include more goalies.

For such an amazing camp, I was shocked to learn that I was the first to actually carry the responsibility of logging video of every goalie. That's something that had never been done before at a Strelow camp, but I'm guessing the only reason for that was due to a lack of resources and time within previous coaching staffs. But aside from resource allocation, money is the source of all potential enhancements.

The same year the Warren Strelow program started, I was hosting my first-annual "Quest for the Crown" charity adult hockey tournament. I created that event from sheer scratch in order to raise money and awareness for the NHL's Hockey Fights Cancer foundation, so I know the pride that comes with seeing an event grow. I also know the importance of reinforcing a strong, solid message.

With that being said, I am thankful that Reiter allowed me to implement an annual "theme" to the camp, as well as provide them with a short writing exercise to get their brains working in a classroom setting. The small group meetings were also a great enhancement, and my only hope is that, regardless of whether I'm involved or not, those things remain intact for future camps.

There's one more section of notes I have in my handwritten pages on the Strelow camp that I am willing to share with everyone. It's the basic structure for the expansion of the Strelow program. This would not be easy to implement, but over the next three or four years, it's definitely plausible.

As I said before, the biggest obstacle right now is the low number of coaches and goalies that are able to share the Strelow program's mission. Very few goalies in the United States know who Strelow even was, or what he means to USA Hockey.

In my mind, that's the first step. We have to transform the Strelow message and mission into something that can extend to goalies and coaches in Arizona, California, Iowa, Florida, Maine, Oregon, Idaho.

We do this by taking the binder that every goalie and coach received at this camp and making it available to everyone. We need to create promotional and informational videos that show some of the drills we used and broadcast some of the presentations held by guys like Reiter and Exter. We need to perpetuate the same themes, principles, and ideologies in youth associations everywhere using the latest technologies and social media platforms.

Once the message begins to spread and more goalies learn about the actual program, you can begin to discuss making Strelow a roving satellite camp. Maybe it's held twice a year, once in Ann Arbor and once in Colorado Springs. From there, maybe it's held on a smaller scale in each district.

This not only helps us spread the message to goalies in smaller markets, but it helps us establish structure that is consistently flowing across the nation.

Unfortunately, this doesn't work unless there's a platform where the distribution and passing-down of information can transpire. This information, at least to start, would be included in that elusive Level 1 Goalie Coaching Certification Program. Inside that program, coaches learn what the Strelow program is all about, and how both grassroots goalies and goalie coaches strive to attend the country's most prestigious goalie camp. But it all starts by stressing the same stuff we stressed on the ice at Strelow camp – a mastery and continual refinement of the most fundamental principles of goaltending.

Getting the budget and financial support from USA Hockey is the hard part. Coming up with the content and getting it out to people is actually the easy part. Yes, it would be time-consuming to create the videos and literature that goes into this, but it doesn't have to be very in-depth, especially in the first few years.

The rest of my hand-written notes were a bunch of lines on a rudimentary map of the USA, showing certain satellite locations for the Strelow program. Expansion would also include adding more information to every Level 1-4 head coach certification clinic, so that the message continued to spread.

The biggest limitation we're facing right now with our ability to expand the Strelow program is a complete lack of online presence. The amount of information online is depressing. There's only a couple of pages on the USA Hockey website about the Strelow program, and you'll find no type of outreach from their corporate headquarters to further advance the impressive success this event has had in just seven years.

I'm so in love with the positive influence and purpose of the Strelow program that I get sick to my stomach when American goalies tell me they've never heard of it before. It's simply mind-blowing that I have to sit here and tell you that the program really has no voice outside of the actual camp. Go ahead and look online for yourself. Check rinks around the country and you'll fail to find any readily-available promotional materials getting into the hands of American goalies. This is a shame, but it can quickly change! Without spending much money, we can do so much to promote Strelow! It only took me a few years to expand the reach of The Goalie Guild, so with my own two hands and a little bit of time, I could and would do the exact same thing for the Strelow program. I just need a green light and a big thumbs up.

Expanding Strelow is one thing, but since it has been so well-run and wildly successful, it further proved to me that, if we could only put that same type of strategic planning into a basic Level-1 goalie coaching certification program, we would have no problem closing the development gap between the two worlds.

22

AMERICAN GOALIE DEVELOPMENT WITH COREY WOGTECH

Corey Wogtech, founder of *W Goaltending* and the goalie coach for the USHL's Bloomington Blaze, has been a good friend of mine for over three years. We originally met at the University of Denver back in 2011 while he was the goalie coach for the University of Omaha-Nebraska Mavericks. At that time, I was working on an article about his time spent training former Anaheim Ducks goalie Dan Ellis.

Since then, we've worked on the ice together at a few camps, most recently the ProHybrid Top-24 USHL Prospects Tour in the summer of 2013. It was during that camp, and the many hours on the bus going to and from different USHL rinks, that I learned just how detail-oriented he was as a goalie coach.

I chose to interview Wogtech for a few reasons. First of all, his intelligence, both as an experienced goalie coach and as someone who understands the ebbs and flows of development on a national scale, is extremely high.

Secondly, he's my age; we both grew up watching all of the same NHL goalies and experiencing some of the same obstacles while trying to develop outside of USA's main hockey hotbeds. Thirdly, he has international playing experience and has coached at all of the top levels in the United States, including the USHL, NCAA, and even with AHL and NHL goaltenders.

Most importantly, however, is that Wogtech is a perfect reflection of the goalie coaching culture in the United States. His popularity and prominence in the American goaltending community rose quickly after he posted a series of instructional YouTube videos, and a few years later, he followed those up with a three-set DVD series on goaltending. Like so many goalies and goalie coaches in the United States, Wogtech single-handedly created a strong coaching reputation through hard work, thousands of hours watching and playing the position, and a strong passion for improving his own game.

In this regard, I was really excited to get Wogtech's opinions and insights on the culture of goalie coaching and development in the USA.

Goldman: For those that aren't familiar with your pro experience, you played internationally, so can you talk real briefly about where you played?

Wogtech: "As a player, I grew up in the St. Louis area and played AAA hockey, Junior-A in the NAHL, then played Division-III college hockey. After that I was fortunate enough to play five years of minor pro hockey, and in that process I played four years in the USA, one year in Europe in two separate countries. Since then I've been coaching and fortunate to work at the NAHL, USHL, NCAA levels, as well as independently with a bunch of NHL goaltenders. In this time, I've been exposed to a number of different coaches, philosophies, locations, and from a coaching aspect, I've had a number of different goalies come across my path from many different nationalities."

Goldman: The year you played in Europe, what two countries did you play in?

Wogtech: "I played in Serbia and the Netherlands."

Goldman: How would you define an American goaltender?

Wogtech: "I'd say it's pretty tough to categorize exactly what an American goalie is technically. I think it's a mix of a number of different styles and techniques. A lot of the times, the high-end goalies have a little more battle or compete to their game then you might see in other countries, but I think that's starting to fade a little bit as time goes along."

Goldman: What do you think about the idea that there's really no defined style for American goalies? Straight up, do you think that's a good or bad thing?

Wogtech: "I think that's probably a good thing because they can create their own game and style if they want to. It's not that you can't do this in Europe, but over there you seem to be surrounded by the same thing over and over again. Even in North America, it's becoming more noticeable that we're being surrounded by the same thing over and over. Once the movement and style and technique is refined, everyone does, for the most part, move around the net in a similar way. I think that's good because most of the time they're making those decisions because they're the most efficient. But I like the idea that any goaltender can pull from the Finnish style, or the Swedish style, or just Europeans in general, as well as what you would consider a North American style. I think that the combination of all those things is what creates an elite American goalie in today's game. I think that each country's 'style' has a disadvantage to it. If you can cut out those disadvantages and implement the advantages, it's going to be extremely beneficial across the board."

Goldman: In your experience, seeing all of these different goalies from different countries, was there one type of goalie or country that had a style that was more successful than any other?

Wogtech: "Not particularly. When I was coming up, Canadian goalies were fairly dominant. But over the course of the past 10 years, you've seen the introduction of more international goalies here in the United States. When I was playing junior and college and pro hockey, I'd say Canadian goalies were dominant, but since I've been coaching, it seems to be transitioning away from North American goalies and more towards European goalies. But as far as their ability as a whole, there wasn't necessarily a country where I could say these guys are more dominant than these guys. Since I started coaching, I've noticed that goalies from certain regions seem to be better at specific situations. So not necessarily the game as a whole, but maybe something like post play, rebound control, fighting for sightlines; each of these categories has a personality of its own in each country. But I've yet to really see many goaltenders in a specific region that has a combination of all of these situational skills."

Goldman: We've talked about this a few times before, and you've brought up a few really good points in the realm of coaching patterns and how they compare and contrast in different countries. Specifically in the USA, where good goalie coaching is at a premium, what's the biggest obstacle for goalies getting to the next level?

Wogtech: "Speaking strictly in regards to coaching in the USA, the biggest obstacle that goalies might face is that there is such an abundance of goalie coaches now. In that process, some goalie coaches have started to try and reinvent the wheel a little bit, and sometimes I think that might be a disadvantage for some of their clients. Sometimes it could be an advantage; goalie coaching needs to continue to evolve. But in general, there are so many goalie coaches – some of which are very high level but are difficult to get a hold of or are very expensive to work with, and some of them are more affordable but may or may not be providing valuable or beneficial coaching depending on the goalie's age and where they are at in their career or development path."

Goldman: You've also mentioned and explained how there is something to be said for goalies in the USA being over-exposed at too young of an age. Now that I've been through the process of scouting for the NTDP, I really agree with your point and I think it's important for goalies, coaches, and parents to understand that it's OK to do your own thing and learn how to manage your own game for a while.

Wogtech: "As far as age is concerned, it's really hard to say when a goalie will or won't benefit from a goalie coach's teachings. I'd say it's valuable to have a coach at a young age to teach you the basics so that you're going about your game, from a movement and puck-stopping standpoint, as efficiently as possible. But I think that it can be a bit of a detriment at a young age because the goalie never really develops their own personality, as to who they're going to be as a goalie. They don't have to struggle how to fix something or analyze their own game, and in that process, they fail to experience what it's like to reach out to someone to get better, regardless of how good the information may be. So it takes away their ability or their willingness to build their own game, and I think it's very important for goalies to have the ability to learn how to manage their own game, so that they can understand what it takes to work through the pitfalls at both the amateur, in-house, travel, and even the college levels. At one point or another, this ability to manage or alter or improve your own game is very important down the line, and you're not relying solely on a goalie coach or a parent to get you through these issues."

Goldman: I love this point and agree with it 100-percent, because I feel goalies that get a goalie coach at too young of an age get forced into playing the position or certain situations a specific way, a way that may not be the most effective for the way their body is structured or moves. But only the goalie himself will know what feels the most comfortable or most effective, and that's something an average or commonplace goalie coach can't necessarily do. So for guys like myself, who grew up without a goalie coach until I was 18, I had to teach myself through the process of failing and learning and training and working and not having an ego. And I know you've said before that a lot of goalies that have had success at the higher levels have gone through a similar process.

Wogtech: "I think we're at a time of transition because it wasn't that long ago that nobody had a goalie coach. I'm 32 and when I was growing up, goalie coaches were very rare. The NHL didn't have them, youth organizations didn't have them. I was forced to seek information and forced to figure things out from level to level. As I started to struggle with different situations or scenarios, it was only my responsibility to learn how to fix those things. Sometimes it was through trial and error at practice, sometimes I'd find information I could read online, and sometimes I'd cross paths with a goalie coach. In between all of that information seeking, I was forced, along with everyone else my age, to build my own game and problem solve. That's actually what got me into goalie coaching; I was continually having to seek information and find ways to fix things that weren't fixable for myself as a goalie. I think now with the amount of goalie coaches there are out there, you don't see goalies have the same workload, or have to work as hard, to find what they need. Usually they have a goalie coach that just tells them what they need to do to fix or change specific areas of their game, and the goalie blindly believes and buys into it. But that's the extent of it. I think goalie coaches are a great resource, but at the same time that could be extremely problematic if at one point or another, you're left to your own devices. This normally happens on teams that don't have goalie coaches, or in the middle of a game when things aren't going your way. If you don't have the intelligence to analyze and figure out what's going on, whether it's physical, technical, or mental, you are basically stuck with the success level that sits in front of you. You don't have the ability to change, manipulate, or improve it. That, to me, is where I think goalie coaching is both extremely advantageous, but also has the potential to be pretty damaging. And that fine line for an individual, figuring out what that means, and knowing how much they should or shouldn't expose themselves to certain coaches, or how much they should do on their own, is very challenging for a goaltender that wants to reach the elite level.

Goldman: So for a goalie coach that has worked most recently with USHL and NHL goalies, can you talk a little bit about how you push an NHL goaltender to know that he could be doing something more effectively, compared to a goalie at the USHL or NAHL level?

Wogtech: "Every goalie has their own personality and every situation and team and level of play carries a personality as well. In the NHL, it's so important that guys feel confident. A lot of times, if you're continuously trying to change things and analyze things and figure out the flaws, it's difficult to stay confident and difficult to believe in your game, because in that process there's a lot of failure and a lot of mistakes being made. So if you're not mentally strong and you can't separate the difference between a Monday or Wednesday practice where you're working on changing your game, or a game-day practice where you have to play within the confines of what you're comfortable and confident with, blending those two lines can be very difficult. At the NHL level, you find that goalies have worked through their game for the most part. There's a few things that they could or should fix, but finding time to do that mentally is tough during the regular season. So often those things are either avoided or ignored for the fact that their skill level is so high, so as long as their confidence is high, they can still be successful. If their confidence is not high, you run the risk of them being unsuccessful because their technical game isn't where it needs to be. So there's a really fine line when you can and can't work on specific things with NHL goalies, especially guys that have established, long-standing careers, guys that have already determined their body limitations and their comfort level. As far as the NCAA and USHL level is concerned, these are kids that are at a stage where they are focused on improving their stock as future pros. So they perceive the games as very important and they don't want to make a lot of changes in that process. The disadvantage is that they're in a developmental league, so it's important that they continually work on improving their technique, their mental game, and their confidence. So you end up spending way more time working with goalies at that level on change. Change on a daily basis is extremely taxing mentally, so it's almost limiting if you have a goaltender that's weak mentally, because you're restricted in how much you can manipulate their technical game, because you can ruin or diminish their confidence week-by-week."

Goldman: Is this why it becomes a double-edged sword in terms of goalie coaching over here?

Wogtech: "Yeah, for me, goalie coaches in North America are the best and worst resource a goalie has. If you're a goalie coach and you don't have the ability to analyze a situation in terms of a goalie's age, development and level at a specific point in time, it's very difficult to know what you should or shouldn't be talking to them about. If you're naturally a technical coach, you may want to continuously work on something, change or improve something. But there are times in a season where that's appropriate and times where that's less appropriate. So it's not necessarily the timeline, but the goalie you're working with that sets those parameters. If they're mentally capable of allowing changes to not affect their confidence or flow within a game a few days later, that goalie is fantastic to work with because you can extend the amount of practice time you're spending on making changes or improvements. If they're mentally weaker, and I don't mean this to sound bad, you

Goldman: Let's discuss another key issue that we've both pinpointed with goaltending in the USA – the issue of over-exposure.

Wogtech: "I think from an elite goaltending standpoint, in order to evaluate talent, there's a general consensus that they bloom and develop later. But the way the USA is set up in terms of evaluating talent, it's so young. You've got college commitments to kids that are freshmen in high school, kids that still have multiple years of high school and junior hockey before they'll enter as freshman in college. The NTDP starts to seriously evaluate talent and NHL potential as early as age 14. From a goalie's standpoint, it's very difficult for them to be at or near their best before they're 19-20, sometimes even 25 years old. That being said, the amount of scouts that are employed and placed into the market are eagerly seeking these 14-15-16-year old kids. So you could be a really skilled AAA goalie at age 16 and have been seen by almost every major D1 program, as well as the majority of USHL and NAHL teams. That's great from an exposure standpoint, but I think it's really difficult to make it all the way to your NHL draft year and still have the support of scouts. When you're seen that early and that often by scouts looking for NHL-caliber talent, it's probably more advantageous for them to see you for the first time when you're 17 or 18 years old, and for the amount of times that they see you to be limited to under 10 times. The more you view someone, the more flaws you might see. The younger the goalie is, the more flaws that naturally exist. When you combine those things together, in both Canada and the USA, it's very difficult for a goalie to become who he is going to become by the time he's 22 or 23 when he's being seen at such a young age. You may not even get the looks because you made so many perceived mistakes when you were 14 or 15. So a lot of these goalies are written off very early in their career in North America. Conversely, in Europe, it's getting worse. There's more scouting and exposure there, but you've seen a trend in the USA where people say goalies are hard to find here, so NHL teams have started going out and getting European talent. But usually they're not looking at 16 and 17-year-olds, they're looking at mid-20 year-olds playing at the highest level in their country, and have gotten to that point and have had the opportunity to fail and succeed at junior and minor-league hockey in Europe before they're being seen, or before NHL teams are making a decision on whether they're worth signing or drafting for development. They may be given another five to six years to make mistakes, develop and alter their game, and then they get their first exposure to NHL teams. So of course if I'm choosing between a guy I've scouted for years with a laundry list of issues, or another goalie that I've recently seen that is playing European pro hockey, and I know his game is more well-rounded and matured, the decision is not a tough one. I'm going to side with the more mature European pro."

Goldman: We've seen this a lot over the past few years with guys like Cristopher Nilstorp, Antti Raanta, Jussi Rynnas, Niklas Svedberg, Jonas Gustavsson, and others. They're all older, their game is fully mature compared to an 18-year-old, and nobody really knows what they're

truly made of, or what they're capable of doing on the smaller ice.

Wogtech: "I'd be very interested to know what current AHL goalies that were drafted at age 17 and were scouted from age 15 or 16 may look like compared to the guys we passed over at that age. The North American goalies that are in the AHL are goalies we made decisions on at age 17 and they may or may not grow. But if we waited to see what they look like for a little bit longer, they may not even be close to having the true potential of an AHL goalie. Making that decision is very complex for any scout at any level, and I think the USA makes it more complex by going younger and younger on what age we're choosing to decide on what kids move on and which kids we pass over."

Goldman: I can speak from my own experience at the NTDP this season that it was so tough because I'm scouting kids that are still growing and understanding their biomechanics and joint function. So how can I evaluate or project who could be a high draft pick in three years during their U-18 season when they're only 15 years old. We're putting so much emphasis on finding the right goalies when we have no clue what that goalie is going to look like a few years later.

Wogtech: "In the end, we're not even pulling most of the NHL goalies right now from our draft lists. We're signing free agents from the NCAA and the European pro leagues to become first, second, third, even fourth goalies in an NHL system. That fact alone says a lot about this idea that we're making decisions on goalies that we place within our top development leagues way too soon. We've deemed them insufficient by the time we need them to be AHL or NHL goalies, because of what you said, because it's too complicated to determine who will be successful five years or five or six levels down the line. I don't know if there's a solution for that, but it does seem like a pretty big problem."

23

THE 2014 USA HOCKEY SELECT 15'S FESTIVAL

As a regional goalie scout for the NTDP, similar to the Strelow camp, I was automatically added to the coaching staff for one of USA Hockey's annual Select Festivals. And since it was my first year with the NTDP, I was assigned to handle goalie evaluations for the youngest age group, the Select 15's.

The 2014 USA Hockey Boys' Select 15 Player Development Camp provided many of America's best players born in 1999 with concentrated on and off-ice training and instruction, while also giving them a chance to compete nationally in a team-oriented environment against other top 1999-born players. It's a key showcase since it is open to scouts from all over the world to attend, but the focus for USA Hockey is primarily on development.

This camp took place July 14-20 at The Northtown Center in Amherst, NY. The facility was nestled in a convenient location, just off Highway 290 and directly across from the University of Buffalo campus. It was my first time in Buffalo, so I really enjoyed soaking in the hockey culture in one of my rare visits out East.

The festival included 12 teams comprised of 18 players each, with two goalies per team. I was mainly responsible for evaluating and writing scouting reports on all 24 goalies in camp, but alongside the rest of the goalie coaching staff, as a group, we had to provide USA Hockey with one final letter grade ranking for each goalie in attendance.

The goalie coaching staff included Reiter, Petraglia, Millar, and then Brennan Poderzay, Jeff Hill, Matt Michno, and myself. Reiter, Petraglia, and Millar were already good friends of mine, so this camp was my first time meeting Poderzay, Hill, and Michno.

Poderzay hails from a small town in northern Minnesota called Tower, so he and I were actually on the same flight to Buffalo, by way of Chicago. It was in the terminal waiting to board our flight that I noticed his Reebok coaching bag, with a GDI business card resting inside the clear plastic sleeve.

"Hey man, my name's Justin. I noticed your GDI card," I said. "You heading to Select 15's?"

"Yes sir. My name's Brennan," he said. "Nice to meet you."

To say that Brennan and I became instant friends wouldn't do the camaraderie justice. I don't know why it happened, but we just got along seamlessly. Brennan was five years my younger and was playing pro hockey in the Netherlands, France, and Austria. I could feel the European culture had rubbed off on him a little bit. He had suave style and his typical "Minnesota Nice" personality shone through effortlessly.

I didn't know this until the first day of camp, but Brennan was actually very close friends with Millar. So the three of us gelled right away, making the entire camp experience way less stressful on me. I never felt so confident being in such an elite scouting atmosphere, and I could tell the wisdom and confidence I gained in Finland and at the Strelow Camp was showing. I no longer had the tiny fragile voice in the back of my mind. I was able to be my dorky self, and it meshed really well with the rest of the goalie staff.

Nevertheless, I was still surrounded by guys that had way, way more experience than me. Aside from a few guys, the entire Select 15's coaching and scouting staff had been doing this for many years. So once again, I was very much considered the rookie and the new face amongst the big boys at USA Hockey, and I made sure to tread lightly. For the most part, aside from when the goalie guys were all together doing goalie scouting things, I only spoke when spoken to.

Along with all of the players, the camp's entire coaching staff stayed in campus dorms, giving the festival an authentic summer camp feel. Being around so many 15-year-old kids in the middle of the summer on a college campus was not a bad way to spend a week on a very serious and stressful scouting grind.

The American Development Model

Before camp got underway, there was a massive briefing held by the festival's head staff, which included Gump Whiteside, Mike Bonish, Al Bloomer, Ken Martel, Ty Hennes, and Kenny Rausch.

This briefing brought the entire Select 15's coaching staff together for a series of pre-camp presentations called the Program of Merit. It was during these presentations that coaches made formal and informal introductions, while also discussing our goals for the camp, the current state of USA Hockey, and the latest developments with the American Development Model (ADM).

The Program of Merit was chock full of information, so I gained a much better understanding of the Select Festival process and the ADM's structure.

In one simple sentence, the ADM is an age-specific program aimed at giving all USA Hockey members a better chance to develop into National-caliber players.

The ADM was launched in January of 2009 and has been steadily gaining traction since then. In some places, the program is recognized as one of the best athletic development models in the world. Focused on age-appropriate competition and training for young hockey players, the model is based around long-term athletic development principles grounded in proven sports science. It's labeled as a "blueprint" and "ladder" for the consistent and efficient improvement of hockey players, regardless of their environment.

One of the presentations held during the Program of Merit was called "Why We Need Change" by Rausch. His insightful look at total registered numbers and how we needed to get more talented kids into the higher levels of regional hockey was eye-opening, especially since I don't focus on skaters at all.

Ty Hennes and his presentation on the current state of the ADM was an excellent listen as well.

"We can't approach today with the same mindset as yesterday," he said.

I wrote that quote in huge letters on my notepad. I knew it would end up in this book. Simple, yet so important, this quote is a facet of the coaching culture we find at all levels (and positions) in hockey. It takes time to advance the thinking of such a large nation, but meetings like these, with key members and major influencers in the world of USA Hockey, are a great place to start.

At the very least, Hennes' presentation spoke to me in a deep-felt way. I got the message, loud and clear.

Ty also explained how the ADM receives funding from the NHL, so their goal moving forward is to keep growing the numbers at the 8-to-10 age range and then retain these kids for as long as possible.

The ADM also wants to expand their model to further focus on developing a blueprint for pro-level players when they reach the ages of 13 and 14. The problem, Hennes explained, is that youth players are vastly under-training and over-competing. The focus in the USA is still centered on immediate outcomes instead of long-term development.

Once again, I saw this as something deeply embedded in our fiercely competitive youth sports culture.

Sure enough, Hennes went on to explain how this was very much a cultural dilemma in the United States, a strong beam of light shining on the scary truth regarding how we train and compete at the youth levels. That means it could take years and years to break those chains, but at least in terms of a team and skater environment, the ADM is becoming the revitalizing winds of change. Over the past few years, the ADM has been adding more youth hockey associations to the mix, so the winds are getting stronger and reaching more kids and hockey families than ever before.

In the most basic format I could write down during Hennes' presentation, the ADM progression looks something like this:

1. *Active Start*
2. *Fundamentals*
3. *Learn to Train*
4. *Train to Train*
5. *Learn to Compete*
6. *Train to Compete*
7. *Train to Win*
8. *Hockey for Life*

Each progression is catered towards an age group. So an "Active Start" is geared towards the 8-Under age group, and the "Learn to Compete" through the "Hockey For Life" progressions are for the most committed Tier-1 junior-aged teens (ages 15-18 for females and 16-18 for males).

As you can see, the emphasis is being steered towards learning how to train first, then focusing on competing and winning a little later on. Right now, kids in many youth travel associations are playing more games than most college programs, and sometimes even more than pro hockey teams. This needs to change, the focus needs to shift towards more practice time. The ultimate goal for our youth hockey players is being lost in a dense fog of over-exposure and over-aggressive parenting and coaching.

The Learn to Compete Stage

In the "Learn to Compete" stage, the objective is to prepare athletes for the competitive environment by further refining and developing their technical, ancillary, and physical skills. All of the objectives of the previous developmental stage (Train to Train) must be achieved before the Learn to Compete objectives can begin, so this stage is all about optimizing a player's fundamentals by becoming more specialized in certain areas, whether that be skating, vision training, or flexibility.

Since training in this stage is fully individualized and customized to the athlete's specific needs, it raises the importance of unbiased scouting reports and evaluation feedback from inner-circle and outer-circle coaches. Monitoring is a key aspect of this stage from the coach's standpoint. During this stage, training volume and intensity increases, as does the importance of performing well in tournaments and showcases. Athletes begin to feel more internal and external pressure from a variety of things, including their friends and family, coaches, and themselves.

As listed in their ADM guidebook, USA Hockey's key focus for this stage includes refining technical skills, gaining confidence in a variety of competitive situations, making good decisions on and off the ice, and making marked improvements in endurance, speed, and strength.

USA Hockey provides Tier-1 and Tier-2 competitive leagues as well as "Hockey for Life" programs like the NTDP that meet each individual's ability. USA Hockey also runs National Player Development Camps for both boys and girls. At the age of 17, players have the opportunity to make a youth-level U.S. National U-18 Team, either through those development camps or the NTDP. The U-18 age level is the initial age where the IIHF holds an official world championship event, so we're fully grooming players for that level.

Alongside the ADM's guidelines for player training, they also incorporate coaching recommendations as well. For this stage, a Level 3 coaching education program (CEP) certification is required. Tier-1 and Tier-2 national tournament bound and 18-Under midget coaches need a Level 4 CEP certification. Additional CEP training and continuing education is encouraged for coaches working within USA Hockey's high performance clubs, but it's also open to any coach that wants to improve their craft.

Within the guidelines for this stage, USA Hockey lays out very specific components for development. Below is a brief explanation of these components.

The first one is the Physical Development, which emphasizes that all athletes need a sufficient level of fitness to withstand the demands of training and competition without suffering injuries or burnout.

The second one is the Psychological Development, which aims to create well-developed mental preparation skills, as well as good pre-game habits in order to perform on demand in key competitive environments. The focus on mental preparation is to help athletes cope with the stresses associated with training and tournament selections.

In this category, I was very pleased to see the ADM include a bullet point that reads, "Athletes are capable of self-coaching and should be encouraged to think for themselves, rather than relying solely on coach feedback."

Next came Training and Competitive Environment. This component was further broken down into the Standard Track and High-Performance Track.

In the Standard Track, the training-to-competition ratio is set at 50-percent training, 10-percent competition-specific training, and 40-percent competition. The training volume is set at 3-to-4 times per week, with session length lasting from 60-to-90 minutes for 18-Under players. Training volume can be reduced for the "Hockey for Life" stage, based on the commitment level of the players involved. Fitness training is set for three times per week. The training year is four weeks per month, for seven months out of the year. The overall activity ratio is set at 50-percent hockey, 40-percent fitness, and 10-percent for other sports. Athletes are encouraged to participate in one complimentary sport, like lacrosse or golf.

In the High-Performance Track, the training-to-competition ratio is the same as the Standard Track. The training volume is increased to 5-to-6 times per week, with the same 60-to-90 minute sessions. They also increase the number of fitness sessions to 4-to-6 per week, including the strength development phase. The training year is increased from seven months to 9-10 per year. The overall activity ratio changes to be 60-percent hockey and 40-percent fitness.

Coaching considerations are focused primarily with a regard to training volume and intensity. Preparation requirements must be detailed and well-communicated. Coaches are asked to make sure players learn to compete with a team-first mentality. They are expected to reinforce the importance of making good off-ice decisions. "Everyone is watching, nothing you post on social media is safe." Displaying accountability, professionalism, emotional stability, and healthy eating is of utmost importance. Sleep and recovery are also emphasized in all aspects of life and hockey.

On the technical side, coaches are emphasizing a mastery of fundamentals and executing those fundamental skills at higher speeds. Detail-oriented tactics and game management are also emphasized.

The Science of the ADM

After breaking down the different stages within the ADM structure, Hennes spent some time explaining the science behind athletic development through what is called the "Window of Trainability" model. This broke down the training process into different age groups, and once again I'll do my best to explain them here in a simple way.

For ages 6-to-8, you have the "Speed 1" window. This is when kids should be taught how to create and improve short bursts of multi-directional speed. This reinforces the importance of small-area games and touches – in this training environment, kids will better learn how to get comfortable using their inside edges, how to transition backwards and forwards, and how to move the puck while skating.

Another window of trainability in the 8-Under age group is called Suppleness. This is all about agility, balance, and coordination. It works hand-in-hand with multi-directional speed bursts. From there, you go into the "Skill" window at the 9-to-12 ages. This is when myelin production is at its highest, so kids have the ability to better adapt, adjust, and improve their natural athletic ability and muscle memory.

Next comes the "Speed 2" window. This is for the 12-to-14 ages and is all about linear speed. From there, you go into the "Strength and Stamina" windows, which account for ages 14-to-18.

I was really impressed with the amount of scientific research that went into creating the ADM. It is based on some very solid facts and studies, and this is the type of stuff that, while I may not have an intimate understanding of the chemistry behind it, I understand that it's necessary for proper athletic development.

I also look at it as a framework for a better future model. Since it has only been around for about five years, the foundation has been laid for more science to be incorporated into the way our head coaches are developing hockey players around the country.

Ultimately, I learned that USA Hockey's message during the Program of Merit was focused on the fact that the number of registered players is rising, but the offensive talent is stagnating. This is accredited to a culture where we place too much value on winning at the younger levels. Too many youth teams are playing too many games. As a result, not only are there not enough practices, but those practices don't include enough "touches" for the players, and there's not enough actual teaching taking place.

Furthermore, while the ADM is programmed to be the problem-buster for these issues, the coaches have to help implement it by acting as advocates for the model within their regions and youth associations.

Coaching Goalies in the ADM

So much great information was provided during the Program of Merit, but as I leafed through my packet, I scanned the final page and let out an audible sigh. Where was the goalie-specific content? Are we expecting head coaches to just lump goalies into the same development patterns as skaters?

I guess so, because at this time, no goalie-specific ADM education for coaches or players currently exists. This is another element that I fully believe has to change as 2015 rolls along.

I know there's very little expertise to draw from here in North America when it comes to knowing exactly how to develop goalies in an age-specific manner, but just like everything else when it comes to creating a structured goalie development program, USA Hockey has to start somewhere. And starting somewhere means trying to make it as basic and as simple as possible.

Even though I was distraught at the lack of goalie-specific content during the Program of Merit, I was really excited to be in the room with so many key USA Hockey coaches. I realized the ADM was breaking ground on a new wave of players and coaching methods, more specifically the "cross-ice" games and "small-area" stations. Even though I may not see any type of significant progress in how they handle coaching goalies for a few more years, it was such a breath of fresh air to know that, as a whole, change – significant cultural change – was taking place.

But one thing really bothered me was the lack of time committed to goaltending. Reiter did get to host a presentation on the Warren Strelow program, but it was such an afterthought compared to the rest of the Program of Merit that half of the coaches didn't even attend. Some were either in the adjacent room at the rink's bar and grill, or they had mentally tuned out, or they were let go to meet with their respective teams.

Reiter's voice, for the most part, went unheard. It was essentially a waste of valuable time, which was a huge problem for me. Part of the issue we're facing as a country is that we need more structure, but if a key moment like this is wasted on things that should already be well-known to every top USA Hockey coach, then we'll never truly progress. The time Reiter was given during the Program of Merit should have been spent solely on helping head coaches understand how to better work with their goalies in practice.

Instead, most of it seemed very redundant and beside the point.

Mind you, not all of Reiter's presentation was worthless. Some coaches listened and raised a few good questions, and there were some good parts regarding head coaches working with goalies, but I was still unsettled and unnerved. It left a sour taste in my mouth as we geared up for the first day of camp.

While I reflected on these presentations that same night, I realized that, as a whole, I was an advocate for the ADM. But I also found myself listing some key obstacles and issues to properly coaching goalies under the current ADM environment. I had some pretty strong feelings here, because I knew we simply had to do more in order to enhance our goalie coaching at the grassroots levels.

I knew that USA Hockey got what they paid for. I knew it all came down to the almighty dollar. But money and budget issues aside, we had the means and we had the minds, we just needed to change the culture.

At the top of my list, I noted that the biggest obstacle in terms of coaching goalies under the ADM was the workload that goalies shoulder in a typical ADM practice. Due to cross-ice scrimmages and small-area stations, many young goalies get tired very quickly. The gear isn't easy to manipulate and wear at that age, so it takes more energy and time to go down, recover, skate, and slide. Yet very few head coaches understand this, so when the goalie gets tired and is pretty much worthless halfway through a practice, he or she is looked down upon, reprimanded, and sometimes even scolded. If the coach is more passive or unobservant, the goalie is just left to his or her own defenses, and at that age, they get scored on so many times in a single practice that they quickly become discouraged.

This doesn't just stymie the goalie's development, it often kills it for good. Some simply quit after their first time in net, and that breaks my heart. As a result, I'm worried we're not retaining as many goalies as we have in past years, because the "sexy" appeal of being a goalie is disappearing. It's too hard and not fun.

Presented with this problem, I tried to detail some potential solutions.

First and foremost, ADM goalies must be allowed to take breaks. That means we need to train a head coach (or a volunteer goalie coach, if a team has one) to be aware of the goalie's situation. If the goalie can skate out of the net and skip a few reps in order to re-hydrate and catch their breath without being reprimanded, their attitudes will remain positive.

Secondly, since many teams under the ADM only have one goalie, I think a head coach should consider putting a shooter tutor on one of their nets. This reduces the strain on the team's sole goalie and still challenges young shooters to pick corners and aim with a purpose.

Thirdly, speaking of nets, there is a lot of discussion regarding their size. I could write an entire chapter on this topic, but at the end of the day, I think this is a subject that is still without answers. There is plenty of merit to having size-oriented nets, but my concern, and one that is shared in Sweden, is the potential for it to make young goalies more robotic. Smaller goalies in a big net are forced to be very athletic because they have to extend, reach, dive, and work hard to catch pucks. But if you put a smaller goalie in a smaller net, he or she will begin to create blocking and space-filling instincts that should not be implemented into their game until they are older and more aware of when, where, and why they block.

I know there is a lot of good scientific research being done that advocates the smaller nets, and I do believe it would stop goalies from being so dejected in ADM practices. But I think the US-born goalie thrives on being extremely competitive and outside-the-box compared to the more purified styles found in Europe. That being said, while keeping the big nets may cause some goalies to drop out, the ones that stick with it and have the toughness to keep competing and battling for pucks eventually develop the fire we want to find in our older and more talented prospects.

Clearly this just scratches the surface of the science behind the size of nets, but my raw opinion right now is that we keep the bigger nets.

Fourthly – and this is the most obvious solution in my mind – is to begin enforcing a rule where 10 minutes of goalie-specific training is included in as many ADM practices as possible. However, this is only realistic if each team delegates a parent or a volunteer to act as the team's goalie coach (especially if the youth association's goalie coach is unavailable). That opens up a whole new dilemma in terms of coaching certification, but if goalies can at least have *someone* competent enough (or certified...hint, hint) to run a few goalie drills, it will eliminate a lot of the problems with retention and slowed development. Young and often emotional goalies need moral and positive support, someone catering to their continued success. We can't just allow them to face a barrage of shots and hope they stick around.

Another one of the many benefits of having goalie-specific training during ADM practices would be the ability to begin instilling key practice and preparation habits at younger ages. This was one of the biggest differences I noticed between youth goalies in Finland. Over there, young kids were incredibly disciplined and regimented with their routines. Over here, kids don't understand the importance of that stuff until they're 14, 15, sometimes even 16 years old.

This falls perfectly in line with what is so desperately needed in order to further expand and strengthen the ADM right now: a basic Level 1 goalie coaching certification program. It would not only be a terrific springboard for amateur goalie coaches to improve their craft, but it would begin to change and shape the culture into something much more beneficial than what we have right now.

If we can reach that point, we'll be able to entrust our parents, volunteers, and amateurs to working with young goalies on the basic skills (mental and physical) and key principles of the position. From there, we not only grow the number of ADM goalies and goalie coaches, but we retain them. We keep them coming back for more.

The Select 15's Experience

Thankfully, with seven goalie coaches, three rinks, and split-team practices, we were able to have one goalie coach on the ice for every Select 15's practice. As a result, there was quite a bit of mentoring and guidance being given to the 24 goalies in attendance. The dark cloud from Reiter's presentation during the Program of Merit was a fast-moving shadow over what was otherwise another unbelievable coaching and scouting experience.

The event was special for me in so many ways. Not only did I get to mentor and build relationships with 24 of the top American goalie prospects born in 1999, but I gained more valuable scouting and on-ice coaching experience in a competitive and high-profile team setting.

Each goalie coach in attendance was assigned two teams to work with for all team practices. Purple and Gold were my assigned teams, and while the Gold goalies struggled and the Purple goalies excelled, all four of them experienced plenty of success in terms of development.

This was a very bright spot in terms of American goalie development.

These 24 goalies all had to manage the same things; traveling before a big scouting event, being tossed onto a team with many strangers, being forced to stay in the dorms with random roommates, and doing so in the middle of the summer. The ones that exhibited some level of maturity, good practice habits, and some form of leadership were the ones that thrived under the pressure of the most elite-level showcase in their age group.

In every game that took place, one goalie coach was responsible for completing a shot chart for each goalie. All shot charts were gathered at the end of each day and punched into a spreadsheet in order to determine each goalie's basic statistics. As you could imagine, all seven goalie coaches knew the limits that came with these team-oriented statistics. They had very little impact on how we rated our goalies overall, but having them posted publically on USA Hockey's website certainly impacted everyone else.

These shot charts were both beneficial and debilitating to the scouting process. On one end, for every game I didn't see, I could look at the shot chart and get a better idea of the goalie's workload, what type of goals they allowed, and where they had success. But for the games I scouted, I spent so much time looking down at a sheet of paper and trying to accurately pinpoint shot locations that I would miss bits and pieces of the game.

Ultimately, there wasn't much I could do to alter that process. I took comfort in the fact that we had two goalie-only practices during the week, which allowed all seven goalie coaches to spend more time getting to know the goalies on the ice. But to put so much emphasis and energy into hand-writing a shot chart for every single goalie in every single game seemed very backwards. Those shot charts could have been compiled by interns. The goalie coaches could have made more detailed notes about style and execution.

Furthermore, there was no video analysis being done at this camp. So, just like I did at Strelow camp, I took my tablet down to ice level for a couple of games and logged some much-needed and very necessary video clips of some of the goalies in camp.

Once again, my mind was blown at the fact that USA Hockey had not set up a system where every goalie was logged into a system that included their stats and a couple of choice video clips, which could be revisited or shared at any time. How can we truly evaluate a goalie's progress from the age of 15 to 18 without any video to support any visual or spoken evidence?

As companies like Double Blue Analytics and Coach's Eye and Vulcan Vision advance their technologies, it is imperative that organizations like USA Hockey use them. Video feedback is the ultimate truth for developing goaltenders; without it, they never really know what they're doing out there.

Don't get me wrong, working with all 24 goalies at the Select 15's Festival was a memorable learning experience. But the lack of video and the time spent filling out game sheets were key problems that could easily be solved moving forward. If so, the entire scouting and development experience will be greatly improved on both sides of the spectrum.

Scouting Biases in a Group Setting

As the week moved along, I started to absorb and learn from some key dynamics that come with scouting goalies as a group. It's always interesting to discover how biases influence decisions, not only for goalies making teams, but on potential goalie coaching or scouting candidates as well.

For example, one goalie coach in Minnesota could have easily been my replacement at the NTDP, but he happened to work with kids in the same age group as the current NTDP players. Although he may very well be a better goalie coach, another candidate who works with goalies that are younger had a definitive advantage, because he is working with kids that would be on the NTDP radar in a few years. He had no bias on kids that could potentially join the program the following year, but had great insight into future classes.

So which one makes more sense? A guy that is working with older goalies, or a guy that will be working with kids that could potentially make the tryout roster in a few years? It's a good question for all of you goalie coaches to ponder.

I learned so much about scouting on a big stage this summer, but one thing that struck me right in the heart when it came to evaluating goalies was the importance of building relationships. And as you build new relationships with young, impressionable goalies, you must learn about the psychological impact of biases – what they are, how they work, and how they influence your own decision-making in a group setting like the Select 15's Festival.

Some biases are harmless. If someone you care about or look up to hates ice cream, you can still like ice cream and be friends. You also do not lose respect for someone just because you love black socks and they happen to own nothing but white socks.

Other opinions and biases are much more powerful, because they have the ability to sway your opinion. That sway depends on the relationship you have with a person, and I was reminded of this when the goalie coaching staff sat down to complete our final rankings for the week.

All seven goalie coaches had tons of notes on the 24 goalies. There were at least two of us in a room at a time for each and every game that took place during the week. We all shared thoughts and gleamed information from each other with every single goalie being discussed. Our rankings, therefore, could be partially attributed to some of the biases that existed within each of us. Some of our rankings looked very similar, and as you will find with all of these group rankings, you have a typical bell curve. There are four or five goalies that clearly belong at the top, a bigger and more ambiguous group of goalies in the middle that could move up or down a few spots, and then a clear-cut group of goalies that belong at the bottom.

I imagined what our rankings would look like if all six of us never spoke to each other about any of the goalies in camp. How different would they look? What then?

"Primeau's a stud," Millar said one morning.

"Hmm," I thought. "He must be doing some impressive things out there that I haven't seen yet. Maybe I'm undervaluing him."

Something as simple as a statement from Millar affirming his thoughts on Cayden Primeau has the power to influence my view of the same goalie. Millar's opinion is one that I trust and value, and since Millar spent the most time with Primeau compared to the other 23 goalies, there is merit in his observations.

As much as I loved scouting goalies with the amazing group of guys at the Select 15's Festival, the whole process still seemed so muddied. But more importantly, I believe you have to share thoughts and opinions and ideas. If you're not doing that, you're not doing everything you can to gain information on a goalie prospect. So I think the key is to simply understand what kind of biases can exist in this type of environment, and how influential another observer can be on your own understanding of a goalie's talent.

Just like I experienced at the Warren Strelow camp, the group of goalie coaches I interacted with was extremely talented. Reiter is always teaching me new things and helping me see things on a deeper level. Millar is one of the most underrated goalie coaches in North America. Poderzay was exactly like me, just so damn enthralled to be there, so he was always willing to go out of his way to get things done. Petraglia stood for pride, his enthusiasm was through the roof. Hill may have been considered the understudy to the rest of the group, but his intelligence and discipline complimented the group extremely well.

These guys reinforced the notion I wrote about earlier – our goalie coaching at the highest levels is underrated and extremely gifted. Now we just need more at the lower levels.

It's actually kind of funny. A country like Finland has amazing structure at the lowest levels, but now they're in a process of adding that structure to the higher levels. Here in the United States, we have amazing structure at the highest levels with our NTDP and our Select Festivals, but now we're hoping to get to a point where we start adding structure at the lowest levels.

It just goes to show that, when comparing goalie development models, "right" or "wrong" is completely relative to the individual country. What works for one does not necessarily work for another, so the only thing that matters is finding solutions to the specific problems we have in the USA.

Fortunately, the Select 15's Festival was exactly the type of platform USA Hockey needed to discuss and determine those problems. And since the coaching staff was so passionate about doing good work, we were able to take advantage of our time together and plant the seeds of change.

Planting the Seeds of Change

Beyond all the coaching I did on the ice, which included one very ugly spill and yard sale in front of a bunch of scouts and coaches, and all the scouting I did off the ice, the Select 15's Festival was a moment of major transition in my personal and professional life. It was during this week that I reflected in the stillness of my sweltering dorm room and made the decision to move back to Colorado in order to start taking over the family business.

In turn, this meant I would be giving up my role as the Minnesota regional goalie scout and mentor for the

NTDP. By no means did I lose the passion for scouting 15 and 16-year-old goalies, but I simply fell in love with a different aspect of goaltending; worldwide development models and the deeper folds of goaltending science, including many topics broached in this book.

At the same time, a new mission arose from the ashes of my role with the NTDP. I wanted to do whatever I could to try and create some sort of structure within USA Hockey goaltending. Whether it was merely getting to update and upgrade USAHockeyGoaltending.com or actually work on implementing a Level 1 Goalie Coaching Certification Program, even if it meant I would not succeed and my tenure with USA Hockey was all over after one short year, I was ready and willing to take the risk.

Since I left Finland, everything I wanted to do in the future finally came to a head at the Select 15's Festival. It was here that I would start planting seeds of progress and promise by going out on a massive limb and openly talking with Reiter and the rest of the goalie coaching staff about the changes we needed. When that camp ended, I was no longer the quiet and peaceful observer. I was outspoken.

The proverbial "massive limb" was informing everyone that I was moving back to Colorado. By doing so, however, I would be in USA Hockey's backyard again, so I would be able to help Reiter make some major changes within our goalie development programs. The next step was to explain to everyone what I learned in Finland, and how I needed them to "buy in" to the idea that we needed to do something to spark the change in our own country.

I don't remember what led me to take this next step, but the next thing I knew, I was hovering over a sheet of white paper with the words "Strelow Buy-In" at the top. I wrote my name in legible print on one side, and then signed my name on the other side. Then I tore it out of my binder and folded it up and stuck it in my pocket.

I knew from the beginning that this near-impossible task would never turn into a perfect solution, but this thought progress and decision to move back to Colorado engaged my motivations and fired me up. There would be so much red tape to break through, but having the goalie coaches from the Strelow and Select 15's camps "buy in" to these ideas might be the momentum I needed to help make a difference. How cool would that be?!

I thought it was going to take a lot more time to get acceptance, but it turns out that Reiter was the only guy I needed to "sell" on these ideas.

Before I approached Reiter, I first spoke to Millar, Petraglia, and Hill. I was honored when, directly following my passionate tirade about Finland and our lack of structure here in the States, which included me waving that little sheet of paper in the air as if it were on fire, Petraglia got up and snatched it out of my hand and signed it with authority. He slammed the pen down, but he was not smiling. He was being serious and adamant for the sake of showing me that he actually gave a damn. He can be intimidating at times, and again, not as intimidating as the one and only Peter Ward, but enough to where I tread lightly.

Petraglia is the most passionate goalie coach when it comes to "The Nation" and has a ton of energy and spirit both on and off the ice. I honestly think of him as the over-protective dad of Strelow. I mean that in a loving and positive way; like I said, he gives a shit, and it always shows. That's why I treaded lightly – the last thing I wanted to do was come off like I'm trying to step in and act like I had all of the answers. I clearly didn't and never will.

I just want to help facilitate change, especially since I still have the time to do so.

Getting 'Trags to "buy in" was huge for me. Having him sign that informal petition with such passion and sincerity gave me the added confidence I needed to do the same thing when I finally sat down with Reiter. I had Hill and Millar sign the sheet as well, and this wrinkled petition still rests silently on my desk, proudly collecting dust as the days turn to months and the ideas that sprung from my trip to Finland transform into legitimate opportunities to revolutionize the way we develop US-born goaltenders.

Millar also honored me when he said he wanted to join me when I sat down with Reiter. I was all for that – I knew I would definitely be more comfortable having him there.

About an hour later, even though I was nervous as hell, I wasn't intimidated. A part of me felt really bad that I was going to drop my move on Reiter during the event, but I wasn't going to hold off and waste any time. So it was the right thing to do, but that didn't make it any easier.

At first, Reiter, Millar, and I discussed potential replacements for my regional scouting gig in Minnesota. We came up with a few names and came to some conclusions and quickly moved on.

Then I pulled out the sheet of paper and poured through everything all over again. I gave Reiter the same exact spiel I had given the rest of the goalie coaching staff, except this time, I was even more assertive with my opinions. I was as honest and as straightforward as I possibly could have been for a guy that rested at the bottom of the goalie coaching totem pole in USA Hockey. I had the smallest voice but a big heart, and a lot of factual evidence to back up everything I had learned over the summer.

I put my balls on the table and let the dominos fall. For nearly two hours, I spoke adamantly with Reiter about the need for a goalie coaching certification program and a basic goalie development handbook. I put it all out there and closed by saying that something needed to be done, and sooner rather than later.

To know that I was able to speak out and have my voice be heard on something as significant as USA Hockey's goaltending development was a huge moment, one that elevated my passion to new heights. The idea that we needed coaches to "buy in" had suddenly begun, the process had started, and at that moment, I once again knew I was meant to be there, meant to move back to Colorado, meant to write this book, meant to help out in any way possible.

After all that passionate speaking, Reiter visibly understood what I learned from my time spent in Finland. He was on my side. He was an advocate for change. To my blissful surprise, not only did he agree with me, but when I asked him if we had to wait to start creating a basic goalie coaching manual, he repeated this phrase three or four times, proving that he agreed change was possible, even if it took a few years.

"No, we don't have to wait," he said. "We're doing this."

24

MITCH KORN, AMERICA'S GOALIE YODA

If you were on a personal retreat deep in the Rocky Mountains and Yoda suddenly appeared in front of you, would he really need an introduction? Affectionately referred to as the Goalie Yoda, Washington Capitals goalie coach Mitch Korn needs no introduction. He's a real-life goalie whisperer, a man I've been honored to call my mentor for the past four years.

For decades, Korn's renowned props and training methods have revolutionized the way goalie coaches around the world have honed their craft. Most recently, his use of medicine balls on the ice with NHL goalies like Carter Hutton, Braden Holtby, and Justin Peters has once again advanced and altered goalie coaching culture, opening the door for creativity to be embraced.

If it was an amateur or lesser-known goalie coach doing this, he or she may have been scoffed at or shunned. But Korn's work in the realm of goaltending is lore. It also transcends all ages and levels; those same medicine balls that he used with NHL goalies have also been used with 12-year-old boys and girls.

Beyond Korn's wizardry of coaching and training goalies, I think his purest wisdom lies in his ability to explain the most complex aspects of development in a simple and visually-appealing way. He's the one true King of the Goalie Metaphor. From the goalie's mind being like a computer filling its hard drive with programs, to his definition of 'goalie geeks' and 'the butterfly', to how he explains the anticipation skills of Dominik Hasek, he gives hockey fans and tenured hockey journalists those elusive 'golden quotes' that leave lasting images in their mind.

Simply put, it is so easy to learn from Mitch, because he excels as a speaker. He presents detailed and complicated goalie information in a vivid and memorable way. Most people are visual learners these days, so I believe his ability to help people visualize the position is what makes him one of the finest goalie coaches and teachers the world has ever seen.

As a writer who strives to reach literary success in the realm of goaltending, all of my conversations, discussions, and phone calls with Mitch have forever resonated in my mind. Every meeting stands out among the rest for these reasons, and the fact he's one of the American forefathers of goalie coaching makes my friendship with him that much more sacred.

Therefore, this book would not have been complete without picking Mitch's brain on everything I had been researching over the summer. Thankfully, for a third straight year, I was able to accept his invitation to be a volunteer goalie coach for one of his youth goalie camps in Minnesota.

This camp was held in Duluth, just off I-35 and close to the Great Lakes. It took place in June, at a time when Korn had just transitioned from Nashville to Washington. As a result, I was in for the experience of a lifetime. Not only did I get my own personal "24/7" behind-the-scenes peek at Korn's first few days as a Capitals goalie coach, but he also let me look over his shoulder as he broke down video of some NHL goalies. The Capitals were seeking a new backup for Holtby, and they relied heavily on Korn for insights as to who would be the best fit.

Not only was Korn willing to let me be in the room when he spoke to guys like Holtby, Pheonix Copley, Olaf Kolzig, Scott Murray, and a few members of Washington's upper management, but he actually gave me a detailed explanation of these conversations. He even asked me for feedback and advice on who might be a good fit for Holtby's backup. As someone who has painstakingly tracked NHL goalie depth charts for a number of years, I have a strong grasp on who has played where, who is available, and where guys are going in all of the minor and junior leagues. It's an asset to know these things, because NHL goalie coaches are way too busy to do that type of research; they're focusing on their own guys and making sure they're prepared for each and every game.

Mitch's camp is a very enjoyable experience for many reasons, but near the top of my list is the fact that it's one of the few times you get to see an NHL goalie coach work with a big group of kids. This happens mainly on a private lesson scale, so to gain insights on how he runs a full-blown camp with kids of all ages is really special and cannot be replaced. It also says a lot about Mitch as a person – he's never too busy or never too proud to work with the youngest kids on the most basic skills.

Without a shadow of doubt, I can tell you that, of all the goalie camps I've ever been to, none has proven to be more organized and streamlined than Korn's. Whether he has 20 or 40 goalies on the ice at one time, every lesson plan and station is strategically placed, and every classroom session is held with a superhuman level of enthusiasm. The man is a solid ball of endless energy and no matter how mentally tired he may be, you'd never know it when watching him give a presentation to his students.

Furthermore, he's a preparation master. From making sure every shooter is on time and accounted for, to putting people he trusts in positions that are considered their 'wheelhouse', he dictates and directs a large goalie camp better than anyone I've ever met.

Korn's camps stress the basics and fundamentals of goaltending, so in my mind, his camp is a different type of learning experience. Instead of video breakdowns and advanced tactics, it's more about the inner-workings of youth goalie development. It's how he teaches the basics in a way that speeds up the muscle memory process. It's the way he engages his kids, holds them accountable, but always makes sure everyone is having fun and moving as much as possible. He will get fierce, but then he'll crack a lewd and obnoxious joke that has you turning to the guy next to you saying, "Did he seriously *just* say that?"

It's pretty damn hilarious.

At the end of the day, what made this interview with Korn so special was the timing of it all. It happened after my trip to Finland and my experiences at the Strelow and

Select 15's camps. As such, I was able to really focus our discussion on the current state of American goalie development, and whether or not a guy like me could actually make a difference in the future.

In fact, this interview was more like a point-counterpoint discussion than a traditional interview. That's another thing I love about Mitch; he really engages me to think about what I'm doing, to figure out a legitimate method and not just fall into madness.

And so it goes for one of the world's finest goalie minds. So many quotable quotes, so many memorable metaphors. If I had to choose one that has left a lasting imprint on my mind, it would be this one:

"Some guys just don't know what they don't know."

This quote keeps me grounded and humble. I know what I know, but I also know what I don't know. I'm still in a place where I'm not ready to call myself an expert. Others are free to call me one if they so choose, but I am still a dedicated student of the position. Any expertise I have is only a result of great knowledge being passed down to me through the teachings of guys like Korn.

A new world awaits the man who turns his mentor's wisdom into knowledge. For more of Korn's wisdom, which I proudly share below, I am eternally grateful.

Goldman: What has been your experience coaching, developing, and mentoring Finnish goalies compared to North American goalies?

Korn: "Well I've actually coached three Finnish goaltenders. We had Markus Ketterer in the Buffalo organization years back. That was almost 20 years ago, so it's very different compared to today. His game unfortunately did not translate over here. He struggled. He was not a big mammoth guy like we see today. But it was interesting, because I had never seen this before; every game, for his pre-game warmup, he'd run the stairs and do sprints. He'd actually play a game almost in terms of energy expulsion before he played the game. It was unusual, because he did that after his normal morning skate. I actually reached out to Markus recently. He's now coaching in the top league back in Finland."

Goldman: And then of course you worked with Pekka Rinne. What was that experience like?

Korn: "When I went over to meet Pekka Rinne for the first time, I watched him practice, but I never saw him play, because he never got into a game. But on practice days, he literally had three practices. He had an off-ice team practice, he had a position-specific goalie practice, and then he had the on-ice team practice. So he did those three things. The goalie practice wasn't really long, but it was still a goalie practice. With Pekka, he was such a late bloomer and a local to his club in Oulu that I don't think he was ever a big part of the federation teams there, like a lot of guys developing today."

Goldman: And then the third?

Korn: "The other Finnish goalie I've interacted with is Juuse Saros, who was drafted by the Preds, and played his first year last year in the Finnish Elite League after excelling in the World Juniors. Our interaction was mostly by text, and he was very diligent with his texts. He speaks great English, he's mature beyond his years, has great 'goalie sense' and he's physically gifted. He's not extremely big, but he's extremely skilled. I guess God doesn't give anybody everything, but he gives everybody something. I broke down games for him last season, so we interacted a fair amount and we had plenty of things to talk about. We never really talked much about the 'Finnish way' and what they do and how they do it. I know when I shared games with my comments with him, I asked him to view and review them with his goalie coach, and they were very willing to do that together and were excited to have my feedback."

Goldman: Was there anything about Juuse or his coach's personality that stood out to you as being different from other NHL prospects you've worked with?

Korn: "The neat thing was that Juuse's coach was always open minded, and welcomed another voice. He was very excited to read my stuff, go through the game and learn with Juuse. Too often here in North America, many goalie coaches would not be that way. I find that many coaching are more close-minded. They get intimidated, and 'shelter' their goalies. I hear of coaches all the time who try to discourage their students from going to one of my summer camps, for example. A lot of young coaches don't know what they don't know. A lot think that they've got all the answers, or are so insecure that they don't want somebody else in their territory, and that may be a very big difference. Here, some of these coaches make their living this way, and are protective of their 'clients'. The 'buy-in' and sharing in Finland, for example, is greater."

Goldman: Do you think that the Finnish goalies have some sort of marked advantage in terms of how they play compared to North American goalies?

Korn: "I think a couple of big things are that, because it's a small country, it is way easier to have uniformity. Secondly, they can adjust much more quickly to new techniques. They have an infrastructure in place, and to the best of my knowledge, there are very few guys that make a living coaching goalies on an independent basis. All information is shared, and there is a large percentage of 'buy-in' there. Whereas I know many people all over North America that run goalie businesses. Therefore, they have their own ideas, they are protective of their turf, there's no accreditation, and they often operate in a vacuum. All they need to do is get an EIN number – if they are even legal – in the United States to run a business. They don't even need to know CPR or basic first aid, let alone follow any minimum standard. I think in some ways it's so cutthroat in some places that they become so protective of their goalies, and they don't want the goalie working with anyone else. It's like figure skating; you're the coach and that's all there is, and that's not the way it should be. A regular hockey player in North America in his career will probably play for 15 coaches, because he goes from team to team to team, and there's no possessiveness by the coach of that player. But in the goalie business, it's very possessive."

Goldman: The way I see it, in Finland, everyone seems to "buy in" to the national program and everyone's willing to share. But here in North America, there's no national certified program to buy in to for goalie development.

Korn: "Right. But even if there was, this country is so diverse, the coach or administrator who currently would be putting it together is also coaching his own teams. It's almost like going coast-to-coast in a political campaign. You have to go to diverse hockey associations, you have to be selling this or that, running seminars, and doing all this kind of stuff. And the guy who would be in charge of that right now simply can't do that. That's a whole new department that needs to be created."

Goldman: I'm glad we're on this topic, because that's where I was headed. After experiencing what Finland has to offer in terms of a manageable infrastructure due to their size, I'm curious what you feel can be done here in the USA in order to help this country create structure or begin to lay a foundation for some sort of future structure. I feel like it's a huge gaping void right now.

Korn: "It is. But I don't know how you do it, because first of all, it's an enormous country. Second of all, we all have to work for a living, so we have to earn money, and USA Hockey is not in a position to compensate these people. And honestly, the best people to share this information are doing too many other things to be in a position to share a lot. Let's say for example there's a small youth hockey association in Florida. How do you reach out to them? Maybe nobody lives there that's in a position to help those kids or volunteer coaches, if there are even goalie coaches to begin with. Finland's such a small country, there's no 'suburbia' to hockey there. Everybody is within regions and reachable. I'm not sure that's the case in this country. Therefore, you need a greater volume of coaches. Take me for example. I'm US-born, but involved in very little with USA Hockey. I have had influence on the people that have done work with USA Hockey though. The joke is, when Joe Exter used to run the Strelow program, that almost everyone he had coaching there had interacted with me at some level, and it's pretty cool to have that influence. But because of what I'm doing professionally, and what I do for my camps, and with my personal life, I am out of time. So I might be one of the more experienced guys to contribute, but how can I do it? The guys that tend to have the time tend to be not as experienced. So it's a catch-22 situation. It's hard, and I don't know how to deal with it or create a solution."

Goldman: So that being said, for someone like myself, someone who is now part of USA Hockey and falls into that category of having the time but not the experience, is there anything...

Korn: "But what you're doing is, because you don't have a wife and you don't have kids yet, you're willing to be on a subsistence level to survive economically. Yet you've still gone to work with Eli Wilson, you've gone to Finland, you've worked with me multiple times, you've worked with Mike Valley, and now you have been present for USA Hockey's annual goalie events. What you have done is what goalie coaches need to do. If you didn't work with me and the other guys, you would be less prepared to be as valuable or as knowledgeable as you have become. So you take that guy who right now is coaching a bunch of kid goalies in Florida; how do we get him to be where you are? I don't know."

Goldman: My answer would be with a goalie coaching certification program.

Korn: "Maybe. But that's a really difficult thing, too. How do you certify the many philosophies that exist on how to handle the posts, how to move the puck, and do we drop and block here, or do we save here? A goalie at 5-foot-7 will play different than a goalie that's 6-foot-4, who will play different if he's in California watching Antti Niemi versus if he's in New York watching Henrik Lundqvist. That goes along with your Shadowing theory. Coaching is not 'just one way' or totally black or white. It's not like being a referee where you read a book, and learn a rule that is black and white."

Goldman: Yes, I'm forever fascinated by the influence of mimicry, because it breaks down cultural and environmental factors. What are your thoughts on that?

Korn: "When I grew up in the New York City area, everyone looked like Ed Giacomin. And I've got friends of mine and kids who work for me now that look like Marty Brodeur. For years, everyone in Quebec resembled Patrick Roy. They all watched their home team exclusively. Today, we're lucky. We have every game on television right at our fingertips, because of satellite dishes that exploded in the late 1980's. I remember installing one of those huge C-Band dishes for my home in 1986, so I was able to watch all kinds of hockey. But at that time, Europeans rarely got to see North Americans. It's not until the recent digital era that all began to happen and evolve. There is definitely a correlation to that."

Goldman: Absolutely. That's something I mentioned to you before. When I was growing up, I saw goalies on TV from different countries, and that influenced my style. But in Finland, kids my age just saw Finnish goalies. So their form and style seems more consistent, whereas in North America, we're a bunch of mutts. So it makes it even more difficult, especially with the size of the country and lack of a coaching certification program. But there has to be some sort of solution to the problem, so for me, first I'm just trying to understand what can actually be done. Any ideas?

Korn: "First off, you need to provide educational material for the grassroots. If they read it, they read it. If they absorb it, they absorb it. If they don't, they don't. But you have to provide that to have a chance. You have to try and get a consistent language. But you can't mandate. You must provide options. Again, there is no 'one way' in all of this. I will say this though: we can criticize USA Hockey all we want, but we've made progress. The Strelow program, for example. The Dave Petersen Camp, the Ann Arbor [NTDP] program for example. The National Development Goaltending camps, both regional when they did them, and national when they do them, at least create some uniformity. The biggest problem I have with that – and this is not to throw anybody under the bus – but those leading are often less experienced than those being brought in at times to coach those camps. And the grassroots get very little support. The learning does not always filter down."

Goldman: Are you talking about the Select Festivals?

Korn: "Yes. I did goalie development camps years ago. I did one when Mike Dunham was 17 and when Tripp Tracy was 16. I worked USA Development camps back then, but sometimes the person we worked for was less experienced than me. So he's supposed to be bringing the uniformity, but instead, you bring a bunch of guys like me together, some who tend to be strong-willed and have different opinions, and sometimes you get that mutt concept. I clearly don't disrespect past leaders, but I would like my leader to be more experienced than me."

Goldman: My fledgling idea is to come up with a sort of 'buy-in' concept, a term you have mentioned a few times in this interview. I would contact all of the head guys associated with the Strelow program and ask them to support the idea that we need to reform and figure

something out before we fall even further behind. And if we can get these guys to buy in, then it's just a matter of putting the pieces together.

Korn: "I don't know how you get everyone to buy in. Can you get a guy in Pittsburgh who teaches 75 kids and a guy in Philadelphia and a guy in Minnesota teaching a hundred kids and maybe also coaching in High School, or the NAHL and USHL to buy in? Do they respect the person they are buying into? Does it negatively affect their business?"

Goldman: Isn't there a way where they could run their private businesses but still support and promote a national program?

Korn: "Is there? Probably. Will they be team guys? Probably. But I suspect it will take some good salesmanship. Any time you bring somebody into the fold and give them a little bit of ownership, they're more inclined to cooperate. But again, there are a lot of coaches out there who just 'don't know what they don't know.' Or they're too busy, or interact with too few, or who themselves do not get mentored. Don't get me wrong, where would our goalies be without the privatization? We need it. But how can we get those teaching close to the same page? I try by taking two 'volunteer' coaches at each of my camps."

Goldman: Right. And I was one of those volunteer coaches three years ago in Edina, and it's something I'm forever grateful for. I guess with that being said,

my goal would be to start going around to influential goalie coaches in the USA and ask them to buy in, saying we need their support, and we need them to help us out.

Korn: "And you have to isolate or identify who those guys are. I don't even know exactly who they are."

Goldman: Well for example, I think John Vanbiesbrouck is one. He's on the board of directors for USA Hockey. Getting him to buy into the fact that Finland and Sweden are way ahead, and even realize Canada is moving forward. What are we going to do? Can you help me figure out a solution? Guys like yourself, or coaches like Joe Exter, Mike Ayers, Kevin Reiter...

Korn: "And all three of them held that same position. But do you notice? They don't stay at that position, because they go on to bigger and better things. The problem is, that position at USA Hockey, it should be the bigger and better thing. Other than the NHL maybe, that should be the bigger thing. The guys who are coaching goalies at universities and colleges should be clamoring to get the USA job, not the other way around. Would you agree with that?"

Goldman: I agree 100 percent. So that's where my dilemma lies after going to Finland and seeing how structured and simple that structure unfolds. It just seems like we are all over the place, but not on purpose. It's just the way things have come about.

Korn: "Well, let's look at it from a World Championships point of view. If you talk to all the Europeans, they have an unbelievable patriotic approach to this tournament. That's the way it is in all these countries. Do you think we have an enormous patriotic approach in the United States? A lot don't understand USA Hockey or feel USA Hockey provides enough grassroots support through its volunteers."

Goldman: No. Everyone's more inclined to focus their attention or their passion on their own needs, private schools, their camps, or the NHL.

Korn: "Or even the pros that are invited to play in the World Championships. Too many turn the USA down compared to the European countries."

Goldman: It's sort of an afterthought.

Korn: "Or the players have had a tough season or did this or did that. The World Championships don't have the same jam to everybody in North America. It does to Canada, but less to the USA. That's why we are a democracy and not a socialist republic. You're suggesting that goalie development become socialized. Goalie coaching is definitely free enterprise."

Goldman: I just wish we could have some of both. I know we'll never get rid of the privatization with the coaches running their camps.

Korn: "And they're doing great jobs! Where would we be without it? We need these entrepreneurial coaches."

Goldman: Right, and they're developing great American-born goaltenders for sure, but can't we also get those guys to buy into a proposed national program? They don't have to get paid by USA Hockey, they just push, promote, and support the Select Festivals and the Strelow program. Look at the USA Hockey Goaltending website – it's a disaster. It's never updated, the information is ancient. Why can't these guys also do a little bit extra for USA Hockey? They already make a living through their own camps and programs, they should be able to do a little extra work for a national model. That's why if you just put a basic program in place and get people to "buy in" to the idea we need a coaching certification and goalie development program, they can still do what they're already doing, but they just help create the foundation and help the network grow.

Korn: "I am all for it. Politics can get in the way, especially regarding the selection process for these programs. But let's take a particular situation, and this is the hard part. There will be a coach who believes you should be loaded and ready to slide on a given play. And maybe I believe you should be on your feet and ready to shuffle on that play. How do you put in a standard?"

Goldman: My answer is to stay away from trying to standardize the advanced techniques and present Option

A and Option B. We don't have to pigeonhole goalies into one set way.

Korn: "I agree and don't think you should, but that's what makes it difficult. If you're 6-foot-7, maybe sliding on that play is the best bet, because when you're on your knees, you're still covering the top corners. But if you're 5-foot-4, I don't think you can do that. So I guess that goes along with the age-specific skill recommendations, or however it's structured. But at the same age, size and skill influence how I coach a goalie to play."

Goldman: Which is what you see in our latest notebook for the Strelow program. Kevin is starting to build like an ADM for goalies. He has that grid that shows what you teach at certain age groups.

Korn: "I get all that. But the people who are at Strelow don't influence enough people below them. How do you get the information down there? How much do these goalie coaches get to share? Not much. I'm lucky enough in the summer I get to share with a lot of young goalies. And I think I'd be on board with what USA Hockey would be teaching in most cases. But most coaches who do what I do in the NHL don't do what I do in the summer. They may go to Strelow, but it stops there. We have to put the information in like a colander, but it has to flow through to people that are teaching kids across the country. We had an assistant coach at my Duluth camp named Eric who teaches high school goalies in Minot, North Dakota. He was there because he wants to learn what we do. How can I teach Eric what I know? How can USA Hockey teach Eric? How can the average volunteer get away like Eric? If it was not me, who can Eric call to get that experience?"

Goldman: That's where I feel the USA Hockey Goaltending website is a big missing piece of the puzzle. If you provide the information and you have guys buying in, all it comes down to is dispersing the information. If Eric could call a Regional Goalie Coach and meet with that guy, or discuss things over the phone?

Korn: "That's how I met Eric [a volunteer goalie coach in Mitch's camp in Duluth]. He sent me an email because he had a problem. I responded to him, I helped him, I called him back, and then I offered him this opportunity. You need lots of regions. You have to divide them up. Minnesota is a big place and there's so many barren areas, too."

Goldman: Like Wyoming and Arizona.

Korn: "It's not easy. I can tell you that in the greater Cincinnati and Oxford area, other than Nick Petraglia and Justin Camuto, I have trouble with local staffing of my camp. I have to bring in coaches from the outside, because there are not enough worthy to work with us. And yet between Columbus, Cincinnati, Dayton, Northern Kentucky, there's maybe 3,000 kids playing."

Goldman: My final question for you is this: how would you define an American-born goaltender?

Korn: "I don't know if there's a typical 'USA' goalie. Jon Quick does not play like Ryan Miller, who does not play like Craig Anderson, just like no two U.S. companies are run the same way. Because we're so big, we're so diverse. I will say that, unfortunately, I think kids that are really good at something often get put on such a pedestal that they become so entitled, and they feel so entitled that sometimes I have to break them down before I can build them up. Some have all the answers, but the problem is that they don't know any of the right questions. These kids have been told for years that they're the greatest things since sliced bread, and many become harder to deal with because of it. Granted, this is a generality – I'm not ripping on North Americans – but I have found that the Euros I've worked with have been pretty good sponges, and act far less entitled. But don't get me wrong, it's not only goaltending, it is part of the culture. But remember this too – all we're seeing is the cream of the crop of the Finns that come over. You're not seeing the ones that might be different. You happen to be here [in the USA], so you can see way more. I know you went over [to Finland] for a few weeks, but you probably only saw it superficially, a small sample size."

Goldman: Yeah, around 30 to 35 goalies total, not including the group of four pro goalies.

Korn: "And those are the 30 that were in this GoaliePro program getting the special attention. I would imagine that the 36 kids that were at Strelow, or the 24 coming out of the Select 15's Festival, have more homogeneity than the masses in the big picture. And I'll bet you Finland is that way too. So there's probably just as much diversity in styles as there is anywhere else. It's just a way smaller country."

Goldman: Well, all of this has been so great, and even though my summer adventure isn't over after this camp, it's a very good conclusion to my dilemma with where USA Hockey currently stands. You can see why I'm so frustrated. There's this huge puzzle with scattered pieces everywhere. I can make sense of what the final picture looks like, but I'm missing the four corners.

Korn: "If you're willing to accept that something's better than nothing, that nothing will be perfect, and that it will always be a work in progress, then you'll be fine. But if you're looking for a neat package that fits perfectly in the box, you're not going to get it."

25

STRUCTURING A GOALIE DEVELOPMENT MODEL IN THE USA

"May this cold sever my face and may the pain weaken my fists. No inner strife will touch me. The only truth is in my heart." –Heaven Shall Burn

The exhausting "Between Two Worlds" summer expedition completely changed my life.

Every trip I took built upon the last. Dots connected. New ideas were born out of deep and intelligent conversations with new friends and wise mentors. I experienced many inner revelations and tons of tiny illuminating moments that revived past interactions. My time in Finland, Estonia, Canada, and different parts of the United States flipped my original views of reality upside down.

But for all the luck and good fortune I've had so far in my career, upon completion of the expedition, I realized I still wasn't satisfied. I simply couldn't come to terms with the culture of goalie development in my little corner of the globe. I couldn't sit idly by while this gap between the two worlds continued to widen. I had to do something beyond writing this book.

I mean, what's the point of learning new things if you can't apply them to anything substantial? These things couldn't just live inside my mind. They had to transform into executable, tangible programs.

In order to make your loftiest goals a reality, just like you did as a child, you have to start by imagining a world where your wildest dreams and ideas readily bloom from the rich soil of your five senses. A single dream can make a change, but you need bravery to see it through. You need willpower and discipline in order to meticulously craft your dreams into resolute and intelligent real-life actions. If you can accomplish this, you'll eventually reach new frontiers that have never been discovered before.

My current lofty goal? To help USA Hockey discover and implement some new structure for their goalie development model. I'm determined to help them do this, and I've been working hard towards realizing this goal since the summer ended and I started writing this book.

I'll be honest; the amount of frustration I've encountered in relation to this massive problem has frayed my mental seams. Not only has progress been excruciatingly slow, but the biggest obstacle is regarding the financial aspects, and there's literally nothing I can do about that.

If I had hundreds of thousands of dollars laying around, I'd give it all to make this change. But I don't. So I can only sit back and hope. If a budget can be allocated to allow many of these changes I document below to take place, I know for sure that USA Hockey will take a deep dive into the hidden sea of progress and come up breathing new life into the thousands of American-born goalies that would benefit from those healing waters.

Under the pride of the stars and stripes, no matter how much frustration I encounter, I'll fight until the end and then fight again. A few months have gone by with no progress, so I've been silently waiting for my chance to have my voice be heard. When that happens, I will say with every ounce of my being,

"Goalie coaches, lay down your arms. A new age is upon us, and the time is now to stand up and fight! This is a calling – this is a new type of war. A war fought without egos and with the pride of a strong hockey nation bringing us together for the sanctity and strength of the USA goaltending brotherhood."

For far too long, we've been a brotherhood fighting each other under too many banners, under too many isolated missions. But that culture of clashing must come to an end. We need an overhaul, we need to initiate a Renaissance, and we need to explore the only option and path to take – the path of change.

If you're in it for the right reasons, you will have no problem joining forces and standing side-by-side. As many of us continue to plant the seeds of change with confidence, I'm doing what I can to approach the decision-makers at USA Hockey.

If you've read everything up to this point, you've learned most of the same things I did over the summer. From the comfort of your home, it's easy to agree or disagree with my thoughts and opinions and ideas, but if you agree we need something more for our goalies, are you willing to stand up? Are you willing to reach out and be an active participant in the eventual solution?

I am willing to do all of this work on a volunteer basis. The building, the rallying, the communicating, the meetings, the writing, the continued research and development, the structuring of the programs, the website revamping. Whatever it takes for as long as it takes, I'll do it. I just need the green light.

There are no more excuses.

With time and location (my office is about 30 minutes away from USA Hockey's corporate headquarters) on my side, and with so many other good-hearted goalie coaches willing to donate their time and lend their support to this fight, it all comes down to the higher-ups at USA Hockey agreeing to allocate the budget and support needed to make it happen.

Let's say money no longer becomes an issue. What then does the solution look like? What is the first thing we need to do in order to revolutionize the way we develop goalies in the United States?

We need a basic Level 1 Goalie Coaching Certification Program.

Before I lay out my plans for this, please understand that when I say "basic" I mean as simple and as barebones as you could possibly imagine. So please don't worry or concern yourself with the finer technical and tactical details that would be included in this program. It's not needed at this level. Remember what Korn said – nothing that is established will be a perfect solution in such a large country.

With this in mind, I firmly believe a Level 1 program is your "Goaltending 101" class for the volunteers, the parents, the head coaches, and the grassroots associations. Therefore, this chapter lays out my ideas in a simple-to-read manner, but it's not all-inclusive. It's more of a basic guide, an introduction so to speak, or a good starting point and example of what could be built in a pretty short amount of time. It should help you realize that this is not as daunting of a process as it may seem. But it will take time.

Without further ado, let's get started.

The Goalie Coaching Pyramid

Again, when creating a structured goalie development program in the USA, I believe it has to start with a rudimentary Level 1 coaching certification program.

"Why this and not a goalie development manual first?" you may be asking.

Well, if we don't have a way to properly train our volunteer goalie coaches and goalie parents how to teach the right things to our youngest goalies, how can we expect those goalies to develop good habits and solid fundamentals at a young age?

If you don't train the men and women that train the most impressionable goalies, everything that comes after that is essentially null and void. You have to start at the bottom and work your way to the top. That means we need to establish a goalie coaching pyramid, one that feeds the knowledge and wisdom of our elite American-born goalie coaches all the way down to the grassroots level.

Here's how the goalie coaching pyramid would look within a USA Hockey framework, starting at the top with a Director of Goalie Development and working all the way down to the volunteer goalie coaches. I've also included a brief summary of each role.

Director of Goalie Development
ADM Goalie Director
NTDP Head Goalie Coach
NTDP Regional Scouts & Mentors
District Goalie Directors
Goalie Leadership Group – Includes 15-18 Board Members
State Head Goalie Coaches
Regional Goalie Coaches
Youth Association Goalie Coaches
Volunteer / Parent Goalie Coaches

Director of Goalie Development: A full-time position based in Colorado Springs. Perfect for a guy like Vanbiesbrouck or Mike Richter, this role needs to be held by someone with exemplary authority in the USA goalie community. It also needs to be someone who could commit the time and energy needed to oversee everyone below him on the coaching pyramid. He would need to act as the voice for the current state of affairs with this country's goaltending. It would most definitely be a full-time job.

The Director of Goalie Development would have a similar role to Magnusson and Nykvist in their respective countries. He would mainly be responsible for putting the right goalie coaches in place, and he would be responsible for updating and enhancing the goalie coaching certification programs and all educational resources (print and web) published by USA Hockey. He would be a vehicle for the promotion of goalie development and would also assist in scouting for the Olympics, World Cup of Hockey, the NTDP, and the U-20 World Juniors team.

ADM Goalie Director: This full-time role would also be based in Colorado Springs. This person would be responsible for structuring and creating the educational resources needed to establish a goalie-specific ADM. His focus would also be on assisting the Director of Goalie Development with various tasks, from scouting to advocating the Warren Strelow program. Someone like Joe Exter, Mike Ayers, or Nick Petraglia would be a perfect fit for this role.

The ADM Goalie Director would also be responsible for communicating with all of the goalie coaches, private and association-based, in the 12 USA Hockey districts. Together with the NTDP Head Goalie Coach, this would create a Goalie Leadership Group comprised of 15 total directors/coaches.

NTDP Head Goalie Coach: I strongly believe Reiter should continue to hold this role. Based in Ann Arbor, Reiter already has an excellent pulse on the top teenage goalies in the nation, so he should continue to work with our best U-17, U-18, and U-20 goalies. His current duties with the NTDP would remain, which is mainly scouting and looking for the next class of NTDP goalies, but a lot of the excess workload he has in terms of preparing the annual Strelow Camp should be shared and pieced out to other goalie coaches involved in this proposed pyramid.

It is important that we include an element of grooming for this position. We need this to be an honorable job for someone to have. In the past, it is one that is so burdened with responsibilities and a lack of support that it has no luster or appeal. It's not a role many guys want to hold for very long.

NTDP Regional Goalie Scouts & Mentors: Part-time roles placed strategically in key regions. I've discussed my role as the Minnesota regional mentor, so I won't re-hash it here. But I believe the number of mentors should be expanded from three to six total. This would allow the NTDP to have top goalie scouts in California, Texas, and then another guy out East. I think it's very important to have someone in California, especially with the rise in talent coming out of that state. Texas is also slowly becoming a breeding ground for talent.

District Goalie Directors: These would be part-time roles, one chosen for each of the 12 Districts. They would be in charge of placing and overseeing State head goalie coaches within their district. They would also oversee the regional and association goalie coaches in their districts. They would hold one district meeting and symposium per year, which would include as many of the association coaches as possible. They would be a main point of contact for hosting Level 1 Goalie Coaching Certification courses throughout the different areas of their district. They would also sit on the Goalie Leadership Board. In order to streamline everything, the six NTDP Regional Goalie Scouts would be, depending on location, invited to also act as the District Goalie Directors.

Everyone holding a role above this line would make up the *Goalie Leadership Group*. They would meet once or twice a year in order to oversee and report on events taking place within their districts, as well as discuss ways to continue developing the coaching certification program.

State Head Goalie Coaches: From there, you fill in these slots with solid and promising goalie coaches that are trustworthy and reputable and willing to volunteer as much time as possible. Maybe you cover their travel expenses for six months out of the year. Some of these roles could overlap, too.

For example, I could act as the Rocky Mountain District Goalie Director, as well as the State Head Goalie Coach for Colorado. As such, I'd be in charge of going around to each association in Colorado and spreading the Warren Strelow mission to each association.

I would also work on locating or placing goalie coaches in each youth association, ensuring they were following the basic guidelines of our Level 1 certification program. I'd be responsible for hosting those certification clinics a few times a year, as well as traveling to different associations to network with the goalie coaches and top goalies in the state.

Regional Goalie Coaches: These guys are basically assistants to the State Head Goalie Coaches. Since some states have much bigger numbers than others, it alleviates some of those issues in places like Minnesota, Michigan, Texas, California, and Florida. Here is Colorado, I'd have one guy handle my role in the mountains, I'd handle the Denver Metro Area, and then I'd have one guy for the Springs area.

The role of *Youth Association Goalie Coaches* and the volunteers/parents are pretty self-explanatory. I think our association goalie coaches just need to do their best at following the structure we put in place with our Level 1 program. We do not expect them to eliminate all of their creative drills, but rather follow the progression for goalies at the youngest ages. At the 8-Under and Squirt levels, we want them to simplify their coaching methods. We want them to reinforce good habits off the ice, good preparation skills, and use consistent terminology.

We also want association goalie coaches to communicate regularly with the State Head Goalie Coach and their District Director. We want them working with volunteer goalie coaches and parents within their organization and get them to buy-in to the Strelow model while still being passionate and creative about their own ideas. We want them to know that they have a chance to develop their coaching skills and work their way up the Goalie Coaching pyramid.

We want the parents and volunteers to learn the basic skills and terminology, a few basic drills, a few mental conditioning elements, and the importance of staying positive, and letting their kids be themselves. We don't want parents trying to over-coach kids, or put all of the focus on winning before they are 12 years old. We want to make sure their kids are playing other sports and have other hobbies and realize there is life outside of hockey.

Once this pyramid is structured, even if it begins with a loose network of mostly volunteer coaches, you are building a framework that will only strengthen as time goes on. From there, you can establish the information superhighway.

A Brief Executive Summary

Below is the introduction to a full-length executive summary I wrote back in September. It rests peacefully inside a notebook and PowerPoint presentation, just waiting to be shared with USA Hockey's higher-ups:

> *"I propose to help USA Hockey create a Level 1 Goalie Coaching Certification Program that will provide the basic educational resources needed for youth association goalie coaches, volunteer goalie coaches, head coaches, and goalie parents to better develop youth goaltenders in a more structured and successful manner. Through a basic one-day Level 1 goalie coaching clinic, USA Hockey not only gets to reinforce the ADM mission, but cater it specifically to grassroots goalies and goalie coaches. This program would cover the basic and essential principles of successful goaltending, while also providing American goalies in rural and less-populated areas with a vital source of information that guides grassroots goalies to the next level in their development. This also helps to bridge the gap between USA Hockey and a few European countries that have been successfully benefitting from goalie development programs for many years." –Goldman*

If this were to be approved, before you actually create the content included in the Level 1, you'd have to determine the best way to unleash it. There are obviously many ways to skin this cat, and there are likely a few really effective methods out there. Below, I'll share a few of ideas I think would work.

First of all, whenever possible, I would have Level 1 goalie coaching certification clinics coincide with regular Level 1 head coaching clinics. That makes it very easy to implement in terms of scheduling, especially since goalie coaches get nothing out of attending a regular head coach clinic.

Secondly, you could consider holding a portion of the Level 1 training take place as an online certification program. This would save money, but it's not recommended, because a big part of growing a network of goalie coaches is being able to build relationships. So while it's plausible, I don't think this would work.

We need human interaction, both on and off the ice. We need a clinic.

The Level 1 Goalie Coaching Clinic

Since the information and education provided in a Level 1 goalie coaching clinic would be very basic and introductory, USA Hockey would be able to automatically certify everyone on the Goalie Leadership Group, as well as all of the State Head Goalie Coaches. These certified coaches would then spread out across the country and help host and facilitate the Level 1 coaching clinics in all 50 states.

That means the only people needing to attend the clinics would be the youth association goalie coaches, and all of the team and volunteer goalie coaches (and parents) out there.

Since I'm living in Colorado again, I could host a 'test-run' clinic right here in Denver and see how feasible it is for everyone involved. Not only is the youth hockey scene small enough to be easily manageable, but I have many years of experience as the former head goalie coach for the University of Denver Junior Pioneers in the CCYHL. I already know some of the members of CAHA, which is the Colorado Amateur Hockey Association, so it would be fairly easy to set everything up.

Thanks to the guidance I received from Hartigan and Ropponen, I know that the first step is to get as many goalie coaches and parents as possible to attend this inaugural Level 1 clinic. That only happens if I have a few keynote speakers and plenty of time to promote the event through necessary channels. This is where I would need USA Hockey's support; they could e-mail every registered youth association and goalie in the state and really boost the exposure and participation.

My idea for a Level 1 clinic includes both on and off-ice sessions. The more interactive this clinic can be, the more it will resonate with the coaches in attendance. Here is a basic mock schedule of a Level 1 coaching clinic to be held in Denver or Colorado Springs:

10:00a - 10:30a --- Introductions and 'Meet & Greet'
10:30a - 11:00a --- Opening Presentation
11:00a - 12:30p --- Coaching Presentation (Classroom)
12:30p - 1:30p --- Lunch Break
1:30p - 2:00p --- Keynote Speaker

2:15p - 3:45 --- On-Ice Goalie Clinic #1
4:00p - 4:30p --- Presentation #2
4:30 - 5:00p --- Off-ice Training or Conditioning Clinic
5:00 - 5:30p --- Closing Words

The 'meet and greet' gives the volunteers and all of those in attendance an opportunity to network with the State or District Leader. It also helps us to establish key lines of communication that are so desperately needed in rural or less-populated areas. Having Reiter essentially give the same presentation that he gave at the Level 5 coaching clinic over the summer further simplifies the process, reinforcing the same basic goaltending principles we try to teach our head coaches.

Once the event ends and the volunteers and amateur goalie coaches are trained and officially certified, it will not be difficult to track their progress. A state like Colorado is not that big in terms of goalie numbers, and holding an annual goalie coaching symposium for Colorado coaches would not be a time-consuming or expensive endeavor.

This annual meeting is important for the sharing of ideas and inclusion of new coaches, and it's an event that has to be held not only on the state level, but on the regional and national level as well.

As you can see, the importance of having an interactive event helps create bridges and tear down walls. If we can't create and implement a one-day certification or training clinic, we have very little hope of establishing the type of development program we need to properly support the thousands of youth goalies that are eager to learn the basic fundamentals of the position.

The Level 1 Handbook

Now that there is structure to the actual goalie coaching clinic, the next step is to actually build the educational materials and resources.

My ability to create a simple digital guide to accompany the Level 1 coaching certification program gives us a chance to not only disseminate information into the rinks and homes of goalies and coaches across the USA, but it's also cost-efficient and environmentally friendly.

This is where I would design a binder or small digital handbook that included the following sections:

Terminology: This section would include a list of the most common terms used in coaching young goalies and provide easy-to-understand definitions for all of them. It would also stress the importance of using and communicating these terms consistently in order to keep young goalies from getting confused. It also streamlines and improves the way we discuss these techniques and terms with everyone. This section would also warn goalie coaches about some commonly misused phrases that can affect the way a goalie perceives how he is being asked to play.

Evaluations: This section would include information on how Level 1 coaches can evaluate young talent. It would explain how to pinpoint weaknesses, reinforce strengths, and write up a basic game report. I do not believe video analysis is necessary at the youngest levels. But it is important that we help volunteer and youth hockey team goalie coaches understand how to better evaluate a young goalie.

On-Ice Training: This section would be the main part of the handbook. It would include an easy-to-follow set of basic drills for all of the fundamental areas of goaltending. That includes very simple angles, positioning, skating, shooting, reaction, and battle drills. This section would also include goalie-friendly drills to use in team practices, how to properly warm up a goalie before games and practices, a collection of basic props (white pucks, deflection boards), a collection of different station-based layouts and practice plans for youth association goalie clinics and multi-goalie practice sessions.

Off-Ice Training: This section would include information on stretching and the importance of pre-game and pre-practice warmups. It would provide details on how to use slideboards, stability balls, tennis balls, and include some details on basic weight training. It would also include information on the importance of nutrition, hydration, proper rest, and playing multiple sports.

Mentoring: This section would include information on how to guide and mentor young goalies. It would stress the importance of helping young goalies instill good habits, both on and off the ice. This section would also introduce Level 1 goalie coaches to key elements like focus, preparation, and confidence.

Parenting: This section is designed specifically for educating parents on different aspects of how to handle success, failure, and other emotional pitfalls that arise with young goalies. It could also include details on how to properly fit their kids in new gear, how they should wear it, and the importance of not putting too much pressure on them to win every game.

USA Hockey: This section would clarify the Warren Strelow program, the annual Select Festival process, the basic mission of the ADM, and explain to Level 1 goalie coaches how they can work their way up the goalie coaching pyramid.

During every Warren Strelow camp, the Goalie Leadership Group would meet to discuss the current program, the information included in the coaching certification handbook, and then, if needed, make updates and enhancements.

With this annual process continually refining the handbook, the brightest minds have a way to implement their ideas in an influential manner. But it will take a lot of give-and-take, and more importantly, a number of years in order to accomplish it all. It may seem like a daunting task, but you have to start somewhere.

Why not here? Why not now? What is the holdup?

Supporting Youth and Minor Hockey Associations

When I was hired by the University of Denver Pioneers in 2006 as the head goalie coach of their youth program, I was excited to get a giant binder with a bunch of drills and lesson plans to work with.

Instead, I got nothing. No drills in a binder, no guidelines, no nothing. I didn't think it was too big of a deal at the time. I knew they needed help with their goalies, but now that I look back at it, the complete lack of educational materials was very disturbing.

Colorado is certainly no hotbed for goalie development, but how many other youth associations have the same problem? How many associations don't have head goalie coaches at all? Too many.

During my time spent with Hartigan, I remember him talking about a youth hockey association in Varkaus, Finland. He said that every season, goalies in that program received one goalie-specific practice, two off-ice goalie practices, and had a goalie coach for almost every team practice and home game. The association didn't just have one head goalie coach, but two, and that every coach on every team was trained and educated under Finland's goalie development program. Every goalie in the entire organization had an equal opportunity to develop.

Furthermore, their emphasis on off-ice training reinforced what very well could be the biggest difference between the two worlds. Over there, it's part of the culture. Over here, it's pretty much nonexistent.

The more I discussed the idea of integrating a development system similar to Finland's in the United States, the more he taught me about the importance of not just certifying grassroots and volunteer goalie coaches, but providing them with a way to take their newfound knowledge and create a program that can be used throughout an entire association.

Again, information included in here is not fully comprehensive, but it gives you a good idea of what Jack taught me about how to create a full in-season and off-season development program for youth associations.

During the season, which is usually from September until March, the following elements should be included within each youth hockey association:

+ *A Level 1 certified goalie coach on the ice for at least two practices per week*

+ *One goalie-specific practice (on-ice) and off-ice training session per week*

+ *A Level 1 goalie coach at most or all home games, along with a written report*

+ *Monthly progress reports with additional feedback on strengths and weaknesses*

+ *For the older goalies, video analysis and feedback at least one game a month*

During the off-season, which is usually from April through August, the following elements should be provided for goalies in a youth association:

+ *Weekly off-ice training sessions or weight training*
+ *One comprehensive on-ice goalie clinic per month*
+ *Opportunities to play in a fun 3-on-3 or friendly league*
+ *One to two week-long goalie camps or clinics*
+ *Time away from the game of hockey*

With these guidelines, youth hockey associations set a new standard for goalie development. Combined with a Level 1 goalie coaching certification program, associations no longer have to fend for themselves. They would be equipped with an enthusiastic and trained goalie coach capable of implementing this new standard, and over time, refining it with new additions and enhancements.

Furthermore, they would be able to create a small library of resources (digital and printed) for future youth goalie coaches that join the association. This is how you build a foundation that actually has the power to change the current culture in a positive and consistent manner across the entire country.

Working Amidst Our Current Culture

Now that I've seen the differences between North America and Finland first-hand, I can safely say that the culture here needs to change. In Finland, goalies are borderline worshipped and glorified. They are the equivalent to our quarterbacks in football. Here in the USA, goalies are the weird, odd, and somewhat antisocial kids. Goaltending simply isn't a priority over here, so they're the obvious scapegoats.

Even more troubling is that non-athletic kids that want to play hockey are often forced into the crease, because there's a belief that if you can't skate, at least you can be a goalie and get away with just standing there. Too many parents and head coaches think that you don't need any talent to be a goalie.

"Just stop the puck," they say.

The high costs of private coaching, traveling to exclusive and popular camps, and the idea that you have to go to Canada in order to get good coaching further stymies the ability to change our current culture. The private goalie training culture will never disappear, which means USA Hockey's system would have to figure out a solution that benefits both sides.

To me, the answer is by certifying and approving private companies, and then having them volunteer their time by supporting youth hockey associations in exchange for getting free exposure to promote their summer goalie camps and clinics.

Either way, I think we're at a point where the solution is very obvious. In the United States and in Canada, there are more and more goalie parents speaking out about the lack of goalie development protocols being executed in youth associations. Because of this, many parents are more than willing to volunteer their time. If we can educate them through a Level 1 goalie coaching program, we're going to make a huge different at the grassroots. Then we'll be able to create a Level 2, 3, and maybe even a Level 4.

The only way privatization could possibly begin to taper off is by giving all kids equal and affordable opportunities to work with solid goalie coaches. This only happens if we put the power of knowledge into the hands of all the goalie dads, the enthusiastic and passionate volunteers and amateurs, and the actual youth associations. If more goalies can get position-specific training during the hockey season, then maybe there will be less importance placed on sending Jimmy to that $2,000 five-day camp in Canada.

This concludes the layout of my framework for a goalie coaching certification program in the USA. There are so many parts that could be expanded on, but the purpose of this chapter is to merely show that the task is not as daunting as it may seem. It's time-consuming, but it's very necessary, so the sooner we start, the sooner we will see results.

I'm very much in debt to Hartigan and Ropponen for their advice and support as I put together some materials to present to USA Hockey when that time came. I presented all of this to Reiter, and then sat back and waited.

And waited...and waited some more.

Two Key Meetings with Reiter

Even though I worked alongside Reiter throughout the 2013-14 season as one of his regional goalie scouts, our friendship didn't really blossom until the Warren Strelow Camp and the Select 15's Festival. The week we spent together in Amherst allowed for us to really bond away from the rink.

Reiter is the epitome of the type of guy we need involved in USA Hockey goaltending. He has the smarts, the enthusiasm, the passion, and the guts. I say guts because that's what it takes to face such a steep mountain of obstacles currently facing goalie development in this country. He's plugging away every day, doing whatever he can to make a change.

Between our time together in Amherst and the start of 2015, Reiter and I met on two separate occasions to discuss the advent of a Level 1 goalie coaching certification program.

The first took place in Blaine, Minnesota during the Dave Peterson Goalie Camp. Following one of the camp's daily sessions, we drove to Chili's and sat there for nearly three hours, pouring over everything you've read in this book; what I learned in Finland, why we need to push forward regardless of what type of budget he has, how I can help, and how we would structure things if we had the glorious green light.

I'll never forget the roller coaster of emotions we shared that afternoon. It was two parts enthusiasm for the future, and two parts frustration for all the pitfalls we're currently facing. But when it was all said and done, I walked away with a memento that I'll probably have until the day that I die.

It was nothing more than a white paper napkin.

On that napkin was a flow chart showing the goalie coaching pyramid I discussed above. Together, Reiter and I drew out exactly how this coaching hierarchy would look if we were able to establish this within USA Hockey. "Head" was the big circle at the top. A line stemmed below it to a smaller circle with "NTDP" for Reiter's position. Below that were four lines extending to four smaller circles, with the following initials: "JG", "AB", JW, and "RG". The first three initials stood for the three regional goalies scouts (myself included) and the fourth, RG, was for another regional goalie scout.

Below each of those four circles were three lines that pointed to "Districts 1-12", which stood for the head goalie coaches named to each district. Below that was an arrow pointing to "One Goalie Coach / State". Another arrow below that pointed to "Association G Coaches" and a final arrow pointing to the final line, "Volunteers & Parents".

I don't know why this napkin meant so much to me, but as I'm writing these very words, I'm staring at the napkin and feeling the hope and the promise for a better future. I hope this becomes a reality someday. I hope the right people see this and realize it's a necessary expenditure for the betterment of USA Hockey. I hope I can have my voice be heard. I hope this all happens, regardless of whether I'm a part of it or not.

The second meeting with Reiter came a few days after Christmas. At this point in the season, a lot of changes had taken place, which you'll read about in the Prologue. I stepped down from my NHL.com writing gig. I had taken on the role as the Vice President for my dad's multi-million dollar cosmetics business. I had agreed to join a new organization called NetWork Goaltending.

As positive as I tried to stay heading into this meeting, it was not as promising as the first.

Stepping Through Another Gate of Change

It was at this meeting, which took place at a hotel in Colorado Springs, that I was told I had no official role with USA Hockey. Despite waiting patiently for some type of update from someone in the front offices, none came. No progress had been made. Nobody outside of Reiter had reached out to me since August.

It was also at this meeting that I learned a lot about the lack of progress being made internally to actually move forward with anything Kevin and I had discussed over the summer. Instead, the ADM was looking to hire someone to act as the head of goaltending for their organization. This person would be paid a salary to act as a proponent for the ADM, while traveling around in order to teach an age-specific curriculum – curriculum that had yet to be created.

It was exciting to hear that USA Hockey was interested in adding another 'goalie guy' to the current group of one, but it was also quite bothersome, because it went against our mutual belief that a coaching certification program needed to be established first. Despite that bit of news, Reiter shared with me his ideas for a "Goalie Coaching Education Program", which he laid out in a PowerPoint presentation format.

This piggybacked off a similar PowerPoint I had created a few months earlier during a weekend writing retreat in Vail. During that retreat, I finalized the information you read above regarding the basic framework for a Level 1 goalie coaching certification program. I chose to share it with Reiter in case he had an opportunity to sit and meet with any of the higher-ups at USA Hockey. Unfortunately, that failed to happen between early-November and early-January. And so still we sit in the same exact predicament as before, with no solutions in sight and no resolutions in place to kick off 2015.

I have to admit, I came away from that meeting somewhat jaded. I had no more patience or time to waste worrying about what may or may not come from everything I had shared with USA Hockey.

Just when I realized one door was closing, I was lucky enough to open another door of my own. Thanks to the very last trip of my summer expedition, an opportunity arose that simply couldn't be passed up. I definitely have not given up on USA Hockey, but if everything I learned continued to fall on deaf ears, why would I struggle to try and help one country when I could possibly help the entire world?

After I was lucky enough to receive amazing guidance from America's Goalie Yoda, I was blessed with a similar exchange with Sweden's Goalie Yoda. Without warning,

Thomas Magnusson suddenly appeared before me in another 'dream-turned-reality' summer experience, and it was due in large part to our time spent together that I knew fate had presented me with a new doorway to open – NetWork Goaltending.

26

THOMAS MAGNUSSON, SWEDEN'S GOALIE YODA

Thomas Magnusson may not be a household name in North America's goaltending community, but anyone who knows him undoubtedly agrees that his reach and influence is both prolific and profound.

Sweden's head of goalie development came from simple beginnings. His passion for hockey flourished at a young age, further nurtured by a few coaches that helped him discover his true calling. As he continued to gain a deep understanding of the position, he would eventually become one of the first goalie coaches in all of Sweden. Some even call him the "Godfather" of European goalie development.

As I stated earlier, meeting Magnusson was not part of my original plan for this book. When I first set out on my *Between Two Worlds* expedition, my sole focus was to write an extensive comparative analysis between Finland and North America. But when I learned that Magnusson would be joining me at the Elite Goalies NHL Camp run by Dallas Stars goalie coach Mike Valley, everything changed.

Gifted with an opportunity to learn from one of the most influential goalie minds in the world, I quickly made plans to interview Magnusson and get his thoughts on his development program, otherwise known as *Malvaktsparmen* or the Swedish goalie bible.

Magnusson was not only kind enough to explain how he spearheaded significant change in a country that was desperate for a goaltending revolution, but he also dropped some unbelievable knowledge regarding the way Sweden teaches certain save selections and modes of playing.

As I reflected on this experience that culminated my surreal summer, I realized that the most beautiful elements of goaltending are the simple ones. A flick of the wrist on a glove save. The glide of a steel blade during a T-Push. The consistent pattern of a freshly taped stick.

Similarly, Magnusson's teachings are some of the most beautifully simple strategies I've ever discovered. In both the way he explains it off the ice and the way he coaches it on the ice, when you're exposed to something so elegantly simple, you can't help but experience a renaissance in your own way of thinking.

If you're a goalie, consider the simplicity of the save process. If you're a coach, consider how simplifying the language makes it easier for students to process what you're trying to teach.

In our haste and desire to create and implement new techniques -- to advance the way we execute certain positional strategies -- I fear it has become too easy to over-complicate all of the simple things that make our position so effortless and smooth.

And as I learned while watching Magnusson work with eight NHL goalies in Madison, the higher the level, the simpler the teachings.

Since returning from Madison, Magnusson's influence has naturally simplified the way I play, scout, evaluate, and mentor younger goalies. Our newfound friendship has had a profound influence on my current role with NetWork Goaltending as well.

Goldman: We just finished an unbelievable week in Madison, and it was my first time meeting you and getting to know you. So I just wanted the readers to get to know you a little bit as a person. How did you first get involved in goaltending?

Magnusson: "Well, I was a goalie when I was younger and started out playing in a local club in Stockholm. I was fortunate enough to have fairly good coaching, but not goalie-specific coaching at that time, because there were no goalie coaches. The coach I had when I was 12-13-14 years old turned out to be an elite coach and eventually a National Team coach in Sweden. His name is Leif Boork and he's meant a lot to me. So after having him as a coach, I grew in confidence in my goaltending ability, and when I was 17 years old, I really wanted to go to North America to play hockey and go to school. I did everything on my own, no organization or anything, and got in touch with some schools in North America through some contacts that I found, and I was actually offered a part-scholarship at a prep school in Massachusetts. I went to this school, Lawrence Academy, for one year and grew even more as a goalie, but especially as a person since I was so very far away from home. And this was of course before internet and texting and things like that. I was at a very good school, so I had my goals set already to either be a top-level goalie, or if I couldn't make it, to work in sports and coaching in some way or another. So I took very high-level courses like anatomy and physiology at the school and was offered a full scholarship to stay for my senior year. Had I done that, I probably would have stayed for another five years, because that would have meant college since the prep school had a 100-percent college placement conversion rate at the time."

Goldman: Just for reference, when was this, and what did you do after your year in North America?

Magnusson: "This was in 1974, which says something about my age – I'm 57 right now. After that year, I went back home and played junior-A at the elite level in Stockholm for AIK. I had two good years at the junior-A level, and I also had some opportunities to practice with the elite team and sat on the bench for I think seven games in the Swedish Elite League. But I felt during those two years that I had reached my potential and limit. It was very hard for me to compete with goalies in those elite teams, and I knew that would mean that I'd have to turn to the lower level, but I wanted to do things at the top level. So after that year, I did my mandatory year of army service and played hockey on a lower level at the same time and stayed with that team for two years. During that time, things grew in me that I wanted to go into coaching. So I applied to the most prestigious school for physical education in Stockholm. It was only a two-year program at the time, but nowadays it's a three-year program. It meant I had a platform to work within sports as a coach or work as a physical education teacher in school. After those two years, I was offered a couple of coaching jobs. I had done all of the certification programs within hockey parallel to my playing days, and I had also started coaching younger goalies in the clubs that I had played with before."

Goldman: And obviously you chose coaching hockey over coaching kids P.E. in school...

Magnusson: "Yes, and having this choice to be a coach for a hockey team in the second level in Sweden was intriguing for me. But I had collected so much information by then that I really wanted to do something about goaltending. There was not a single goalie coach in Sweden at the time, so it was not a career path or anything. So what I did was, I got in touch with my old coach, who at the time was the coach of Djurgarden, the Swedish championship team, and I brought up my ideas for coaching goalies. I knew the organization was really progressive and he was into new things, so I wanted him to hire me to coach goalies at the elite level. I started on a semi-professional, semi-volunteer basis. I was with the team three times every week for practice. I went to all the home games. I started doing all the scouting and also providing the feedback for the goalies. We didn't have the iPads back in those days, so it was all writing. I started with that for one year to try things out, and it ended up being my role for the next 21 years of my life, winning five National Championships. After my second year, I was coaching goalies and acting as the team's assistant coach. I was also a part-time PE teacher parallel to this, but after my fourth year with the club, I went into full-time goalie coaching. During those 21 years, I was often asked to do things for the Swedish Federation, because there was nothing in place at the time – no educational material, no goalie coaches for the National teams."

Goldman: Is that how you got involved in structuring goalie development for Sweden?

Magnusson: "Well, I was in and out of different National teams starting actually in 1987. I went to the Under-20 World Championships in Czechoslovakia, which is has widely been known for the big, big bench-clearing brawl in the finals between Canada and Russia. During that tournament I had my first assignment for the federation as an assistant coach and goalie coach. I've been a goalie coach for a number of Swedish national teams since then, but I always criticized the Swedish Federation for not giving goaltending the necessary attention. I was working in a club system where we really focused on the goaltenders and I didn't think the federation was doing enough in that field, and I especially thought they were lacking a long-term perspective on goalie development. In our club system, in Djurgarden, we really focused on the goalies, the top names as well as the juniors and the younger goalies in our system. After a couple of years, we had our goalies representing Team Sweden in the U-20 World Championships eight years in a row. So that was something we were proud of that we could achieve, and we were surprised that no other teams tried to copy what we were doing."

Goldman: So what did you do next?

Magnusson: "You know we had this big national evaluation and a complete makeover of Swedish hockey in 2002 when everyone involved in our sport got together to discuss what had to be done about our poor results in international competition. We were lagging behind and were not close to any medals in the U-20 or U-18 Worlds or anything. So we got together – all the coaches, all the different districts and everyone involved like agents and scouts, everyone was there. We pinpointed 10 different things we had to work on in Swedish hockey, one of those being goaltending. It was never giving us an opportunity to win tournaments. At that time, Tommy Boustedt, another old friend of mine that I had been working with on the club level had been appointed as the director of development for the Swedish federation. He reached out to me and asked if I would become the director of goaltending development, meaning that I would be developing goaltenders for our national team program, our player development program, but most importantly, creating a whole set of new educational materials, along with a program to get that implemented into our system with our coaches. We had had some kind of goalie coach education system with a one-day and a supplementary two-day course, but in

2005, we implemented our certification program, which is a three-level system for goalie coaching. It also includes one basic coaching part and two different physical training parts, so in reality, there are six steps or levels you have to go through to be a certified goalie coach in Sweden."

Goldman: So that's a pretty awesome background story and a really cool evolution of who you are and everything you've accomplished. Knowing that you have done so much for the structure of goalie development in Sweden when they really needed it, what was the best part for you, or the most rewarding experience?

Magnusson: "The best part for me was finding the level of success we had by reaching out to the grassroots. We did a lot for our national teams and our player development programs and everything like that, but we started out in 2006 by doing a whole set of new educational material with a binder of printed materials and some DVD's and we wanted to reach out with that to our clubs in the Swedish hockey system. We have around 350 clubs that organize hockey programs from the youngest kids to juniors, and in most cases a first team, all with a single national system of divisions from the Swedish Elite League down to regional and local divisions at five or six different levels. Here, teams can qualify up, but also be relegated down within the system. We set up a program where the clubs could apply for money to pay for educational material and to have trained goalie coaches – who we certified in the system that we built – come out to their organization and work with their goalies and their goalie coaches twice a year over a period of two or three years. As it turned out, I think around 200 out of the 350 clubs joined the program. What's really neat about it was that it's for the clubs, for the players, and it's all for free, because we have a grant from our government to set up different programs and have the money funded for the teams to use. So that's the thing I'm most proud of, and I really enjoyed reaching out to the grassroots. That has meant that today we have very well-educated goaltenders in our system, because they get opportunities to work with well-educated goalie coaches. So up until now, from 2005 until now, more than 160 goalie coaches have gone through the entire certification process. That's not very many every year, but enough for us since two years back, we were able to introduce demands on the clubs at all levels to have goalie coaches certified at least to the second level. And the clubs with teams in the top two divisions, and those competing in the major junior leagues must have a level-three certified goalie coach."

Goldman: It's great to hear this background information on your development program, because not a lot of people in North America have had a chance to really understand how things have evolved in Sweden. In terms of the progression of your career, it's just an awesome story. But now that we're at this point, I wanted to ask you about the Swedish "style" from your perspective. First and foremost, what makes a Swedish goalie different from goalies in other countries?

Magnusson: "First of all, I am of the opinion that there are as many styles as there are goalies. I don't really buy into what you call a butterfly goalie, because today all goalies use the butterfly, which I like to refer to as a save technique or stance. I consider each goalie an individual. I really don't see all that many similarities really in Sweden or in Finland, because every individual is playing his or her own game. But of course there are some things that are common for Swedish goalies. I think one would be that Swedish goalies in general are well-educated. Most of them get in touch with goaltending coaches who are pretty much all on the same page, which means that they work very much on their fundamentals and on the basics, so they usually are very good skaters. They're good at moving on their skates while standing, with their down movements on the ice, and so I think most Swedish goalies build out from their strong mobility, from being good movers."

Goldman: I hear a lot of people say, "Swedish goalies all play really deep like Henrik Lundqvist."

Magnusson: "No, they don't. I think since he's the big star and hero, more and more goalies try that game, but he hasn't played that way for very long. He changed that after coming to North America. Before 2005 when he left, he was really, really aggressive. He was playing way, way out. Moving a lot, forward and backward. That's the way he played over here too at first. So he started to change his game, I believe, maybe five years ago, and it's just in the last three or four years he has been playing the way he does now. So now more and more Swedish goalies are picking up on that.

Not just because of him, but because of Swedish goalie coaches also realize what we're talking about with the good things that come from playing that way. You actually get less movement since you don't have to move that much when you play inside the crease. And if you can be aggressive just at the last instant, you can cover as much net as when you start out there. So he's playing an inside game, but you can see that he's able to be really aggressive and challenge the shooter sometimes when it's needed. See what I mean?"

Goldman: Yeah, absolutely. A lot of what people discuss in North America is what they see from one or two guys like Henrik Lundqvist, or what they read in articles, but very few people really get the exposure on a personal level, which is why I went to Finland in the first place -- to see it and experience it for myself. I didn't want to go on hearsay and see Finnish goalies like Kari and Kipper play in North America. So being able to talk to a guy like yourself and Hannu to help me shred some of those misperceptions and help people understand what the real philosophy and ideologies are.

Magnusson: "What I mean by Swedish goalies being well-educated is what we're doing with these top NHL goalies here [in Madison]. We're talking to them about their own game plan. You can do that with a 15-year-old. Almost any 15-year-old goalie you can talk to in this way, and they will be able to describe how they want to solve different situations."

Goldman: So how do they get so smart? You can't do that with an average 15-year-old in the States. Is it because coaching is so much better at a younger level?

Magnusson: "Yes. And also, the way we coach is by trying to make the game simple. We don't complicate the game. Our mission is to make each individual grow as much as possible to their potential, but also to give them tools to simplify their game. I find a lot of goalie coaches – and there are coaches like this in Sweden too – who do the opposite. They complicate the game. Like I say, and I don't know if I said it when you were there, but I think goaltending is about very few things. You have to be in the right position each time for each instance. To do that, you need to move. So goaltending is about moving, getting into position, save selection, executing the save, and playing each situation through to the end, which is rebound control and what you do with the puck afterwards. Each of these three different things – moving, positioning, and saving – there are of course different variations, but they are not that complicated and there aren't that many things you have to do. So moving is how you move down on the ice and standing, and it's also about movements from your feet to the down position, and from the down position back up to your feet. Then you have different tools and different techniques, and when it comes to making saves, I look at it in three different ways. The old fashioned way is the aggressive way. You catch pucks, you make saves with your pads by the low corners, you extend. You react and act, making the save by extending. That's one way you're making a save, when extending is necessary to reach the puck. You can also do it to gain control by using your glove, which is also reacting and acting. The other opposite or counterpart in goaltending is often referred to as the blocking game. But I don't buy into the idea that you can only choose between the reactive or the blocking save movement. I think there's the reactive game that I described, which is extending. And then there's the blocking game, which is basically the full blocking save, when you cover the whole net with a butterfly or an SMS or in other compact stances. But there's also a third way of making saves, which is reacting and blocking. Because the full block is the passive way of getting in the way of the puck, usually before the shot is taken. Today, however, goalies make huge use of making saves in blocking stances after reacting and then moving into a blocking stance. So those are the three different ways you can make saves, that's pretty easy to look at it that way."

Goldman: So just so I understand this correctly, you're reacting into a blocking mode?

Magnusson: "Yes, exactly. When you have full coverage, or full box control as we call it in Sweden, you can make a full blocking save and it doesn't matter which part of your body the puck is hitting. You fill the whole box. Then you can make a passive blocking save. But you can also elevate the success level if you put an element of trying to hold onto the puck into that passive blocking save; to smother it, to hold it to your body with the glove, to cradle it with your body. But the other one, the reactive blocking save, you move into the puck's trajectory. You don't cover that part of the net from the beginning.

So standing and going down into the butterfly is often a reactive blocking save, and an even better example is perhaps a center shift, where you react to the puck's trajectory and move laterally to make a blocking save."

Goldman: Because you're reacting to a shot being taken, but all you're doing is filling space.

Magnusson: "Yes."

Goldman: This concept, or this explanation of how you break down the three basic types of saves is really, really different compared to how things are being explained or taught in North America. Yours is three-dimensional, but ours is two-dimensional, because it's either block or react. And nobody wants to have just a blocking goalie, but you're teaching me and all of your other students to understand what you really mean by a blocking technique. So the Reverse-VH, and correct me if I'm wrong, but what I learned during your presentation is that you can't allow it to only exclusively be a passive blocking save.

Magnusson: "You don't want it to be only a passive blocking save. What happens sometimes is that the goalie is in a really low position, ready to come down into a VH position, but your knee isn't on the ice. Then you react and drop the knee to the ice, which is a reactive blocking save. But also, you want to be able to stay reactive in case you don't cover the whole net. If you have a player on the wall, and you're playing in a blocking position like a VH, and the puck is moving to the center and you're not quick enough to be in position, then you have to be able to react and block if he's shooting the puck far side."

Goldman: And this is what you have been teaching in Sweden since you came on board?

Magnusson: "Yes, since 2005. The ideas have been there and have been around, but they haven't been put into books and teaching videos until after 2005. It's an ongoing process of course, but between 2005 and 2008, we reached out to all of the clubs in Sweden and gave them the opportunity to apply to have a goalie coach come to their club twice a year for free to work with the goalies and their goalie coaches, or their goalie coach prospects, those who wanted to become goalie coaches. So we reached out to all 350 clubs and, as I mentioned, somewhere around 200 clubs responded and took part in this."

Goldman: Was it difficult to get coaches to buy in to the idea that you needed a goalie coaching certification program?

Magnusson: "Not at all."

Goldman: How hard was it to get full support from the Swedish Hockey Federation?

Magnusson: "None. It was no problem, because this is what we have for our regular coaches, who must have a certification to coach. So why shouldn't goalie coaches? The only reason we didn't have this before was that we didn't have this level of goalie coaching education. We didn't have a way to start certifying goalie coaches until we introduced this system in 2005. The demand for the clubs to have goalie coaches at certain levels having certain certification requirements was only completed two years ago, because before that, we couldn't have those demands on the clubs because there weren't enough goalie coaches. The number of goalie coaches were too low at that time."

Goldman: So with this eight-year process in terms of structuring the goalie development in Sweden behind you, how are you feeling about where things are at right now, and what are the current challenges?

Magnusson: "I think we are right now at a point where we have reached the numbers we expected and probably more goalie coaches and goalies that are well-educated. So the biggest challenge right now is that the material we have is already getting old. That's mostly looking at the pictures. The ideas are still the same, and what has changed is that some new techniques in the toolbox have to be added, because goalies have discovered and developed new ways of making saves or moving and playing the position. Like the SMS for example. It wasn't there and didn't have a name eight years ago. So that's not in our material. And the pads don't look exactly the same today, so young goalies need pictures of goalies they can relate to with names and equipment and some of the technique. I can't think of anything that I would take out of it or change actually.

So that's one thing. We need new pictures, new material, we need to add some writing and some pictures and film on some of the new techniques, which is basically only the SMS. And I think what I mentioned yesterday, we also need to further work on the concept that I told you about. Not drills, but methods of practice."

Goldman: Oh yes! Can you explain that to readers? When you guys [the coaches in Madison] were sitting in the locker room coming up with today's progressions, just the way that you guys were explaining it was so different and really amazing. It's just a totally different way of not only seeing things, and that's what is scary. Very few goalie coaches in North America beyond the pro levels don't use pre-prescribed drills. They pick drills within a theme and a certain area, but it's not your end-to-start philosophy.

Magnusson: "It was so cool how we understood each other directly, you know? I didn't have to go into very much detail before everyone understood exactly what I meant. This was different from what I'm used to, because coaches in general, and specifically goalie coaches who are really into detail, they always want drills. 'Can you hand me this drill' or 'Can you show me some drills I can use?' Almost ever since I started as a goalie coach, and especially since I worked with some really good head coaches in most of the 1990's, I didn't think so much about drills and I never save anything. I don't write down very much. I think of it as, 'what technique or what tool or what situation are we going to practice today?' Then I think of that within the situation, which could be just a shot. Then I think backwards from that shot. What do I want to do before that? Maybe I want a goalie to move like there's a pass. So I think of it that way. I also consider what happens after the shot. So what do I want the goalie to do afterwards? Is he in full control? Does he have the puck in his glove or against his body? Then I probably want him to put it on the ice and pass it somewhere. Is it a controlled rebound? If so, I probably want him to move so he's prepared in the best stance I can think of, at least in that situation, for the next shot. Is there an uncontrolled rebound? Then I want him to gain control of the situation and recover to the best possible stance for that situation. If there's enough time, it could be moving back to his feet. Usually you refer to it as the save process, and a lot of things happen before that. You position yourself, you choose your stance, and then you have these three different ways of making the save. One really important part of making the save is that you play the situation through to the end, so you either gain full control or you need to move yourself to a new position or stance to be ready for the next shot. Thinking of each situation in this manner -- the 'before, during, and the after' of a save – not only makes it easy to analyze a game situation, but it also gives you a set of tools to create or expand drills as you go along. It's an easy way to build new progressions while you're working with the goalie on the ice."

Goldman: Well I'm really excited because it sounds like we're going to become good friends and work on some projects together with the goalies and coaches in this camp. I am so excited to also be able to share this

information with all of the goalie fans out there like me that want to soak up this information and knowledge from a master of the position. But I also do want to get your thoughts on the NetWork camp. We touched on it briefly, but I'm curious what comes out of this for yourself?

Magnusson: "It was definitely a huge learning experience for me. Which I realize it is every time I step on the ice. It's not that big of a deal if it is eight NHL goalies, or I go to a goalie camp with twelve 10-year-olds, I learn from these goalies all the time because they are doing different things. But of course, at this level, the level of learning is higher, both from being around these goalies and being able to work and communicate with them. But also the coolest thing I think is their communication with each other. How they bond and look at each other, how they talk to each other, how they show each other, how they learn from each other. That's the coolest thing for me, and that gave me a chance to learn a lot from them by listening and seeing what they did. Also, the way they are receptive to feedback, which is not at all different from younger goalies. Someone would expect that these guys know it all, but they realize you never know it all, it's a learning process. That's also something I take with me from this. Another thing is the great experience working with this group of coaches, including yourself, David Alexander, Mike Valley, and my counterpart from Finland, Hannu Nykvist. We've been having a great time and it has been a great learning experience for all of us, and we've been sharing just like all of the goalies have been. That's probably the most important message I would give to your readers; the importance of sharing, which has always been part of the way I look at working in goaltending. Being able to share your experience and knowledge always gives you something back, makes you grow. I really saw this sharing between all of the coaches but as well as among the goalies. How they understood and really wanted to share."

Goldman: It's one thing to have the capacity as a human being to share and want to be open, but often it's harder to be in an environment where sharing is really cultivated. This environment was one where it was easy to share and open up and want to kick ideas back and forth and you don't find that very often, especially here in North America, is rare. I talked on your podcast about the power of this event and this camp and how it all ties together. I started this summer on this journey for this book and I had so many questions about different styles and regions, and without this environment this week, I wouldn't have come up with the eloquent and beautiful answer you gave me, which is that there are as many styles as there are goalies. That's what this whole week and my whole summer has been about. I don't gain that wisdom unless you're able to share it in an environment created here.

Magnusson: "It's been my pleasure, Justin and I hope we can keep this up and continue to work together in the future."

27

THE GENESIS OF NETWORK GOALTENDING

"Something moving in the emptiness, something drew me near. Someone told me of my future deeds, whispered them in my ear." –Amorphis

I've never needed proof to believe in fate and I've never struggled with whether or not things happen for a reason. Years ago, I realized that there will simply be moments in life where I was blessed to find myself in a certain place at the right time. I wouldn't be writing this book if that wasn't the case. End of story.

Being invited to the Elite Goalies NHL Camp on the University of Wisconsin campus in Madison was one of those moments. In fact, of all the interconnected and synchronistic experiences I've had in my life, none was more intense as my week spent at this camp. It was not only the final adventure of my summer expedition, it was the absolute pinnacle of my professional career.

Eight NHL goaltenders joined forces with four of the world's finest goalie coaches in the final week of August to create a "fantasy" camp unlike the world has ever seen. For five days, the 13 of us worked together at the Kohl Center in preparation for NHL training camps, which were only two weeks away.

The participating goaltenders ran the gamut of different NHL roles and included Kari Lehtonen, Ben Bishop, Brian Elliott, Anders Lindback, Jake Allen, Dan Ellis, Jussi Rynnas, and Michael Hutchinson.

The coaching staff included Elite Goalies founder Mike Valley (Dallas Stars), Magnusson (you know him already), Nykvist (you know him as well), and David Alexander (Syracuse Crunch).

Valley asked me to be their fifth man. Just as I did for the Strelow camp, I'd be in charge of handling all of the video and scouting duties. That would allow us to capture video of every goalie doing a few reps of every single drill for the entire week, then provide each of them with a memory stick full of their drills and video feedback. Talk about a no-brainer. I paid my way out there, paid for my hotel and rental car, and didn't ask to get paid a single penny. The experience was worth more than anything money could buy.

Valley worked very diligently to bring these goalies and coaches together at a time when things started to get crazy for the NHL pre-season. Obviously we had developed quite a strong friendship over the years, especially after successfully publishing *The Power Within* at the start of 2014, but considering the coaches and goalies involved, I did not expect to be included in his plans. I was honored when he formally invited me in June, but at no point in the second half of the summer did I have the time or the ability to truly grasp the magnitude of what would eventually transpire in Madison.

Seeing an international all-star goalie coaching staff instantly galvanize with themselves and the eight NHL goalies was unlike anything I had ever seen before. It was as if everything I hoped to find on my summer adventure in terms of positive coaching and smart on-ice development had manifested itself into this surreal world inside a prestigious and NCAA facility. Being on the ice with so much talent, especially after everything that had happened to me over the summer, was pure mind-blowing ecstasy.

Valley's NHL goalie camp coincided with the UW Pro Alumni Camp, so close to 20 other pro players (including Joe Pavelski) held a "pre pre-season" camp at the same time, giving the eight NHL goalies a chance to play in some scrimmages that further prepared them for training camps.

All I could do was try to soak everything in, but I was not a spectator at this camp; I had a job to do, and it was one that I would not take lightly. I was so drained from such a tiring summer, so I put every last fume of energy I had into collecting the best video I could possibly capture.

Supporting these eight NHL idols and evaluating their movements and reactions on the ice for the first time in my life was tough to grasp. I think it had a lot to do with the fact I was watching them through so many different lenses, but from a distance of inches and feet. Loaded up like a packing mule with video equipment, I had my iPad

Air, Asus Transformer tablet, Nykvist's white Samsung camera, David's tiny GoPro, and my Samsung S3 phone. Watching the goalies through all of these different lenses was very similar to my everyday reality – watching NHL goalies through TV's and computer screens. But when my eyes lifted off the screen and I saw these goalies in the raw, everything I thought I knew changed. A veil lifted and the accompanying adrenaline rush created a completely new experience that indulged my five senses and caused my brain to release large amounts of serotonin. I was on a totally different planet.

During the first on-ice session, I gained an immense amount of respect and admiration for these goalies. To see their genetically superior levels of body control, vision, and kinesthetic sense from such a close and intimate distance was like looking through a deep space telescope at thousands of hidden stars, or looking into an electron microscope to find the true stuff cells are made of. It was such a significant shift to my usual perception of the NHL goaltender that it instantly transformed the way I evaluated nightly performances I had been previously over-analyzing on social media platforms for nearly six years.

If you've ever been on the ice with an NHL goalie before, you likely understand what I mean when I say that having success at this level is seemingly impossible. Shooters are so damn good these days. Things happen so freaking fast. The pressure is so suffocating. It's a miracle a goalie has the capacity to pitch a shutout, win 30 games in a season, and withstand the rigors and mental stresses of an 82-game season.

Experiencing this sudden and drastic shift in my perspective caused me to hate a small part of my past self. I almost nauseated myself when I thought of all the hundreds of times I scoffed at a goalie for allowing a weak goal, or for undermining their capabilities when breaking down a play.

"What in God's name was I thinking?!" I said this under my breath on the ice as the 6-foot-7 Lindback ripped a puck out of the air from 12 feet away. "It's not like that at all."

But that's the magic of self-discovery at age 32; you're often punched in the face with the fierce reality that you're never too old to learn, never too wise to change your way of thinking.

What I Learned On the Ice

I cherished so many moments during the Elite Goalies NHL Camp in Madison, but what I learned on the ice and in the classroom was irreplaceable. Instant wisdom was injected into my mind, and as this new lifeblood flowed through my veins, I was exposed to the highest level of coaching that anyone could possibly find anywhere in the world.

What I learned was the brilliant simplicity of training NHL goalies. The situational drills were easy to read and execute. The explanations were easy to understand. The skating and movement drills were recognizable – probably very similar to ones you did in high school. Everything was so simple that it almost felt embarrassingly remedial to the goalies.

This first-hand revelation that drills and explanations at the NHL level are often simpler than what you'll find at amateur goalie camps reinforced a notion I've discussed a few times in this book. It proved once again that there are no secrets out there being hidden from the masses. It's not what you teach, it's how you teach it, how you communicate information and feedback to the goalie, how you help them receive the message.

Goalie coaches that don't share their drills or methods because they think it creates a competitive advantage on someone else, or coaches who try to unnecessarily over-complicate or re-package things are completely missing the point and ultimately damaging the culture of goalie coaching in North America.

I also learned about the extreme importance an NHL goalie places on having a strong belief system in his own positional strategy (especially heading into a new season). This does *not* mean he is closed off from suggestions or from making changes, but rather that he must feel a high level of confidence in his decision-making, his technical execution, and his tactical reads. For every scoring situation he will face, he must have an absolute and unwavering faith in his ability to play it the right way.

I will never forget one of the classroom sessions we held during the camp. It was hosted by Magnusson and focused on the ever-popular reverse-VH technique. Magnusson went into great detail on the origins of this technique, how it was popularized and mastered in Sweden, and how the post integration progression evolved. Afterwards, the goalies (there were two groups of four) spent close to 30 minutes discussing their own positional post-play strategies.

For example, Bishop discussed how he used the Reverse-VH technique in an "extreme" manner compared to the rest of the NHL goalies, but that was because nobody could match his frame. As a result, he explained how he was able to get away with dropping into that post seal much earlier in an attacking sequence due to his sheer net coverage. It was also a comfort thing; he said he felt more comfortable getting down early and then moving out from there, as opposed to having to drift back and "find" the post with a little backward momentum.

Elliott, on the other hand, explained how he played it much differently. Then Lehtonen chimed in and explained how he played it differently from both of them. Then you had Ellis, quietly soaking it all in, until he finally said how he was still just trying to grasp the technique and naturally integrate it into his game.

As these goalies discussed the advanced components of this positional strategy in a myriad different situations, I'll never forget when Elliott sarcastically responded to Bishop's strategy by saying, "Well, yeah you can go down early. You're like 14 feet tall!"

Everybody laughed.

It was at that moment I comprehended the magnitude of this camp. These guys were blazing a trail for the next evolution of NHL goaltending. With eight of the world's top 60 goalies (just over 13-percent) working together to understand the intricacies of post integration, a "think tank" of immeasurable size was established. I was drowning in the knowledge being shared in this unprecedented exclusive symposium.

As I sat back and took a few notes on these classroom discussions, I also realized that it was not the coaches that advance the technical game at this level, but the goalies. They're the ones analyzing each other, trying different things in practice, and getting a better feel for what works and what doesn't. The coaches are the facilitators, the guides, the ones that move things along. But the goalies blaze the trails.

This was just one of many memories that comprised the learning experience of a lifetime. The coaches and goalies held so many conversations that fueled the progress of the position in unforeseen ways, and they masterfully created a learning environment where everyone graciously worked together to find different solutions to some of the more tricky situations each goalie faced in the crease.

As the week went on and I started to get over the sheer shock of it all, my mind was open to absorb a lot more information. I quickly became very familiar with the subtle kinetics and movements of each goalie. By the end of the week, I had established a deeper understanding of their playing style, work habits, personality, and overall skill sets. As a result, I gained even more confidence in my idea that the different functional movement disciplines I explained in "The Science of Shadowing" would eventually become more prevalent and more widely accepted and understood in the goaltending community.

At this level, a true mastery of the core principles of goaltending is so innate and intuitive that practicing them is more about routine and keeping certain mechanical and mental elements sharp. But in terms of actually improving and sharpening their skills and senses, over time, more pro goalies will begin to realize the importance of using visualization and imagery to enhance (Ideokinesis) their movement performance. It reinforces the lesson that Josh Tucker taught us in the chapter on Vision Training. No matter how skilled you are as a goalie, there is no such thing as perfect vision. It can always be enhanced and strengthened. The same goes for functional movement.

For example, when you have a guy like Pavelski lining up on the other side of the Royal Road and you only have a split second to get across, using a reinforced foundation of movement and visual acuity system through methods such as Ideokinesis and Pilates gives the goalie an edge that they don't get in other realms. You can only sharpen your skates or tweak your gear so much. Furthermore, these are methods that have been around for nearly 100 years, yet they have almost never been used to give an elite goaltender that extra edge they need to beat passes, have a slightly smoother lateral transition, or a slightly easier time feeling that puck into and off of their body as they follow through on an initial save.

I think that's what it all comes down to at the highest level – it's way less about the mastery of a skill and way more about getting that right "feel" to execute the mastered skill properly. When you have that right "feel" in the crease, you're thinking less, because you know you're comfortable. You're moving with more precision and awareness. You're reading stick blades with less blur and more definition. Your reactions and net coverage completely match the puck's trajectory.

But in order to help these feelings and that kinesthetic sense fall into place, with such a fine line between nailing it and being "slightly off" or "fighting it" at the NHL level, this camp taught me that discovering those functional movement disciplines was the "new realms" of goalie development reflected in this book's title. I honestly feel that there will come a time when elite goalie coaches will realize what I did a few years ago; these are result-driven ways to enhance the solid skills of an elite goalie.

If these are "secrets" that we thought no longer existed, they're not secret any longer. But all new ideas are considered unfamiliar at first. It's only when they are properly implemented that they are accepted. That's exactly what happened with Korn's use of medicine balls with Hutton and Holtby.

I also think this is very revealing with a term I call *Displacement.*

Displacement is when a goalie initially establishes the proper angle and squareness prior to a shot being taken, only to have that angle and shot trajectory change between the time the goalie sets his feet and the time the puck is actually released off the stick blade.

One example of this is when a player winds up for a slap shot while the puck is still moving laterally, toward, or away from the goalie. That slight change in the puck's location – it could be anywhere from six to eight inches or a few feet – "displaces" the goalie's proper squareness and net coverage. That forces them to need to adjust, shift, lean their body or body part(s) in order to fill the space that was eventually opened due to the puck's altered location.

So it's not just the angle change of the puck that can throw you off, but it's a bit of a catch-22. Setting your feet nails you to that crossfire, but pucks may still be moving, and shooters are getting better at disguising releases, or subtly altering them instantaneously with their release. When that crossfire changes, the goalie often has to change, including how he or she reacts, or what save selection is chosen.

What was originally a tight butterfly save with the hands in front of the body was suddenly turned into a half-butterfly extension with the glove or blocker tight to the hip, just above the pad. But the time it took the puck to displace the goalie's squareness is like vapor – you can't see it. It happens so fast, in the blink of an eye. Ask a goalie how he deals with this idea of displacement and many will tell you that the only way to truly process that alteration and adjust accordingly is by subconsciously "feeling" it. Instincts, man.

In order to enhance a goalie's ability to manage the various forms of displacement, or the different types of speed changes in a game, I honestly believe it is less about technique and more about mind-body awareness at the highest levels. That improved awareness sharpens the "feel" you get from making certain movements and reactions, including tracking the puck, anticipating shot trajectories and where pucks will end up going through screens and tips, and reading the speed alteration on a puck deflected in the low slot.

That is why these things – Yoga, Pilates, Ideokinesis, and Meditation – matter. They can enhance even the best levels of coordination, equilibrium, fine-motor skills, and muscle balance. On top of all this, the latest advancements in athletic neuroscience will continue to open the door for these disciplines to filter into goalie development at all ages.

Displacement "aside" (no pun intended), I was surprised at the simplicity but effectiveness of the skating and movement drills. One drill had goalies hopping from one foot to the other, engaging their edge awareness and balance. They also worked on getting a "good feel" for their inside edges as they made extended c-cut after extended c-cut down the ice and back again. They were asked to be methodical with their movements, and to move slowly.

Once again, these drills reinforced the notion I discussed above about having that "feel" out there.

Another drill saw Valley standing in front of one of the benches, using a stick to point in different directions. The goalies had to read the stick and then react with a short off-center butterfly drop and a fast recovery back to their skates. They had to feel their feet setting and feel the sharp push back to center.

In each and every drill, I was immersed in so much precision. Everything these guys did was so close to perfect that I become enthralled with the biomechanical mastery of it all. Their eyes tracked pucks better than anyone I had ever seen on the ice. They had an eerie and almost alien-like 360-degree awareness of where their body and pads were placed in relation to the puck.

They were such fine-tuned athletes, but they looked like organic creatures instead of metallic machines. I did not see the mechanical roboticism that some believe to be prevalent at the NHL level. Instead, I saw the natural fluidity of their movements and the aura of elite unconscious competent reactionary skills.

As a result of all this, I pretty much had zero feedback to give anyone. But I also knew it was not my place to do so.

Instead, I kept my mouth shut for almost the entire week and focused on collecting my video.

As the week went along, I never lost the sense of awe and amazement, but I did begin to feel more comfortable being on the ice with these guys. My eyes continued to adjust and I continued to see more as time went on. I was the observer peeking out from behind cameras and tablets, learning as much as possible about the training dynamics of a goalie camp that included international coaches and NHL talent.

I still did not want to speak to anyone. I did not want to interfere with the majesty of their training rhythm.

A Sense of Belonging

My comfort level on the ice grew as the week continued, but off the ice was a bit of a different story. Part of me wanted to leave the goalies and coaches alone to do their own thing every night, but another part of me didn't want to pass up the opportunity to build friendships and get to know them away from the game.

That being said, a couple of off-ice experiences stood out among the rest.

The first took place on a midafternoon following one of the day's on-ice sessions. During the camp, UW students were starting to move back into their dorms and apartments, so the campus was jam-packed with people. The buzz of a new school year was in the air. Everything was freshly painted and prepared. Gorgeous girls were tanning in vibrant bikinis, smiling at the sky through oversized sunglasses. Distracted guys were purposely tossing footballs and throwing Frisbees right next to them, clearly aware of their immediate surroundings. I was drowning in a deep sea of Badger red, and I couldn't have been happier.

Scheduled to take a private tour of the UW football stadium and training facilities before going out for the night, we all had to walk from the Kohl Center to the football stadium, which was about a mile away.

Instead of walking, a few of the goalies decided they would rather rent public bikes and ride to the stadium in comical style. These bikes were the ones you pull out from a sidewalk docking station, you know, the ones you use for an hour and then lock back into any number of places scattered around the campus. They looked silly instead of sporty, with small baskets on the front and chromed handlebars that curved in a way that made me feel uncomfortably effeminate around a bunch of pro goalies.

But the guys thought they were hilarious, so the few that originally rented them biked back to the Kohl Center where the coaching staff was waiting.

Hilarity ensued. Pictures were taken. Laughter was shared.

"What the hell is even happening," I said to myself as I watched these monsters wheel around on these tiny bikes. How were they not breaking into a million pieces, and what kind of spectacle am I witnessing? At no point in the rest of my life will I ever see a group of NHL goalies on cheesy rental bikes, cruising through a college campus.

I took zero photos. I said nothing on Twitter. I respected their privacy. I just wanted to be a part of this.

A few minutes later, the rest of us decided to rent bikes as well. Mike, David, Hannu, Thomas, and I found the nearest docking station, chose our chromed carriers, and joined the goalie caravan as we rolled down the street, one behind the other, ringing bells and checking out all the cuties without a worry in the world.

Only one problem, though. Everyone's legs were way, way stronger than mine.

I almost burst a lung trying to keep up. I thought my bony kneecaps were going to explode out of my skin and my toothpick ankles were going to snap. I pedaled as hard as I possibly could to the point where I was either going to get blindsided by some dimwit college student in a Scion, collide with a melancholy mom seeing her baby son off, or fall so far behind that my only option would be to meet them back at the hotel later on. Oh, the embarrassment I would have felt had that happened.

Fortunately, I stayed within range and didn't get caught in any traffic or stuck at any red lights. Despite a sweaty back, dead legs, and messy hair, gasping for air, I made it.

The rest of the tour was awesome. We walked down the tunnel to the football field and took more group photos. I was always the photographer in these situations for obvious reasons, but I didn't care. I was still there. I was still a part of the group.

It may have just been a tour of the UW football facilities, but since I was together with the guys in a leisurely manner, I really felt like I belonged. None of the goalies really knew much about me except that I was the guy from The Goalie Guild, but I did feel accepted. I didn't feel like they saw me as a media-type, or someone that would be publicizing their every move.

The following day, pretty much out of nowhere, I received a staggering vote of confidence from Valley and the rest of the coaching staff. We were sitting in the locker room preparing for a session, when suddenly Valley looked at me while tying his skates.

"I was just in the locker room telling the guys about tonight," he said. "Your name came up."

"What? Me? Why? Ugh…please don't tell me I fucked something up."

"No, not at all," Mike said with a laugh. "We were all just talking, and some of the guys mentioned how it was great having you out here with us."

"Oh. Wait…really?"

"Yeah. You know how these guys are. They're all smart guys. They definitely took a few days to see what you were all about," he said a-matter-of-factly. "A couple of them had heard about you, but this was the first time any of them met you. They all like you. They're happy to have you here. You should be proud."

I was speechless. I stood there, dumbfounded, not moving, with a peeled banana staring me right back in the face. All I could think to do was to thank the coaches for allowing me to attend. I was not only instantly energized, but more importantly, depressurized. I finally relaxed.

For all the work I had done capturing video all week, I think the coaching staff sensed this was my little moment of glory. It was their way of proverbially patting me on the back and further including me.

I never liked the feeling of knowing I'm being watched, but due to my large audience on Twitter, I know that many people I've never met before pass judgments every day. I am totally fine with that, it's a part of life in a world that is becoming increasingly saturated by social media. But to know that the eight NHL goalies were collectively happy to have me there, and to know that they had accepted me as the coaching staff's "fifth man" was a quiet and conscious moment of great personal achievement.

I guess I had done it. I guess I no longer had to feel like I needed to prove to anyone that I belonged, or that I was capable of scouting or supporting goalies at the highest level imaginable.

From that moment on, it was so much easier to talk to the goalies on the ice. I could tell they were more open to speaking to me as well. We shared jokes, we discussed drills, and we definitely talked gear. The weight of the world lifted off my shoulders. I was able to be myself in a place where I never thought I'd ever belong.

The Garden of the Gods

One of the players at the UW Pro Alumni Camp was Adam Burish. Formerly with the Dallas Stars, he was friends with Valley and therefore one of the main shooters we used during our training sessions. Knowing that many of the guys were in Madison for the first time, Adam was kind enough to invite all of us to come out to his family's summer home on Lake Wisconsin on Thursday for a night of grilling and boating.

Later that afternoon, Dave, Mike, and I drove out to Adam's place in Mike's truck. We first stopped at Costco to pick up everything we'd need for the night, then traveled north of Madison on Route 113 until we reached the lake's shoreline. We lost phone reception, but made it without any trouble.

The eight goalies, Hannu, and Thomas arrived at Adam's an hour later in a limo.

Adam's plot of land was as picturesque as it was sprawling. Nestled within his family's wooded property was a huge authentic log cabin, which was originally built in British Columbia, then shipped down and placed perfectly on the edge of what had to be close to 20 acres. The place was very private, with no other houses in sight for miles, and the drive up to the property was like snaking through a crooked Grand Canyon creek.

Upon seeing this slice of pristine Upper Midwest land, I couldn't believe Adam was kind enough to invite everyone to hang out. I mean, I understood why he would invite the goalies, but I was a complete stranger. But he was still the most gracious host. He never once looked like was worried or concerned when he allowed all of the guys, including myself, to take his jet skis and pontoon boat out for a spin.

Since Dave, Mike, and I got there an hour before the rest of the guys, we busied ourselves by helping Adam prepare the dinner feast. I think I thanked Adam about five times for allowing me to come over and join everyone. Dave did an awesome job preparing all the food and I just did whatever I could to help out.

Soon after, I took a look around Adam's house. Winding down a narrow staircase with polished wooden guardrails,

I dropped into his basement, where his parents had a huge collection of Adam's hockey memories. It included jerseys, newspaper clippings on his accomplishments, trophies, medals, and more.

"Whoa. I'm in the middle of an authentic American hockey family home," I thought. "How in God's name did I even get here?!"

The bliss was starting to settle in.

When the players finally arrived, it didn't take long for all of us to get out on the water. Jussi, Kari, and Hannu took turns riding jet skis across the serene lake. Other guys walked back and forth along the dock, dipping their feet in the water. I just hung out on the back patio, relaxed, observed, and smiled.

As the daylight slowly faded, it felt as if Burish's lake house had lifted off the ground and rested far above the mortal sphere. It was like the vernal equinox was transpiring right before my very eyes; the sun beamed down directly on the property and perfectly split my world between day and night, reality and a dream. Unable to explain how I got there, I struggled to maintain a grip on the normal world I knew.

The entire experience was like being amongst the mythological Greek gods. On this special afternoon, I joined them as they retreated to their lofty chambers to eat, drink, and celebrate their dominance over the entire goalie dominion. Feasting together after another day of toiling on the ice, amidst the lingering light of another perfect Wisconsin summer day, these eight goalie gods shared their stories of victory and defeat, of peace and war, of glory and future goals. They strengthened friendships and reveled in the immortality of being some of the most elite hockey players in the universe.

And there I stood. Skinny legs, tired eyes, pale skin, and permanent smile. Happily engaged in my own intoxicating and dizzying array of the ever-blooming green groves of goalie greatness, I released my grip on reality and let go. I let myself drown in it.

After a bunch of the guys took Adam's Sea-Doo out for a spin, I took a quick rip around the lake. For some reason though, as soon as I docked, I felt guilty. It was like I snuck out on a prized golden chariot belonging to one of the NHL gods. But nobody cared. A couple of guys even asked if I had a good time.

"Hell yeah," I said. "It's perfect out there."

Just before the sun dipped the outer rim of its golden bowl into the lake's glassy horizon, the goalies and coaches joined Burish on the pontoon boat for a slow, seraphic sail. I stayed behind for this one. I wasn't about to intrude on that relaxing moment for the guys. Plus someone had to keep an eye on everything.

During their time on the pontoon boat, all I could do was sit on the back patio and write. I wasn't paralyzed, but for some reason, I didn't have the conscious ability to actually *do* anything. I guess I was too enamored with my surroundings and too caught up in warming energy of the oncoming dusk to write anything specific. Instead, I just wrote down little moments.

"Handing 20 fresh, crisp ears of corn to David."
"Cleaning Adam's massive stainless steel grill."
"Brian and Jake bullshitting about fishing trips."

"Petting Brian's dog and feeding him a chip."
"Listening to Hannu talk about classic rock."
"Watching Hutch smile about nothing at all."

A few minutes later, I looked up and everyone was suddenly getting off the boat. Time to eat. The feast ensued, good conversation continued, and while the food helped bring me back to reality, I chose not to reel myself back in. When we finished eating, everyone wound down before firing it up and going out later that night. Coincidentally, it was my favorite time of the day, where the glow of the setting sun still lingers in the air, and the rays of light track back up towards the moon.

It was twilight.

Suddenly, out of the corner of my eye, a tiny glob of golden light softly flashed and disappeared. A few feet to the right, the same thing. Then one slight below that, and then another one above and to the left.

A firefly! I hadn't seen one of those in years, probably since I was a kid living on my ranch in Texas.

I jumped up from my chair on Adam's deck and hovered over to the middle of a big plot of thick grass, which stretched about 30 yards from the end of his elevated deck to the water's edge. I dropped down to my knees with a narrowed butterfly and took a look around.

To my left, a few guys were in the hot tub, laughing about whatever. To my right, nothing but pine trees and the sound of crickets, rubbing their feet together in a smug symphony of faint chirping. Behind me, a few guys were quietly talking on the deck. In front of me, a pair of wooden Adirondack chairs conjoined by a small tabletop.

In the left seat was Dan. In the right seat was Thomas. On the small table joining them was a laptop.

In the final moments of visible light, Thomas and Dan were breaking down some of the video I had recorded earlier in the day. Together, they were looking at ways to improve his post integration skills. Nothing but Lake Wisconsin in front of them, I snapped a photo of this perfect scene.

Then I fell flat on my back and stared up through the pine trees protecting Adam's property.

Between the glow bugs dancing around my field of vision and the scene directly in front of me, it was at this moment I had a slight out-of-body experience. The force of gravity released itself from my body's skeletal chamber. From the earth's soft soil I rose, until I joined the goalie gods in their lofty chambers and saw everything through my third eye.

This was the culmination of all things.

On this burnished throne of serene nature I sat side-by-side with the goalies, the vault of the arching sky now within reach. Genetically superior cells cast forth their energy onto my entire being. I was fully interconnected with so much goaltending talent and wisdom that it made me feel god-like. I felt immortal.

During that ephemeral moment, I changed. I transformed into a new form of biologically optimized pulsating determination, more effective and confident than all of the previous me's. Illuminated by the stars above and the glow bugs below, my spirit exulted.

A life-long dream had suddenly become the definition of my identity. This was the closest I would ever get to being an NHL goalie. It had nothing to do with talent, but everything to do with opportunity, hard work, perseverance, and trusting one's path.

As the moon lifted from the shadows of the twilight, I felt the moment of bliss starting to fade. I slowly parachuted back down into reality. In my weakest moment of my entire summer, amidst all the aches and pains and exhaustion I never felt so alive.

I knew this night wouldn't last forever, but that didn't dissipate the energy I felt from spending a night in the Garden of the Gods.

The Genesis of NetWork Goaltending

With the surreal experience from Burish's house still fresh in my mind, it became quite clear to me that the coaching staff had created something very special in Madison, both in terms of the way the camp was run, and the environment in which it existed.

I was not alone in my thoughts. Everyone agreed that we wanted to continue working together. But how?

The following afternoon, the five of us tossed ideas back and forth about different ways to work together. By the end of the brainstorming, Mike had presented us with an opportunity to form an organization, an international collection of coaches that would focus on four tenants: sharing ideas, educating coaches, developing goalies, and bringing the goalie community together.

Naturally, everyone started to think of a name for this proposed organization. I came up with a few hilariously brutal names, but it was Magnusson who came up with a clever way to connect our newfound mission with a little play on words.

"NetWork Goaltending."

Everyone loved it. Done and done. We all smiled, talked amongst ourselves, and engaged our creative side for a few more hours. It appeared that we had found a way to accomplish something that may had never been done in North America before; a couple of elite coaches let go of their ego, invited goalie coaches from other countries to work together, and shared information in an open manner. There was no over-protective energy, no sense of trying to one-up or discredit the other, and no pissing matches.

I think everyone had slightly different ideas of what NetWork Goaltending would eventually become, but the foundation had been laid. I was excited to help these guys create something new, especially something that would become quite influential.

By the end of camp, we had agreed to work towards creating two experiences. The first was by hosting one international summer goalie camp for aspiring pros in a manner very similar to the NHL goalie camp. The second was by trying to host a few coaching symposiums that would allow goalie coaches from all walks of life to come together and experience the same sharing environment we did in Madison. It would not only break down some of the cultural barriers currently existing in North America, but it would give everyone an opportunity to learn new techniques and training methods, which makes everyone better.

Lastly, we wanted to find a way to integrate this sharing environment on the internet. That's where ideas can quickly spread, so we came up with the idea known as "NetTalks", which was similar to the same concept you find on Ted Talks. Goalie coaches from all over would share videos and ideas and help others to share their ideas as well.

I was too intoxicated and exhausted from the blissful experience in Madison to really visualize it all in my head. But I was so committed to helping these guys create their brainchild that I refused to let the opportunity fade from the front of my mind. Even though I was so busy getting my life in order back in Colorado, I sat down and built the website. Again, I did this without asking for any money, because I just wanted to continue to be a part of what these guys were doing.

Never did I imagine that, just a few months later, NetWork would become a full-blown website with a solid mission statement and a ton of believers. It was a very exciting new professional endeavor, and as much as I was still dedicated to trying to help USA Hockey in some way, I asked myself one question.

"Why settle for helping one country with their goalie development when I can help the whole world?

The Hard Return to Reality

When the camp came to a close and everyone left the hotel in Madison, I experienced a very hard mental and emotional crash. I came to the realization that I was not only going to complete the process of uprooting my entire life after spending the past two years in Minnesota, but that I was at the end of my amazing summer adventure. Training camps were only a few weeks away, and I had to prepare for another year of writing fantasy hockey articles for NHL.com.

I was exhausted to the point that my entire body was numb to all the aches and pains. My mind was also numb to the fact that I now had to gather myself and write the book.

It was really, really tough returning to my regular everyday life.

For five days in Madison, I was in a perpetual state of nirvana. I shared ice, meals, car rides, memories, ideas, and opinions with a group of goalie gods that had fully accepted me into their brotherhood. I was gifted with the ultimate boost of confidence, a pair of wings needed to soar way above my everyday life and experience a regal sense of my own hubris.

Like Icarus, I realized I had flown too close to the sun. The wax from my wings melted and I crashed into the proverbial sea of depression. The sliver of bliss was suddenly torn from my grasp, so I forgot that it was ultimately my responsibility to get over it, appreciate the experience for what it was, and push forward. I had to fight to move on. I had to remind myself that Madison was not real life, and while it may come around again, it would only be for a few fleeting days.

I sulked for one night, maybe two. But after getting over it, I felt eternal gratitude. To this day, I still thank Valley for inviting me to his camp. It changed my life.

Filled with so many amazing revelations, nothing impressed me more than the lack of egos and the pure camaraderie between everyone in Madison. The creativity and sharing flowed, the work ethic was visibly high, and the training environment was very productive. It was a tribe of brothers and fathers, of warriors and chieftains, all working together in a sacred environment to get the most out of each other.

The whole thing was very much a spiritual experience.

28

THE NETWORK GOALTENDING ROUNDTABLE

Author's Note: *On the eve of the final day of the Elite Goalies NHL camp, the four coaches and I met up in the hotel lobby and spent a few hours discussing various aspects of the camp's successes, snags, and our ideas for working together in the future. Luckily, I was allowed to record most of this roundtable discussion for the book, giving you a further glimpse into the genesis of NetWork Goaltending.*

Goldman: "So what was everyone's expectations heading into camp?"

Valley: "My expectations were extremely high, so I think on the ice, we've met my expectations. I knew it was going to be really good. I just knew that's the quality I wanted and anything less would've been disappointing. So it's been high, but again, I knew that both of you guys [Nykvist and Magnusson] were going to bring everything you had, and I knew Dave [Alexander] and Justin would as well. It's kind of the standard I wanted. The thing I'm very pleased with was all of the off-ice things that came together. So as you sit down and plan out all these little details, everything just worked well. The things that are out of my control – these guys bonding and going out and having a good time like picking up bikes – that exceeded my expectations. I guess the other thing that exceeded my expectations was the amount that the athletes enjoyed it. I knew they would think it was fun, but they think this is awesome and they all want to come back. I knew with these guys it had to be a balance of hard work and a lot of fun. We achieved that."

Magnusson: "I didn't really have any expectations, because I didn't know how these guys would be practicing on the ice together. I had no expectations at all."

Nykvist: "For me it was a little bit of diving into darkness."

Goldman: "What about your expectations in terms of teaching NHL goalies something? How did you feel being able to communicate with this elite group of goalies?"

Magnusson: "From my earlier experiences working with pro goalies, I knew that these guys would be willing to pick up new ideas, learn things, and feed off each other. So in that case, this camp was about what I expected. I didn't think very much about the bonding, but I'm not surprised at all, because when we had elite camps in 2007 I think it was, we had all of the best goalies in the 18-20 year range in Sweden. Then the elite team goalies were together in that camp, which included almost anyone who was an NHL goalie in that age bracket. Enroth, Svedberg, Owuya, Eddie Lack, Gustavsson, Liv, Lindback, Markstrom; they were all there. And they bonded just the way all goalies seem to do when they get the opportunity to get together. No matter what age or level. And so did our guys here. It's been awesome."

Valley: "I said to David that this is probably the coolest experience that I've been involved in. It's probably the coolest week that I've been a part of."

Magnusson: "You will see that with kids in goalie schools how they bond. And I expected this with the group here like the kids do, because they're all goalies. And when goalies get together, it's a special breed."

Alexander: "Goaltending is like a subculture, you know?"

Valley: "So all in all, everything went – and I know it's not over and we'll finish strong tomorrow – but everything went great. There's nothing where I wished something else would have happened. Today when we didn't have as many shooters as we had hoped for, it didn't bother me, because I knew we had the ability to work around it. Actually, when I'm doing sessions or working with my guys, often I don't even want shooters. If you get too many, it draws away from a lot of the details that I need to have happen with a goalie, because there's such a fine balance in trying to keep the shooter interested, but it takes away from my goalie.

So sometimes we only want one or two guys with Kari, or maybe not even any."

Magnusson: "It's funny. You often hear goalie coaches saying that they like to shoot, but they find it so hard to watch the goalie the same time they are shooting. I feel the opposite. When I do all the shooting, I get a better feeling for the goalie."

Valley: "With a young goalie coach, one of the important things is that you know how to shoot."

Alexander: "I remember you told me that, what, six years ago? I've been working on my shot ever since. This year was great because the pro rink is empty. So at night, I would literally go with a bucket of pucks and practice shooting."

Valley: "It's so important. You gain a little more respect that way, you can do more drills, and you're not handcuffed. If you can't shoot, you have to find someone who can. I've had times during the season though where my shoulder hurts, and it's a matter of time before your shoulder goes and you need surgery."

Magnusson: "As a goalie coach, you're very rarely warmed up. You have to do things instantly, especially if someone tells you that you have 5-to-10 minutes to work with the goalies. After 25 years, my shoulders were gone. The last seven to eight years, I haven't been on the ice enough and haven't kept it going, so my shot is completely off."

Nykvist: "The biggest thing for me is that I believe we did a good job on the ice, but I still loved it the most when the guys were together and spending time with each other. Now when they start to play against each other, there are friendships and relationships between them."

Goldman: "That was my favorite part as well. I've seen NHL goalies play for years, but I've never been in an environment where they are relaxing and enjoying life together, especially in this manner. I seriously want to watch every game where these eight guys are playing each other."

Valley: "I guess it's safe to say that it exceeded everyone's expectations. Obviously from how the goalies bonded, but the chemistry between us as well. We thought it was going to be good, but the way we fed off each other and worked off each other was better than I expected."

Nykvist: "If we can manage to do this again next year, we can already discuss this camp, what's been happening during the season, then it's so much easier to get things going again."

Author's Note: *At this point in the interview, Nykvist pulled out that same copy of the Finnish Goalie Development Handbook that I first saw in Helsinki. My eyes lit up as he started to show it off to the rest of the roundtable. Some parts here were lost in the mix since we were all talking over each other, but the direction of the roundtable moved towards the content found within.*

Valley: "It doesn't matter what content you provide, it's the execution of that content and that plan, and those who are teaching it."

Magnusson: "There are not a certain number of different styles. Each goalie is unique, having their own personal style. Then they use different tools that are similar, but the way every goalie applies those tools, those technical parts, and uses them in a tactical way, everyone is unique. I learned that for the first time after coaching Tommy Soderstrom and our next goalie was someone else, two completely different goalies."

Goldman: "So if there's one thing that's different, it's not the styles, but the way the goalies are being taught."

Valley: "It's also the environment that they've been put in."

Magnusson: "And how we look upon the game of goaltending, and how that can be taught."

Goldman: The environmental factors are important because we're a product of our environment, and our thoughts are like the food we put in our body. So it's the same thing, that same theme keeps coming up. It's not where you're from, it's what you do with the tools and the coaching you're given."

Magnusson: "Right. What he does with the information that you feed him."

Goldman: "Seeing this wonderful Finnish goalie development manual for a second time, it brings up so many things regarding where USA Hockey is at. David, how do you feel about where Canada is at right now in the process?"

Alexander: "I think hockey Canada is in a good spot. Yes, they are under the spotlight, but to be honest, they can either see this as a setback or a springboard. From what I can tell, they have assembled some great minds and are taking the springboard approach; they're looking to get better and continue to be a great place to develop goalies. What I find most intriguing is that, I see them developing an egoless mindset like I saw when I visited Sweden this summer. Hockey Canada is starting to reach out to other countries and more coaches across Canada to try and get the most input possible when it comes to developing new curriculum and the best practice teaching methods. To me, this doesn't show weakness, but strength in acknowledging they want to learn. They are multiplying their learning. Through this whole process, I'm sure they have been their own biggest critic, but by the end, they're going to deliver in a big way. I think it's an exciting time for Canadian goaltending."

Goldman: "Mike, what are your thoughts about everything going on? It definitely seems like there's a clear shift taking place with more European goalies in North America. I kind of agree with what David is saying in terms of a lack of talent, just how it's being handled."

Valley: "Well, I think it kind of goes back to my point from yesterday. What are we comparing them to? Are we saying that a 17-year-old in Sweden or Finland is better than a 17-year-old in Canada? Or are we looking at the end result, which is an NHL goaltender at the age of 26? One of the major reasons why we're seeing more Europeans in the NHL is because the process allows them to be good, it allows them to develop over time. Whereas the system within North America will push you out by the time you're 18 or 19 if you're not good enough. You have no options. You can continue to play, develop, and then get good coaching, at a time when you really need it [in Europe]. When we're drafting goalies at 18, I tell our scouts that they're trying to draft a goalie before a goalie has even found himself. That's really what it is. You don't even know. You don't have the slightest clue – I don't care who you are – how to play goal when you're 18. Anybody that turns 26 and is playing at a high level will tell you that. There's so much to learn and it takes time, so I think you're comparing apples to oranges; it just doesn't work. So I think it's unfair to say a 17-year-old in Europe is better over there. Hey, there are good goalies all over the place. It's how you manage it, and how the opportunities you get grow over time. I did that little breakdown for scouts. The average NHL goalie that played in the top-30 in minutes broke into the NHL at 24.8 years old. You have the majority of the goalies, 30-percent, coming from Europe. A little less come from major-junior and then it was college. The average round draft pick of the top-30 goalies playing in the NHL was the fifth round. The average success rate from a major junior goalie was drafted in the top 1.8 rounds. So why is that?"

Goldman: "Because they just have to be superlatively superb athletes."

Valley: "When we draft a player in the top two rounds, after major junior, where do you put them?"

Goldman: "In the AHL."

Valley: "Right. You're not putting him in the ECHL. So what is he getting in the AHL? Coaching and a higher quality of competition. That's automatically going to make you better. If you're drafted in a lower round, you're likely going to the ECHL or maybe even the CHL. So guys that play at a higher level will develop at a higher level. So what about a European guy who gets to stay in Europe? All of a sudden he gets to play and develop over there without those pressures. So it's often where we place guys and the opportunities that they get. Look at Viktor Fasth, Niklas Backstrom, and Pekka Rinne. Those goalies, if they had been Canadians playing our system, may not be playing. So at that critical age when you have to either continue to develop or quit the game. What's an 18-year-old kid that doesn't make junior hockey going to do? He's done. He's got nowhere to go. Yes I believe that the coaching and the evolution and the system they have in place in Europe is better, but there's so many things to look at, you can't even really start comparing."

Magnusson: "When you're out in smaller areas in Sweden, you almost don't pay anything at all. If you are in one of the bigger clubs, you probably pay like SEK 20,000 a year, which is still less than $3,000 dollars a year."

Valley: "If you play Midget-AAA hockey in Dallas, it costs you thousands of dollars. I wouldn't be able to play hockey if it cost more than $500. When I played, if you were a goalie and you owned the equipment, you didn't have to pay the association fee. But that's changed, so there's just so many environmental factors involved."

Nykvist: "I totally agree with you. And even inside the country there's variety. In Finland it's a little bit different up in the north compared to the major cities. It's really dependent on just where you're born. Like Antti Niemi. I think he got his first National Team game in the Olympics, after already winning the Stanley Cup. He was in a Finnish B-League team, and meanwhile he was making some money by driving the Zamboni, and then he got his opportunity. So he's a really good story."

Goldman: "What is even more interesting is that now you have companies in North America teaching the Finnish style. And then my question always becomes, well what does that really even mean?"

Valley: "But even that's wrong then. You're teaching an athlete. You're teaching the mechanics of movement. You're not teaching a style. This is almost like the flavor of the month. We're going to give a Finn or a Swede an opportunity because that's what everyone else is doing, so it must be right. So this is the message we've been sending these guys all week, it's not the nationality, it's the goalie."

Nykvist: "When you look at the newspapers and articles, people who don't really understand what they're talking about will use some type of adjective, then you go into nationalities or styles, and that justifies your opinion. That's what I've found."

Valley: "Or when you're evaluating goalies, let's look at the current flavors of the month. Well, it's being European or a big goalie. So maybe we're eliminating a lot of really good goalies out there just based off of the fact he doesn't fit the mold we're looking for. But you're not trained to see beyond the flavors."

Nykvist: "It starts and ends with the goalie. I start with the glove hand side, and take the same shot, and you see the same mistakes in Canada as you do in Finland. The net is the same size."

Valley: "That's right. The other thing is how much ice time we get to train. That's another big thing. I went to Sweden at age 17 because if I would have stayed in Canada, I would have skated three times a week. In Sweden, I was on the ice eight times a week. It's that simple. So all of a sudden I went from being an average 17-year-old goaltender, to going over and training really hard for one year, coming back and then being a Junior-A star and getting nine scholarship offers. It's huge."

Nykvist: "Those must have been exciting days for you when you went over there."

Goldman: "So Hannu, what was the best part of this experience for you?"

Nykvist: "The best thing about this week for me is that between all of these guys, there's now some kind of bond. Between us and everyone. We have done something special, something unique that has never been done before. That's one of the coolest things. It's never been done before."

Goldman: "I think the first day or two, it was, 'holy shit, I'm on the ice with eight NHL goalies.' Now I think the coolest thing for me is hearing Mike and you guys say how it's the coolest experience you guys have ever been a part of. To know that I've been able to be a small part of it, to interact with everyone, to offer up my services, is totally unreal. The whole experience has been amazing."

Magnusson: "It's hard to tell, but I agree, it is the best experience in my career."

Valley: "That's so cool to hear. You know what else is cool to hear? I've looked up to him [Magnusson] for so long, so to be able to hear him be so excited about something is so cool."

Goldman: "Now that I'm hearing you guys say all of this, I know I'm going to miss this so much. I don't want anyone to leave. I've gained so much confidence just by being here."

Magnusson: "I also wanted to say this too, but I really appreciate, and I'm not exactly sure how to put it, but watching what you're doing on the ice with the goalies, I see a lot of myself in what Mike is doing, 20 years ago. I don't mean the goaltending instruction, but the passion, the drive, and also the big picture you have of everything you're doing. And that makes me feel really, really good in my heart. It made an impression on me."

Nykvist: "Kari is really lucky to have you as a coach."

Goldman: "What about you, David?"

Alexander: "You know what, it's kind of a weird situation, because Mike and I have done this stuff together before. I have kind of done something like this in Maine with Bishop and Howard and Allen, so I kind of have an idea of how we roll. We have exceeded my expectations for sure. I'm not surprised with it because I know how this was bound to happen. But what has hit me the most, and it's only described as gratitude for being here, but I'm grateful for being surrounded by our staff and the goalies because of how selfless this whole experience has been. Everybody is kind of in it for everyone else, which is really weird to me. Remember, I come from a country where some goalie coaches will prohibit video cameras. Two weeks ago, I had one of my competitor's wives sitting in the rink watching my camp for a day trying not to be noticed. So she was spying on my camp. It's just weird. But when you get to this level where Mike has been in the NHL for six years now, and you have him saying it's the coolest thing he's done, and people like you guys saying the same thing, to think that we're at such a high level and it's so selfless, it's very intriguing to me. It's a very special week. The stars have aligned, you know?"

Magnusson: "The selfless part of it you mentioned is all credit to Mike, because of the group he has picked, because of the way he is and the people he wants to surround himself with."

Valley: "It all goes back to the term I used at the start of the week, vibrational frequency. It's what you are attracted to. Like why did we connect in Malmo? Because we're on the same wavelength and same page at the same time."

Goldman: "I think it ultimately becomes a very powerful thing. When you have a situation like this, where everyone is egoless and vibrational frequencies are flowing together and you have the right coaches with the right goalies, everything that comes from this is so timeless and poignant. It makes so much sense. I never would have expected the information to flow so smoothly in terms of how you guys build the drills and progressions. Everything you guys discussed just came together, almost like the puzzle pieces were already pre-arranged. That blows my mind because it's Finland, it's Sweden, and it's Canada. Everyone comes from such different areas, but when it came time to work together, to create lesson plans, it just locked in. And I'm just amazed at the flow of information and the refining. It's a credit to you all."

Alexander: "A lot of people can't let go, and that's part of it to. Yes we agree on a lot of things, but you'll get to camps where someone wants to have control of everything. Mike and I do the exact same drill and the same methods are being taught, but there are a lot of control freaks out there that would have a tough time with the small variances, like the puck starting five feet to the left in that drill. I've been to a number of camps myself as well, and they can't let go."

Nykvist: "I also think we also have a responsibility to provide the best learning experience for these goalies. So we can't have disparity between each other."

Goldman: "And that's the power behind it! Everything that comes out of this is so above and beyond what is being learned. I always think of Hutchinson in this regard, because he's the most 'green' goalie of the group, except maybe Jussi [Rynnas]. So he's probably the most impressionable, and for him, this must open his mind to all sorts of stuff, and I can't imagine what he's picking up consciously and subconsciously."

Nykvist: "I also love the process of getting to know these goalies. For me it's so interesting to see how certain goalies respond to things we say, and then when you start to learn a little more here and there what they've been through with their lives, I'm so interested in that."

Valley: "The coolest thing was just seeing the discussions that you guys were not even forcing, but guiding them into. You just had to set the table, and they ate it up. Thomas, during your presentation, Brian [Elliott] jumped in, took a marker, went up to the dry erase board, started diagramming things, then Ben jumped in with his comments, Kari did the same, and that's just how it worked. So the position was literally evolving right in front of our own eyes, and that was really cool."

Nykvist: "One thing that is so interesting for me. Even these big stars and these guys playing at the highest level, but still you can see how vulnerable they are and how fragile they are. They're still people."

Goldman: "So Mike, what was your goal for the camp in the first place?"

Valley: "The goal of the camp was to get eight motivated NHL goaltenders into one place with four world-class coaches in order to create a great learning environment for the goalies and the coaches as well. There wasn't really a set plan other than creating something that would be really cool that hadn't been done before in an environment where we could all continue to learn and grow."

Goldman: "Now that the camp is over, how do you see it growing from here?"

Valley: "I don't think it does grow. What we accomplished this week is what we'd want to do every year. Part of the success this week is that it was catered to eight guys with the intention of the coaches giving everything we had, and sharing it with them to make them better. So there was no ego involved in trying to grow something, it was just about giving something."

Alexander: "I think it will mature naturally. I don't know how, but the reason it will is because we've now spent a full week together with each other. We've gotten into a work flow, we know how each other works. I'm sure a lot of the same goalies will be back next year, and that being said, I think naturally the camp will get better because our ability to communicate and our styles will grow. As far as my role with the camp next year, I can't imagine where else we would go with our roles. Not to toot our own horn here, but we maximized our output at the rink and away, so I don't think we can do much more."

Magnusson: "I agree with Mike that we don't necessarily have to grow. This is a perfect format. It's a perfect mix of Finland, Sweden, Canada, USA; we all bring different things to the table from a hockey and goaltending standpoint, and also from other parts. Like Justin handling video, and David, your part with the structure and order of things. Of course there are details we can work on and expand upon, but the whole concept is there, and it doesn't necessarily need to grow that much. From my standpoint, I would definitely like to be able to do this on a yearly basis, because I think it's something that makes the goalies grow and it does something really good to them at this point of the year. And of course we all agree that this is an exceptional learning and sharing experience for all of us."

CONCLUSION: I AM ETERNALLY GRATEFUL

"Our lives are filled with meeting wonderful people. Make sure those that have become a part of your life hear your words of appreciation." –Ace Antonio Hall

Upon returning from Finland and then Madison, I battled through a lot of emotions. I was so sad to be leaving a world where I was surrounded and enraptured by an intoxicating aroma of effective goalie development. Unprepared and unwilling to face this realization, I was slightly depressed when I had to leave all of my new friends behind, without any assurance that I would ever see them again.

Depression is such an unsettling emotion for me, because I'm rarely ever in that state of mind. I've always been a very happy person, mainly due to the fact I've survived a handful of tragic near-death experiences. But those are stories for another time, I suppose.

On the return flight from Finland, a small TV on the back of the seat in front of me included on-demand videos. As a geeky guy that loves learning about science, I was drawn to Ted Talks. If you're not familiar with Ted Talks, I highly suggest looking them up. They're short, digestible lectures from some of the world's best public speakers and experts representing a variety of psychological and technological fields.

With my bony elbows digging into my sides, I leaned forward and scrolled through the list of Ted Talks until I found one that grabbed my attention. A succinct title and a synchronicity with my current emotional state caused me to tap the screen without hesitation.

It was titled, *Be Grateful.*

In this lecture, Brother David Steindl-Rast, a monk and interfaith scholar, discussed how happiness is born from gratitude.

In today's world, everyone has a different idea or preconceived notion of happiness. For some, it is just financial stability and security in an economically-driven world. For others, it's falling in love and getting married, or proving other people wrong. No matter what you imagine happiness to be, you want it. Badly.

But as Rast explained at the beginning of his lecture, humans are programmed at an early age to believe that when we are happy, we are grateful.

"But is it really the happy people that are grateful?" he asked.

We all know people that have plenty of nice things and good lives – they're not all happy. They may have wealth, all of the new goalie gear you could ask for, numerous luxuries, good looks, job security, and intelligence. But even all of those things still don't make them truly happy, and if you're like me, you probably don't enjoy being around those type of people.

On the flip side, many people are faced with perpetual waves of bad luck. Some are born into it; maybe they have genetic defects or develop a disability in their early years.

Others manifest it through bad habits and abuse. Others suffer terrible tragedies and never recover, no matter how hard they try. Yet these people can still radiate and maintain natural happiness for many years.

This happens because they bask in the light of a different mindset; a grateful one.

"So it is not happiness that makes us grateful," Rast says, "but gratefulness that makes us happy."

Upon hearing this, I thought about my current situation. I was given a golden opportunity to finally visit my favorite country through the GoaliePro coach mentoring program. I didn't buy my way into the opportunity, it was given to me, and it was of real value to my life's lofty pursuits. When these two things joined forces, then gratefulness appeared.

The key to this, Rast says, is the fact that gratefulness isn't just a single experience that may transpire a few times, but rather that it has the potential to be a way of life, or as he called it, grateful living.

And how can we live gratefully? By having an awareness that every moment in life is a gift, and that these moments are gifts with the potential for new opportunities.

"A gift within a gift," Rast says.

Every moment is a gift – we either utilize it or misuse it. The choice is ours, but the power to choose what we do with those moments is another gift that only humans can experience in our wide spectrum of emotions. That gift is free will, which can make even the most spoiled man a grateful one. Moment by moment, we hold the key to unlock a certain natural happiness that comes from just being alive.

Since I have had four near-death experiences, whenever I'm forced into a moment of depression or sadness, or when I fail in certain areas of life, I never sulk for long, because I'm genuinely grateful to be here. So while I had already naturally found a way for living gratefully, Rast's speech taught me how I could begin to transform my current mental and emotional state.

"It's so simple that it's actually something we were told as children when we learned to cross the street," he said. "Stop. Look. Go."

Stop. If I don't take the time to stop and reflect on special experiences like this one, especially one that really altered my life's path, I would've missed the learning experience. It would've slipped through my hands like water, voiding any chance I had to quench my thirst for true gratefulness.

Look. I looked back and remembered how grateful I was when I first started playing ice hockey. Never before had kids in Texas been able to do this before 1993, so each and every skate, practice, and game made me so happy, because it was a gift. The gratefulness I felt was what made it so easy for me to be happy, regardless of the wins or the losses. As I got older, playing all the time made it harder to be as grateful. So many things were happening in life that it routinely became a blur, and without the time to look back and appreciate this simple act of playing hockey, my gratitude dissipated. Now, at the age of 32, the gratitude had returned, because I'm on the ice and in my pads a lot less frequently.

Go. I decided to go to Finland to enjoy this opportunity that Ropponen and GoaliePro gifted to me, and that has manifested itself into this book. It was a creative spark that planted a seed inside me, and that act was so powerful, because it significantly changed my life and my view of the world I live in.

Stop. Look. Go...and do what you love!

Since that flight back from Finland, I've done a lot more meditating, journaling (this book), and reflecting. I've worked hard at appreciating the gift and thanking my friends. That also included opening up my heart in order to help others, which is something I did for a dear friend that was very sick and unhealthy throughout the winter and into February of 2015. Even though she did not have much to offer in return, I was there for her.

Giving up my time and energy in a selfless manner was something I explained thoroughly in *The Power Within's* chapter on Egolessness, as well as the role of the spirit. Some of these gifts bestowed upon you are not solely for your benefit, but for the purpose of helping others. That is another reason why I put so much time and effort into writing this book – so that you hopefully got inspired by what I had learned.

As Rast continued to give his lecture on being grateful, I became even more aware of the synchronicity between my trip to Finland and my quick attitude adjustment – from being sad about leaving to being so happy to have had the opportunity to do this in the first place.

I would have that same exact experience returning from Madison.

The more I thought about it, the more I realized that there was a key tie-in between gratefulness and Finland's willingness to share. If you're grateful, you're not fearful.

And if fear doesn't hold you back from being open with your ideas and insights, then you're happy to help educate and support others. You act out of empathy instead of selfishness, and you're willing to share and appreciate the differences between some worlds in order to find ways to improve others.

I'm grateful for the experiences that helped me realize these two life-altering affirmations: The importance of sharing and the importance of relationships.

The lesson here stays true; I'm happy right now because I am so grateful for the opportunity to have a much better idea of the current state of goalie development in Finland and North America. With a much stronger awareness and bigger world view, I've been exposed to new truths, and that has allowed me to put together a sensible plan of action for improving goalie development in the United States.

The Only Constant is Change

Shortly after the 2014-15 NHL season got underway, I realized I no longer had the passion to continue working my NHL.com gig.

It's not that I was no longer grateful for the opportunity, but rather I felt as if it was suffocating my creativity. Since I had to spend so much time focusing on watching games nightly and dissecting stats, it didn't leave much time for me to learn new things or do much research. It was the same thing every week. The same word count, the same perspective on who was playing well, and who was struggling. I had done this every week during the hockey season for nearly four years. It was time to move on.

I felt really bad for quitting my role mid-season, but my editor Matt Cubeta was very understanding. It was not an easy decision to make, but it was the right one. My future was in book writing. In NetWork Goaltending. In doing more consulting, research, and development.

I also came to the realization that my future with The Goalie Guild was changing. Instead of being a for-profit company, I wanted to gain non-profit status so I could raise funds to help goalies overcome some of the same obstacles I had faced on my path of development as a youth.

Good goalie coaching is hard to find. I realized that this summer. I also realized that costs were rising. Private coaches were charging more. Camps were getting more expensive. Gear was getting more expensive. With those rising costs, while some could continue to afford attending camps, many others would be unable to do so. Furthermore, with so many good goalies popping up in rural areas across the globe, I felt I had an opportunity to provide undereducated and underprivileged goalies with training opportunities that they wouldn't regularly receive.

And so my new mission statement for The Goalie Guild was born. I decided to transform my entire business model into something that would raise awareness for goalie development and alleviate the costs associated with training and educating goalies around the world.

A Special Thanks to My Friends

If you've made it this far and you've read this entire book from cover-to-cover, I want to thank you. This book was winding, looping, and maybe in some instances, a little all over the place. But I did my best to compile thousands and thousands of learning experiences, memories, interactions, and stories from my life-changing summer.

I hope you enjoyed all of the insights the coaches shared. I hope you got an opportunity to reflect on your own thoughts and ideas regarding goalie development. I hope you picked up something new. I hope this inspired you to start sharing more. I hope you take a moment to reach out to me and introduce yourself. I'd love to hear from you, I'd love to discuss our experiences, and I'd love to help you in any way possible!

My favorite metal band, Kalmah, is known for infusing heavy riffs with soulful lyrics. In their song titled *Outremer*, one stanza goes like this:

> *"We are the fuse, we are the fuel. What can we do to stop the fire? The answer will be found from our brains, not from the books or from the tales."*

This is why we must share our experiences. The answers I uncovered this summer weren't found in any books or manuals. They were found in the minds and through the words of those I met. Magnusson answered one of them with a simple phrase that will forever be the lead sentence of this book's synopsis.

> *"There are as many styles as there are goalies."*

When we share our experiences with others, we create bonds. When we create bonds, we feel empathy for each other. When we feel empathy, we are willing to do more than ever before to help one another.

Another stanza from one of my favorite metal songs stuck with me at the moment of writing this final section. Suidakra's album *Eternal Defiance* is all about the realities of war in a world where respect is so hard to earn on the battlefield. I think, as goaltenders and goalie coaches, we have so much empathy for each other, because so many of us deal with this lack of respect and appreciation on a regular basis. I know I have. I know you have, too. So that's why we should always stick together.

> *"Side to side with banners high, to the last one they would fight. Relentless, fearless to the end. Each one of them he called his friend."*

I may have never met you before, but if you've read all of these words, no matter who you are, where you're from, or what you think about everything I've written in this book, I'm definitely calling you my friend.

Made in the USA
Lexington, KY
22 July 2018